TEACHING NOTES

WORLD LITERATURE

Holt, Rinehart and Winston
Harcourt Brace Jovanovich
Austin • Orlando • San Diego • Chicago • Dallas • Toronto

ACKNOWLEDGMENTS

For permission to reprint copyrighted material, grateful acknowledgment is made to the following sources:

Robert Alter: From "Poetry in Israel" from *After the Tradition: Essays on Modern Jewish Writing* by Robert Alter. Copyright © 1961, 1962, 1964, 1965, 1966, 1967, 1968, 1969 by Robert Alter.

The American Association of Teachers of Spanish and Portuguese, Inc.: From "Machado de Assis: Short Story Craftsman" by Donald M. Decker from *Hispania,* vol. XLVIII, no. 1, March 1965. Copyright © 1965 by The American Association of Teachers of Spanish and Portuguese, Inc.

The American University in Cairo Press: From "Introduction" by Mursi Saad El Din from *Wedding Song* by Naguib Mahfouz. Copyright © 1984 by The American University in Cairo Press.

Arnold-Heinemann Publishers (India) Pvt. Ltd.: From *Santha Rama Rau* by S. K. Desai. Copyright © 1976 by S. K. Desai.

The Asia Society: From *A Thousand Years of Vietnamese Poetry,* edited by Nguyen Ngoc Bich, translated by Nguyen Ngoc Bich with Burton Raffel and W. S. Merwin. Copyright © 1962, 1967, 1968, 1969, 1970, 1971, 1972, 1974 by Asia Society, Inc.

Associated University Presses: From *Initiation: Translations from Poems of the Didinga & Lango Tribes* by J. H. Driberg. Copyright 1932 by The Golden Cockerel Press, London.

A & C Black Ltd.: From *A Literary History of Rome* by J. Wight Duff, edited by A. M. Duff. Copyright © 1960 by A. M. Duff.

Basil Blackwell Ltd.: From *The Style of La Fontaine's Fables* by Jean Dominique Biard. Copyright © 1966 by Basil Blackwell.

George Braziller, Inc.: From *Maupassant* by Michael G. Lerner. Copyright © 1975 by Michael G. Lerner.

Cambridge University Press: From *History/Writing* by Albert Cook. Copyright © 1988 by Cambridge University Press. From *Reading Greek Tragedy* by Simon Goldhill. Copyright © 1986 by Cambridge University Press. From "Turn of a century: modernism, 1895–1925" by Evelyn Bristol from *The Cambridge History of Russian Literature,* edited by Charles A. Moser. Copyright © 1989 by Cambridge University Press.

Cassell PLC: From *Symbolists and Decadents* by John Milner. Copyright © 1971 by John Milner.

Chicago Review: From "Pablo Neruda at Macchu Picchu" by Agnes Gullon from *Chicago Review*, 27:2, 1975.

Copyright © 1975 by Chicago Review.

Columbia University Press: From pp. 60–61 from *The Pleasures of Japanese Literature* by Donald Keene. Copyright © 1988 by Columbia University Press. From pp. 449–450 from *Sources of the Japanese Tradition*, Volume I, compiled by Ryusaku Tsunoda, Wm. Theodore de Bary, and Donald Keene. Copyright © 1958 by Columbia University Press. From "Introduction" from *The Complete Works of Chuang Tzu*, translated by Burton Watson. Copyright © 1968 by Columbia University Press. From *Early Chinese Literature* by Burton Watson. Copyright © 1962 by Columbia University Press.

Cornell University Press: From pp. 52–53 from *Socrates, Ironist and Moral Philosopher* by Gregory Vlastos. Copyright © 1991 by Cornell University Press.

Doubleday, a division of Bantam Doubleday Dell Publishing Group, Inc.: From *The breast of the earth* by Kofi Awoonor. Copyright © 1975 by Kofi Awoonor.

E. P. Dutton, an imprint of New American Library, a division of Penguin Books USA Inc.: From pp. 4–6 from *The Tao of Pooh* by Benjamin Hoff. Copyright © 1982 by Benjamin Hoff; text and illustration from *Winnie-the-Pooh* and *The House at Pooh Corner*, copyright 1926, 1928 by E. P. Dutton; copyright © 1953, 1956 by A. A. Milne.

S. Fischer Verlag: From *Conversation with Kafka* by Gustav Janouch, translated by Goronwy Rees. Copyright © 1953 by S. Fischer Verlag.

Fitzhenry & Whiteside Ltd.: From pp. 178–179 from *Northrop Frye on Shakespeare*, edited by Robert Sandler. Copyright © 1986 by Northrop Frye.

Fromm International Publishing Corporation: From *Rainer Maria Rilke: Letters on Cézanne*, edited by Clara Rilke, translated by Joel Agee. Translation copyright © 1985 by Fromm International Publishing Corporation.

Grove Press, Inc.: From pp. 335–336 from *The Book of Songs*, translated by Arthur Waley. Copyright © 1937, 1960 by Grove Press, Inc.

Harcourt Brace Jovanovich, Inc.: From "Introduction" from *Italian Folktales*, selected and retold by Italo Calvino, translated by George Martin. Copyright © 1956 by Giulio Einaudi editore, s.p.a. English translation copyright © 1980 by Harcourt Brace Jovanovich, Inc. From "Introduction" from *Microworlds: Writings on Science Fiction and Fantasy* by Stanislaw Lem, edited by Franz Rottensteiner. Copyright © 1984 by Stanislaw Lem. Introduction and bibliography copyright © 1984 by Harcourt Brace Jovanovich, Inc. From *Lectures on Don Quixote* by Vladimir Nabokov. Copyright © 1983 by the Estate of Vladimir Nabokov.

(Acknowledgments continue on page viii)

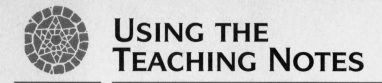

USING THE TEACHING NOTES

For each unit introduction in the *World Literature* student text, *Teaching Notes* provides a corresponding introduction. This introduction includes further discussion of background presented in the student's book as well as additional information of related interest. The *Teaching Notes* also includes suggested unit projects that address both individual selections and the unit as a whole.

Each literary selection or, in some cases, group of selections in the *Teaching Notes* includes a brief summary. The teacher may use the summaries in initially planning the course syllabus. The summaries can also serve as quick memory-refreshers for the main points of plot in a narrative, the key elements of a poem, and so on. The next feature in this section of the *Teaching Notes* supplies further information about the author, the selection, or the culture involved. "A Critical Comment," a direct quotation about the selection or the author by a noted critic or other secondary source, gives the teacher an idea of a prevailing interpretation of the selection, offers additional insight into the work, or presents an interesting view of the selection. The commentary also provides an opportunity for students to read literary criticism firsthand. "For Further Reading" is a brief bibliography that guides the teacher to additional

critical material on the selection, and in most cases provides the original source for the selection itself.

At the end of the *Teaching Notes* is a section devoted to pedagogical articles on various teaching strategies. These articles include interesting, up-to-date research on such important topics as the teaching of writing; holistic and other forms of assessment; the use and evaluation of student portfolios; the implementation of peer-response groups; the use of various critical thinking strategies; skimming, scanning, and close-reading strategies; writing to learn; timed writing; reading development among high-school students; collaborative learning; vocabulary building; journal writing; Readers' Theater; self- and peer evaluation; and a host of suggested classroom activities that will enhance the teaching of literature and language in the high-school classroom. In addition, this section of the *Teaching Notes* includes various assessment scales, an assortment of forms that can be used for peer and self-evaluation, and a chart of correction symbols for use in composition instruction. The section also includes "For Further Reading" suggestions to the teacher and information on where to obtain audiovisual resources.

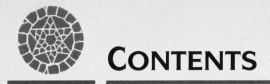

CONTENTS

(Continued from page ii)

HarperCollins Publishers, Inc.: From "The fruits of conversion" from *Tolstoy* by T. G. S. Cain. Copyright © 1977 by T. G. S. Cain.

HarperCollins Publishers Limited: From p. 231 from *Classical Persian Literature* by A. J. Arberry. Copyright © 1958 by George Allen and Unwin Ltd. From *The Poetry and Career of Li Po* by Arthur Waley. Copyright 1950 by George Allen and Unwin Ltd.

Heinemann Publishers (Oxford) Ltd.: From *The Writing of Wole Soyinka* by Eldred Durosimi Jones. Copyright © 1973 by Eldred Durosimi Jones.

Hollym International Corporation: From *A Guide to Korean Literature* by In-sŏb Zŏng. Copyright © 1982 by In-sŏb Zŏng.

Henry Holt and Company, Inc.: From *The Folktale* by Stith Thompson. Copyright 1946 by Holt, Rinehart and Winston, Inc.

Houghton Mifflin Company: From "Introduction" by Robert A. Pratt from *The Tales of Canterbury* by Geoffrey Chaucer, edited by Robert A. Pratt. Copyright © 1974 by Houghton Mifflin Company.

International African Institute: Proverb from *Jabo Proverbs from Liberia: Maxims in the Life of a Native Tribe* by George Herzog. Copyright © 1936 by the International African Institute. Published by Oxford University Press (UK).

Kodansha International Ltd.: From "The Pillow Book: Sei Shōnagon" by Makura no sōshi from *A Reader's Guide to Japanese Literature* by J. Thomas Rimer. Copyright © 1988 by Kodansha International Ltd.

The Labyrinth Press: From "Introduction" from *The Lais of Marie de France*, translated by Robert Hanning and Joan Ferrante. Copyright © 1978 by Robert W. Hanning and Joan M. Ferrante.

Macmillan Publishing Company: From pp. 21–22 from *The Indian Way* by John M. Koller. Copyright © 1982 by Macmillan Publishing Company, Inc. From "Psalms" from *Dictionary of the Bible* by John L. McKenzie, S.J. Copyright © 1965 by Macmillan Publishing Company, Inc.

McFarland & Company, Inc., Publishers, Jefferson, NC 28640: From "The Short Story Writer" from *Chekhov Criticism, 1880 Through 1986* by Charles W. Meister. Copyright © 1988 by Charles W. Meister.

William Morris Agency: From *The Ramayana* as told by Aubrey Menen. Copyright © 1954 by Aubrey Menen.

New American Library, a division of Penguin Books USA Inc.: From "Introduction" by Archibald T. MacAllister from *The Inferno* by Dante Alighieri, translated by John Ciardi. Copyright © 1954 by John Ciardi. Introduction copyright © 1954 by New American Library, a division of Penguin Books USA Inc.

New Directions Publishing Corporation: From pp. 94–95 from *Li Ch'ing-chao: Complete Poems*, edited and translated by Kenneth Rexroth and Ling Chung. Copyright © 1979 by Kenneth Rexroth and Ling Chung. From *Bird in the Bush* by Kenneth Rexroth. Copyright © 1947, 1955 by New Directions Publishing Corporation, copyright © 1959 by Kenneth Rexroth. From "Introduction" from *The Selected Poems of Tu Fu*, translated by David Hinton. Copyright © 1988, 1989 by David Hinton.

New York University Press: From "Poetry" from *Gabriela Mistral: The Poet and Her Work* by Margot Arce de Vazquez, translated by Helen Masslo Anderson. Copyright © 1964 by New York University Press.

Nilgiri Press: From "Introduction" and from "The War Within" from *The Bhagavad Gita for Daily Living* by Eknath Easwaran. Copyright © 1975 by Blue Mountain Center of Meditation.

Northwestern University Press: From *An African View of Literature* by Peter Nazareth. Copyright © 1974 by Peter Nazareth.

W. W. Norton & Company, Inc.: From "Introduction" from *The Song of Roland*, translated, with an Introduction, by Frederick Goldin. Copyright © 1978 by W. W. Norton & Company, Inc. From "Introduction" from *The Arabian Nights*, translated by Husain Haddawy. Copyright © 1990 by W. W. Norton & Company, Inc.

Norvik Press: From pp. 242–243 from *Ibsen & Meaning* by James McFarlane. Copyright © 1989 by James McFarlane.

Oxford University Press, Inc. (NY): From 2 Esdras 8:41 from *The New English Bible: The Apocrypha*. Copyright © 1970 by The Delegates of the Oxford University Press and The Syndics of the Cambridge University Press. From "Octavio Paz" from *Modern Latin American Literature* by D. P. Gallagher. Copyright © 1973 by Oxford University Press, Inc. From "The Creation" and from "The Trickster" from *The World of Myth*, edited by David Adams Leeming. Copyright © 1991 by Oxford University Press, Inc.

Oxford University Press (UK): From "Baudelaire" from *Countries of the Mind, Essays in Literary Criticism* by John Middleton Murry. Copyright 1922, 1931 by Oxford University Press. From pp. 80–81 from *Goethe* by T. J. Reed. Copyright © 1984 by T. J. Reed.

Pantheon Books, a division of Random House, Inc.: From pp. 7–10 from *African Folktales* by Roger D. Abrahams. Copyright © 1983 by Roger D. Abrahams. From *Federico García Lorca: A Life* by Ian Gibson. Copyright © 1988 by Ian Gibson.

The Pennsylvania State University Press: From *Baudelaire as a Literary Critic: Selected Essays*, introduced and translated by Lois Boe Hyslop and Francis E. Hyslop, Jr. Copyright © 1964 by The Pennsylvania State University.

Princeton University Press: From *The Hero with a Thousand Faces* by Joseph Campbell. Copyright © 1949 by Bollingen Foundation Inc., New York, NY. From pp. 65–68 from *Thucydides* by W. Robert Connor. Copyright © 1984 by Princeton University Press.

Random House, Inc.: From *Forewords and Afterwords* by W. H. Auden, selected by Edward Mendelson. Copyright © 1973 by W. H. Auden. From pp. 6–7 from *Medieval Romances* by Roger S. Loomis and Laura H. Loomis. Copyright © 1957 by Random House, Inc. From pp. 52–54 from *"Isak Dinesen" and Karen Blixen: The Mask and the Reality* by Donald Hannah. Copyright © 1971 by Donald Hannah. From pp. 18–19 from *A Jew Today* by Elie Wiesel, translated by Marion Wiesel. Copyright © 1978 by Elirion Associates, Inc.

Revista Vuelta: From "In Time's Labyrinth" by Octavio Paz. Copyright © 1986 by Octavio Paz.

Schocken Books, published by Pantheon Books, a division of Random House, Inc.: From *The Legend of Krishna* by Nigel Frith. Copyright © 1975 by Nigel Frith.

Scholars' Facsimiles & Reprints, Inc.: From "Introduction" from *The Rubaiyat of Omar Khayyam*, translated by Parichehr Kasra. Copyright © 1975 by Scholars' Facsimiles & Reprints, Inc.

School of Oriental and African Studies: From *Sunjata: Three Mandinka Versions* by Gordon Innes. Copyright © 1974 by Gordon Innes.

Charles Scribner's Sons, an imprint of Macmillan Publishing Company: From "Greek Lyric Poets" by Glenn W. Most from *Ancient Writers: Greece and Rome*, T. James Luce, Editor. Copyright © 1982 by Charles Scribner's Sons. From "Introduction" by Abioseh Nicol from *Africa is Thunder and Wonder* by Barbara Nolen. Copyright © 1972 by Barbara Nolen Strong.

Servant Publications, P. O. Box 8617, Ann Arbor, MI 48107: From *Daily Life in the Time of Jesus* by Henri Daniel-Rops, translated by Patrick O'Brian. Copyright © 1962 by George Weidenfeld and Nicholson, Ltd.

Simon & Schuster, Inc.: From pp. 34–35 from *Popol Vuh: The Mayan Book of the Dawn of Life*, translated by Dennis Tedlock. Copyright © 1985 by Dennis Tedlock.

Soundings: From "Two Women in a Man's World: A Reading of the Book of Ruth" by Phyllis Trible from *Soundings* 59, Fall 1976. Copyright © 1976 by Soundings, An Interdisciplinary Journal.

State University of New York Press: From Chapter 8 from *The Goddesses' Mirror* by David Kinsley. Copyright © 1989 by State University of New York.

Three Continents Press: From p. 17 from *Achebe's World* by Robert M. Wren. Copyright © 1980 by Robert M. Wren.

The Times Literary Supplement: From "Wising Up" by Ike Onwordi from *Times Literary Supplement*, no. 4313, November 19, 1985. Copyright © 1985 by The Times Literary Supplement.

Charles E. Tuttle Co., Inc., Tokyo, Japan: From *Zen Flesh, Zen Bones*, compiled by Paul Reps. Copyright © 1957 by Charles E. Tuttle Co., Inc.

Twayne Publishers, an imprint of Macmillan Publishing Company: From *Selma Lagerlöf* by Vivi Edström. Copyright © 1984 by G. K. Hall & Company. From *Alexander Solzhenitsyn* by Andrej Kodjak. Copyright © 1978 by G. K. Hall & Company. From *James Joyce* by A. Walton Litz. Copyright © 1966 by Twayne Publishers, Inc. From *Voltaire* by Peyton Richter and Ilona Ricardo. Copyright © 1980 by G. K. Hall & Company. From "Book of Songs" from *Heinrich Heine* by Hanna Spencer. Copyright © 1982 by G. K. Hall & Company. From "Conclusion" from *Alexander Pushkin* by Walter N. Vickery. Copyright © 1970 by Twayne Publishers, Inc.

U.S. News & World Report, Inc.: From "An Embargo that Backfires" by Mark Mathabane from *U.S. News & World Report*, vol. 109, no. 1, July 2, 1990. Copyright © 1990 by U.S. News & World Report, Inc.

University of California Press: From the "Introduction" by B. A. van Nooten from *Ramayana* by William Buck. Copyright © 1976 by The Regents of the University of California. From *Ancient Egyptian Literature, Three Volumes* by Miriam Lichtheim. Copyright © 1973–1980 by The Regents of the University of California. From "Introduction" by Sigurdur Nordal from *The Prose Edda of Snorri Sturluson*, edited and translated by Jean Young. Copyright © 1964 by The Regents of the University of California.

University of Chicago Press: From *The Sumerians* by Samuel Noah Kramer. Copyright © 1963 by The University of Chicago. From *Letters from Mesopotamia*, translated by A. Leo Oppenheim. Copyright © 1967 by The University of Chicago.

University of Michigan Press: From "Margaret Atwood: Beyond Victimhood" from *Parti-Colored Blocks for a Quilt* by Marge Piercy. Copyright © 1982 by The University of Michigan.

University of South Carolina Press: From pp. 198–199 from *Understanding Albert Camus* by David R. Ellison. Copyright © 1990 by the University of South Carolina.

University Press of America, Inc.: From *A Kì í: Yorùbá Proscriptive and Prescriptive Proverbs* by Oyekan Owomoyela. Copyright © 1988 by University Press of America, Inc.

University Press of Kentucky: From "The Voyage beyond the Map: 'El ahogado más hermoso del mundo'" by Mary E. Davis from *Kentucky Romance Quarterly* 26, no. 2 (1979):25–33. Copyright © 1979 by University Press of Kentucky.

University Press of New England: From pp. 72–73 from *Encounters with Chinese Writers* by Annie Dillard. Copyright © 1984 by Annie Dillard.

Vikas Publishing House Pvt. Ltd.: From *History of Arabic Literature* by K. A. Fariq. Copyright © 1972 by Indian Institute of Islamic Studies.

Viking Penguin, a division of Penguin Books USA Inc.: From "Introduction" by Thomas Bergin from *The Decameron* by Giovanni Boccaccio, translated by Mark Musa and Peter Bondanella. Translation copyright © 1982 by Mark Musa and Peter Bondanella; Introduction copyright © 1981, 1982 by Thomas Bergin. From "Introduction" by Bernard Knox from *The Iliad* by Homer, translated by Robert Fagles. Translation copyright © 1990 by Robert Fagles; Introduction and notes copyright © 1990 by Bernard Knox. From "Introduction" from *The Metamorphoses* by Publius Ovidius Naso, translated by Horace Gregory. Translation copyright © 1958 by The Viking Press, Inc.; copyright renewed © 1986 by Patrick Bolton Gregory.

Wallace Literary Agency, Inc.: From "Introduction" from *The Mahabharata* by R. K. Narayan. Copyright © 1978 by R. K. Narayan.

Wayne State University Press and Beongcheon Yu: From pp. 16–17 from *Akutagawa* by Beongcheon Yu. Copyright © 1972 by Wayne State University Press.

Yale University Press: From "Poem 13" from *The Literature of Ancient Egypt*, edited by William Kelly Simpson, with translations by R. O. Faulkner, Edward F. Wente, Jr., and William Kelly Simpson. Copyright © 1972 by Yale University Press.

Ehsan Yarshater: From "Introduction" by Dr. Amin Banani from *The Epic of Kings: Shah-Nama the national epic of Persia* by Ferdowsi, translated by Reuben Levy. Copyright © 1967 by The Royal Institute of Publication of Teheran.

UNIT 1: WORLD MYTHS AND FOLKTALES

(Textbook page 2)

Unit Introduction

Myths and folktales tell about the beginnings of things. They include marvelous or supernatural events and tell of the deeds and adventures of gods and goddesses, heroes and heroines. They explain the origins of various rituals that people follow. They are passed down from generation to generation by word of mouth. Most important of all, however, they explain the human experience. They tell us, in poetic, imaginative terms, the most important things that we can communicate to one another: who we are, where we came from, and what we believe in.

BACKGROUND

WHAT ARE MYTHS AND FOLKTALES?

At the most basic level, myths and folktales are simply the stories of a culture. They are oral narratives, usually of anonymous authorship, that are repeated from one generation to the next. On a more complex level, myths are the history, psychology, religion, philosophy, and sociology of a culture. They fill the psychological and emotional needs of the individual as well as the collective.

Although belief in the particulars of a mythology will rarely span from one culture to another, the basic structures of most of the world's mythologies are remarkably similar. Virtually every society has mythological constructs: Its heroes are Gilgamesh, Prometheus, Coyote, Hercules; its gods are Zeus and Thor. The similarity of mythological patterns, or archetypes, from culture to culture has elicited a variety of responses and several popular theories. In the eighteenth century, mythologies were thought to have evolved from a single source, lent and borrowed as cultures came into contact with one another through migration and invasion. The original source was at one time thought to be India, and at another time Africa. This theory, however, is currently held as too simple, and myths are now thought to have developed independently of each other. Many mythologists conclude that the similarities stem from the fact that humans, regardless of culture, will ask the same questions: Who are we? Where did we come from? How was the universe created? Why does the sun rise and set?

The universal existence of mythology and folktales suggests that there is an essential human need for them. Mythology provides the explanations which give order to a universe that seems to have no order. Mythology also unites the peoples of a culture by providing them with a common ancestry and a shared destiny. Experts view mythology as having deeper, symbolic uses. Within the stories of creation, of birth and rebirth, lies the symbolic regeneration of a society, experienced to some degree with each retelling. Other myths are viewed as metaphors for experiences shared by all human beings: birth, death, tragedy, luck, betrayal, fertility, war, fate, evil—the list is endless. The myth "Osiris and Isis," for instance, is symbolic of both the planting associated with the annual flooding of the Nile and the cyclical birth, death, and regeneration of life.

CREATION MYTHS

Creation myths, examples of which are found in the first section of this unit, "Tales About Beginnings," are particularly essential to a culture, because they answer the most fundamental questions: How was the universe created? How were humans made? Why is there death? The myths retold in this section are representative of the many hundreds of myths that answer these questions. These myths invariably involve a god or gods. The methods of creation and the resources available to the creator vary, often by climate and geography. For instance, in the northern countries, the empty world might be ice-covered, while in the southern hemisphere the creator might use the mud of a flower-banked river. Creation myths may also serve to answer questions of lesser importance: Where did the buffalo come from? Why are monkeys so much like humans?

THE GOLDEN AGE

Myths about a lost Golden Age seem to reflect a basic human need to believe that the inadequacies we see around us are not integral to the world, for when the world was first created, these flaws did not exist: The world was perfect. In many mythologies, the gods, who are perfect themselves, are incapable of creating an imperfect world. How, then, do we explain pain, suffering, and limitation in this life? At some point there is an inevitable fall from a perfect state, which explains the negative aspects of existence. An example from Greek mythology is the story of "Pandora's Box," in which all the evils of the world are liberated by the curious Pandora.

A related theme is the destruction of the world as we know it with all its evils. This destruction sets the stage for the re-creation of a more perfect world. These myths reveal two common traits of mythology: hope for a more perfect world and fear of the great power of the gods (or the unknown).

THE TRICKSTER

The trickster is a favorite archetype. He commonly possesses the most unattractive, nonspiritual human traits. His role in folklore is to account for the ills in the world, as well as to provide unbeatable entertainment value. Coyote in Native American mythologies is a typical trickster, as is Brer Rabbit of African American legend, and the modern-day cartoon characters Bugs Bunny and Wile E. Coyote.

FOLKTALES

The "tales" of the "folk" develop naturally from the mythology of a culture and, accordingly, folktales and myths are often grouped together, or even assumed to be the same. Folktales, however, tend to focus on the narrative of the hero's adventure rather than on supernatural creation. Their function is considered to be entertainment, rather than explanation. Very often the tales will be legendary in nature—that is, their heroes were probably once real people who performed extraordinary deeds, and through the ages, stories of their accomplishments were magnified, exaggerated, and embellished with each new storyteller, like a game of "telephone."

THE MONOMYTH: THE ARCHETYPAL HEROIC ADVENTURE

Whether the hero is Jason, Robin Hood, Gilgamesh, or Indiana Jones, the tale of the hero is eagerly devoured as one of the finest and oldest sources of entertainment. What is it that makes the hero/quest story so attractive? How does it relate to the basic situation of humankind?

Like the other archetypes of myths and folktales, the hero and the quest follows a fairly specific pattern that is remarkably unchanging regardless of the culture from which it springs: The hero is born,

goes on a danger-fraught adventure on which he successfully shows off his or her prowess against powerful enemies and low odds, and returns to the community bearing the fruits of the journey.

Preeminent mythologist Joseph Campbell uses the term *monomyth,* borrowed from the Irish writer James Joyce, to describe the common structure of the heroic myth. In the theory of the monomyth, the hero follows a standard path of adventure: separation, initiation, return. The hero, often (in myths, at least) the offspring of a god and a mortal, is born in the midst of regular folk. Unusual circumstances usually surround his birth, and he usually demonstrates superhuman abilities at an early age. At some point in his youth, the hero receives a "call" to adventure. Accepting the call, the hero leaves his or her protective community for the outside world to begin the adventure, which is usually connected with a quest of some kind. During the quest, the hero encounters many obstacles, often in the form of evil monsters, and successfully conquers them. The hero receives a boon (a beautiful woman, knowledge) and eventually returns to his or her community, bringing to it the knowledge or other life-giving aspect it was formerly missing. There are, however, deviations to the pattern. For instance, the hero may decide to ignore the call to adventure, or, having gone to the trouble of embarking on the quest, may return to his or her community and be rejected. These versions highlight the prices and the risks of adventure and help to keep the stories of our heroes fresh.

A LARGER-THAN-LIFE REFLECTION OF HUMANITY

It is the character of the hero or heroine, in addition to the excitement of the journey, that attracts our attention. The hero is everything we want to be—he or she is bold, courageous, intuitive, attractive, and strong. The hero is our representative in a world full of dangers where success is attainable. We share certain characteristics with our hero. Born into a regular family, perhaps no different from our own, a folktale hero might be dismissed as ordinary. This is a situation we are familiar with. His or her travails are our travails. We also want to be associated with his or her success. We hope to be rewarded for all our troubles, just like the hero is.

But, as well as having character traits we admire, the hero also has faults, character deficiencies— Tomotada, for instance, in "Green Willow," falls in love and strays from his mission. Character deficiencies help us sympathize with the hero. We can appreciate the admirable and not so admirable traits of heroes of another culture. Hence, what partially makes myths so universal is the unchanging nature of human pathos.

THE MYTHIC VS. THE FOLKTALE HERO

The heroes of myths and folktales have many similarities, but their differences are reflected at birth. The heroes of myths have extraordinary births; Theseus, for example, born to a princess, is really the unknown son of the King of Athens, but is thought to be the son of the god Poseidon. Sometimes the hero-child will be born to a virgin, inheriting his or her divine nature from the unnamed father. In folktales, the young hero is born into a family of lower status, orphaned or rejected at birth, and dismissed by his or her culture as worthless. At a certain age, both types of heroes begin to show superhuman or out-of-the-ordinary characteristics.

THE HERO'S CALLING

Soon after discovering his superior powers, the hero receives the "call" to adventure. For the servant in "The White Snake," the call is a direct result of the discovery of power. In the occasional myth, the hero will ignore the call or become sidetracked, as Tomotada does in "Green Willow." The result is a great loss—for Tomotada the loss of his identity. The hero without the fulfilled adventure is incomplete, symbolically lacking the deep knowledge of the inner self necessary to be whole.

THE HERO'S QUEST

Often there is a quest involved in the adventure: the hero is after something that is either lacking in him or her or in the community. Isis, for example, has a very specific quest: the rescue of her husband/brother Osiris. For many heroes the quest is simply for experience or knowledge, as for the servant in "The White Snake." In other tales, reunion with the father figure symbolizes not only the attainment of knowledge and wisdom, but also the reclamation of one's family heritage, as represented in "Theseus" by Theseus' quest to find his father Aegeus. The distant biological father may also be symbolic of the supreme being, and to know the father is, ultimately, to enter into a relationship with the deity. The father figure is also used to represent the hero's national heritage, which is particularly useful on a cultural level. In addition, the search for the father helps to answer one of the most basic questions posed through mythology: Where do we come from?

In order to find the object of the quest, the hero who does answer the call will surmount difficulties of all kinds—horrible monsters, impossible labyrinths, travel to distant lands, and so forth. The quest itself is often seen as a symbol for the journey of life; its obstacles are the difficulties and rites of passage all humans endure in a lifetime. The quest also brings ultimate good, the object in question, and may bring some wish fulfillment along the way. Like the quest, one's journey through the physical world begins at birth, and it is for this reason that the community which the hero leaves behind is

often seen as the womb of the mother. But the quest is really set in motion when the hero leaves home.

OBSTACLES AND DIVINE INTERVENTION

Frequently the hero will be aided by some being. In myths, this being is usually a god (or gods); for example, Theseus prays to Aphrodite, who responds by facilitating Ariadne's love. In folktales, assistance might come in the form of magical fairies or animals: the servant of "The White Snake" is aided by the fish, ants, and birds he meets in the forest. Often aid will be offered by females: Ariadne and her ball of string; the Queen of Byblos.

The hero's quest often involves an excursion into a dark place: Theseus' descent to the underworld, Isis' (and the Grimms' servant's) into a forest, and Tomotada's into the mountains. This part of the hero's journey has its parallel in the more unpleasant experiences in life. Psychologically, this aspect of the trip also represents the darker side of human nature, the unconscious. Once the darker side is known and conquered, the hero, now whole, may return to his community.

Sometimes the obstacles are too great, or the hero's strength is not great enough. A common obstacle is the temptress, or *femme fatale*. For Tomotada, Green Willow serves as a temptress (though she is good and motivated by love, unlike the *femme fatale*), making him swerve from his obligations and dooming him to life as an outcast.

THE HERO'S RETURN

When the hero completes his or her journey, he or she returns to the native community. For the mythical community, the hero's return is always life-giving in some way—a return to order, a spiritual booster, ultimate knowledge. The hero always comes away with some special gift or a "boon," which frequently is representative of the natural phenomena a culture appreciates. For instance, Isis' reunion with Osiris is symbolic of the yearly flooding of the Nile and the subsequent growth of crops.

HEROIC ADVENTURERS FROM AROUND THE WORLD

The myths and folktales in the second half of this unit are stories of heroes and heroines from around the world: "Theseus" (Ancient Greek), "Osiris and Isis" (Ancient Egyptian), "Green Willow" (Japanese), and "The White Snake" (German). The first two are classical and well-known, the third will probably be unfamiliar to students, and the last may be known by those familiar with the works of the Brothers Grimm. Each, however, is a fine example of the hero/quest genre. Other heroic quest stories may be found in different units of the book: selections appear in Unit 2 (*Sundiata*), in Unit 3 (*Epic of Gilgamesh*) and in Unit 5 (the *Ramayana*).

UNIT PROJECTS

1. Choose a hero from one of the tales in this unit or from another myth or folktale that you know and create a short comic strip version of an important episode in the hero's adventure.

2. With another classmate, plan a debate about the pros and cons of myths and folktales and present it to your class. One of you should cite the benefits of being familiar with myths and folktales and the other should argue the negative aspects or lack of importance. Select a moderator to manage the debate. Allow each debater the same amount of time to present his or her side of the issue and also allow time for rebuttals. The moderator should ask the class to vote for the side that presents the strongest case.

3. Build a diorama of a scene from your favorite myth or folktale. You could, for example, create a scene of Theseus in the underworld, Isis reviving Osiris, or the samurai Tomotada on his quest in the Japanese countryside. Refer to art and history books for visual references, if necessary.

4. Write a one-act play using the plot of one of the myths or folktales. Ask your classmates to act the parts and direct them in rehearsal. When your actors are prepared, present the play to the class.

5. From your library borrow some books on the ancient arts of various cultures (African, Egyptian, Celtic, Norse, Japanese, Chinese, and so on), particularly those that deal with mythological gods. Write brief narratives of the gods you have been studying. While you present your narratives to the class, pass the books around the class with the appropriate pages flagged.

6. Write a television commercial or copy (words) for an advertisement promoting a product endorsed by a hero of your choice. Be sure to allude to specific traits that make your hero the ideal promoter of the product. Present the written ad to your class or have classmates perform the commercial. Find out from your audience how well your ad would sell. Which aspects work best? What should be changed?

7. From the library select a variety of collections of myths and folktales. Skim the books and spend some time reading the stories that interest you. Imagine that you have been selected to create an anthology, or collection, of world myths and folktales. Which tales will you include in your anthology? Why do you choose those tales? Write a list of your favorite selections and explain why they would go together well in an anthology.

8. Compose a rap song or another kind of song to present to the class. Base your composition on the adventures of one of the heroes you have been studying or another hero of your choice. Use a chorus or back-up singers if appropriate.

9. Design an "instruction manual" for the heroic quest. Outline the "steps" of a heroic quest. Include the *do's* and *don'ts* that a hero must follow while on a quest. Illustrate your manual and share it with the class. Alternatively, you could design a "travel guide" for a heroic quest to a fantastic setting of your choice.

10. Suppose you are a television talk-show host. You have as your guest one or more of the gods or heroes from your favorite selection(s). Present an interview with your guests. What were the hero's fears as he embarked on his quest? What motivated a god to either create or destroy a person or people? In what ways do the gods use their superhuman powers? Write the script for your talk show and, with classmates, present the show to the class.

HOW THE WORLD WAS MADE

Retold by Alice Marriott and Carol K. Rachlin ▾ (Textbook page 11)

SUMMARY

Maheo, the All Spirit, is living alone in a world that is a void. First he creates a great body of water. Then he creates creatures to live in and on the water and a bottom of mud for his lake. In order to see the things he has made, Maheo creates light. With the help of the creatures he has created, Maheo sets out to create land. Only the coot, one of the humblest of creatures, is able to dive to the bottom of the lake to procure mud. As Maheo holds the mud in his hand it grows until it is too large for him to hold, and Maheo lays it on top of the shell of the Grandmother Turtle, who holds the weight of the earth above the water. Maheo designates the Earth as female and fertile, and from her grow trees and flowers. To keep the Earth company, Maheo takes a rib from his right side and creates man. From his left side he creates woman. As the descendants of this pair begin to populate the earth, Maheo creates all the other animals to feed or clothe human beings. At last Maheo creates one animal to provide for all human needs: the buffalo.

MORE ABOUT THE CULTURE

The Cheyenne, a Native American Nation, are particularly known as having been a warrior people.

They fought with other Native Americans as well as with white settlers who encroached on their territory. The Cheyenne's first recorded encounter with European Americans was in 1804 near the Black Hills of South Dakota, when Lewis and Clark made their famous expedition to the West Coast. The Cheyenne are noted for being crucial to the defeat of Custer and his troops at the Battle of the Little Bighorn in 1876. However, skilled as they were, the Cheyennes suffered the same fate as most Native Americans: They were forced to give up long-held lands under the squeeze of white expansionism, and by the late 1800s they were subjected to living solely in the Indian Territory of Oklahoma.

Peace Chiefs, central to the organization of the Cheyenne Nation, led the individual bands and were selected every ten years. Like many other Native American peoples, the Cheyenne's philosophy focuses on the Circle of Life, which is prevalent in many tales. Traditionally oral, Cheyenne myths of religious importance were told by Elders over long periods of time. These myths typically accompanied religious rituals—before battle, for example—and were told at night.

A CRITICAL COMMENT

"A myth of creation, a cosmogony (Greek *kosmos,* meaning "order," and *genesis,* meaning 'birth'), is a story of how the cosmos began and developed. Typically, though not always, cosmogonies include the creation of the world, the creation of humankind, and the fall of humankind from a state of perfection, or the struggle in heaven between various groups of immortals.

"Each person's birth is the subject of a story that is somehow revealing about that person. The events surrounding one's birth are a celebration of the miracle of individuality. The same applies to cultural myths of origin. Origin stories are sacramental—outward and visible signs of an inner truth about the individual or culture in question. Mircea Eliade has called the creation myth the 'narration of a sacred history,' the story of the 'breakthrough of the sacred' into time (*Myth and Reality,* page 6).

"That the creation story is a metaphor for birth is indicated further by the frequent presence in cosmogonies from around the world of the motifs of the primal egg or the primal waters. These essential female symbols remind us that it is the Great Mother, perhaps breathed on by an intangible ultimate source, who gives form to life. It is she who is the *prima materia* without which life cannot be born:

> The mother of us all,
> the oldest of all,
> hard,
> > splendid as rock
>
> ('The Hymn to the Earth,' *Homeric Hymns,*
> trans. by Charles Boer, p. 5)

In the analogous mythic motif of the hero's birth, even God, if he chooses to participate in the human experience, must be born of a Maya or a Mary or an Isis, the living embodiment of Creation itself. . . .

"The creation myth, then, establishes our reason for being, the source of our significance. As such, it is often used to help individuals or groups to regain health or order. . . ."

—*from* The World of Myth,
David Adams Leeming

FOR FURTHER READING

Campbell, Joseph. *The Power of Myth.* Ed. Betty Sue Flowers. New York: Doubleday, 1988.

Coffin, Tristram P., ed. *Indian Tales of North America.* Philadelphia: American Folklore Society, 1961.

Dooling, D.M. and Paul Jordan-Smith, eds. *I Become Part of It.* New York: Parabola Books, 1990.

Edmonds, Margot and Ella E. Clark. *Voices of the Winds.* New York: Facts on File, 1989.

Hamilton, Virginia. *In the Beginning: Creation Stories from Around the World.* San Diego: Harcourt Brace Jovanovich Publishers, 1988.

Leach, Maria. *The Beginning: Creation Myths Around the World.* New York: Funk and Wagnall's, 1956.

Leeming, David Adams. *The World of Myth.* New York: Oxford University Press, 1990.

Marriot, Alice, and Carol K. Rachlin. *American Indian Mythology.* New York: New American Library/Mentor, 1972.

POPOL VUH: THE WOODEN PEOPLE

Translated by Dennis Tedlock ▼ (Textbook page 18)

SUMMARY

This creation myth depicts a failed attempt on the part of the gods to create adequate human beings. In the first two attempts, the gods had created the animal kingdom and a man of mud that disintegrated immediately. On the third try, they create the wooden people, who are durable, but lacking in hearts and minds, and especially in the ability to remember and appreciate their creators. Heart of Sky, the father god, creates a flood that brings about the destruction of the manikins. During the flood, various creatures rise up in rebellion and destroy the wooden people. Even inanimate objects such as pots and pans join in the murder of the wooden people. After the destruction, monkeys are left behind as the only remnants of the failed human creation.

MORE ABOUT THE CULTURE

The tale of the wooden people is related in the Popol Vuh, the pre-Columbian "bible" of a people closely related to the architects of the great Mayan ruins. The four parts of the Popol Vuh relate the stories of the first peoples, the conflicts of the Hero brothers with Earth Giants, the duel between upper-world heroes and the nether-world demonic powers, the rise of the sun, and how Death is overcome in his own lair and by his own wiles ("the harrowing of Hell.").

The Mayan civilization, known both for its art and sophisticated architecture, came to its height between 300 and 900 A.D., after which some groups were thought to have moved to the coast and to the hills. The Popol Vuh, one of only a few written works that survived the European invasion (in which native texts were burned in the interest of propagating Christianity), seems to have been transcribed some centuries after the prominent Mayan civilization had fallen. In the early 1700s, a Spanish priest found the only existing version of the Popol Vuh, written in hieroglyphics. He translated it into Spanish. There is little doubt, however, that the myths related in the Quiché book had been orally communicated for generations before the Europeans discovered them.

A CRITICAL COMMENT

"For the gods, the idea of human beings is as old as that of the earth itself, but they fail in their first three attempts (all in Part One) to transform this idea into a living reality. What they want is beings who will walk, work, and talk in an articulate and measured way, visiting shrines, giving offerings, and calling upon their makers by name, all according to the rhythms of a calendar. What they get instead, on the first try, is beings who have no arms to work with and can only squawk, chatter, and howl, and

whose descendants are the animals of today. On the second try they make a being of mud, but this one is unable to walk or turn its head or even keep its shape; being solitary, it cannot reproduce itself, and in the end it dissolves into nothing.

"Before making a third try the gods decide, in the course of a further dialogue, to seek the counsel of an elderly husband and wife named Xpiyacoc and Xmucane. Xpiyacoc is a divine matchmaker and therefore prior to all marriage, and Xmucane is a divine midwife and therefore prior to all birth. Like contemporary Quiché matchmakers and midwives, both of them are *ahᴣih* or "daykeepers," diviners who know how to interpret the auguries given by thirteen day numbers and twenty day names that combine to form a calendrical cycle lasting 260 days. They are older than all the other gods, who address them as grandparents, and the cycle they divine by is older than the longer cycles that govern Venus and the sun, which have not yet been established at this point in the story. The question the younger gods put to them here is whether human beings should be made out of wood. Following divinatory methods that are still in use among Quiché daykeepers, they give their approval. The wooden beings turn out to look and talk and multiply themselves something like humans, but they fail to time their actions in an orderly way and forget to call upon the gods in prayer. Hurricane brings a catastrophe down on their heads, not only flooding them with a gigantic rainstorm but sending monstrous animals to attack them. Even their own dogs, turkeys, and household utensils rise against them, taking vengeance for past mistreatment. Their only descendants are the monkeys who inhabit the forests today."

—*from* Popol Vuh,
Dennis Tedlock

FOR FURTHER READING

Nicholson, Irene. *Mexican and Central American Mythology*. London: Paul Hamlyn, 1967.

Bierhorst, John. *The Mythology of Mexico and Central America*. New York: William Morrow and Company, 1990.

Tedlock, Dennis, trans. *Popol Vuh: The Mayan Book of the Dawn of Life*. New York: Simon and Schuster, 1985.

COYOTE AND THE ORIGIN OF DEATH

Retold by Richard Erdoes and Alfonso Ortiz ▼ (Textbook page 23)

SUMMARY

The story begins with a village meeting in which people are discussing what to do about the overpopulation of the world due to the fact that there is no death—everybody lives forever. The first

suggestion made is that people should die for a limited period of time and then be brought back, but Coyote suggests that people should die permanently. His idea is vetoed and the village's medicine men build a grass house in which to resurrect all the people who die. When the first man dies, the medicine men gather in the grass house and sing. After about ten days, a whirlwind soul comes to enter the grass house. Seeing the returning soul, the coyote shuts the door to the house, thus making death permanent. The coyote, recognizing the immensity of what he has done, runs away, and is still skittish to this day.

MORE ABOUT THE CULTURE

The Caddo, a Native American nation, were centered in the area of the Red River, where the Southern central states (Louisiana, Texas, Arkansas, and Oklahoma) are now located. Farmers primarily of corn, the Caddo grew a variety of vegetation, as well as hunted to ensure their existence. When the French settled in the area, the Caddo began to function as liaisons in trade between the Europeans and the other native groups, also helping the white people with the unfamiliar land. Prior to European invasion, the Caddo numbered more than eight thousand. However, during the 1800s, the population declined sharply due to war and disease. The treaty of 1835 saw the retreat of the Caddo into Texas, and later into Mexican territory. Eventually they returned to the Southwest and were allotted land under the Dawes Act. But with their reintroduction to a country quickly becoming Westernized, came the inevitable disintegration of their traditional culture. Caddo oral tales are historically preserved in the form of traditional dances.

A CRITICAL COMMENT

"One of the most popular archetypal motifs in myth and literature is that of the trickster. Whether he be Hermes in Greece, Krishna in India, Loki in Northern Europe, Coyote or Raven among the Native Americans, or related popular figures such as Aesop's and La Fontaine's fable animals, Davy Crockett on the American frontier, Brer Rabbit in the American South, Inspector Clouseau in the film, "The Pink Panther," or any number of animated-cartoon characters, the trickster is at once wise and foolish, the perpetrator of tricks and the butt of his own jokes. Always male, he is promiscuous and amoral; he is outrageous in his actions; he emphasizes the "lower" bodily functions; he often takes animal form. Yet the trickster is profoundly inventive, creative by nature, and in some ways a helper to humanity. Jung sees in him a hint of the later savior figure (*Four Archetypes,* p. 151).

"The trickster, then, speaks to our animal nature, to our physical as opposed to our spiritual side, and reflects what Jung calls "an earlier, rudimentary stage of consciousness" (*Four Archetypes,* p. 141). He has the charming if sometimes dangerous appetites of the child, as yet untamed by the larger social conscience. And, of course, he is almost always funny."

—from The World of Myth,
David Adams Leeming

FOR FURTHER READING

Erdoes, Richard, and Alfonso Ortiz, eds. *American Indian Myths and Legends.* New York: Pantheon Books, 1984.

Radin, Paul. *The Trickster: A Study in American Indian Mythology.* New York: Schocken Books, 1972.

Bierhorst, John. *The Mythology of North America.* New York: William Morrow and Company, 1986.

THESEUS

Retold by Robert Graves ▾ (Textbook page 29)

SUMMARY

During a visit to Corinth, the King of Athens, Aegeus, marries the Princess Aethra. To ensure the safety of their son Theseus from crown-aspiring nephews, his identity is kept secret. On Theseus' fourteenth birthday, Aethra tells him who his father is. Theseus moves a huge boulder to find a sword and sandals that belonged to Aegeus. Aethra sends her son to Athens to deliver his father's possessions. Theseus fights and destroys several monsters—a giant, a wild sow—and Procrustes, an evil innkeeper. He finally arrives in Athens and ascends the throne, but he is attacked by the King's jealous nephews. Theseus manages to slay them all.

The Athenians, angry with Theseus for killing his cousins, demand that he face the Cretan Minotaur. Ariadne, Minos's daughter, helps him slay the Minotaur after he vows to marry her. However, on the way back to Athens, Theseus loses Ariadne to the god Dionysus. He forgets to replace the black sails on his boat with white victory sails, and King Aegeus, spotting the black sails and thinking that Theseus has been killed, drowns himself out of grief. Theseus immediately assumes the throne. Some years later, Theseus makes a trip to Hades to help a friend, Peirithous, win the goddess Persephone. The two confront Hades, the King of the Dead, who tricks them into spending eternity in Hades stuck to a bench.

MORE ABOUT THE MYTH

According to the findings of art and archaeology, some of the stories of Theseus seem to be based on fact. Other stories, however, appear to have little if any basis in reality, and are more likely the result of tall-tale telling and romanticizing. For this reason, Theseus may be thought of as something of a legend, like John Henry or Paul Bunyan, as opposed to a purely mythic figure.

Much of our knowledge of Theseus' exploits comes from works of art from the classical Greek period. Vases provide detailed pictorial accounts of stories, both mythical and real. Of course, original written material is also helpful. Theseus is mentioned in Homer's epics, the *Iliad* and the *Odyssey* (written in the ninth century B.C.). The *Theogony* of Hesiod, from the eighth century B.C., which is the earliest organized collection of myths and legends, relates in a written form that which was previously handed down orally. The dramas of Aeschylus, Sophocles, and Euripides also provide source material, especially for myths involving the gods.

Using archaeological sites and chronological references, some historians are attempting to piece together at least a general outline of Theseus' life. He may have been born at Troezen during the Bronze Age. Although there is a rock there that is claimed to be "Theseus Rock," there is no indication now that this rock is more likely to have hidden Aegeus's accouterments than any other rock in the area. The land on which Theseus was thought to have met the pine-bending Sinis is now completely bare of trees and seems to have been the same in Theseus' time, thus relegating this portion of the hero's adventure to the realm of myth. Researchers have found that the great palace at Minos would have been large enough to confuse most citizens, and could easily have been the Minotaur's labyrinth. The Minotaur itself is suspected of being simply a bull, since bulls were often used in ancient Greek rites and appear frequently in art of the time.

Many of the heroics attributed to Theseus seem to parallel the feats of the famous Attic hero Heracles (Hercules), and mythologists suspect that Athenians endowed the already renowned King of Athens with conquests and stories to compete with Heracles.

A CRITICAL COMMENT

"The standard path of the mythological adventure of the hero is a magnification of the formula represented in the rites of passage: *separation— initiation—return*: which might be named the nuclear unit of the monomyth.

"A hero ventures forth from the world of common day into a region of supernatural wonder: fabulous forces are there encountered and a decisive victory is won: the hero comes back from this mysterious adventure with the power to bestow boons on his fellow man.

"Prometheus ascended to the heavens, stole fire from the gods, and descended. Jason sailed through the Clashing Rocks into a sea of marvels, circumvented the dragon that guarded the Golden Fleece, and returned with the fleece and the power to wrest his rightful throne from a usurper. Aeneas went down into the underworld, crossed the dreadful river of the dead, threw a sop to the three-headed watchdog Cerebrums, and conversed, at last, with the shade of his dead father. All things were unfolded to him: the destiny of souls, the destiny of Rome, which he was about to found, 'and in what wise he might avoid or endure every burden.' He returned through the ivory gate to his work in the world. . . .

"Everywhere, no matter what the sphere of interest (whether religious, political, or personal), the really creative acts are represented as those deriving from some sort of dying to the world; and what happens in the interval of the hero's nonentity, so that he comes back as one reborn, made great and filled with creative power, mankind is also unanimous in declaring. We shall have only to follow, therefore, a multitude of heroic figures through the classic stages of the universal adventure in order to see again what has always been revealed. This will help us to understand not only the meaning of those images for contemporary life, but also the singleness of the human spirit in its aspirations, powers, vicissitudes, and wisdom."
—*from* The Hero with a Thousand Faces,
Joseph Campbell

FOR FURTHER READING

Burn, Lucilla. *Greek Myths*. Austin: University of Texas Press, 1990.

Campbell, Joseph. *The Hero with a Thousand Faces*. Princeton: Princeton University Press, 1968.

Graves, Robert. *The Greek Myths*. Baltimore: Penguin Books, 1960.

Hamilton, Edith. *Mythology*. Boston: Little, Brown and Company, 1969.

OSIRIS AND ISIS

Retold by Padraic Colum ▼ (Textbook page 35)

SUMMARY

Osiris is Lord of all things. His sister and wife, Isis, reigns with him over the land. Thout, the Wise One, is their brother, and reigns over arts and reckoning. Two other siblings are Nephthys and Seth, the Violent One. Seth resents Osiris' rule. He builds a wooden casket made of fragrant woods and at a banquet, Seth tricks Osiris into the chest. The casket is then thrown out to sea. It finds its way to a wooded area in Byblos, and a tree grows around it. The King and Queen of Byblos cut the tree down and take its trunk to their palace, where, casket and all, it guards the royal child's nursery.

Isis hears about the tree and poses as a nurse to the Queen's child. She takes the form of a swallow and mourns the tree. Isis discloses her immortal identity and the King frees the casket from the tree-column. Isis returns to Egypt with the casket and breathes life into Osiris.

One night Seth attacks the revived Osiris and tears him to pieces, bringing death to the land. Isis searches for and finds the pieces of Osiris and puts them together. She is then informed by a divine voice that Osiris lives in the underworld where he judges those who die. Isis has a son by Osiris named Horus, who avenges his father's death by bringing Seth to his mother's mercy. Isis demotes Seth to the position of a lesser god.

MORE ABOUT THE CULTURE

The ancient Egyptians believed strongly in the afterlife. Their tombs and temples, elaborate and filled with riches and provisions for travel in the hereafter, provide evidence of this. In addition, from sources such as inscriptions and the Pyramid Texts, we find the diverse tales which suggest the rich faith of ancient Egypt. Typically, the story of Isis and Osiris is not available to us in complete form; it was instead pieced together from a variety of sources and references. Plutarch, in first-century A.D. Greece, took on the monumental task of gathering the parts of the Egyptian myths and assembling them to create the first-known text of complete Egyptian myths. This compilation is the basic source for most renderings of the myths.

Sources from earlier times suggest that Egyptians worshiped animals as gods, and that divinities varied with locality, or later, with each pharaoh. Gods were eventually endowed with human attributes, and, in later times, developed into more human forms, though still closely related to animals. A good example is the facility with which Isis metamorphizes into a swallow in this selection. Other Egyptian deities appear as jackals, cats, falcons (Horus), or ibises (Thout). Most people are familiar with the part-human, part-animal depictions of various Egyptian deities.

Pharaohs were considered half-human, half-god (like many of the heroes in these selections) and represented a direct connection between the people and their deities. As such, only pharaohs were permitted the divine right of entrance and worship in the temple of a god.

Although certain gods were common to all parts of Egypt (the gods of the sun, the moon, the Earth, and the Nile), each area had a specific god who was protector of that locale. Osiris seems to have been the god worshiped in an area known as Busiris. He later attracted a large following, and it is because of this later popularity that we know him. Osiris was not only the god most closely associated with death, but also with vegetation. The planting of seeds is symbolized by the burial of his body parts. His rebirth, of course, is associated with the annual renewal of vegetation. This symbolism took a ritual form at the end of each flood season: the shape of Osiris was traced on the ground and the interior planted with seeds. In spring, vegetation would sprout in the shape of Osiris. This ritual was also performed for funereal ceremonies. The Osiris of Vegetation has been found in several tombs.

A CRITICAL COMMENT

"During the first few centuries of its history, one of the most powerful rivals to Christianity in the Greco-Roman world was the religion of the goddess Isis. During these centuries, she was widely worshiped throughout the Mediterranean world for a variety of blessings: health, fertility, family security, and immortality. She was popular among the nobility as well as among the lower classes and was especially dear to women. She was widely known for her warm approachability as well as her great cosmic power. . . .

"In the context of Egyptian religion, this myth seems to have two primary meanings—one associated with the Nile River and the other with the birth, death, and rebirth of the pharaohs. . . .

The myth of the birth, death, and resurrection of Osiris, in part at least, suggests the rhythm of agriculture and vegetative life. Like the crops, Osiris grows to maturity, is then slain (harvested), only to be reborn in the spring. In the context of Egyptian geography, the rebirth of vegetation (the rebirth of Osiris) is inextricably bound up with the flooding of the Nile before spring planting. Indeed, the land would not be renewed, the crops would not be reborn, if the Nile did not annually swell its banks and renourish the land. This periodic flooding is caused by the tears of Isis when she laments for her dead husband. In the myth, Isis brings back life through much effort, after a long and trying search, and after much mourning and shedding many tears. Osiris (vegetation) is revived through both Isis's emotion (her tears) and her efforts. . . . In the myth as it relates to Egyptian geography, then, Isis may be said to be the land itself, which is left barren without the annual rebirth of vegetation, while Osiris is the spirit of the crops, the fecund power that yields food from the land.

"The other fundamental meaning of the myth of Osiris and Isis in the context of ancient Egyptian religion concerns the periodic death and rebirth of the pharaohs. In Egyptian political mythology, when the pharaoh died he was identified with Osiris, while the new pharaoh, usually young and inexperienced, was identified with Horus. . . . Through the effort, love, and magic of Isis, the powerful, divine genius of the pharaoh as a fructifying and civilizing force was transferred or recycled in refreshed form from the dead pharaoh to his successor. . . .

"In her role as protector, nourisher, and mother of all pharaohs, Isis is represented by a hieroglyph that has as its basic element the throne of the pharaohs . . . So basic was she to the well-being

and power of the ruler that she was understood to be the seat of his power, quite literally. It was she who had given him birth, continued to nourish him in his vulnerable infancy and youth, and sustained and invigorated him in his maturity and old age. As the fertile land itself, Isis was the ground upon which the pharaoh sat, and he was the genius of fecundity, the presence of order and civilization that made her habitable, beautiful, and ever fruitful."

—*from* The Goddesses' Mirror,
David Kinsley

For Further Reading

Budge, E. A. Wallis. *The Gods of the Egyptians.* New York: Dover Publications, 1969.
——————— *Egyptian Religion.* New York: Carol Publishing Group, 1987.
Grimal, Pierre. *Larousse World Mythology.* New York: G. P. Putnam's Sons, 1965.
Kinsley, David. *The Goddesses' Mirror.* Albany: State University of New York Press, 1989.
Wolkstein, Diane. *The First Love Stories.* New York: HarperCollins, 1991.

Green Willow

Retold by Paul Jordan-Smith ▾ (Textbook page 41)

Summary

A young Japanese samurai is sent by his lord on a special mission to the Lord of Kyoto. During the journey, the samurai, Tomotada, facing a heavy snowstorm, stops at a humble mountain cottage. He is received by an old couple and their beautiful daughter, Green Willow. Tomotada requests her hand in marriage, and the old parents enthusiastically give their permission. Riding with Green Willow toward Kyoto, Tomotada is overcome with anxiety about his proposed marriage. He is not allowed to marry without the permission of his lord, and he also fears that his bride-to-be is so beautiful that she will be stolen from him. Forgoing his mission, Tomotada retreats with Green Willow into the mountains where they live happily together. Five years later, Green Willow suddenly takes ill and dies. Many years later, a wandering monk stops at a stream to drink. On the bank of the stream he sees two old willow trees and one young one, next to which is placed a stone memorial. The monk inquires about the stone from an old neighborhood priest, and the priest tells him the story of Green Willow. When the monk inquires about Tomotada, the priest, who has been lost in

thought, explains that he was thinking about a young samurai.

More About the Culture

Crucial to understanding this tale of love is a knowledge of the socio-economic structure of medieval Japan and the nearly irreconcilable social differences between the samurai and his peasant bride. During the time of this tale, Japan was ruled by an emperor who resided at the capital (now known as Kyoto). The emperor, however, was often placed on the throne as a child and rarely held actual power. In reality, Japan was ruled by the office of the shogun, the chief officer for the emperor, and was often controlled from behind the scenes by the royal family. The imperial family, the aristocracy, the samurai, and the wealthy landowning families constituted the upper class.

The country was divided into provinces, each of which was presided over by a special envoy, or governor. In the provinces a feudal system developed on the local level and continued to thrive until 1867 when Emperor Meiji abolished it. Samurai, akin to the knights of medieval Europe, served the lords in the provinces and at court. As part of the upper class, Samurai generally kept their distance from the peasants, farmers, and merchants who made up the rest of Japan's citizenry. Thus, the union between Tomotada and Green Willow would most likely not have been looked upon favorably.

Shintoism, Japan's central native religion, is based on the existence of many gods and the ritual worship of ancestors. Although Buddhism, brought to Japan from China, has had a great influence on the social practices of the Japanese, Shintoism has remained strong. Another influence from China was Confucianism, in which social order is perceived as bringing stability. A doctrine known as *bushidō* (the "way of the warrior"), which developed from a mix of Shintoism and Confucianism, outlined a code for warriors. *Bushidō* demanded that a samurai serve his lord with unwavering loyalty and stay true to principles of self-discipline, including a willingness to meet death in the performance of duty. Hara-kiri, or ritual suicide, was mandated should the samurai fail in duty or lose in battle. Thus, in marrying Green Willow and not carrying out his duties to his lord, Tomotada commits the triple sin of disobeying the *bushidō*, not performing hara-kiri, and marrying a commoner.

A CRITICAL COMMENT

"The teller of stories has everywhere and always found eager listeners. Whether his tale is the mere report of a recent happening, a legend of long ago, or an elaborately contrived fiction, men and women have hung upon his words and satisfied their yearnings for information or amusement, for incitement to heroic deeds, for religious edification, or for release from the overpowering monotony of their lives. In villages of central Africa, in outrigger boats in the Pacific, in the Australian bush, and within the shadow of Hawaiian volcanoes, tales of the present and of the mysterious past, of animals and gods and heroes, and of men and women like themselves, hold listeners in their spell or enrich the conversation of daily life. So it is also in Eskimo igloos under the light of seal-oil lamps, in the tropical jungles of Brazil, and by the totem poles of the British Columbian coast. In Japan too, and China and India, the priest and the scholar, the peasant and the artisan all join in their love of a good story and their honor for the man who tells it well. . . .

"Although the term 'folktale' is often used in English to refer to the 'household tale' or 'fairy tale' (the German *Märchen*), such as 'Cinderella' or 'Snow White,' it is also legitimately employed in a much broader sense to include all forms of prose narrative, written or oral, which have come to be handed down through the years. In this usage the important fact is the traditional nature of the

material. In contrast to the modern story writer's striving after originality of plot and treatment, the teller of a folktale is proud of his ability to hand on that which he has received. He usually desires to impress his readers or hearers with the fact that he is bringing them something that has the stamp of good authority, that the tale was heard from some great storyteller or from some aged person who remembered it from old days. . . .

"It is clear then that the oral story need not always have been oral. But when it once habituates itself to being passed on by word of mouth it undergoes the same treatment as all other tales at the command of the raconteur. It becomes something to tell to an audience, or at least to a listener, not something to read. Its effects are no longer produced indirectly by association with words written or printed on a page, but directly through facial expression and gesture and repetition and recurrent patterns that generations have tested and found effective.

"This oral art of taletelling is far older than history, and it is not bounded by one continent or one civilization. Stories may differ in subject from place to place, the conditions and purposes of taletelling may change as we move from land to land or from century to century, and yet everywhere it ministers to the same basic social and individual needs. The call for entertainment to fill in the hours of leisure has found most peoples very limited in their resources, and except where modern urban civilization has penetrated deeply they have found the telling of stories one of the most satisfying of pastimes. Curiosity about the past has always brought eager listeners to tales of the long ago which supply the simple man with all he knows of the history of his folk. Legends grow with the telling, and often a great heroic past evolves to gratify vanity and tribal pride. Religion also has played a mighty role everywhere in the encouragement of the narrative art, for the religious mind has tried to understand beginnings and for ages has told stories of ancient days and sacred beings. Often whole cosmologies have unfolded themselves in these legends, and hierarchies of gods and heroes."

from The Folktale,
Stith Thompson

FOR FURTHER READING

Campbell, Joseph. *The Masks of God: Oriental Myth.* New York: Penguin Books, 1962.
Davis, F. Hadland. *Myths and Legends of Japan.* Singapore: Graham Brash, 1989.
Piggott, Juliet. *Japanese Mythology.* London: The Hamlyn Publishing Group, Ltd, 1969.
Tyler, Royall, ed. and trans. *Japanese Tales.* New York: Pantheon Books, 1987.

THE WHITE SNAKE

Retold by Jakob and Wilhelm Grimm ▾ Translated by Jack Zipes ▾ (Textbook page 47)

SUMMARY

An unnamed servant, curious about what his king eats every night, discovers that his master secretly eats a white snake. Upon tasting the white snake, the servant discovers that he has gained the ability to understand what animals are saying. When the queen loses her ring, the servant is accused of the theft; the king orders him to find the thief or be put to death. The servant retrieves the ring using his newfound power, and the king grants the young man's wish to see the world.

During his travels, the servant aids three distressed groups of creatures: fish, ants, and birds. All vow to remember and repay him. Soon the traveler comes to a city where he declares himself a suitor for the king's daughter. Before her father will consider him, the servant must perform an impossible task: He must retrieve a gold ring from the ocean. The three fish whose lives he had saved recover the ring for him. The proud princess demands another feat, which is performed by the ants he helped during his travels. The princess demands yet another impossible task: procure the golden apple from the Tree of Life. The golden apple is brought to him by the three young crows he had saved. The princess then accepts the young man and the couple lives happily for many years.

MORE ABOUT THE AUTHORS

Although known worldwide for their *Fairy Tales,* the Grimms were two of Germany's most famous nineteenth-century scholars. Their major areas of study were the development of language and the preservation of the Germanic cultural heritage. Of their many academic achievements, several were exemplary. One was their conception of the *German Dictionary,* a work which not only defined words but also provided for each word an etymology spanning a four-hundred-year-period. The Grimms underestimated the magnitude of this project and were unable to complete it, but it was eventually completed in thirty-two volumes over one hundred years later by many dedicated individuals.

In contrast, the *Fairy Tales,* three slender volumes containing some two hundred selections, brought the Grimms immediate acclaim and international recognition. In the 1812 preface to the first volume, the Grimms spoke eloquently for themselves and their motivation for compiling the *Tales.* They realized that a wealth of early German literature had never been written down and was subsequently lost for all time. The folk and fairy tales, as well as folksongs, were probably the only vestiges of a rich and once-thriving literary tradition.

Because they had compiled, translated, and published a number of scholarly treatises on the folklore of other countries, the Grimms realized the innate importance of the tales they were collecting. The also knew that many of the same themes and plots had evolved in tales of other cultures. Other ancient peoples related tales of their Cinderellas and Sleeping Beauties, although with different names. The Grimms understood the importance of preserving ancient folk wisdom and myths for generations to come.

This, however, was not the attitude of the Grimms' contemporaries. The study of folk literature was not only considered irrelevant, but almost disreputable. Many of the scholars thought of folktales as the superstitious inanities of ignorant peasants. In contrast, the Grimms believed they contained inherent wisdom and universal truths. Their respect is evident in the immense amount of time and attention that went into collecting the tales.

A CRITICAL COMMENT

"Many deplorable features of modern life, irrationalism, nationalism, idolization of mass-feeling and mass-opinion, may be traced back to the Romantic reaction against the Enlightenment and its Polite Learning; but that same reaction is also responsible for the work of Jakob and Wilhelm Grimm who, with their successors, made the fairy story a part of general education, a deed which few will regret.

"There are quite a number of people who disapprove of fairy tales for children, and on various grounds. Let us take the most reasonable first: those who claim that the fairy tale as we know it from Grimm and Andersen is not viable in modern culture. Such tales, they argue, developed in a feudally organized society which believed in magic, and are irrelevant to an industrialized democracy like our own. Luckily the test of viability is a simple one. If a tale is enjoyed by the reader, or audience, it is viable; if he finds it boring or incomprehensible, it is not.

"The second charge against fairy tales is that they harm the child by frightening him or arousing his sadistic impulses. . . .

"Lastly there are the people who object to fairy stories on the grounds that they are not objectively true, that giants, witches, two-headed dragons, magic carpets, etc., do not exist; and that, instead of indulging his fantasies in fairy tales, the child should be taught how to adapt to reality by studying history and mechanics. I find such people, I must confess, so unsympathetic and peculiar that I do not know how to argue with them. If their case were sound, the world should be full of Don Quixote-like madmen attempting to fly from New York to Philadelphia on a broomstick or covering a telephone with kisses in the belief that it was their enchanted girl friend. . . .

"If such a tale is not history, what is it about? Broadly speaking, and in most cases, the fairy tale is a dramatic projection in symbolic images of the life of the psyche, and it can travel from one country to another, one culture to another culture, whenever what it has to say holds good for human nature in both, despite their differences."

—*from* Tales of Grimm and Andersen,
W.H. Auden

FOR FURTHER READING

Manheim, Ralph, trans. *Grimm's Tales for Young and Old*. New York: Doubleday, 1983.

Michaelis-Jena, R. *The Brothers Grimm*. London: Routledge, 1970.

Peppard, Murray B. *Paths Through the Forest*. New York: Holt, Rinehart and Winston, 1971.

Stern, James, ed. *The Complete Grimm's Fairy Tales*. New York: Pantheon Books, 1976.

Zipes, Jack, trans. *The Complete Fairy Tales of the Brothers Grimm*, Volumes I and II. New York: Bantam Books, 1987.

NOTES

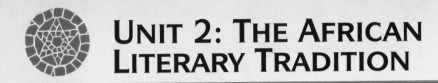

UNIT 2: THE AFRICAN LITERARY TRADITION

(Textbook page 64)

Unit Introduction: African Literature

African literature is as old as the pyramids. Written literature on the African continent began with the ancient Egyptians, and many of their literary traditions have counterparts in African literature today.

BACKGROUND

EGYPTIAN WRITING

The earliest known African writings, brief Egyptian hieroglyphics identifying people, places, events, or possessions, date from the period between 3500 B.C. and 3000 B.C. The art of writing was considered holy, and it was originally used only for pharaohs, who were thought to be the living representations of deities. The first written texts were Offering Lists, inscribed on the walls of royal tombs dating from the First Dynasty (c. 3000 B.C.) and listing the foods, fabrics, and ointments to be offered regularly to the pharaoh after his death. By the beginning of the Old Kingdom period (c. 2700 B.C.), nobles too were constructing elaborate tombs and writing Offering Lists. These lists grew in length, including not only detailed specifications about offerings but also lengthy explanations of the ranks, titles, and achievements of the tomb-owner and members of his family. Eventually the Offering Lists were replaced in pharaohs' tombs by briefer, formalized prayers for offerings. But in nobles' tombs, instead of being replaced by a more concise form, the Offering Lists grew into full-fledged autobiographies, one of the most important and widespread genres in Egyptian literature. Thus, the prayer and the autobiography were the first true literary genres to evolve in ancient Egypt. Both forms reached their highest level of sophistication during the Fifth Dynasty (c. 2450–2300 B.C.).

Meanwhile, a third genre was also developing, one involving writings recorded not on tomb walls but on papyrus scrolls: the instruction genre. The instructions, too, achieved a recognizable form during the Fifth Dynasty, when they gained a popularity that would not wane until well past the New Kingdom (1600–1100 B.C.). The instructions, also called Instructions in Wisdom, consisted of strings of maxims presented within a simple narrative frame, usually one in which a father was instructing his son in the proper virtues. Instructions were always attributed to a famous sage or pharaoh—just as the maxims of the Hebrew Bible's Book of Proverbs are attributed to the wise Solomon and the wisdom of the Chinese *Analects* is attributed to Confucius. Over the course of centuries, the original texts of the instructions were expanded and edited repeatedly.

The culturally flourishing Fifth Dynasty produced a fourth significant genre: the Pyramid Texts, forerunners to the New Kingdom Book of the Dead. These groupings of myths and spells were intended to aid the soul of the dead pharaoh in his journey to the afterlife and his reunion with the gods. These texts were inscribed on the walls of tombs and were often formulated as poetry. By the Middle Kingdom (c. 2000–1800 B.C.), these had become the much more elaborate Coffin Texts, inscribed not on tomb walls but on individual coffins. Hymns, or poems in praise of the gods, and lyrics, or songs, were two other poetic forms that first appeared during the Middle Kingdom. These forms were refined during the New Kingdom (c. 1600–1100 B.C.), which also saw the emergence of the love lyric. The narrative prose form also originated during the Middle Kingdom. These narratives included adventure tales like "The Tale of the Shipwrecked Sailor"; wonder tales, like the five usually grouped under the title "King Cheops and the Magician"; and the hero tales such as "The Story of Sinuhe," which featured the ideal Egyptian hero: modest and moderate, conscientious and law-abiding, living in harmony with the divine order.

THE GROWTH OF LITERARY TRADITIONS THROUGHOUT AFRICA

As Egypt's power waned during the early centuries before and after the start of the Christian era, North Africans such as Apuleius and St. Augustine, writing in Latin, offered literary contributions that would profoundly affect Western literature and thought. It was also during this period that the chivalric warriors and troubadours of the Fasa people roamed the grasslands of the Sahel region (between Africa's Sahara and Sudan deserts). The members of this nation, who apparently had a well-developed oral literary tradition, clashed repeatedly with the Fulbe (Fulani) people until they finally subdued them in the third century A.D. The exploits of the Fasa are commemorated today in fragments of the Soninke oral epic *The Dausi*, which reached its present form in the sixteenth century but probably existed in some form at least three centuries earlier; those of the Fulbe are recounted in the later, and also fragmentary, oral epic *The Baudi*. Other African oral epics, complete but more difficult to date, are *Sundiata* of Old Mali, recited among speakers of the Mande family of languages throughout West Africa; the *Mwindo Epic* of the Bantu-speaking Banyanga, who live in the Congo Republic in central Africa; and the epic of Shaka Zulu, the last great Zulu king, known in many parts of southern Africa.

African Literary Genres

In addition to epics, the African oral tradition embraces many types of myths, tales, songs, poems, and dramas. The conventional genre classifications of Western literature are neither helpful nor relevant when discussing the oral literatures of Africa; instead, some scholars classify types of African oral literature by their functions: historical, religious, ceremonial, didactic, social. But because the religious, social, and political arenas are all thoroughly integrated into daily life in most traditional African cultures, even these classifications blur and overlap. In this unit, for example, the proverbs function both aesthetically as poetry and didactically as teaching tools. The cradle song, "Song of a Mother to Her Firstborn," fulfills a practical domestic function as a lullaby but also functions as a ceremonial praise poem. And the ritual poem "Ogun Kills on the Right" is at once religious, ceremonial, and social in function.

Writing Systems in Africa

Writing systems were known in Africa from early times, for trade routes through the Sudan Desert provided opportunities for the exchange not only of goods, but also of cultural knowledge. Salt from northern Africa, mentioned by Herodotus in the fourth century B.C., was traded for West Africa's gold; goods from the Mideastern world were exchanged for raw materials and spices from Africa's continental interior; and archaeological evidence confirms that goods from China were traded as far south as Zimbabwe. When much of Sudanic Africa accepted Islam in the eighth century A.D., the Arabic writing system was also introduced, as Muslim law stipulates that the Koran must be written and recited only in Arabic. Many African cultures adopted writing systems for such purposes

as bookkeeping, but African literatures remained oral.

The Features of African Orature

One reason that writing was seldom used for literary purposes in Africa involves the tonal qualities of African languages. In the majority of African languages (and, incidentally, in many others, such as Chinese), words change meaning depending on the tones in which the syllables are spoken. For example, in a Bantu language spoken in Cameroon, one word can mean "payment" if spoken in a high tone and "crossroads" if spoken in a low tone. Some African languages employ up to eight fixed tones, with additional rising and falling tones. The complexities of such highly tonal languages, and the difficulties of accurately transcribing them, are difficult for speakers of English (an atonal language) to grasp, but they are significant.

Another, more compelling reason that writing never became the medium of choice for literature in Africa was that the oral tradition worked so well and was so strongly developed. In West Africa, for example, griots—community bards and historians who were often members of hereditary castes or clans—learned rhetorical skills passed down through generations. They were highly educated in many disciplines, and they memorized vast bodies of literature, law, and traditional material, presenting certain works verbatim, as tradition required, and performing others with their own individual enhancements. These "speaking documents" preserved and furthered a uniquely living literature.

The Future of African Oral Literatures

The combined effects of colonialism, urbanization, and advanced technology are to a certain extent eroding Africa's oral literatures. Griots in West Africa, for example, were traditionally supported by patronages from aristocratic families. Today, however, the patronage system is gone, and many griots have turned to public entertainment to earn their livings. Some have regular radio programs; others perform at weddings and parties, inducing wealthy guests to pay them handsomely for reciting their praises. Furthermore, as oral literature is taped and/or transcribed, it is both fixed and, over time, removed from the oral tradition. African groups today are addressing these issues and searching for ways to preserve their oral traditions. Several modern African authors are experimenting with ways to synthesize African oral traditions and the traditions of written literature. The modern poets Chinweizu of Nigeria, Kofi Awoonor of Ghana, and the late Okot p'Bitek of Uganda are three who have been instrumental in this effort.

UNIT PROJECTS

1. **Creating a Diarama.** With a group of other classmates, create a diorama showing the troops of Sundiata and Soumaoro massed for the battle of Krina. Use details about the battle from passages in *Sundiata*, and draw information about setting, dress, and weapons from other references about the Mali Empire. When you finish your diorama, display it for the rest of the class. Include an explanatory label and map.

2. **Presenting a Newscast.** Imagine that you are a newscaster for a television channel broadcasting a live report about one of the events from a selection in this unit. For example, you could report on the village disturbance in "Talk." Or you could give a blow-by-blow account of the battle between Sundiata and Soumaoro at the battle of Krina from *Sundiata*. Provide background about the event you choose, drawing on details in the selection. You may want to research the culture in question to lend accuracy to your eyewitness report. Present your newscast before the class.

3. **Drawing a Portrait of the Aten.** After consulting art books that contain photographs of statues, paintings, or bas-reliefs of the Aten, the sun-god worshiped by Akhenaten, draw your own portrait of the Aten. Reread "The Great Hymn to the Aten" for ideas about what the sun-god might be wearing, holding, or doing and about which objects to put in the background of your portrait. Use your imagination as well as your research to make your portrait different from those you have seen. When you have finished your portrait, show it to the class along with other representations of the Aten.

4. **Researching Hieroglyphics.** Go to your school or public library and do some research on hieroglyphics, consulting books, encyclopedias, and audio-visual tapes. Present your findings to the class in the form of an oral report. If possible, find samples of hieroglyphic writing (with translations) and copy several characters onto notecards to show to the class.

5. **Producing a Skit.** With other classmates, prepare skits that illustrate the theme(s) of one of the selections in this unit. For example. you might use several of the proverbs as the basis for a skit. Choose or create props that will evoke appropriate settings and details, and write dialogue that is relevant to the selection's theme. After practicing your skits, present them to the class. Let class members guess which selection each skit illustrates.

6. **Playing "proverb charades."** Write your favorite African proverbs on separate slips of paper, and put the slips into a container. Divide the class into two teams and let one member of each team draw a paper from the container. Without speaking or writing, the team member who has drawn the paper must pantomime clues that will enable the other members to guess the proverb. Whichever team can correctly guess its proverb first wins the round. After playing, discuss which proverbs were hardest to guess, and explore the reasons for the difficulties.

7. **Giving a Choral Reading.** With other classmates, plan a choral reading of one of the following selections in this unit: "Song of a Mother to Her Firstborn," "The Great Hymn to the Aten," a New Kingdom love lyric, or. "Ogun Kills on the Right." Select appropriate music to accompany the reading, and decide which lines or phrases should be read by a single voice and which should be read by several voices. Decide, as well, which lines should be read loudly or softly, and which phrases should be emphasized. After planning your choral reading, practice it and then present it for the class.

8. **Writing a Rap Song.** With several classmates, pick one of the selections in this unit and compose a rap song about the events, theme, and/or character(s) in the selection. Let each of your partners "emcee" a different part of the rap. You may also create accompanying music and a dance for the rap. Present your finished product to the class.

9. **Writing a Crossword Puzzle.** Using your imagination and the selections in this unit, create a crossword puzzle for your classmates. Use clues about characters, plot, themes, or other context clues. For example, the clue for "one, down" might read, "When he laughs, others run for cover" (answer: *Ogun*).

10. **Inventing an Oral Tale.** Get together with a few classmates and create a short oral literature tale, using conventions of African orature, such as repetition, refrain, alliteration, and chants. You may choose an incident from your own experience or make one up. When you have outlined your tale, have each member of your group take turns telling the tale, recording each telling on an audio or video tape recorder. Present the different taped versions to the class. Were there any changes, additions, or deletions? Where did they occur?

THE GREAT HYMN TO THE ATEN

Translated by Miriam Lichtheim ▾ (Textbook page 73)

SUMMARY

In general, praise poems are characterized by a string of complimentary descriptions of a god, followed by a plea for protection or an affirmation of the god's favor. This praise poem is addressed to the Aten (the sun, worshiped as the sole god and the creator of all things).

The god is described as a bringer of light and a giver of life. The speaker contrasts the somber and threatening nighttime, when the god is absent, with the bright and festive daytime, when living things rejoice and thrive in the god's presence. A river bustling with ships, fields and flocks being tended, towns large and small, and a multitude of diverse peoples are all images evoked to demonstrate the scope of the sun god's dominion and his watchful care. The poet praises the god's works, commenting especially on the variety among life forms and on the god's foresight as a provider. For example, the god has made the Nile to irrigate arid Egypt, along with seasonal rains to irrigate other lands.

The poet ends the hymn with a reminder that the pharaoh is the god's son, that he is virtuous, and that he and his queen will live forever.

MORE ABOUT THE AUTHOR

Whether or not it was actually written by Akhenaten, "The Great Hymn to the Aten" reflects the prosperity that prevailed during this pharaoh's reign. It also reveals the tolerance toward other peoples and the enjoyment of daily life that, according to researchers, characterized upper-class Egyptians of the New Kingdom. Akhenaten himself appears to have been an unusually intelligent and enlightened pharaoh. Archaeological evidence suggests that he was a deep thinker; a talented writer, architect, and patron of the arts; and an egalitarian reformer whose institution of new religious rules and appointment of a new order of nobles replaced many oppressive social constraints. He encouraged unprecedented artistic freedom and significantly reduced the authority that the old nobles held over the working people and peasants. Scholars have theorized that Akhenaten's religious and social reforms, along with the radical step of constructing a new capital, represented a shrewd attempt to regain some of the political power which had gradually passed from the monarchy to the priesthood and the old orders of nobles in Thebes.

The ruins of Akhenaten's well-planned capital at Tel-el-Amarna, four hundred miles north of Thebes, confirm the idea that his reign was a period of enlightenment. Tel-el-Amarna extended for eight miles along the Nile, boasting lakes, painted pavements, public and private gardens, and buildings decorated with brightly colored, naturalistic scenes of everyday life in the New Kingdom. Today the murals and reliefs on Tel-el-Amarna's buildings and tombs are important sources of information about New Kingdom lifestyles. The center of the city was the huge Temple of the Aten, its innovative, open design possibly conceived by the pharaoh himself. Near it was the royal palace, almost eight hundred yards long, open and filled with light, fronting the river. Judging by the palace murals depicting the day-to-day activities of the royal family, Akhenaten enjoyed his home life and was relaxed and affectionate with his wife and children.

Whether because he was less robust than earlier pharaohs (his odd appearance—elongated skull, drooping shoulders, pot belly, and heavy thighs—is thought to indicate a glandular disease) or because he was preoccupied with domestic affairs, Akhenaten did not often venture far from his capital, and he neglected Egypt's foreign holdings. By the end of his reign, the Hittites, pressing from the east, had won control of many Egyptian provinces. After Akhenaten's death, his religious and social reforms were quickly abolished, and the disorder in the provinces was addressed by those advising his successor, Tutankhamen. This boy-king ascended the throne at the age of nine and was ritually married to one of Akhenaten's six daughters. Probably under pressure from his powerful advisors, he hurriedly reinstated the old gods and moved the capital back to Thebes.

A CRITICAL COMMENT

"The *hymns to the gods* are . . . [a] genre in which the New Kingdom built on the foundations of the Middle Kingdom and went beyond them. . . .

"The largest number of hymns are addressed to the sun-god in his several manifestations. [Early examples] show the widened universalist conception of sun worship and also the inclusion of the sun disk, the Aten, among the manifestations of the sun-god. This was the point that the worship of the Aten as a distinct deity had reached in the time of Amenhotep III.

"*The Great Hymn to the Aten* recorded in the tomb of the courtier Ay presents in pure form the doctrine of the sole god worked out by Amenhotep IV, Akhenaten. The king had taught it to his followers, and it is only through their hymns and prayers, carved in their tombs at El Amarna, that his monotheistic teaching has reached us. The Great Hymn and the shorter hymns and prayers in the Amarna tombs show how completely the doctrine of the one god had been enforced at Amarna. In recording their hopes for a blessed afterlife, the courtiers could no longer turn to Osiris and related comforting beliefs. Only the king, the son of the Aten, remained as a guarantor of their survival. . . .

"*The Great Hymn to the Aten* is an eloquent and beautiful statement of the doctrine of the one god. He alone has created the world and all it contains. He alone gives life to man and beast. He alone watches over his creations. He alone inhabits the sky. Heretofore the sun-god had appeared in three major forms: as Harakhti in the morning, as Khephri in midday, and as Atum in the evening. His daily journey across the sky had been done in the company of many gods. It had involved the ever-recurring combat against the primordial serpent Apopis. In traversing the night sky the god had been acclaimed by the multitudes of the dead who rest there; and each hour of the night had marked a specific stage in his journey. Thus the daily circuit of the sky was a drama with a large supporting cast. In the new doctrine of the Aten as sole god all these facets were eliminated. The Aten rises and sets in lonely majesty in an empty sky. Only the earth is peopled by his creatures, and only they adore his rising and setting.

" . . . Akhenaten had dedicated his new city to the Aten, and the public worship of the god must have been the central feature in the daily life of the court. . . . [The courtiers] could no longer pray to Anubis for protection; nor could they look toward passing the judgment before Osiris and being welcomed by the gods. All that a courtier of Akhenaten could hope for was to be granted a tomb and that his *ka* would survive by virtue of his association with the king. It is no wonder that after the death of Akhenaten his followers hastily abandoned his teaching and returned to the comforting beliefs in the many gods who offered help to man in life and beyond death."

—*from* Ancient Egyptian Literature, *Miriam Lichtheim*

FOR FURTHER READING

Lichtheim, Miriam. *Ancient Egyptian Literature: A Book of Readings, Volume II: The New Kingdom.* Berkeley: University of California Press, 1976.

Maspero, Gaston. *Popular Stories of Ancient Egypt.* Trans. A. S. Johns. New Hyde Park: University Books, 1967.

Simpson, William Kelley, ed. *The Literature of Ancient Egypt: An Anthology of Stories, Instructions, and Poetry.* New Haven: Yale University Press, 1972.

NEW KINGDOM LOVE LYRICS

Translated by William Kelley Simpson ▼ (Textbook page 81)

SUMMARY

In "The Voice of the Wild Goose," the speaker says that she is caught in the snares of love, just as the wild geese she traps for her mother every day are caught in her nets. Today she is immobilized by love, unable to perform her daily task, and she wonders what to tell her mother when she returns home with no catch.

In "Most Beautiful Youth Who Ever Happened," the speaker confides her dream of sharing a home with her beloved, describing her feelings of love, the sense of well-being she derives from spending time with her lover and from knowing that he is well and happy, and her desolation—approximating a state of death—when she is separated from him.

MORE ABOUT THE SELECTIONS

Scholars have discovered very little about ancient Egyptian courtship practices, and only four manuscripts containing Egyptian love lyrics are known. The two lyrics in this selection come from a battered New Kingdom papyrus containing three sets of love lyrics, now in the British Museum. The lyrics were probably sung to musical accompaniment at dinner parties and other festive occasions. Murals and reliefs show that the elaborate parties of wealthy New Kingdom Egyptians included entertainment by singers, dancers, acrobats, and musicians playing harps, flutes, lutes, and drums.

"The Voice of the Wild Goose" is one of a set of eight poems which can be read independently of each other but which share themes and images of country life—wild geese being lured with grain and then netted, a dove calling at daybreak, a garden gate through which one's beloved is expected to arrive. The eight poems are unified under a common heading: "Beginning of the delightful, beautiful songs of your beloved sister as she comes from the fields." (It was standard practice in ancient Egypt for lovers to refer to each other by familial terms like sister, brother, or cousin.) The pastoral imagery in these lyrics may indicate that the sophisticated courtiers who composed the poems had an idealized view of life in the countryside—just as many city dwellers have today.

In "Most Beautiful Youth Who Ever Happened," the speaker's straightforward statement that she wants to "take [her beloved's] house as housekeeper" may reflect the matter-of-factness of New Kingdom marriage customs. According to scribal household and temple records that have survived, if a man and woman decided to marry, the man would obtain the consent of the woman's father and a conventional legal agreement would then be executed. Researchers have found no records of religious ceremonies associated with marriage. Both the woman and the man had the right to initiate divorce proceedings, simply by taking the legal steps necessary to dissolve the contract. Yet, in spite of this business-like approach to marriage, many Egyptian love lyrics reflect attitudes that modern Americans find romantic and familiar: hope that the loved one will remain faithful, fear of neglect, and veneration of the loved one. In "Most Beautiful Youth Who Ever Happened," for example, the speaker expresses the idea that being separated from her lover is as painful as dying and says, touchingly, that her heart seeks him out. (In the original, the poet probably used the term "liver" instead of "heart," for ancient Egyptians thought that the heart housed the intellect and the liver housed the emotions.)

A CRITICAL COMMENT

"Lyric poetry was well developed in the Middle Kingdom; but *Love Lyrics* seem to be a creation of the New Kingdom. At least, no love poems older than the New Kingdom have come to light. The love poems are misunderstood if they are thought to be naive and artless. For they are rich in elaborate wordplays, metaphors, and rare words and thereby indicate that they are crafted with deliberation and literate skill. The actual situations of life from which the poems may have arisen are concealed from our view. We do not know enough about the position of women, especially of young unmarried girls, to know how to interpret the free relations of the lovers that are depicted in so many of the poems. . . .

"We have seen continuity with the earlier periods in terms of the principal literary categories: private autobiographies, royal historical inscriptions, hymns and prayers, instructions, mortuary spells, and tales. The New Kingdom broadened the genres and added new themes, attitudes, and motifs. It also created two genres: school texts and love lyrics. . . .

"*'Le temps conserve de preference ce qui est un peu sec.'* [The climate tends to preserve things that are somewhat dry.] This remark by Jacques Chardonne . . . seems eminently applicable to the literature of ancient Egypt. Having been physically preserved by the dry sands of the desert, these ancient works endure by virtue of their sober strength. Even at their most lyrical, as in the love poems, the writings are never cloying or sentimental. Up to the end of the New Kingdom, the literature mirrors a society whose members lived in harmony with themselves and with nature. The cares of life could be met with confidence, for the gods ruled the world firmly and justly. Life was both hard and good. . . .

"In their introductory titles some of the collections are called 'sayings,' others are called 'songs.' Calling them 'love poems' rather than 'love songs' is not meant to deny the probability that many of them were sung, but is designed to emphasize their literary origin. The freshness, immediacy, and universality of these poems should not mislead the reader into believing them to be spontaneous outpourings of unlettered young lovers. Their style, prosody, and choice of words all bear the stamp of deliberate, literate artistry. . . .

"Though sophisticated in the context of their own times, the [love] poems have the conceptual simplicity and terseness of language that are the hallmarks of ancient Egyptian literature. That simplicity and terseness must be retained in the translations. Some recent renderings of Egyptian love poems exhibit a typically modern lush and mannered eroticism which is quite alien to the ancient Egyptian. . . ."

—*from* Ancient Egyptian Literature,
Miriam Lichtheim

FOR FURTHER READING

Beier, Ulli. *African Poetry.* Cambridge: Cambridge University Press, 1966.

Lichtheim, Miriam. *Ancient Egyptian Literature: A Book of Readings, Volume II: The New Kingdom.* Berkeley: University of California Press, 1976.

Pound, Ezra, ed. *Love Poems of Ancient Egypt.* Trans. Noel Stock. New York: New Directions, 1962.

Simpson, William Kelley, ed. *The Literature of Ancient Egypt: An Anthology of Stories, Instructions, and Poetry.* New Haven: Yale University Press, 1972.

AFRICAN PROVERBS

(Textbook page 85)

SUMMARY

The selection includes a sampling of proverbs from representative groups in sub-Saharan Africa. Western African groups represented include the Jabo of Liberia, the Ashanti of Ghana, and the Yoruba of Nigeria. Central Africa is represented by the Baganda of Uganda, eastern Africa by the Masai of Tanzania and Kenya, and the southern tip of the continent by the Zulu of Zululand, South Africa. Each set of proverbs offers general insights into human nature and the way of the world and are often expressed with wry humor. In addition, each set contains specific references to familiar animals, objects, and activities from the people's daily life. For example, Masai proverbs mention zebras, lions, and elephants, all of which are common sights for these herders from the high plains of eastern Africa. A Zulu proverb cautions against talking about a rhinoceros unless there is a tree nearby, evoking a vivid image of one hazard faced by these people of the southern savannas.

Through the proverbs of each group vary in content, their form is consistent and similar to the form of English-language proverbs. Each consists of only one sentence. Some utilize repetition and contain balanced, parallel phrases or clauses, such as the Ashanti "One bird in your hand is better than ten birds in the sky." Others are as brief and striking.

MORE ABOUT PROVERBS

One mark of a proverb is that it can be understood both literally and figuratively. Some of the proverbs presented in this selection employ relatively abstract imagery, such as the Ashanti "No one knows the story of tomorrow's dawn." Others rely on imagery that is more concrete, such as the Baganda proverb that says the one who withholds beans from you saves you from having indigestion. But regardless of whether their imagery is concrete or abstract, all the proverbs have more than one level of meaning.

It is partly because of their multiple levels of meaning that proverbs in oral literatures have uses ranging far beyond the uses of proverbs in written literatures. English-language proverbs, for example, are fairly simplistic and are often used automatically as clichés. However, among some African groups, the proverb is close to a poetic form, reminiscent of a Japanese haiku. Among most groups, the proverb serves as a rhetorical aid, and among many, it also serves as a shorthand way of discussing complex philosophical concepts. Most African groups have a huge body of proverbs, many quite subtle in meaning. The appropriate and creative uses of

these proverbs are seen as indicators of intellect and rhetorical skill. Skill at using proverbs can also increase a speaker's power within the society. For example, proverbs adroitly used in a legal proceeding can sum up precedents and thus influence the outcome of the case. Similarly, political candidates can sway public opinion by using proverbs in a way that reveals their depth of insight into national and international affairs.

Among some African groups, it is considered inappropriate for children to quote proverbs in the presence of adults, on the theory that children cannot comprehend the subtleties that most of the proverbs contain. Similarly, only the simplest proverbs, those that convey the most basic cultural values, are quoted to children. These proverbs are considered so elementary that anyone quoting them in speaking with adults would be seen as inarticulate.

Though the proverbs in this selection, taken at face value, may seem clear, they in fact may have meanings that are missed by those unfamiliar with the cultures the proverbs come from. For example, the Yoruban proverb "However large the ear, it cannot hear seven speeches at once," might seem to be a warning against trying to do too many things at once. However, in the Yoruban culture, the proverb is instead used to dismiss a braggart. Its logic is based on the fact that the size of people's ears has no relationship to their hearing acuity, and its meaning is that an impressive appearance does not necessarily indicate quality or effectiveness.

Because many African languages are highly tonal, spoken proverbs may be accompanied by specific melodies, and the melodies of the proverbs can convey various meanings. For example, the Jabo of Liberia traditionally used "One does not embrace the leopard" as an honorary title for a warrior, implying that his enemies feared and avoided him as if he were a leopard. The melody of the proverb, played on the horn, might indicate that a certain warrior was arriving or that his praises were being sung.

A CRITICAL COMMENT

"In the years of elective political rule in Nigeria before the first of the series of coups that have now become endemic, the Yoruba politician, Chief S. L. Akintola, controlled the allegiance of a massive following largely because of his almost unparalleled facility in supplying fresh and telling proverbs in any given situation.

"Like other non-literate cultures, the Yoruba encourage and celebrate invention and artistry in conversation, just as literate cultures do in their forms of literature. Proverbs have widespread appeal in this regard because of their brevity, their wit, and their generally fresh and apt observations on life and reality. The user appreciates their economical metaphors, and the hearer enjoys a surge of delight, especially when after a brief period of disorientation resulting from the *prima facie* disjunction between the matter under consideration and the literal statement of the proverb, he or she recognizes the common elements in the metaphor and the situation under reference. Arguably, proverbs derive their authority primarily from the aesthetic pleasure they give, which induces their appreciative audience to award rhetorical points to the accomplished user. Support for that suggestion comes from the most popular of Yoruba proverbs: Proverbs are the horses of discourse; when communication is lost, one resorts to proverbs to retrieve it.

"Their brevity serves important cultural and sociological ends: it obviates long arguments and explanations in many instances, especially when all that is necessary to make a point is to direct attention to an aspect of an issue that may not be immediately obvious, or to make a cryptic reference to an experience the speaker and the hearer share, leaving the latter to flesh out the details. . . . The Yoruba, who . . . loathe 'speaking with the whole mouth' (that is, without delicacy, reticence or tact), appreciate this means of finding direction by indirection, and of communicating in delicate situations by suggestion. As they say, Half a statement is all one makes to a well-bred person; when it gets inside him it becomes whole."

—*from* A Kì í Yorùbá Proscriptive and Prescriptive Proverbs, *Oyekan Owomoyela*

FOR FURTHER READING

Courlander, Harold. *A Treasury of African Folklore*. New York: Crown Publishers, 1975.

Njururi, Ngumbu. *Gikuyu Proverbs*. Nairobi: Oxford University Press, 1983.

Ol'Oloisolo, Massek A., and J. O. Sidai. *Wisdom of Maasai*. Nairobi: Transafrica Press, 1974.

Owomoyela, Oyekan. *A Kì í: Yorùbá Proscriptive and Prescriptive Proverbs*. Lanham: University Press of America, 1988.

SONG OF A MOTHER TO HER FIRSTBORN

Translated by Jack H. Driberg ▾ (Textbook page 90)

SUMMARY

In this free-verse cradle song, a mother speaks to her newborn baby, playfully and tenderly addressing him as if he might answer. In the first two stanzas, the speaker describes the baby's laughing, shining eyes, and his hands, small but strong. She also describes her hopes for him, imagining him as a spear-wielding warrior and a famous leader.

In the third and fourth stanzas, the speaker speculates about what name the baby will be given. She describes the favors the gods have bestowed on the baby—beauty, strength, and wisdom—and assures him of their concern for him. The speaker refers to the traditional Didinga and Lango beliefs in reincarnation—central to the naming ceremony to come—when she asks the baby which ancestor's spirit resides in him.

In the fifth stanza, the speaker describes the joy that the baby has brought her. She is happy and proud because, with the birth of this first child, she is honored by her husband and feels secure in his love.

In the sixth stanza, the speaker describes the joy that the baby has brought, and will continue to bring, to his father. The child will tend the father's shrine, guaranteeing immortality to the father's spirit. The child's own future offspring, she says, will also bring immortality to her husband.

MORE ABOUT THE SELECTION

Cradle songs in the oral tradition can be of two general types. The first, most common type is brief and relatively simple, like English-language nursery rhymes and lullabies. The second type, of which "Song of a Mother to Her Firstborn" is an example, is longer and more complex. Cradle songs of this type may be either traditional or spontaneously composed, and in several respects they are similar to praise poems. As in a praise poem to a god, the speaker enumerates and celebrates the baby's characteristics and refers to the benefits that the baby is expected to bestow upon her and her husband.

"Song of a Mother to Her Firstborn" reflects many details of the Didinga and Lango cultures as they were during the early years of the twentieth century, when the translator, a British civil servant with a strong bent for anthropology, stayed for extended periods among both groups. The groups were mainly pastoral at that time, and the raising of cattle provided an important part of their livelihoods, though they also made raids on other groups to insure their survival. Evidence of their lifestyle can be found in the poem. The mention of "Lupeyo's bull-calf" in line 3 refers to a black calf that the speaker and her husband had received from an uncle, Lupeyo; a bull calf was an especially valued gift, and the speaker emphasizes the baby's worth and potential by comparing his eyes to the calf. The speaker's several positive references to warriors, spears, and shields demonstrate the high respect that was earned by members of successful raiding parties.

The speaker's insistence that, with the birth of this child, she is "now indeed" a wife reflects specific social customs among the Didinga and Lango. Among both groups, married women had more social status than unmarried women. However, a married woman was not considered truly married, and was not called "wife" by her husband, until she had borne a child. (After the birth of a child, the woman might even be called "Mother-of-[child's name]," rather than being called by her own name.) If no children were born within a specified time period, the husband could, and usually did, annul the marriage. The speaker in the poem is happy not only because she loves the baby, but also because her status as a married woman is now affirmed.

Certain religious beliefs of the Didinga and Lango come to light with the speaker's reference to the child's future diligence in tending his father's shrine and to the children that the child himself will someday have. Among both groups, ancestors were held in reverence, and their spirits were thought to continue to live as long as they were remembered and their shrines were tended. For this reason, a dutiful child, preferably one who had many children and raised them to be dutiful as well, was highly valued.

A CRITICAL COMMENT

"A word of explanation for these poems is, perhaps, necessary. I do not care to call them translations, though that word would most accurately describe them. Many of them are translations in the strictest sense. . . .

"[I]t is obviously clear that a song or hymn heard once or twice only could not be recorded with complete accuracy, but my transcriptions are as near to the originals as circumstances allow. They at least do not include anything, either in imagery or in sentiment, that I did not hear. This applies . . . to the Mother's Song to Her First-born ["Song of a Mother to Her Firstborn"]. . . .

"Only in one point have I departed from the originals. In many hymns and chants it is customary for the leader to intone a line or a stanza (I use our own terms quite arbitrarily to designate the pauses which divide the hymns into their different sections), and then for the participants to repeat the last few words of the concluding sentence in a tense murmur of great impressiveness. It would have been quite impossible to reproduce this method in English, or at any rate to reproduce it in such a way as to preserve the correct feeling and the deep sense of religion, which action and sound give words which might be banal in themselves. I have therefore felt it necessary to cut out an element which would be distracting and only relevant as a religious exercise."

—*from* Initiation: Translations from Poems of the Didinga and Lango Tribes, *Jack H. Driberg*

FOR FURTHER READING

Chinweizu, ed. *Voices from Twentieth-Century Africa.* London: Faber and Faber, 1988.

Driberg, Jack H. *Initiation: Translations from Poems of the Didinga and Lango Tribes.* Great Britain: The Golden Cockerel Press, 1932.

Rutherford, Peggy. *Darkness and Light: An Anthology of African Writing.* London: The Faith Press Ltd., 1958.

Trask, Willard, ed. *Classic Black African Poems.* New York: Eakins Press, 1971.

OGUN KILLS ON THE RIGHT

Translated by Ulli Beier and Bakare Gbadamosi ▾ (Textbook page 95)

SUMMARY

Ogun is the bloodthirsty god of iron. He is shown killing suddenly and silently, both outdoors and indoors. The god kills guilty people, such as a thief and the owner of a house in which stolen goods are hidden; but he kills innocent people as well, such as a child carelessly playing with an iron implement.

Ogun is next described as a forest god whose generosity is as boundless as his fury: for example, he gives away his clothes to various forest birds, which use the bark of different trees to dye their clothes. Even the laughter of Ogun makes his enemies scatter, just as butterflies in the forest

scatter when a leopard approaches. The speaker requests Ogun's forbearance and protection, emphasizing the god's fierce, unpredictable nature and the fact that he is never to be taken for granted. The poem closes with an affirmation that the god will not reject the speaker because the speaker is both an instrument and a child of the god.

MORE ABOUT THE SELECTION

This oral poem, with its rhythmic, repetitive lines, was used in Yoruban hunters' ceremonies. The dangers faced by hunters were considerable, not only because of the ferocity of the animals hunted, but also because of the wildness of the forest itself. Any injury, whether from an attack by the animal being hunted, from a fall or a snakebite, or from a hunter's carelessness in handling his own weapon, could quickly cost the hunter his life. Under these circumstances, hunters must have felt a strong need to ensure the protection of Ogun, their patron god.

Basically, like "Song of a Mother to Her Firstborn" and "The Great Hymn to the Aten," "Ogun Kills on the Right" is structured as a praise poem. The first few stanzas, through line 21, describe the god in a way that is intended to mollify and flatter him: he is fierce, held in awe, unassailable; his actions are of huge proportions; his laughter invokes terror; and it is difficult even to look at him. The speaker in the poem, who as a hunter is also a priest of Ogun, asks for a first favor in line 22: simply to be allowed to behold the god. The speaker then reaffirms his deep respect for Ogun, emphasizing that Ogun is not to be trifled with (lines 24–28), before asking the god, in lines 31 and 33, for a second favor: to pity him and spare him.

In the final stanza, the speaker builds up an image of himself as someone important to the god. He draws analogies between Ogun's relationship to the hunter and a weaver's relationship to a spindle, a dyer's relationship to the cloth being dyed, and the eye's relationship to the things it sees. These analogies imply that the hunter, who is Ogun's subordinate, is also useful to Ogun, and for that reason Ogun should protect him, or at least not turn against him.

A CRITICAL COMMENT

"This poem represents a lively acknowledged salute to Ogun, one of the most colorful gods of the Yoruba pantheon. His divinity encompasses all acts of bravado, of reckless disregard of danger, of delirious heroism, of death by blood, for he is the lord of the cutting edge of iron. He is heat and vengeance, a god of excesses who knows no moderation. . . .

"The poem begins with a typical repetitive recounting of the terrible attributes of Ogun. Though he is the god of laughter and debauchery, he is reputed to possess a terrible temper that sweeps over every offender without remorse. His laughter disguises his terrible temper. The cumulative listing is ended with the brief but poignant line 5, "Ogun kills in silence." This perhaps attempts to contrast him with the god Shango, who kills in thunder and lightning. His ability to kill at home and in the field connotes the unexpectedness with which iron instruments—machetes, guns, in the days of flintlock guns—inflict fatal wounds upon even their users. Lines 6 to 8 state Ogun's abhorrence of thieves. Workers in iron cannot steal or receive stolen goods, for the punishment from

Ogun can be dreadfully severe. It is widely held in areas where Ogun worship still obtains—notably Yorubaland, Dahomey, and Eweland—that the most honest members of the community are the ironworkers. Line 8 emphasizes Ogun's sheer love of blood; his sign is blood, with which, after killing those who offend him, he paints the spot where they fall. Lines 9 to 13 emphasize Ogun's love of colors. He is the most flamboyantly dressed god, next perhaps to Eshu-Elegba, the trickster-god. He is friend to the birds of the forest with whom he shares his clothes. The paradox of Ogun, the god of blood, retaining the purity and innocence of the undyed cloth in its whiteness emphasizes the victorious aura that encompasses Ogun the warrior. This is stressed in the simplicity of line 14, "Ogun's laughter is no joke." Line 15 reaffirms the fearsome awe that typifies Ogun's laughter. He is the god of preternatural vengeance, marked by an endlessly destructive cunning that is expressed through that laugh which is one of mockery and anger rather than of joy. His vengeance is so embracing that he hardly distinguishes those who offend him from his own devotees. . . . The god of war is also a god of brightness, an essence of the Supreme God that he shares. But it is the brightness of spears and machetes, weapons of war, rather than of pristine innocence. And, like the men of blood, the warrior and the hunter, whose clothes are soaked in blood, it is hard to distinguish the frenzied redness of his eye. Pounded yam of line [24] suggests utter helplessness, the dependence and uselessness that is associated with the pounded yam ready for feasters to knead into any shape. Line [27] suggests the ease and nonchalance with which the beggar tosses a coin into his cap, or perhaps more precisely, the way in which the giver tosses the coin into the beggar's cap. These lines suggest the . . . opposites of the active malevolence of Ogun when challenged. Ogun's lunacy is always emphasized by his addiction to silly games and quarrels, his unpredictability, and his ability to dissemble. He is the god who will punish an offense even after seven hundred and eighty years, inflicting punishment upon the descendants of the offender."

—*from* The Breast of the Earth, *Kofi Awoonor*

FOR FURTHER READING

Awoonor, Kofi. *The Breast of the Earth*. Garden City, New Jersey: Anchor-Doubleday, 1975.

Beier, Ulli, ed. *Yoruba Poetry: An Anthology of Traditional Poems*. Cambridge: Cambridge University Press, 1970.

Chinweizu, ed. *Voices from Twentieth-Century Africa*. London: Faber and Faber, 1988.

Hughes, Langston, ed. *Poems from Black Africa*. Bloomington: Indiana University Press, 1963.

TALK

Retold by Harold Courlander ▾ (Textbook page 98)

SUMMARY

In this prose narrative, a farmer sets to work in his field to harvest yams. As he digs, one of the yams speaks up, scolding him for neglecting to weed the yam patch. The farmer turns in astonishment to see if perhaps his cow has spoken. The cow is silent, but the farmer's dog casually explains that the yam has spoken and that it wants to be left alone. The farmer, passing from astonishment to indignation, cuts a palm frond to beat the dog, but the palm tree orders him to set the frond down—softly, the frond stipulates, as the startled man prepares to fling it away. The man sets the frond on a stone, which sharply tells the farmer to remove it. At this, the farmer takes off at a gallop for his village.

As he runs, the farmer encounters first a fisherman with a fish trap, a weaver with a bundle of cloth, and a man swimming in a river. Each asks why the farmer is running, and each time the farmer repeats his story. The men scoff at the farmer's overreaction, but when first the fish trap, next the bundle of cloth, and then the river itself each speaks up, each man becomes terrified and joins the farmer in racing toward the village. In the village, the chief has his ceremonial stool brought out, and he sits down to listen to the four frantic men. After listening to their improbable accounts, the chief rebukes them, admonishing them to get back to work and stop their foolishness. The four men, chastened, trudge off. The chief mutters scornfully about their wild story, and the chief's ceremonial stool exclaims, "Imagine, a talking yam!"

MORE ABOUT THE SELECTION

"Talk" is humorous, and its primary purpose among the Ashanti was most likely to provide entertainment. However, it also reflects certain underlying values and assumptions that are found in the traditional tales of many of the peoples of sub-Saharan Africa. First, like many traditional African tales, "Talk" illustrates negative consequences of immoderate speech. Many African groups, while valuing rhetorical skill, also stress the importance of restraint and decorum in speech. Certainly, when people live in close-knit communities, unrestrained verbal outbursts can have any number of disastrous effects. With the emphasis on controlled and even reticent speech, the farmer in "Talk," babbling wildly, is made to look ridiculous. Another general African feature of the tale is its portrayal of areas outside the village as dangerously chaotic and unpredictable, places where mysterious things can happen (a yam can talk, one's own dog can order one around, a fish trap or even a river can poke fun). The village, in contrast, is portrayed as a place where order and predictability are maintained (once the men are in the village, the chief steps in and halts their wild flight, and his levelheaded attitude reduces their terrifying experiences to mere foolishness).

Other, more unusual elements of the tale contribute to its humor. One of these elements is its broad characterization. As more Africans move to cities, the purpose of storytelling changes. What was, in villages, a discreet and indirect means of commenting on social and interpersonal issues becomes for citydwellers more of a general diversion. For this reason, storytellers in African cities adopt styles that will appeal to wider and more impersonal audiences; their characters tend to become more standardized (the priest, the chief, the country bumpkin)—types who will be recognized even by people of diverse backgrounds, as opposed to the quirky individuals who would be recognized as specific neighbors by villagers. "Talk" may reflect this trend, for all its characters are relatively broadly sketched. Another unusual element is the story's punchline. Very few traditional African stories have punchlines that introduce the kind of ironic surprise ending found in "Talk." The last lines of most tales sum up or continue ideas that have been made obvious much earlier in the stories. To add to the humor, the punchline in "Talk" turns the tale's more traditional features upside down. When the chief's ceremonial stool speaks, the village suddenly becomes just as unpredictable as any outlying area. The stool's comment also mocks the chief, with his carefully controlled speech (he listens politely to the men's tales and restrains himself from snorting in derision, though his scowl makes his true feelings clear). When his own stool does what he has just dismissed as impossible, the proper and dignified chief is made to look at least as ridiculous as the four babbling men.

A CRITICAL COMMENT

"[African folktales] were first recorded in a form intended to be used either for learning the language of the subject people or for the enjoyment of an audience back home already accustomed to reading folktales. But because the folktales already known were of an especially literary type—the marvelous tales of the Grimms, the more exotic *Thousand Nights and a Night* [also known as *A Thousand and One Nights*], other Oriental tales, and later Joel Chandler Harris's collection of jocular trickster tales of the American South—the first collector-translators of African stories may have adopted the literary style already shown to excite the common reader. . . .

"The contemporary anthologizer, facing the question of whether these early efforts reflect the tales most characteristic of the world of Black Africa, must acknowledge that they do so only in part. They represent only the kind of stories that would be told to missionaries and colonial officials. . . . They are the most public sort of story, and moreover the kind most easily understood. But with greater study of various cultures. . . . it becomes ever clearer that these tales are only one segment of the African ocean of story.

"Recent inventions have made it possible to record actual tale-telling sessions and probe the broad spectrum of types more satisfactorily. Through them we have learned a good deal about the performance of these fictions: who performs for whom, under what conditions, and what the stories reveal about the lives of the people they belong to. However, when tales recorded in this way are transcribed verbatim, the first thing that impresses the reader is that they are often abundantly unreadable, even boring. The text, even when translated with some sense of style, is full of the repetitions and hesitations that are the rule in an oral performance, but hardly to be expected in a written one. Fortunately, a few recent collectors have taken such problems as a challenge, and have given us translations that are not only faithful transcriptions of stories as performed, but have rendered them in a wholly readable and enjoyable style. . . .

". . . [S]torytelling—as pure narration—seldom arises by itself in this part of the world. Stories involve a singing, a dancing, an acting-out of themselves. The audience participates actively in the singing and the dancing songs; the acting-out, through impersonation and masking and comic costuming, imposes a kind of distance through performance mastery. . . .

"It is precisely the way that the storyteller 'grabs your shirt' and thrusts you into the tale that isn't there in the folktales we read in literary collections such as those of the Brothers Grimm, where what we find on the whole is a record of stories as remembered by old people who no longer tell them actively. In contrast, the African stories . . . were recorded while still flourishing in social and cultural environments in which the artful employment of speech in all dimensions of community is encouraged and applauded."
—from African Folktales, *Roger D. Abrahams*

FOR FURTHER READING

Abrahams, Roger D., ed. *African Folktales.* New York: Pantheon Books, 1983.

Beier, Ulli, ed. *Black Orpheus.* New York: McGraw-Hill, 1965.

Bowen, Elinor Smith. *Return to Laughter.* New York: Anchor-Doubleday, l953.

Courlander, Harold. *A Treasury of African Folklore.* New York: Crown Publishers, l975.

---

from SUNDIATA

D. T. Niane ▼ Translated by G. D. Pickett ▼ (Textbook page 105)

SUMMARY

This prose excerpt from the Mandingo (also called Mandinka) epic opens when Sundiata, legendary hero-king of thirteenth-century Mali, is seven years old. Sundiata's father, King Maghan Kon Fatta of Mali, has died. Although the old king had named Sundiata as his successor, the young prince and his mother and sister are forced to live in poverty because the old king's first wife, Sassouma Bérété, has ousted them and has installed her own son on the throne. Few people believe in a prophecy which points to Sundiata as a future hero, for the young prince, at the age of seven, cannot yet even walk.

Sassouma Bérété consistently makes fun of Sundiata's mother and her "backward" son. One day she mocks Sundiata's mother because Sundiata cannot fetch any baobab leaf, a condiment used in cooking. Weeping, Sundiata's mother scolds her son for his "uselessness," and Sundiata reacts to his mother's shame and fury by taking his first steps. He shows his strength by bending an iron bar into a bow, uprooting the baobab tree, and bringing it back to his mother.

From that day on, Sundiata's superhuman strength and skills increase rapidly. Sassouma Bérété exiles Sundiata, and the hero journeys to the distant kingdom of Mema. There Sundiata grows to young manhood. Meanwhile, an evil sorcerer-king, Soumaoro Kanté of Sosso, is gaining power in West Africa. Soumaoro invades Mali, and Sundiata gathers an army and sets out to free his native land. His decisive battle against Soumaoro comes at Krina, a plain in the valley of the Niger River.

On the eve of the battle of Krina, Sundiata and Soumaoro engage in a ritual exchange of threats and boasts, using supernatural powers to call upon magical owls, who carry the dialogue between the distance that separates the two warriors. Afterwards, Sundiata is joined by his loyal half-sister and his griot, Balla Fasséké, whom Sassouma and her son had banished to Sosso at the time of Sundiata's exile. Sundiata's half-sister has learned the secret of the evil Soumaoro: to conquer the sorcerer-king of Sosso, Sundiata must wound him with a wooden arrow pointed with the spur of a white cock. Sundiata and his helpers prepare the arrow. The next morning, the battle begins, but Sundiata's forces cannot overcome Soumaoro's. When Sundiata nicks Soumaoro with the special arrow, Soumaoro flees, and the victory goes to Sundiata's warriors. Sundiata pursues Soumaoro into a mountain cave, but there the evil sorcerer disappears.

The next day, Sundiata's troops march on Sosso, Soumaoro's capital. Sundiata's troops quickly defeat the Sossos and storm the city. In Soumaoro's palace, Sundiata and his friends find the evil sorcerer's magic chamber in disarray; the power that maintained the magic chamber has dissipated, indicating that the sorcerer has indeed lost his magical power. Sundiata's troops completely raze Sosso. Sundiata then takes his rightful place as ruler of "the world" (the Mali empire).

MORE ABOUT THE SELECTION

The version of *Sundiata* used for this selection is one of several; the epic is told among all West African groups speaking languages of the Mande family, with the hero variously referred to as Sundiata, Sunjata, Son-Jara, and the Lion of the Manding. This version is outstanding for its rich descriptive and narrative detail, for its skilled characterization, and for its literary style, maintained through the versatile diction of Mamoudou Kouyaté, the griot who recited it to D. T. Niane sometime during the 1950s. D. T. Niane describes Kouyaté as "an obscure griot from the village of Djeliba Koro," but also as one of "the most authentic traditionists of Mali." Niane, a native Guinean fluent in French and a scholar affiliated with the Institute of Black Africa in Dakar, was researching oral sources of Mali history when he came to know Kouyaté and other griots from several remote villages in the area that once had been the ancient capital of Old Mali. The translator describes his profound respect for these griots, referring to them as "masters" and as "speaking documents" and explaining that they were trained in the tradition of the "royal" or "court" griots who, by memory alone, had preserved the constitutions, histories, traditions, and laws of their kingdoms through the centuries.

A striking feature of the epic is the stress it places on fate, prophecy, and sorcery, which play the roles that gods and goddesses play in the epics of pantheistic cultures. The epic stresses repeatedly that each person's fate is set before birth, and that no one can alter fate. Prophecy is presented as a way of discovering what fate has ordained, and sorcery is presented as a powerful tool, but only for helping people achieve what they are fated to achieve. The epic makes it clear from the outset that Sundiata's fate is bound up with the fate of

Mali and that Sundiata can in many ways be seen as embodying Mali. Like Sundiata, Mali had a long and difficult "childhood," for Sundiata was preceded by sixteen kings with varying fortunes; and like Sundiata, Mali had grown great and would grow greater still.

Sundiata achieves victory partly through sorcery, partly through the aid of his family and his people, and partly because of his heroic character: he is brave, strong, and resourceful; he respects his people and treats his enemies fairly; he is articulate (a key value among the Mandingo). But underlying all other reasons for his success is the idea that he was fated to succeed. Similarly, in the haunting passage which closes the selection, describing the barren wilderness where Sosso once stood, the implication is clear that even Soumaoro's great wealth and power could not change fate.

A CRITICAL COMMENT

"Though Sunjata [Sundiata] is undoubtedly stronger and braver than we are, he is nevertheless a human being like ourselves. The qualities which he has are the qualities which we ourselves have, in however diminished a form. . . . Even if we could never aspire to equal the deeds of Sunjata, nevertheless we feel our stature . . . is enhanced by the knowledge of what . . . Sunjata could achieve. Before a battle [in West Africa], a griot would narrate the Sunjata epic to the king and his followers. This narration encouraged the listeners to excel themselves when battle was joined, not so much by inspiring them to emulate Sunjata, but by making them feel that they were capable of greater things than they had previously thought possible. By reminding them of what Sunjata could do, it raised their estimate of what they themselves could do. . . . [L]istening to the Sunjata epic not only gives a man a feeling of intense pride, but also makes him look at his own life—what has he achieved, has he acquitted himself in a way befitting a man in his position, has he enhanced the family name, or at any rate not diminished it?

"The behavior of the audience listening to a griot relate the Sunjata epic is different from that of an audience listening to fictional tales. In the latter case, members of the audience will utter exclamations from time to time to encourage the narrator. Indeed, an expert storyteller will have a friend in the audience who will utter "Namu!" or some other expression of approval and support after virtually every sentence. And the whole audience will of course sing the refrains of the songs which occur in so many tales. In contrast to this, an audience listening to a griot recounting a historical narrative listens in silence, without interjection or interruption of any kind. . . .

"For Mandinka listeners, Sunjata is not some figure remote from their everyday life. His career is a source of great pride, and a griot's narration can rouse a deep emotional response. But for the

Mandinka, Sunjata is also the man who established the social framework of present day society. The network of family relationships is described in terms of common descent from Sunjata or from one of his generals; settlement, and hence ownership, of land is attributed to Sunjata's generals. Thus Sunjata's influence is felt to impinge directly on life today. But the old values are changing; political power is now in the hands not of independent kings but of elected representatives of the people; education and wealth are increasingly important factors in determining a man's place in society. In view of such changes . . . it seems likely that the Sunjata epic will tend to appear increasingly remote from people's everyday experience. It will probably continue to be told for a long time yet, increasingly preserved in print and on tape, but will lose its relevance to contemporary life and become merely an entertaining old story."

—*from* Sunjata: Three Mandinka Versions,
Gordon Innes

FOR FURTHER READING

Biebuyck, Daniel, ed. *The Mwindo Epic: From the Banyanga (Congo Republic)*. Trans. Kahombo C. Mateene. Berkeley: University of California Press, 1969.

Innes, Gordon. *Sunjata: Three Mandinka Versions*. London: School of Oriental and African Studies, University of London, 1974.

Mofolo, Thomas. *Chaka*. Trans. Daniel P. Kunene. London: Heinemann, 1981.

Niane, D. T. *Sundiata: An Epic of Old Mali*. Trans. G. D. Pickett. London: Longmans, Green and Co. Ltd., 1965.

NOTES

UNIT 3: THE ANCIENT MIDDLE EAST

(Textbook page 128)

Unit Introduction: The Literature of Ancient Mesopotamia

The literature of ancient Mesopotamia survives on thousands of clay tablets inscribed with cuneiform, a writing system based on wedge-shaped markings. The political systems of Mesopotamia were not stable, and the scribal class bore a heavy responsibility for the preservation and perpetuation of the written word. Scribal writing reflected the integration of different cultures, such as Babylonian and Assyrian, that converged in Mesopotamia over the centuries. The writings that survive include hymns, fables, proverbs, letters, and the Epic of Gilgamesh, which may be the world's oldest epic.

BACKGROUND

Much literature has survived from ancient Mesopotamia. The volume and variety of ancient Mesopotamian literature can be attributed to several factors: the existence of the sophisticated cuneiform writing system; the fact that a succession of dominant powers intermixed with and adopted the literature of the peoples they conquered; and the fact that the Mesopotamians valued the written word to the extent that they developed a scribal class to preserve the languages and literature of the earliest to the latest Mesopotamian peoples.

THE LEGACY OF THE SCRIBES

So many ancient tablets have been unearthed that scholars have been able to determine the stages by which cuneiform developed. It began as word pictures, such as an ear of corn, a fish, or a palm tree, drawn in wet clay with a pointed stick. But pointed sticks created unwanted ridges, so scribes began instead to impress the marks with cut reeds. Because the reeds were triangular in cross section, they created wedge-shaped marks. These marks, in turn, led to simplification and stylization of the picture-signs.

In order to convey a broader range of ideas, scribes gradually extended the meanings of the pictures by association. Much as we read the heart symbol on a bumper sticker as "love," they extended the sun sign to mean "day" or "bright," and the star sign to "god" or "sky." Finally, to express abstract words, scribes adapted certain signs to represent only the first syllable of the word originally depicted. The end result was a "logo-syllabic" writing system, containing hundreds of signs for specific words and syllables, that was capable of recording not just commercial transactions, but also myths and poems of great spiritual, intellectual, and emotional depth.

Since ethnic divisions were largely ignored in ancient Mesopotamia, the stories and poems of earlier peoples were expanded rather than lost. People of Sumerian ancestry continued to coexist with later peoples of Semitic ancestry, and those peoples (Akkadians, Babylonians, and Assyrians) made Sumerian literature their own. They both recorded and retold Sumerian stories in their own languages, and they preserved Sumerian as a literary language that was taught in their schools.

Only sons of the aristocracy attended the *edubba* or "tablet house," the scribal academy. Although the curriculum included sophisticated mathematics and a range of skills, its core was the copying and memorizing of bilingual word lists. These "dictionaries" listed all of the terms in a given category, such as glassmaking, in both Sumerian and Akkadian or Babylonian. Accumulation of such lore theoretically prepared a graduate to select from a broad range of professions: priest; secretary to a military commander; or clerk in a business, temple, or government bureau. Additionally, the many years training stimulated scribes' interest in both preserving traditional literature and creating new works. The scribes were a cohesive class that existed independently of the rise and fall of political powers. For nearly three millennia, scribes provided the continuum through which the social, intellectual, and literary traditions of Mesopotamia were preserved and diffused throughout the Middle East.

Unearthing the Key to a Culture

The variety and extent of the scribal contribution is recognizable even today, thanks to the nearly half a million clay tablets found to date. Particularly revealing of the fabric of ancient life are tablets containing correspondence. In his *Letters from Mesopotamia,* A. Leo Oppenheim translated dozens of such pieces, on topics as varied as business worries, a son's complaint to his mother, and astrological reports to the king.

One merchant writes to two investors:

I keep hearing reports that you have sent merchandise to Ina-Sin and to Inarawe. Both these men are dead! Although I searched for evidence for the arrival of any silver, there isn't any. One of you should come here from where you are, or else the silver belonging to your father will be lost.

A young man, apparently away at school, complains to his mother that the clothes of the other young gentlemen—even those of the son of his father's assistant—grow finer and finer, while she lets his clothes become "more scanty." "You do not love me!" he concludes.

An astrologer in the service of a king informs him:

The eclipse of the moon moved from the eastern quadrant and settled over the entire western quadrant of the moon. The planets Jupiter and Venus were visible during the eclipse until it cleared. This is propitious for Your Majesty, and (portends) evil for the Westland.

Given such a profusion of written records, it was possible for the Assyrians, the last great rulers of Mesopotamia prior to the rise of the Persians and then the Greeks, to amass huge libraries of inscribed tablets. An important nineteenth-century discovery was the library at Nineveh (in modern Iraq). Unearthed documents range in size from tiny fragments to multi-column tablets inscribed with hundreds of compact lines. The literary compositions range from brief hymns to myths approaching a thousand lines. The most famous works of literature are the *Enuma Elish,* a creation account, and the *Epic of Gilgamesh.* Samuel Noah Kramer, a noted scholar of ancient Sumer, writes eloquently in his book *The Sumerians* of the importance of these documents as source material for understanding the spiritual and intellectual concerns of all cultures of the ancient Middle East:

"As literary products, the Sumerian belles-lettres rank high among the aesthetic creations of civilized man. They . . . mirror the spiritual and intellectual life of an ancient culture which would otherwise have remained largely unknown. Their significance for a proper appraisal of the cultural and spiritual development of the entire ancient Near East can hardly be overestimated. The Akkadians, that is, the Assyrians and Babylonians, took these works over almost *in toto.* The Hittites, Hurrians, and Canaanites translated some of them into their own languages and no doubt imitated them widely. The form and content of the Hebrew literary works and, to a certain extent, even those of the ancient Greeks, were profoundly influenced by them."

Unit Projects

1. **Drawing a Comic Strip.** Create a comic book adaptation of the *Epic of Gilgamesh.* Plan the pictures and dialogue for one episode of the story. You may set the story in a different time and place: Gilgamesh as a modern superhero, like the comic book version of the Norse god Thor, for example. Draw and color at least one page of the comic book, and supply a synopsis of the comic book as a whole.

2. **Preparing a Dramatic Reading.** Prepare an audiotape of background music to accompany a dramatic reading of one episode from the *Epic of Gilgamesh.* The music may be classical, rock worldbeat, jazz, or any other musical form that matches the mood of the episode. Time the music against an oral reading of the episode and record it so that you can play it as you read your episode to the class.

3. **Researching Ancient Mesopotamian Culture.** Find out more about some aspect of the people, history, and culture of ancient Mesopotamia, and prepare a report to deliver to the class. Consider the following topics, or another topic of your choice: the use of animal symbolism in ancient Mesopotamian cultures; the architecture of the ancient Mesopotamians; the Mesopotamian view of the afterlife and how it compares with the ancient Egyptian view; the art or music of ancient Sumeria; the development of cuneiform; the story behind one of the great archaeological discoveries in the Middle East; the Hanging Gardens of Babylon; the scribal class in ancient Mesopotamia; the biography of one of the famous rulers of ancient Mesopotamia. Narrow your topic, and write a brief report to deliver to the class. Supplement your presentation with visual aids.

4. **Building a Model.** Build a scale model of one of the following: a ziggurat; a middle- or upper-class Sumerian's house; a walled Sumerian city; or the boat constructed by Utnapishtim. Find books from the library to help you make your model. You may use whatever materials seem appropriate: paper, cardboard, clay, wood, papier-mâché, and so on. You may make a two-dimensional rendering on paper instead, but try to show your subject from all sides.

5. **Adapting the Epic for Children.** Adapt the story of Gilgamesh and his quest as a

children's book. Rewrite the epic, or a portion of the epic, as a simple story that could be read aloud to children ages 6–9. Keep the episode simple and easy to follow, and use vocabulary that young children can easily understand. Provide some pictures and create a *Gilgamesh* picture book. (You may work with a partner or team to create a picture book.) If you can arrange it, read your simplified Gilgamesh story to a classroom of children.

6. **Researching the Quest for Eternal Youth.** Do some research into other stories—books, movies, or episodes of television programs—that deal with the theme of the search for eternal life or eternal youth. (Some possibilities are the Oscar Wilde novel *The Picture of Dorian Gray,* the movie *Cocoon* and its sequel, and any classic science fiction and horror novels and films, such as old *Twilight Zone* episodes and stories by Ray Bradbury.) What are some of the recurring themes of such stories? Does the quest for eternal life end in a positive or a negative way? Report your findings to the class.

7. **Carving a Cylinder Seal.** Ancient cylinder seals contained recessed carvings. Rolling the cylinder across wet clay produced a raised picture. Draw the design for a cylinder three-fourths of an inch in diameter and one inch tall. The left and right edges must meet to form a continuous picture when you roll the paper into a cylindrical shape. If you work in ceramics, cut your design into a cylinder of clay, fire it, and use your cylinder seal actually to make an impression in wet clay.

8. **Researching the Mesopotamian Pantheon.** Create a chart showing the ancient Mesopotamian pantheon, or family of gods and goddesses. Research to find out who they were and what they were like. What were their special powers, and what forces or places did they rule? Draw a "family tree" of the gods and goddesses, or write brief biographies of your favorite deities.

9. **Researching Supernatural Creatures.** Research the types of half-human, half-animal creatures, as well as other supernatural beings mentioned in the mythology of ancient Mesopotamia. (Remember the Man-Scorpion in *Gilgamesh*.) Choose a supernatural being and create a "museum display" that includes a drawing or three-dimensional model of the being accompanied by a placard that explains its nature, origin, and significance to the ancient Mesopotamian culture.

10. **Creating Epic Music.** Obtain a copy of the N. K. Sandars translation of the *Epic of Gilgamesh*. Notice that the epic contains several poems or songs, each set off from the text in italics. (A song about the flood appears on page 148 of your textbook.) Choose one of these poems and set it to appropriate music. You might, for instance, want to set Gilgamesh's lament for Enkidu in "The Death of Enkidu" to an appropriately melancholy melody. Or, write a ballad that relates the adventures of Gilgamesh. Sing the ballad to a tune you already know, or compose special music for it. Include a recurring refrain.

from the EPIC OF GILGAMESH
Translated by N. K. Sandars ▾ (Textbook page 136)

SUMMARY

The arrogance of Gilgamesh, king of Uruk, is curbed by the gods' sending him an equal, the wild man Enkidu. After a fierce wrestling match, the two become friends. Together they destroy Humbaba, the demon who guards the great Cedar Forest, and the Bull of Heaven sent by the goddess Ishtar to ravage the land. The gods decree that one of the disrespectful heroes must die.

Mortally ill, Enkidu tells Gilgamesh his dream of a man-bird who took him to the palace of Irkalla, Queen of Darkness. There, all are reduced to an existence of eternal drudgery. When Enkidu dies, Gilgamesh goes into the wilderness to mourn. As a result of his friend's death, Gilgamesh seeks to learn the secret of everlasting life from Utnapishtim, survivor of the great deluge. At Mount Mashu, the half-human, half-dragon "Scorpion" guardians urge Gilgamesh to abandon his quest. He shows such determination that they grant him entry to the mountain. There, in the garden of the gods, the sun god Shamash tells Gilgamesh he will never find eternal life. Siduri, goddess of wine, urges him to relish the life span allotted to mortals, but directs him to Urshanabi, the ferryman. Urshanabi conducts Gilgamesh across the waters of death to Dilmun, home of the immortal Utnapishtim and his wife. When Gilgamesh asks for the secret of eternal life, Utnapishtim promises to reveal the secret, but first recounts the tale of the flood.

Utnapishtim challenges Gilgamesh to prove his worthiness of eternal life by prevailing against sleep for six days and seven nights, but Gilgamesh immediately falls asleep. Discouraged, he accepts water to clean himself and clothes that will remain like new all the way home. Utnapishtim's wife urges her husband to give Gilgamesh a gift. Utnapishtim reveals the secret of a thorny underwater plant that restores youth. Gilgamesh salvages the plant and plans to share it with the old men of Uruk. But that night, while Gilgamesh is bathing, a serpent snatches the plant and immediately renews itself by shedding its skin. Gilgamesh abandons his quest and returns with Urshanabi to Uruk where he engraves the story of his travels on a stone.

MORE ABOUT ARCHAEOLOGICAL DISCOVERIES

Since 1912, a number of German expeditions have excavated Uruk, the city-state ruled by Gilgamesh. Now called Warka, Uruk was once a 200-acre, bustling city with official buildings, houses, and gardens and cemeteries. The site is dominated by the stump of a ziggurat dedicated to the sky-god, Anu. The ruins of Uruk have yielded hundreds of small clay tablets and cylinder seals inscribed with the crude pictographic beginnings of Sumerian cuneiform writing.

The principal tablets on which translations of the *Epic of Gilgamesh* are based come from the library of Assurbanipal at Nineveh. The site across the Tigris from the Iraqi city of Mosul was identified as Nineveh early in the nineteenth century and was extensively explored from 1820 on. The site is surrounded by a brick rampart, now partially restored, more than seven miles long. The Palace of Sennacherib, excavated between 1849 and 1851 by English archaeologist Austen Henry Layard, rises from a level plain to a height of ninety feet. It is about a mile long and 1,950 feet wide. Besides spectacular winged bulls and other works of art, Layard unearthed tablets and columns that enabled language scholars to decipher ancient Persian and Akkadian.

Continuing Layard's work in 1852–1853, Turkish archaeologist Hormuzd Rassam unearthed more than 25,000 fragments of cuneiform tablets constituting the library of Assurbanipal. The tablets were taken to the British Museum, where George Smith discovered that they included a Babylonian version of the well-known biblical flood story. In 1872, Smith published a general outline of the *Epic of Gilgamesh* and a partial account of its flood story.

Other literature from the library of Assurbanipal includes the Babylonian creation epic, *Enuma Elish,* and a large body of wisdom literature: parables, poems, and proverbs. The wide popularity of Mesopotamian literature in the ancient Middle East was attested in 1955 by the discovery in central Israel of a cuneiform tablet containing forty lines of the Gilgamesh epic. A shepherd chanced upon it in the rubbish dump of an American expedition at the ruins of Megiddo.

A CRITICAL COMMENT

". . . Sumerian epic poems consist of individual, disconnected tales of varying length, each of which is restricted to a single episode. There is no attempt to articulate and integrate these episodes into a larger unit. There is relatively little characterization and psychological penetration in the Sumerian material. The heroes tend to be broad types, more or less undifferentiated, rather than highly personalized individuals. . . . Mortal women play hardly any role in Sumerian epic literature, whereas they have a very prominent part in Indo-European epic literature. Finally, in the matter of technique, the Sumerian poet gets his rhythmic effects primarily from variations in the repetition patterns. He makes no use whatever of the meters or uniform line so characteristic of Indo-European epics. In spite of all these differences, it is hardly likely that a literary form so individual in style and technique as narrative poetry was created and developed independently and at different time intervals in Sumer, Greece, India, and Northern Europe. Since the narrative poetry of the Sumerians is by all odds the oldest of the four, it is not impossible that it was in Sumer that the epic genre first originated and that it spread from there to the lands around. . . .

"[Five Sumerian epic tales] revolve about the best known of Sumerian heroes, the hero without peer of the entire ancient Near East, Gilgamesh. . . . [One of the best preserved is] 'Gilgamesh, Enkidu, and the Nether World,' which depicts him . . . in turn as a chivalrous knight, an oppressive bully, a despairing whiner, a counseling sage, a loyal master, and a saddened mortal anxious to learn about life in the nether world. His servant Enkidu plays the role of a faithful and courageous friend. . . ."
—from The Sumerians, *Samuel Noah Kramer*

FOR FURTHER READING

Dalley, Stephanie, trans. *Myths from Mesopotamia: Creation, The Flood, Gilgamesh, and Others.* Oxford: Oxford University Press, 1991.

Gardner, John, and John R. Maier. *Gilgamesh.* New York: Random House, 1985.

Kramer, Samuel Noah. *The Sumerians: Their History, Culture, and Character.* Chicago: The University of Chicago Press, 1963.

Mason, Herbert. *Gilgamesh: A Verse Narrative.* New York: New American Library, 1970.

Pfeiffer, Charles F., ed. *The Biblical World: A Dictionary of Biblical Archaeology.* New York: Bonanza Books, 1966.

Sandars, N. K. *The Epic of Gilgamesh.* Middlesex: Penguin Books Ltd., 1960.

Wolkstein, Diane, and Samuel Noah Kramer. *Inanna: Queen of Heaven and Earth.* New York: Harper and Row, 1983.

Unit Introduction:
Hebrew Literature

(Textbook page 154)

Hebrew literature is the literature of an exiled people whose religion provided them with a sense of cultural identity and spiritual unity. The Hebrew Bible, known to Christians as the Old Testament, serves as a written record of the Hebrews' exile, the formation of Jewish tradition, laws, and belief, and the political struggles of the Israelites. These biblical writings include such literary forms as historical narratives, psalms or sacred songs, proverbs, and stories.

BACKGROUND

For centuries, the Hebrew Bible served Western peoples as their major source of knowledge of the ancient Middle East. Recent discoveries confirm the historical accuracy of considerable portions of books set after about 1000 B.C., books such as Kings, Chronicles, and the Book of the Prophet Nahum. (Nahum describes the destruction of the Assyrian city of Nineveh.)

THE BIBLE
AND MODERN ARCHAEOLOGY

Scholars of the past frequently attempted to derive historical dates for the Creation and the Flood from Genesis. Archaeologists sometimes worked with a spade in one hand and the Book of Genesis in the other. In the 1920s, for example, when Sir Leonard Woolley came across an unusual formation while excavating the Sumerian city of Ur, he cabled London, "We have found the Flood." Discoveries have since revealed the occurrence of many floods between 4000 and 2500 B.C.

Twentieth-century archaeology does, however, confirm the existence of previously unknown peoples whom the ancient Hebrews mentioned briefly in Genesis; the Hittites, from whom Abraham buys a tomb (Genesis 23), are one example. Turkish excavations and records from Syria and Egypt now show the Hittites dominated Anatolia (Turkey), Syria, and Canaan from about 2000 to 1200 B.C. Egypt alone rivaled them as a world power.

Major advances in our understanding of Genesis and other books of the Hebrew Bible began between 1947 and 1960 with the discovery of the Qumran texts or "Dead Sea Scrolls." Found in more than a dozen caves at seven different sites along the northwest shore of the Dead Sea, and written in several different scripts between the third century B.C. and the first century A.D., the texts include entire scrolls and tens of thousands of fragments. Consisting of biblical books, commentaries, and non-religious documents, the texts shed light upon the development and transmission of the Hebrew Bible, and on the social, political, and literary background of the New Testament.

ARCHAEOLOGICAL FINDS: CONTEXT
FOR THE HEBREW BIBLE

Further spectacular findings began to occur in 1964 at Tell Mardikh, south of Aleppo, Syria, where Italian excavators unearthed Ebla, the capital of a Canaanite empire that existed about the time the Akkadians overwhelmed the Sumerians (c. 2400 B.C). In 1975, the expedition discovered some 15,000 clay tablets baked hard by a disastrous fire. Written in cuneiform symbols adapted from those of Sumer, the tablets primarily concern Ebla's treaties and commerce with other cities. But they also include Sumerian-Canaanite dictionaries, and literary texts that include Creation and Flood stories. Furthermore, the tablets mention personal names that also occur in the Bible, such as Abraham, Ishmael, and David. While the names may be coincidental, scholars speculate that some biblical stories may enshrine half-forgotten memories of this great Canaanite empire.

All such discoveries have led scholars to recognize Hebrew literature as reflecting, in a more complex manner than previously imagined, the history and literary traditions of the empires of the ancient Middle East. In 1992, on the occasion of the quincentennial of the arrival of Columbus in North America, American historians began to reassess the traditional interpretations of the history of the United States. Just so, on a far grander scale, the assemblers of the Hebrew Bible sought to reinterpret and clarify their own identity.

UNIT PROJECTS

1. **Performing Scenes from Genesis.** With two or three classmates, plan and present a Reader's Theater performance of any portion of "In the Beginning" or "Noah and the Flood" from the Book of Genesis. You may wish to add recorded background music, timing it beforehand so that it meshes well with your live reading. Or you might

use live music played on guitar, flute, or another portable instrument. Enhance your reading with a background slide show of nature photographs and works of art, if you wish.

2. **Comparing Portrayals of Satan.** In the Book of Genesis, a slithering serpent leads Adam and Eve into temptation. Find reproductions of several paintings based on the stories of the Garden of Eden and the Fall. How is the serpent portrayed in each? The serpent in Genesis is often seen as Satan. Try to find other works of art (you will find some in your textbook) that portray Satan, and compare and contrast the various portrayals. If you wish, draw your own picture of what you think the tempting serpent looked like in the Garden of Eden *before* God condemned him to crawl on his belly.

3. **Creating a Diorama.** With a classmate, create a diorama of either the Garden of Eden or Noah's ark. Include as many details as you can: vegetation and animals for the Garden of Eden, and the ark, Noah and his family, and numerous pairs of animals for "Noah and the Flood."

4. **Researching Women in the Bible.** Ruth is not the only powerful female character in the Bible. Both the Hebrew Bible and the New Testament give us tantalizing glimpses of the lives of many women. Read about and report to your classmates on one or more of the following biblical women: Sarah (Genesis 12: 10–20 and Genesis 17: 1–21); Hagar (Genesis 16: 1–16 and 21: 1–21); Rebecca (Genesis 24 and 27); Leah and Rachel (Genesis 28, 29, 30, 31); Rahab (Joshua 2 and 6); Deborah and Jael (Judges 4); Esther (the Book of Esther); Mary and Mary Magdalen (the New Testament Gospels). In your report, summarize the role of each woman and comment on any similarities that you see between the lives of women in the Bible and the lives of contemporary women.

5. **Illuminating a Psalm.** In the Middle Ages, scribes often painted initial letters and other decorative elements of their manuscripts with images from the Bible. These illustrations, or illuminations, were usually stylized and ornate. Find some books that reproduce illuminated manuscript pages from the Middle Ages. Then choose a psalm, either from your textbook or from a bible, and create an illuminated manuscript page. Carefully print the psalm or handwrite it using calligraphy, then add whatever decorative touches (an initial letter, for example, or birds) seem appropriate to you. Share your illuminated manuscript page with the class.

6. **Studying Biblical Art.** Throughout the ages, the Hebrew Bible and the New Testament have been rich sources of inspiration for artists. Look through art books for reproductions of paintings that are based on stories from the Bible such as Leonardo da Vinci's *The Last Supper,* Peter Paul Rubens' *Daniel in the Lion's Den,* Caravaggio's *The Conversion of St. Paul,* and Michelangelo's Sistine Chapel ceiling. Choose one work of art and research the bible story on which it is based. Summarize the story for the rest of the class as you display the artwork. Be sure to mention any special details or symbolism in the artwork that might shed light on the significance or meaning of the story.

7. **Researching Music Based on Psalms.** Many of the psalms from the Hebrew Bible have been set to music, either as parts of worship services or as separate pieces of music. Locate some recorded versions of psalms by various composers (some will be in Latin) and play them for the class. If you are musically talented, you might prefer to compose your own melody for the psalm of your choice.

8. **Drawing a Mural.** With a small group of your classmates, create a mural that depicts several stories and poems from the Hebrew Bible and the New Testament. Each panel should contain images based on a specific selection, such as the Creation, the Twenty-third Psalm, or the parable "The Talents."

9. **Dramatizing a Parable.** With at least three classmates, write a script for, rehearse, and then present to the class a dramatization of any parable from the New Testament. You may wish to have one member of your group serve as prop manager or director rather than as an actor.

10. **Writing a Biblical Memoir.** Choose a character from the Hebrew Bible or the New Testament and write a biography of that person. Describe his or her life as revealed in biblical stories and comment upon his or her significance in the Bible. If you wish, draw or paint a portrait of that person and include it with your biography.

IN THE BEGINNING
from Genesis

King James Bible ▾ (Textbook page 163)

SUMMARY

In the beginning, the spirit of God moves over chaos, and God speaks the universe into existence. The first day, God creates light and divides it from darkness. The second day, God creates the firmament, and divides the waters below it from those above it. The third day, God gathers the waters under the firmament into seas, causes dry land to appear, and has the earth bring forth vegetation. The fourth day, God establishes the sun, moon, and stars as markers of days and seasons. The fifth day, God causes creatures of the sea and air to appear. The sixth day, God creates land creatures, and, in the divine image, male and female human beings. God rests on the seventh day.

"The Garden of Eden" begins abruptly, explaining that on the day God creates heaven and earth, no humans exist to till the earth. God forms one from the dust of the ground, breathes into his nostrils the breath of life, and places him in charge of tending a luxurious garden. In the midst of the garden God plants a "tree of life" and "the tree of knowledge of good and evil." The man is forbidden under pain of death to eat of the tree of knowledge. So that the man (Adam) will not be alone, God forms the beasts of the fields and air and has Adam name them. But none proves a suitable partner for Adam. God casts him into a deep sleep, takes one of his ribs, and from it builds a woman (Eve).

In "The Fall," the serpent assures Eve that she and Adam will not die if they eat of the forbidden tree, but will become godlike, understanding both good and evil. She and Adam eat the fruit, realize their error, and try to hide from God. In penalty, God condemns the serpent to crawl upon its belly, Eve to suffer pain in childbirth, Adam to suffer pain and sorrow in working the earth, and human beings to die and return to dust. God drives the humans out of the garden and sets warrior angels to guard the tree of life.

GENESIS COMPARED TO OTHER CREATION ACCOUNTS

Interestingly, Genesis is filled with motifs also found in Babylonian, Hittite, and Canaanite stories. The Hebrew accounts differ from those of their neighbors in striking ways, however. The classic Babylonian creation account is found in the Mesopotamian epic *Enuma Elish,* thought to be based upon earlier Sumerian traditions. In the beginning, chaos reigns, personified as the male fresh-water deity, Apsu, and the female salt-water deity, Tiamat. These two beget the gods, but hostility arises between parents and offspring, and

Apsu is slain. Tiamat is now revealed as a monster, the dragon of chaos, and she is also killed in combat; the visible universe is created from her carcass. Other heavenly bodies become the seats of deities, and the god Marduk builds himself a heavenly palace whose earthly counterpart is the temple of Babylon. Mankind is made of clay mixed with the blood of a slain god, Kingu, an ally of Tiamat.

Similarly, Canaanite myths of origins depict the universe as arising from combat between Baal (equivalent of Marduk) and at least two other adversaries, Mot (death) and a monstrous dragon called Sea-River. Hittite stories contain the same theme of combat with a primordial monster, but because the Hittite empire (c. 2000–1200 B.C.) covered mountainous areas of Turkey and Syria, the stories give greater prominence to mountains and to storm gods.

In Genesis 1 the earth is a flat disk resting upon the waters of a lower abyss, with the sky arching overhead like an inverted bowl. As in *Enuma Elish,* light appears from primeval chaos, the firmament is created, dry land and luminaries appear, human beings are created, and the deity rests. The Hebrew word for chaos is even distantly related to the Babylonian word *tiamat.* The Hebrew creator is a single deity, and the heavenly bodies are not seats of divinities, but mere instruments for telling time. Even light, which in Babylonian stories represents Apsu or Marduk himself, is a creation of God. In addition, human beings, however, attain greater significance than in Babylonian myth. Formed in the image of God, they are given dominion over the rest of creation.

Genesis 2 also contains motifs common to Middle Eastern stories. The garden of Eden reflects both the Babylonian garden of the gods and the Sumerian paradise of Dilmun, described in the *Epic of Gilgamesh.* As in the *Enuma Elish,* the human beings in Genesis 2 are made from clay, but the divine element in humanity comes from the breath of God, not from the blood of a slain deity.

FOR FURTHER READING

Achtemeier, Paul J., et al., eds. *Harper's Bible Dictionary.* San Francisco: Harper & Row, Publishers, 1985.

Friedman, Richard Elliott. *Who Wrote the Bible?* New York: Summit Books, 1987.

Magnusson, Magnus. *Archaeology of the Bible.* New York: Simon and Schuster, 1977.

Trawick, Buckner B. *The Bible as Literature: The Old Testament and the Apocrypha.* 2nd ed. College Outline Series. New York: Barnes & Noble Books, 1970.

NOAH AND THE FLOOD
from Genesis
Jewish Publication Society of America ▾ (Textbook page 171)

SUMMARY

"Noah and the Flood" tells of an ancient deluge that occurred in Mesopotamia. Seeing that human wickedness has corrupted the earth, God resolves to destroy all humanity, except for the six-hundred-year-old Noah. God directs Noah to build an ark and to board it with his wife, his three sons, their wives, and two of each kind of animal. It rains forty days and nights, until water covers the highest mountains. Then God causes the rain to stop and a wind to blow; the waters begin to subside, and the ark comes to rest on Mount Ararat. Noah sends out a raven, but it returns to him, having found no place to rest. A dove also returns. A week later Noah sends the dove again, and it returns with an olive leaf. A week later, the dove does not return, and the people and animals leave the ark. Noah builds an altar and offers burnt sacrifices to God. God promises never again to destroy every living being, but makes demands of human beings as well: they may eat meat but not drink the blood of animals, they must punish murderers with the death penalty, and they are commanded to multiply. God sets a rainbow in the clouds as a sign of this covenant.

The sons of Noah are named Shem, Ham (Canaan), and Japheth. One day Noah becomes drunk with wine made from the grapes of his own vineyard, and lies naked in his tent. Ham comments on the situation to his brothers, but the two courteously cover their father while averting their eyes. Noah curses Canaan, but blesses Japheth and Shem for their behavior. Noah lives another 350 years, until age 950.

COMPARING ACCOUNTS OF THE FLOOD

Tales of a great flood abound in world literature, but the most striking parallels occur between biblical and Mesopotamian accounts, which arose from the same literary tradition. In Mesopotamian literature, one man is spared from the flood; in the Bible, too, God spares Noah. Both heroes are directed to build vessels and save themselves and representative pairs of all living creatures. Both arks come to rest on a mountaintop. The Mesopotamian hero sends out a dove, a swallow, and a raven; Noah sends out a raven and a dove. Both heroes offer sacrifice to their gods, who respond with commandments for humankind to follow.

Three major cuneiform versions of the Flood story have been found, all of them pre-dating Genesis: a Sumerian story, an account within the *Gilgamesh* epic, and the Atrahasis epic. In the fragmentary Sumerian story, the hero is rewarded with immortality. In the *Gilgamesh* epic, the flood story demonstrates that Gilgamesh cannot attain immortality, because the circumstances of Utnapishtim's immortality were unique. In the Atrahasis epic, it is overpopulation by human beings that prompts Enlil and the other gods to send plague, drought, famine, and ultimately, a destructive flood. One god, Enki, ordered Atrahasis to build an ark in order to survive the flood. After the flood, further overpopulation is controlled by Enki's initiation of safeguards such as barrenness and miscarriage for some women.

In contrast, the hero of the biblical story is not rewarded with immortality, nor is the flood a response to overpopulation, as in the Atrahasis epic. In fact, God commands human beings to multiply upon the earth. The flood arises because of the progressive pollution of the earth by the misdeeds of humanity. After the Flood, God gives Noah and his family some basic laws to prevent the recurrence of such despoliation. The idea that moral misdeeds can contaminate the earth is important in the Hebrew Bible, for Israel believed that it had inherited the land of Canaan because the previous inhabitants had polluted it through idolatry. Ultimately the Hebrew prophets came to believe that Israel, too, had polluted the land, and therefore merited the Babylonian Exile.

Despite numerous attempts to find archaeological evidence for a universal deluge, no conclusive evidence has been found, although localized flood levels have been discovered in various Mesopotamian cities.

FOR FURTHER READING

Achtemeier, Paul J., et al., eds. *Harper's Bible Dictionary.* San Francisco: Harper & Row, Publishers, 1985.

Magnusson, Magnus. *Archaeology of the Bible.* New York: Simon and Schuster, 1977.

Pfeiffer, Charles F., ed. *The Biblical World.* New York: Bonanza Books, 1966.

THE BOOK OF RUTH

King James Bible ▾ (Textbook page 178)

SUMMARY

In Chapter 1, famine drives a family from Bethlehem in Judah to the country of Moab: Elimelech, his wife Naomi, and their sons Mahlon and Chilion. Elimelech dies in Moab, and Mahlon and Chilion marry Moabite women, Ruth and Orpah. Later, Mahlon and Chilion also die. When Naomi sets out for her home in Judah. She urges her daughters-in-law to return to their mothers' homes and to find new husbands. Orpah leaves, but Ruth insists on accompanying Naomi and adopting Naomi's people and god as her own. They arrive in Bethlehem at the beginning of the barley harvest.

In Chapter 2, Ruth supports herself and Naomi by gleaning wheat missed by the reapers. She happens to choose a field owned by Boaz, a man so impressed by Ruth's industry and her devotion to Naomi that he tells her to glean only with his servants. He gives her a meal and instructs his men not to bother her and to leave extra grain deliberately for her. When Ruth reports that she worked in the fields of Boaz, Naomi calls blessings upon him and identifies him as a close relative.

In Chapter 3, at the end of the harvest, Naomi, who wishes to see Ruth settled, tells her that Boaz will be spending the night at the threshing floor. Ruth is to go to the threshing floor, and, when Boaz has fallen asleep, lie down under the covering at his feet and wait for him to tell her what to do. That evening, Boaz awakens out of a sound sleep to discover Ruth lying at his feet. Explaining that they are close relatives, she asks him to marry her. Boaz says that he will, unless a more closely related man wants to do so. At dawn, he sends her home with a cloakful of barley.

In Chapter 4, Boaz goes to sit at the town gate among the town elders. "Levirate" marriage laws of the times obliged a close relative of a childless dead man to marry his widow and raise sons in the dead man's name. He asks Naomi's dead husband's nearest male relative whether he will buy land once belonging to Elimelech and marry Ruth as duty dictates. The man tells Boaz to redeem the property himself. Boaz agrees, and the witnesses bless the marriage and pray that it will be fruitful.

Boaz and Ruth marry, and Ruth bears a son. The women of Bethlehem tell Naomi that her devoted daughter-in-law has proved better to her than seven sons. Naomi becomes the child's nurse, and the women give her the name Obed for him. He becomes the father of Jesse, who becomes the father of King David.

MORE ABOUT THE SELECTION

Critics have long praised the two heroines of the Book of Ruth, who courageously rebuilt the house of Elimelech. More recently, scholars have noted the feminist manner in which Naomi and Ruth focus on making their own lives rather than on honoring the dead man. In Chapter 1, the men immediately disappear, and Naomi and Ruth take center stage. In Chapter 2 it is not a man, but Ruth who takes economic control of her life and Naomi's. Even in Chapter 3, when Ruth approaches the sleeping Boaz according to Naomi's instructions, she does not wait for Boaz to tell her what to do. Instead, she asks him to marry her. Only in the scene at the city gates (Chapter 4), a gathering limited to male participants does emphasis switch from the welfare of living women to justice for dead men. Boaz's contention that Naomi has property to sell comes as a surprise, for Naomi has not mentioned it. Everytime Naomi has urged marriage upon either daughter-in-law, it has not been for the sake of a dead man's estate or lineage, but for the sake of the woman herself. And Ruth has shown no interest in remarrying until Naomi urged a plan upon her. At the end of the story, even the male orientation of Chapter 4 yields to the women of Bethlehem. They identify the newborn not as a man's child but as the son of Ruth who bore him and Naomi who nurtures him. And they, not the male elders, name the child.

A CRITICAL COMMENT

"With consummate artistry, the book of Ruth presents the aged Naomi and the youthful Ruth as they struggle for survival in a patriarchal environment. These women bear their own burdens. They know hardship, danger, insecurity, and death. . . . They themselves risk bold decisions and shocking acts to work out their own salvation in the midst of the alien, the hostile, and the unknown. . . .

"From a cultural perspective, Ruth has chosen death over life. She has disavowed the solidarity of family; she has abandoned national identity; and she has renounced religious affiliation. In the entire epic of Israel, only Abraham matches this radicality, but then he had a call from God. . . . Besides, Abraham was a man, with a wife and other possessions to accompany him. Ruth stands alone; she possesses nothing. No God has called her; no deity has promised her blessing; no human being has come to her aid. She lives and chooses without a support group, and she knows that the fruit of her decision may well be the emptiness of rejection, indeed of death. Consequently, not even Abraham's leap of faith surpasses this decision of Ruth's. And there is more. Not only has Ruth broken with family, country, and faith, but she has also reversed sexual allegiance. A young woman has committed herself to the life of an old woman rather than to the search for a husband, and she has made this commitment not 'until death do us part' but beyond death. One female has chosen another female in a world where life depends upon men. There is no more radical decision in all the memories of Israel."

—from God and the Rhetoric of Sexuality,

FOR FURTHER READING

Achtemeier, Paul J., et al., eds. *Harper's Bible Dictionary.* San Francisco: Harper & Row, Publishers, 1985.

Trawick, Buckner B. *The Bible as Literature: The Old Testament and the Apocrypha.* College Outline Series. 2nd ed. New York: Barnes & Noble Books, 1970.

Trible, Phyllis. *God and the Rhetoric of Sexuality.* Philadelphia: Fortress Press, 1978.

PSALMS 23, 104, AND 137
from the Book of Psalms
King James Bible ▼ (Textbook page 187)

SUMMARY

The Twenty-third Psalm, probably the most often recited psalm, compares God with a kind shepherd and with a lavish host. Psalm 104 praises the Creator. In addition to parallelism, it uses evocative metaphors, similes, and sensory images, as it describes God and his gifts to humanity. It celebrates the continuous, creative generosity of God, without whom mortals return to the dust. Psalm 137 expresses the sorrow of the Jews during the Babylonian Exile.

MORE ABOUT ANCIENT HEBREW LITERATURE

Just as the biblical Creation and flood stories resemble those of Mesopotamia, so other biblical literature resembles that of additional peoples with whom the Hebrews intermixed. The story of the temptation of Joseph by Potiphar's wife (Genesis 39), for example, strongly resembles a tale that first appears in Egyptian literature about 1200 B.C. Similarly, Hebrew poetry often connects with that of Egypt and of Ugarit, a small Canaanite kingdom.

An especially famous Egyptian poem, "The Great Hymn to the Aten" (see textbook page 73), written c. 1345 B.C., shows numerous parallels with Psalm 104 in both content and poetic techniques. The hymn speaks, for example, of Aten setting in the western horizon, casting the earth into darkness, when men must be wary of lions and other night beasts. Psalm 104 addresses Yahweh, who makes the darkness in which the beasts of the forest creep forth, and lions roar after their prey. "The Great Hymn to the Aten" describes ships that sail up and down, the fish leaping before Aten; Psalm 104 speaks of ships that move upon, and the creatures that play in, the sea.

As strongly as some psalms resemble Egyptian poetry, however, twentieth-century discoveries have shown that Hebrew poetry is even more deeply rooted in Ugaritic literature. Discovered by chance in 1928, the ruins of Ugarit lie at a Syrian site now called Ras-Shamra, on the Mediterranean coast. Ugarit was the administrative center of a small Canaanite kingdom that fell under the influence of the Hittites and, for many centuries, Egypt (beginning c. 1900 B.C.). It was destroyed by the Philistines c. 1200 B.C. Literary remains include hundreds of political, diplomatic, commercial, religious, and mythological texts written not only in cuneiform Akkadian, Egyptian, and Canaanite, but also in a Ugaritic alphabetic script.

The religious and mythological texts of Ugarit exhibit stylistic devices such as parallelism, and a vocabulary often taken over with little change by Hebrew authors. Ugaritic texts tell of the deeds of Canaanite deities known to Israel (Baal, El, Asherah, Anat), and even mention a legendary patriarch, Danel, known in the Hebrew Bible as Daniel. Other Hebrew names, such as Absalom, Solomon, and Jerusalem, contain the name of the Canaanite god of the evening star, Solom.

Of special interest are the many identical phrases found in Ugaritic and Hebrew poetry. Both the Canaanites' Baal and the Hebrews' Yahweh "mount to the clouds" in their chariots; they speak in thunder and storm; they stand "at the head of the assembly of gods." The Ugaritic monster Lotan becomes the Hebrew Leviathan of Psalm 104; the Ugaritic notion of the recesses of the North as the seat of the deity appears in Psalm 48; and a Ugaritic blessing with the dew of heaven and the fat of the earth recurs in Genesis 27:28.

The texts of Ugarit have been helpful, too, in deciphering biblical passages obscured through millennia of copying. The famous but enigmatic words of the exiled poet in Psalm 137, "If I forget thee, O Jerusalem, let my right hand forget her cunning," are more prosaically clarified in the Ugaritic parallel, "let my right hand wither." Similarly, some of the puzzling notations that accompany the first lines of various psalms are now recognized as musical directions, such as the tone in which the poem is to be sung, or the instrument to be used as accompaniment.

That the psalms are thoroughly rooted in the milieu of the ancient Middle East is attested not only by parallels such as these, but often by their very content. In that time, there was nothing improper about a prayer that included violent curses against an enemy and a frank longing for revenge, as in Psalm 137. Such notes, like the name Yahweh, simply reveal the psalmists as people of a specific cultural milieu. The Hebrew poets adapted to their own unique perspective both content and form of the literature of the world in which they lived.

A CRITICAL COMMENT

"It is difficult to speak of the 'teaching' of the Psalms. The book is a collection of the spontaneous popular piety and beliefs of Israel from the monarchy to the postexilic period. It is not prophetic or wisdom in conception and style, but lyrical; in one sense the Psalms are a summary of all the beliefs of the Old Testament, but in another sense only the entire Old Testament is a sufficient commentary on the Psalms.

The themes of the Psalms are rather implicit and presupposed; one does not expound in prayer, especially when one's prayer is a song. One may note, however, that the dominant themes of the Psalms flow naturally from the [themes of other biblical literature]. Yahweh is conceived in the hymns as a God of power and the savior of Israel. In the lamentations He is conceived as the savior of the individual Israelite, merciful and forgiving, faithful to His promises. . . . Israel in the Psalms is the people of election and covenant. Man is viewed in the lamentations as miserable and helpless, utterly dependent on Yahweh for his deliverance from evil. . . . Israel, collective and individual, lies under the obligation of the moral will of Yahweh and is governed by His action in history. . . ."

—*from* Dictionary of the Bible,
John L. McKenzie

FOR FURTHER READING

McKenzie, John L. *Dictionary of the Bible.* New York: Macmillan Publishing Company, 1965.

Romer, John. *Testament: The Bible and History.* New York: Henry Holt and Company, 1988.

Trawick, Buckner B. *The Bible as Literature: The Old Testament and the Apocrypha.* College Outline Series. 2nd ed. New York: Barnes & Noble Books, 1970.

THE PRODIGAL SON, THE SOWER, AND THE TALENTS
from the New Testament
New English Bible ▾ (Textbook page 199)

SUMMARY
THE PRODIGAL SON

In teaching his listeners about the generous love of God, Jesus tells the story of a man who has two sons. The younger requests his inheritance, turns it into cash, and leaves home for a distant country where he squanders the money. When famine falls upon that country, he finds work tending pigs. He would have been glad to eat the pods the pigs were given, but no one gave him even that much. Coming to his senses, he decides to confess his sinfulness to his father and beg to be treated as a hired servant. While he is still a long way off, the father sees him coming. He runs to greet the young man, flings his arms around him, and welcomes him with a lavish feast. When the older son complains that the father has never thrown such a party for him, the father explains that everything he possesses already belongs to the older son, but his brother had been lost, essentially dead to his family, but now had returned and was reclaimed.

THE SOWER

Jesus tells a story about a sower who spreads his seed. Depending upon where the seeds have fallen, they either wither or take root and flourish. After telling the parable, his disciples privately ask Jesus to explain its meaning. Jesus explains that the seeds represent the word of God, and the fate of the seeds in the various locations where they fall represents the way the words are received by different people. Some people no sooner hear the words than Satan steals them from their hearts, just as the bird steals the seeds that fall on the footpath. Some hear the words with joy but have not prepared their hearts to truly accept their meaning; like seeds that fall on poor soil, the words cannot take root in their hearts. Some let worldly cares turn their thoughts from the words they have heard, just as thistles choke the seeds' growth. But others who hear the words accept them wholeheartedly. Just as seed that falls on good soil comes to bear rich fruit, these people are blessed.

THE TALENTS

Jesus compares God to a householder who expects responsible behavior from his servants. Earlier translations of this story used the word "talent," the name of a valuable gold coin, instead of "bags of gold." The kingdom of God is like a householder going abroad, who entrusts his capital to his servants. To one he gives five bags of gold, to another two, and to another one, each according to the servant's capacity. The first two men invest and double their money. The third man, fearing the master's harshness, buries the gold. When the master returns, he praises the first two servants and gives them greater responsibility. He condemns the third man as a lazy rascal who could have banked the money and earned interest. That servant is cast out into the darkness.

MORE ABOUT THE PARABLES

Parable is an English version of the Greek word *parabol,* understood in the Hellenic world of New Testament times as a story used by an orator to demonstrate or illustrate a point. The Gospel writers, however, were educated in Jewish rather than in Greek oratory. In the Jewish culture, several skills were expected of the gifted speaker. First, the speaker was expected to employ quotations or allusions from the Hebrew Bible in an appropriate manner. Secondly, the speaker should produce a great number of developments on a theme, much as a musician improvises on a theme. But most of all, the speaker had to be an expert in the *mashal,* a literary form that included not only the moral story, but an entire range of literary types. The Hebrew name for the Book of Proverbs, for example, is Meshalim (the plural form of *mashal*); and the term *mashal* is applied to writings as varied as a song of triumph over the fall of Babylon in the Book of Isaiah, messages from God spoken by a prophet in the Book of Numbers, and a riddle posed by the hero Samson in the Book of Judges. The book of the prophet Ezekiel uses every kind of *mashal* from popular sayings to historical allegories, songs of derision, oracles, and the performance of symbolic actions, as well as the telling of stories with a moral.

One hundred years before the Gospels began to be written, the rabbi (teacher) Meir was already famous for producing inventive *meshalim* with a fox as the chief character; he is said to have composed three thousand of them. The Talmud, a collection of commentaries on the Hebrew Bible, contains hundreds of these stories. One commentator on Genesis, for instance, compares God with a man who mixes boiling water with cold in a basin before pouring the water into his jug, lest he crack the pottery. Other stories are almost identical to the fables of the legendary Greek storyteller, Aesop.

Jewish people of New Testament times were thoroughly grounded in this tradition of *meshalim.* Unlike modern readers, who tend to treat Gospel parables as isolated units, Jesus' listeners would have interpreted his stories in the context of the entire oration and, indeed, the context of the whole body of Hebrew literature. The parable of "The Sower," for example, would have called to mind Ezekiel's elaborate allegories of vines and trees, and a parable-*mashal* from the Second Book of Esdras:

The farmer sows many seeds in the ground and plants many plants, but not all the seeds sown come up safely in season, nor do all the plants strike root. So too in the world of men: not all who are sown will be preserved. (New English Bible, 2 Esdras 8:41)

Parable-*meshalim* were more than simple stories drawn from the daily life of New Testament times. A speaker's artistry lay in his ability to use them to evoke the entire range of Hebrew religious and literary experience.

A CRITICAL COMMENT

"It is abundantly obvious that Christ [Jesus] was acquainted with the *mashal* and that He used it. It would have been quite impossible for a Jew of His time not to have heard one of these ingenious little tales either uttered spontaneously or repeated by someone who had heard it. In fact, the Talmud contains some parable-*meshalim* which are almost the same as His: there is one, for example, on the wedding-guests, and another about the foolish virgins. Our Lord employed the *mashal* in all its forms. The 'Physician, heal thyself' of Saint Luke's Gospel [4:23] is a *mashal;* so is the apophthegm [pithy instructive saying] in Matthew [15:11] about what makes a man unclean: and among the *meshalim* parables there are several different kinds, varying much in length and nature.

"But when one compares the parables of the Gospels with those of the Talmudic tractates it is at once apparent that their character is new. There is nothing stereotyped or conventional about them: one feels that the comparison has sprung naturally from the mouth of the speaker; it is simple and exact, and . . . the tone is one that cannot be copied, it is a wholly personal style. . . . From the literary point of view it is artless, and yet in its emotional power it goes far beyond the most elaborate literary artifice. It does not so much amaze as persuade; it does not merely conquer, it convinces."

—*from* Daily Life in the Time of Jesus, *Henri Daniel-Rops*

FOR FURTHER READING

Daniel-Rops, Henri. *Daily Life in the Time of Jesus.* Trans. Patrick O'Brian. Ann Arbor: Servant Books, 1980.

Drury, John. *The Parables in the Gospels: History and Allegory.* New York: Crossroad, 1989.

Rhein, Francis Bayard. *An Analytical Approach to the New Testament.* Woodbury, NY: Barron's Educational Series, Inc., 1966.

NOTES

Unit 4: Greek and Roman Literatures (Textbook page 214)

Unit Introduction: Greek Literature

The ancient Greeks' efforts to define themselves and their universe fed a wellspring of Greek literature, a literature that helped to shape many of the later cultures in the West. The epics, with their brooding heroes and colorful array of deities, provided the first energetic and cohesive statement of Greek cultural values. Greek lyric poetry, drama, and historical writing investigated the private and public struggles of the individual. And the Greek philosophers, who speculated on the composition of the universe and postulated the existence of the atom, stamped all of Western thought from the classical era to the present.

BACKGROUND

THE GREEK LEGACY

Along with the Hebrew Bible, perhaps no other literature has had a greater impact on the development of Western thought and culture than that of the ancient Greeks. Thanks to the Romans (and their Hellenized descendants, the Byzantines, and after them the Arabs), Greek literature was preserved and cherished for its high artistic and intellectual achievement. Accordingly, it survived to influence, either directly or indirectly, the entire course of literary history in the West, especially since the Renaissance. Even in ancient times, however, as the Greeks' political dominance of the Mediterranean world was being assumed by the Romans, the indelible influence of Greek literature had already been established.

Early on, the Romans—as much out of aesthetic admiration as spiritual need—had appropriated the Greeks' pantheon and myths along with their temple architecture. The exploits of the gods and heroes—even in today's simplistic, popularized versions—remain as entertaining and inspiring as when the stories were first recorded in the Homeric hymns, Hesiod's *Theogony,* and Homer's epics of war and wandering. Perhaps the reason for the enduring power of the Greek myths—as in any mythology—lies in readers' understanding that the tales are essentially metaphors for the impenetrable mysteries of creation. The Greek myths convey insight into the workings and interrelationships of the divine and human realms.

As with the mythology, the other genres in which the Greeks excelled—epic, fable, lyric poetry, drama, historical writing, philosophical treatise— were all adopted, studied, imitated, and ultimately enshrined as "classics" by the Romans and their successors. The Greek literary heritage has so permeated Western thought, so entered the general psyche, that a Wall Street brokerage firm recently used TV adaptations of Aesop's fables to attract "wise" investors. Greek culture infuses our pop culture: We purchase Nike shoes, buy pop psychology books about the Graeco-Roman god and goddess archetypes within us, and listen to rock stars like Sting singing about being caught between Scylla and Charybdis. And while Oedipus probably appears today more often in the psychiatrist's office than on the stage, his "complex" attests to the broad cultural influence of Sophocles' character. Though there is much in Greek literature that may be alien to us, there is a large portion that remains compelling and wholly familiar.

THE HOMERIC EPICS

Perhaps the two most enduring texts in all of Greek literature are Homer's epics. They are the prototypes for most other epics in the Western tradition and have been the subject of a voluminous stream of criticism and analysis that stretches from the Renaissance to the present. Not surprisingly, Homer appears as one of the presiding geniuses in the contemporary American poet James Merrill's great epic poem *The Changing Light at Sandover.* Even more indicative of the enduring dominance of Homer are the many new translations that continue to appear, speaking with renewed vigor to each succeeding generation. Within the last few years, for example, new English renditions of the *Iliad* have been published by Christopher Logue and Robert Fagles. They join a long line of eminent

Unit Introduction **43**

translators of Homer's epics, including George Chapman (1611), Alexander Pope (1715–1720), William Cowper (1791), Andrew Lang (1882), Samuel Butler (1898), Richard Lattimore (1951), and Robert Fitzgerald (1961), whose translation is used in the textbook.

The Lyric Poets

In Greek lyric poetry, we generally hear the intimate, personal voices of individuals rather than the lofty, public voice that characterizes Homer's epics. In ancient times, the poems were customarily accompanied by music played on a lyre or some other instrument and were intended to be experienced primarily as performance and not as written texts. Greek lyrics consisted of two main kinds. Sappho's poems, for example, were monodies—songs for single voice—whereas the odes of Pindar and Baccylides were mainly choral. These choral poems were of several types and were performed at different public occasions: the dirge, for example, at funerals; the paean at triumphal military processions; and the epithalamium at weddings. The distinctive metrical and stanzaic forms that Greek lyric poets developed or popularized often bear their names: Sapphics, for example, after Sappho; Alcaics after Aclaeus; Asclepiads after Asclepiades of Samos; and so on. They were widely imitated in ancient Greece and later adopted by the Romans. Various poets over the centuries have tried with varying success to adapt Greek meters to English prosody. For instance, Sidney, Swinburne, Pound, and most recently the American poet Timothy Steele have all written poems using Sapphics.

Historical Writings

The keeping of historical records in Greece in the form of annals can be traced back to the end of the second millennium B.C. Tablets inscribed in Minoan script, for example, detailing municipal records have been found in Crete. However, the writing of history as we know it today developed in Greece alongside and then in opposition to the mythic and epic traditions. Writing in prose rather than verse, the first true historians, such as Hecataeus of Miletus and Herodotus, emerged at the beginning of the fifth century B.C. More than merely scribes, they were travelers and geographers who carefully recorded their observations and were willing to submit local legends to rational scrutiny. In this they were following the empirical lead of physicists and mathematicians like Pythagoras; nevertheless, they did not always arrive at "the truth." Even the "Father of History," Herodotus, has been criticized for credulity in his monumental *Histories*. In contrast, slightly later historians like Thucydides in his *History of the Peloponnesian War* and Xenophon in his *Anabasis,* are generally shrewder observers and better interpreters of political motivations and of cause and effect.

The Philosophers

The works of the Greek philosophers stand as towering achievements of rationalism and speculative thought. For the Greeks, "philosophy" encompassed not only physics, astronomy, geometry, and arithmetic—in short, "sciences" that probe the physical nature of the universe—but also subjects with a decidedly human focus or application, such as ethics, political theory, aesthetics, and theology. Later on, the Greeks' notion of philosophy grew to include epistemology (the theories of knowledge), logic, and other branches dealing abstractly with thought and language. So influential were the groundbreaking discoveries and theories of the Greek philosophers that their names are inextricably linked with concepts that every student must still grapple with at some stage of his or her education: Pythagorean theory, Socratic method, Aristotelian logic, platonic love. Democritus's atomic theory, Heraclitus's notion of reality as flux, Parmenides' conclusion that the sensory world is illusion, Plato's belief in the immortality of the soul—all these theories have had a permanent impact on how we view the world and conduct our lives. The textbook's selection from Plato's *Apology*, in which Socrates reaffirms his loyalty to the pursuit of the truth, is a testament to all these thinkers.

Timeless Dramas

Greek drama, represented in the textbook by Sophocles' *Oedipus Rex,* had its origins as religious ritual in honor of Dionysus—the fertility and vegetation god associated with winemaking. The all-male actors and chorus proclaimed their lines from behind masks (a common prop in Dionysian ceremonies) and moved in highly stylized, dancelike patterns. The plays, in which the playwright himself often performed, were composed in verse and were formally structured, befitting a religious occasion; nevertheless, they were never considered direct acts of worship in themselves. The general impression was probably similar to that of Japanese Noh drama (page 596).

The annual Dionysia in Athens attracted thousands of people from the surrounding countryside. It began with a solemn procession in which the god's statue was carried from his temple in the Academy to another temple adjacent to the theater on the southern slope of the Acropolis. After ritual sacrifices, young men would then carry the statue by torchlight into the theater, where it would preside over the dramatic performances. In addition to the playwrights' competition—a series of tragedies interspersed with comic and often bawdy satyr plays—spectators would witness choral performances of lyric odes and the formal presentation of armor to the sons of soldiers who had been killed in the latest war. Thus the spectacle of the Dionysia had religious, political, social, and aesthetic aspects. That the plays of Aeschylus,

Euripides, and Sophocles have retained their power to move modern audiences attests to the timelessness of their vision. Ultimately, we do not need to understand fully the particular religious, political, and social contexts in which the Greeks wrote their plays. They reach across the millennia—as do the Greeks' myths, epics, poetry, histories, and philosophy—to engage that part of us which is immutable: our common humanity.

UNIT PROJECTS

1. **Illustrating a Scene.** Homer's *Iliad* and *Odyssey* were favorite subjects of Greek vase painters. Consult art books to learn about how the Greeks decorated their pottery with mythological and everyday scenes. Look especially for renderings of Homer's heroes. Then try your hand at illustrating a scene from the *Iliad,* such as the death of Hector, in the style of an ancient Greek artist. Display your illustration in class.

2. **Creating a Chart.** Greek pottery came in many shapes and sizes depending on its intended use. Some pots were used commercially, as in the wine industry. Others had household uses or were reserved for religious rituals. After doing library research, prepare a chart showing the different shapes and sizes of Greek pottery. Include captions that identify each pot and explain its use.

3. **Creating a Historical Map.** Create a wall map of ancient Greece and the surrounding lands of the eastern Mediterranean Sea. Indicate important features, such as the following: major cities, such as Athens, Thebes, and Sparta; reputed birthplaces of major writers, such as Homer and Sappho; places associated with Homeric legends, such as Troy, Mycenae, and Ithaca; religious centers, such as Delphi, Delos, Ephesus, and Olympia; and major battlefields, such as Marathon, Thermopylae, and Salamis. If space permits, include brief annotations explaining the significance of each site.

4. **Devising a Labyrinth.** According to Greek legend, King Minos of Crete ordered an elaborate maze, called the Labyrinth, to be built to hold the ferocious Minotaur, a half-man, half-bull monster. So complicated was the Labyrinth that anyone entering it supposedly could not find his or her way out. Build or draw a model of the Labyrinth as you imagine it may have looked at the time of King Minos. To help give your design an authentic look, you may want to find out more about Minoan architecture.

5. **Making a Collage.** Countless drawings, sculptures, and paintings, both from ancient and more recent times, exist of the Greek gods and goddesses. Prepare a collage of Greek deities, using images from various historical periods. Try to include all the major gods and goddesses,

especially the twelve original Olympians (Zeus, Hera, Poseidon, Demeter, Athena, Artemis, Apollo, Aphrodite, Hephaestus, Ares, Hermes, Hestia) and the late-comer Dionysus.

6. **Setting a Lyric Poem to Music.** The lyre was a stringed instrument resembling a small harp and was used to accompany poets as they recited or sang their poems. Choose one of Sappho's poems and set it to music. You may either compose your own melody or find existing music that you think is appropriate. Arrange a performance of the poem for the class.

7. **Preparing a Funeral Oration.** A mastery of the art of public speaking was one of the aims of education in ancient Greece. Using Thucydides' "Funeral Oration of Pericles" as your model, write a speech that a modern American politician might deliver at a public funeral for a notable citizen, such as a war hero, humanitarian, or outstanding artist or scientist. What particular ideals embodied by the citizen might the politician want to persuade his or her audience to uphold? Record or videotape your speech and have it played for the class.

8. **Building an Architectural Model.** Greek architecture has had a lasting impact on Western civilization. Modern racecourses, for example, are derived from ancient Greek stadiums, and many public buildings incorporate the imposing columns and mathematical proportions of Greek temples. Build a model of an ancient Greek stadium, temple, amphitheater, or other public structure. Study the diagrams of ancient Greek structures to make your model as authentic as possible. Prepare a brief explanatory talk to accompany the presentation of your model to the class.

9. **Designing Costumes and Scenery.** Imagine that your school is planning a production of Sophocles' *Oedipus Rex*. Working with other classmates, prepare sketches for the various characters' costumes and for the scenery. Use your school library to research the architecture and dress of ancient Athens as a basis for your designs. Display your designs in class.

10. **Dramatizing a Scene.** Working with a classmate, write a dramatization of the minutes leading up to Socrates' death from drinking hemlock after having been found guilty of impiety and the corruption of Athenian youth. Consult Plato's dialogue *Phaedo* for specific details of the event.

11. **Preparing an Illustrated Program.** The ancient Olympics, which inspired our modern version, were held every four years at Olympia from 776 B.C. to A.D. 261. Do research to find out what the ancient Olympics were really like: What was the purpose of the games? What

special ceremonies would a spectator see? In what events did athletes compete? What were the rules, and who was eligible to participate? Who determined the winners? Prepare an illustrated program to help an imaginary time traveler to the fifth century B.C. better understand and enjoy the various Olympic events.

from the ILIAD
from Books 1, 22, and 24
Homer ▾ Translated by Robert Fitzgerald ▾ (Textbook page 229)

SUMMARY

from BOOK 1

In the opening lines of Book 1 of the *Iliad,* the poet/speaker invokes the inspiration and aid of the Muse as he begins to sing of the destructive wrath of Achilles. Agamemnon had angered the god Apollo by refusing to ransom Chryseis, the daughter of Apollo's priest, Chryses. Apollo unleashed a terrible plague on the Greek host. After nine days, Achilles called an assembly, at which the seer Calchas revealed that the plague would not cease until Agamemnon restored Chryseis to her father.

The angry Agamemnon says that he will surrender Chryseis only on the condition that the army chiefs give him a substitute prize. This demand in turn angers Achilles, and the quarrel of the two men swiftly intensifies. Achilles accuses Agamemnon of greed and cowardice, while Agamemnon accuses Achilles of trying to trick him and usurp his power. Achilles is about to strike Agamemnon with his sword, but the goddess Hera sends Athena to intervene. Achilles then swears that Agamemnon and the other Greeks will regret the day that they angered him and caused him to withdraw from the battle against Troy.

Nestor, the oldest of the Greek warriors, urges both Agamemnon and Achilles to compromise, but the chiefs continue to wrangle bitterly. Achilles agrees that he will surrender to Agamemnon his own prize, Briseis, as a substitute for Chryseis, but he threatens deadly resistance if he is robbed of any other prize.

Agamemnon dispatches Odysseus as the leader of an expedition to return Chryseis to her father. He then commands his heralds to go to Achilles' tent to fetch Briseis. Achilles sits apart by the seashore, calling tearfully in prayer to his mother, the sea nymph Thetis. When Thetis appears, Achilles begs his mother to intercede with Zeus in his behalf. Thetis sorrowfully laments Achilles' destiny to die young. She agrees that she will ask Zeus to take the Trojan side in the war so that her son's honor can be avenged.

BOOK 22

Angered by the death of his friend Patroclus at Hector's hands, Achilles has at last rejoined the battle. In Book 22, Achilles reluctantly abandons his pursuit of Apollo when the god tells him that it is fruitless for humans to strive against immortals. As Achilles runs across the plain toward the town, both Priam and Hecuba entreat Hector not to fight with Achilles. After deliberating about his course, Hector decides to stand firm, but when Achilles has almost reached him, Hector's nerve cracks and he flees, with Achilles close behind in pursuit.

The sight prompts Zeus to pity Hector, and he exhorts the other gods to find a way to save the Trojan hero. Athena, however, remonstrates with her father, reminding him that even the gods may not change destiny. Zeus yields to Athena. As the pursuit continues, Zeus weighs his golden scales, and Hector's fate sinks down. Apollo deserts Hector, and Athena intervenes to trick him, assuming the shape of one of Hector's favorite brothers, Deiphobus. Encouraged by this unexpected support, Hector stands to face Achilles. He dodges Achilles' first spear, but Athena supernaturally returns Achilles' spear to the Greek hero. Hector's spear rebounds from Achilles' shield. When he turns to Deiphobus for another spear, his "brother" has vanished, and Hector now realizes his doom. He desperately charges Achilles with his sword, but he is fatally wounded by Achilles' spear thrust to the throat.

As he dies, Hector begs Achilles to ransom his body to his parents, but Achilles—maddened by rage for the death of his friend Patroclus at the hands of Hector—scornfully refuses. After the Greek troops stab the corpse, Achilles attaches it to his chariot and drags it by the feet around the city walls. Watching from the walls, Priam and Hecuba lament their son's death. The last to learn of his fate is Hector's wife Andromache, who runs to the walls like a madwoman, only to view the hideous sight of her husband's body being dragged by the chariot horses at a gallop toward the Greek ships.

from BOOK 24

In Book 24, Priam journeys by night from the city of Troy to the tent of Achilles, hoping to secure Hector's body with a huge ransom. The god Hermes accompanies the old king and advises him on his mission.

Priam enters Achilles' tent, kneels down, and kisses the Greek hero's hands in supplication. He urges Achilles to remember his own father and to revere the gods. Both Priam and Achilles weep. Achilles reflects on the mixed destiny of good and evil that Zeus has given to mortals. He agrees he will ransom Hector's body, but he warns Priam not to vex him by pressing his entreaties too hard. Achilles orders his attendants to prepare the body. Priam and Achilles then eat supper. Achilles has Priam's bed prepared, and all retire to sleep.

Hermes reappears to Priam, reminding the king that if he is discovered and detained inside the Greek camp he may himself be held for ransom. Hermes urges Priam to depart secretly so that he may return to Troy in safety. When Priam arrives within the gates, Hector is lamented by his sister Cassandra, his wife Andromache, his mother Hecuba, and finally Helen of Troy. Priam orders the funeral pyre to be built, and the Trojans perform Hector's funeral rites.

MORE ABOUT THE AUTHOR

The authorship of the *Iliad* and *Odyssey* has been one of the most researched and controversial questions in classical studies for several centuries. Many scholars of the nineteenth century inclined to the view that the two poems were the amalgamation of shorter poems by a number of different composers. How else, these scholars reasoned, was one to explain the repetition? In the late 1920s and 1930s, however, the research of the American scholars Milman Parry and Albert Lord firmly established that repetition was an integral feature of the style of *oral* poetry. Parry's brilliant and convincing arguments that the *Iliad* and *Odyssey* were orally composed had a radical effect on the question of authorship. Repetition, as well as certain other stylistic features, could no longer be used as support for an "analyst" view of the epics as a collage of smaller narratives that had been stitched together. Parry and Lord supported their view with some intriguing parallels from orally composed, Serbo-Croatian heroic songs, which they researched and recorded in the field on several extended trips to Yugoslavia.

It is now generally accepted that the Homeric epics are the products of oral composition. The overwhelming artistic unity of both the *Iliad* and the *Odyssey* has been emphasized in many modern scholarly works that tend toward a "unitarian" view—namely that a single author (sometimes called the "monumental poet") was responsible for most of the epics as we now have them. It seems likely that this poet lived in the eighth century B.C., toward the end of a long oral tradition that may have stretched back for three or four hundred years to the time of the Trojan War itself. The monumental poet was surely able to build on the oral tales of his predecessors and to manipulate the formulaic diction of traditional epic with consummate skill. We may as well call this poet Homer, even though we know next to nothing for certain about a historical person by that name. Precisely how, when, and why the poems were first written down is a question that is still hotly debated.

A CRITICAL COMMENT

"Homer's Achilles is clearly the model for the tragic hero of the Sophoclean stage: his stubborn, passionate devotion to an ideal image of self is the same force that drives Antigone, Oedipus, Ajax and Philoctetes to the fulfillment of their destinies. Homer's Achilles is also, for archaic Greek society, the essence of the aristocratic ideal, the paragon of male beauty, courage and patrician manners—'the splendor running in the blood,' says Pindar, in a passage describing Achilles' education in the cave of the centaur Chiron. And this, too, strikes a tragic note, for Pindar sang his praise of aristocratic values in the century which saw them go down to extinction, replaced by the new spirit of Athenian democracy.

"But it seems at first surprising that one of the most famous citizens of that democracy, a man whose life and thought would seem to place him at the extreme opposite pole from the Homeric hero, who was so far removed from Achilles' blind instinctive reactions that he could declare the unexamined life unlivable, that Socrates, on trial for his life, should invoke the name of Achilles. Explaining to his judges why he feels no shame or regret for a course of action that has brought him face-to-face with a death sentence, and rejecting all thought of a compromise that might save his life (and which his fellow citizens would have been glad to offer), he cites as his example Achilles, the Achilles who, told by his mother that his own death would come soon after Hector's, replied: 'Then let me die at once—'rather than 'sit by the ships . . . / a useless, dead weight on the good green earth' (18.113–23).

"And yet, on consideration, it is not so surprising. Like Achilles, he was defying the community, hewing to a solitary line, in loyalty to a private ideal of conduct, of honor. In the last analysis, the bloodstained warrior and the gentle philosopher live and die in the same heroic, and tragic, pattern."

—from the Introduction to Robert Fagles' translation of the Iliad, Bernard Knox

FOR FURTHER READING

Edwards, Mark W. *Homer, Poet of the Iliad*. Baltimore: Johns Hopkins University Press, 1987.
Finley, M. I. *The World of Odysseus*. London: Chatto and Windus, 1964.
Griffin, Jasper. *Homer on Life and Death*. Oxford: Oxford University Press, 1980.

Homer. *The Iliad.* Trans. Robert Fitzgerald. New York: Anchor Press, 1975.

Homer. *The Iliad.* Trans. Robert Fagles, Jr. London: Penguin Books, 1991.

Kirk, G. S. *The Songs of Homer.* Cambridge: Cambridge University Press, 1962.

Moulton, Carroll. *Similes in the Homeric Poems.* Gottingen: Vandenhoeck & Ruprecht, 1977.

Stanford, W. B. and J. V. Luce. *The Quest for Ulysses.* New York: Praeger, 1974.

Wood, Michael. *In Search of the Trojan War.* New York: Facts on File, 1985.

SAPPHO'S LYRIC POEMS

Translated by Mary Barnard ▼ (Textbook page 281)

SUMMARY

The speaker in "You Are the Herdsman of Evening" addresses Hesperus, the evening star, metaphorically comparing him to a herdsman who drives sheep, goats, and children home to their mothers as darkness falls.

In "Sleep, Darling," the speaker is a mother who tenderly lulls her small daughter Cleis to sleep. Cleis is as precious to her mother as a golden flower. The speaker says she would not accept all the riches of Croesus in exchange for her daughter.

In "We Drink Your Health," the speaker acclaims a lucky bridegroom in a toast to his health. The loveliness of the bride proves that the goddess Aphrodite herself has favored the bridegroom.

The speaker of "To an Army Wife, in Sardis," is a soldier who is posted far away from his wife Anactoria. Some say that a cavalry corps or the ships of a fleet are a fine sight, but the soldier affirms that the finest sight on earth is the object of a person's love. He cites Helen of Troy as a proof who yielded to love when she eloped with Paris?

In "You May Forget But," the speaker tells another of how someone in the future will think of them.

In "Tonight I've Watched," the speaker sadly reflects on her loneliness and her passing youth as the moon, and then the Pleiades, set in the night sky.

In "Don't Ask Me What to Wear," Cleis's mother tells her daughter that she has no embroidered headband to give her, the way her own mother gave her a purple ribbon. The mother tells Cleis that the most becoming headdress for her blonde hair would be fresh flowers.

MORE ABOUT THE AUTHOR

It is important for the modern reader of Sappho to remember that Sappho is a figure whose reputation has been clouded by two thousand years of gossip and incomplete information. Sappho was a member of a thriving, literate society in which many people wrote and performed poetry, and the notion of Sappho as a lonely or necessarily unusual figure is inaccurate. Sappho was well-known in her day, which explains why there are so many different versions of her life. Apparently, women poets and performers of religious ceremonies were very common in Greece during Sappho's lifetime. Yet only Sappho's material survives, and it comes to the modern reader in fragments that have been transcribed and translated again and again over a period of 2500 years.

Sappho's poetry was ostensibly public poetry—wedding songs and celebratory poems—yet the surviving fragments strike the modern reader as intensely personal and private in nature. Still, the style of the fragments is neither sentimental nor encumbered with emotion; Sappho's writing is at once clean, precise, and unornamented, and yet touching. The contradictions of Sappho's life and poetry make translation difficult; the translator Mary Barnard was careful to preserve Sappho's "Greekness" and provide clues for modern readers to the woman who wrote them. She also decidedly compressed the fragments, rather than fill them out to "make" a poem.

A CRITICAL COMMENT

A critic comments on "Tonight I've Watched": "We respond to the grammatical simplicity of the clauses, in which emotion seems to express itself without mediation, and to their straightforward coordination, whereby each clause slips past as gently but irrevocably as the hours of loneliness. We also imagine in all its distinctness the implied situation: an evening toward the end of winter (in Greece, the season when the Pleiades set in the middle of the night), against whose familiar chill (and hints of future warmth) the girl reacts with a desire for love. She waits and watches, and not finding the object of her desires on earth she seeks complicity in the most feminine of celestial bodies; abandoned finally by these too when they vanish below the horizon, she follows their motion downward and inward into her bedroom and into herself; here she first becomes fully aware of the extent of her solitude, recognizing that, when all nature has retired, she alone remains awake. The girl feels herself both a part of wider natural processes and irremediably divorced from them. In the moon and stars she has found a companionship that her loved one has denied her, but she has been disappointed in the end by them as well. We recall that the Pleiades were once girls, who turned into stars in order to escape the amorous pursuit of Orion—who, now himself a constellation, forever follows them to the horizon in vain."

—from "Greek Lyric Poets,"
Glenn W. Most

FOR FURTHER READING

Bowra, C. M. *Greek Lyric Poetry*. 2nd ed. Oxford: Oxford University Press, 1961.

Finley, M. I. *Early Greece, The Bronze and Archaic Ages*. 2nd ed. New York: W.W. Norton and Co., 1982.

Most, Glenn W. "Greek Lyric Poets." *Ancient Writers: Greece and Rome*. Ed. T. James Luce. New York: Charles Scribner's Sons, 1982.

Sappho. *Sappho: A New Translation*. Trans. Mary Barnard. Berkeley: University of California Press, 1984.

Webster, Thomas B. L. *Greek Art and Literature 700–530 B.C.* Westport, CT: Greenwood Press, 1959.

FUNERAL SPEECH OF PERICLES
from History of the Peloponnesian War
Thucydides ▼ Translated by Benjamin Jowett ▼ (Textbook page 286)

SUMMARY

In his funeral oration, Pericles first calls attention to the difficulty of his task: it is hard to say neither too little nor too much on such occasions. He urges his listeners to remember the achievements of their ancestors, who bequeathed them a free state. Pericles summarizes the principles of action that aided the Athenians in their rise to power. He praises Athenian political democracy and the relaxed and elegant Athenian way of life. Comparing the Athenians' training with that of the Spartans, Pericles emphasizes Athenian superiority. He also singles out Athenian decisiveness, generosity, and confidence as values worthy of praise. Summing up, he calls Athens the "school of Hellas."

Pericles explains that he has dwelt upon the greatness of Athens so that his listeners may have a clear image of the kind of city for which they are fighting and which claims their loyalty. He praises the courage of the dead, asserting that they have honorably made the supreme sacrifice for their country. He comforts the parents of the dead, and he urges the sons and brothers of the dead to emulate their heroism. He admonishes the widows to bear their grief in a dignified way. Pericles closes his speech by reminding the audience that the state will maintain the young children of the dead until they are grown. When the mourners have duly lamented their own dead, they should depart.

MORE ABOUT THE SELECTION

One of the most remarkable features of Thucydides' *History* is the author's style. One feature is Thucydides' use of poetic and archaic words. Another distinguishing trait is his extreme conciseness (the ancients called it "swiftness"). A third characteristic is his use of a large number of abstract nouns to express his ideas. Some of these nouns, in fact, first appeared in ancient Greek in Thucydides' *History*. Finally, Thucydides often emphasized his ideas, especially in the speeches, with a highly distinctive use of antithesis.

This figure of speech normally expresses sharply contrasting ideas in parallel phrases or structures—as can be seen at several points in the English translation. What is not easy to translate, however, is Thucydides' manipulation of antithesis so that his prose comes close to, but actually avoids, precise formal balance. The contrasting elements are approximately parallel but not exactly so. An example in English might run as follows (with apologies to Alexander Pope): *"To err* is human; *forgiveness,* divine." In English, the slightly disturbing effect of substituting an abstract noun for an infinitive in the second, antithetical phrase would be regarded as a stylistic fault. Thucydides boldly used such asymmetrical constructions to create jarring, memorable effects. It is as if his urge to clarify distinct ideas by juxtaposing them conflicts with his belief that the direct opposition of two concepts may oversimplify them.

A CRITICAL COMMENT

"The Funeral Oration provides an ideal setting for the development of the commonplaces about the need for individual sacrifice for the common good. Such topics are inevitable in the genre and not surprising in their context. More remarkable is another aspect of the relationship between the citizen and his city: Pericles' emphasis on the relaxed quality of Athenian life. While paying tribute to former generations of Athenians who, among their other accomplishments, turned back the Persian invasion and won the Athenian empire, the speech emphasizes the confident amateurism of Athenian life. This point is developed by a rhetorical strategy unparalleled in other extant funeral orations. Pericles passes over the customary survey of Athenian history, real and mythic, and concentrates instead on those habits, civic arrangements, and dispositions that stand behind Athens' growth to greatness. . . .

"This substitution of a discussion of patterns of Athenian life for the traditional material of funeral oratory opens the way for a discussion of the difference between Athenian ways and those of other Greek cities . . . The contrast between Athens and the unnamed 'others' gradually concentrates on her differences from the disciplined and regimented life of Sparta, so much admired, though only rarely imitated, by other Greeks. . . .

"This picture of the spontaneous bravery and commitment of the Athenians carries on the contrast between them and the Spartans that the Corinthians drew in the first book (esp. 1.70), but new contrasts and a further function emerge. Athenian society is now viewed according to its contribution to the individuals who comprise it: 'To sum up I say that this city taken collectively is an education for Greece and that at an individual level a citizen among us, it seems to me, dexterously attains in the largest number of respects and with all graciousness full self-sufficiency.'"

—from Thucydides,
W. Robert Connor

FOR FURTHER READING

Connor, W. Robert. *Thucydides.* Princeton: Princeton University Press, 1984.

Kagan, Donald. *The Outbreak of the Peloponnesian War.* Ithaca: Cornell University Press, 1969.

Rawlings, Hunter. *The Structure of Thucydides' History.* Princeton: Princeton University Press, 1981.

Thucydides. *Thucydides Translated into English.* Trans. Benjamin Jowett. Oxford: Clarendon Press, 1900.

from the APOLOGY
from the Dialogues
Plato ▼ Translated by Benjamin Jowett ▼ (Textbook page 295)

SUMMARY

At his trial in Athens, Socrates asserts that he does not wish to demean himself by weeping and lamenting or begging the jurors to acquit him. He prophesies to those who condemned him that they will experience a far more severe punishment than they have inflicted on him. To his friends, Socrates says that he is confident that he has followed the right course. His proof of this is the silence of his inner voice or oracle, which has not opposed anything he has said or done during the trial.

Socrates asserts that there is good reason to hope that death is a good, rather than an evil. To support his optimistic outlook, he offers two analogies for death: first as a state of utter unconsciousness or sleep, and second as a journey in which the soul migrates from one world to another. In either case, Socrates argues, death is beneficial. He looks forward to meeting in the underworld the judges of the dead and the souls of past heroes. Finally, he asks his judges to correct his sons if they should in adulthood prefer riches to virtue or to think too highly of themselves.

MORE ABOUT THE AUTHOR

In addition to the *Apology,* Plato wrote several other dialogues in which he chronicled and dramatized the last days of Socrates' life. In the *Crito,* for example, Socrates refuses to cooperate with a plan devised by some of his disciples for his escape from prison. In this dialogue, Socrates argues that, just as children must obey their parents, obedience to the laws of the city is every citizen's duty. In the *Phaedo,* which recounts Socrates' last hours and his death by drinking the poison hemlock, Socrates gives some of his most interesting and important arguments about the immortality of the soul.

A CRITICAL COMMENT

"Mastery of the resources of a new literary medium which suits so well Plato's dramatic flair challenges his artistic gifts. He tries his hand at it, produces little masterpieces, and delight in successful creation keeps him at it year by year. But the artist in Plato could not have displaced the philosopher. We must assume that philosophical inquiry was the *primum mobile* in the composition of those earlier dialogues no less than of any he was to write thereafter, and that throughout this first phase of his writing Plato remains convinced of the substantial truth of Socrates' teaching and of the soundness of its method. But the continuing harmony of the two minds, though vital, is not rigid: the father image inspires, guides, and dominates, but does not shackle Plato's philosophical quest. So when he finds compelling reason to strike out along new paths, he feels no need to sever the personal bond with Socrates. And when these lead him to new, unSocratic and antiSocratic conclusions, as they visibly do by the time he comes to write the *Meno,* the dramatist's attachment to his protagonist, replicating the man's love for the friend and teacher of his youth, survives the ideological separation. And so, as Plato changes, the philosophical persona of his Socrates is made to change, absorbing the writer's new convictions, arguing for them with the same zest with which the Socrates of the previous dialogues had argued for the views the writer had shared with the original of that figure earlier on."

—from Socrates, Ironist and Moral Philosopher, *Gregory Vlastos*

FOR FURTHER READING

Brickhouse, T. C. *Socrates on Trial*. Oxford: Oxford University Press, 1989.

Friedlander, Paul, ed. *Plato*. Vol. 1. New York: Pantheon, 1969. 3 vols.

Havelock, Eric A. *Preface to Plato*. Cambridge: Belknap-Harvard University Press, 1963.

Plato. *The Works of Plato*. Trans. Benjamin Jowett. New York: Modern Library, 1928.

Vlastos, Gregory. *Socrates, Ironist and Moral Philosopher*. Ithaca: Cornell University Press, 1991.

OEDIPUS REX

Sophocles ▾ Translated by Dudley Fitts and Robert Fitzgerald ▾ (Textbook page 307)

SUMMARY

PART 1

As the play opens, the city of Thebes is ravaged by a devastating plague. Citizens gather to beseech King Oedipus for aid. A priest reminds Oedipus that once before he saved the city from the monstrous Sphinx by correctly answering her riddle. Oedipus replies that he has sent Creon, the brother of Queen Jocasta, to the oracle of Apollo at Delphi. Creon returns from Delphi and announces the utterance of the oracle: Thebes will be delivered when the Thebans find and punish the murderer of the former Theban king, Laius. Oedipus promptly resolves to begin an investigation of the crime, and demands that anyone with information about the murder of Laius should come forward. He then consults the blind seer Teiresias. But when he is ushered in, however, the seer stubbornly refuses to reveal what he knows. Growing increasingly frustrated and angry, Oedipus at first cajoles and then denounces Teiresias, accusing him of joining in a conspiracy with Creon against him and the city. The seer hints as he departs that Oedipus will one day find out the truth about his own past—and that this truth will destroy him.

Creon is angry and upset at Oedipus's unjust accusation of conspiracy, and the two men quarrel. Jocasta enters and begs Oedipus to relent. He yields to her pleas and those of the Choragos, reluctantly allowing Creon to leave. Jocasta tries to set Oedipus's mind at ease by recalling the ancient oracle that had predicted that Laius would die at the hands of his own son. Jocasta tells Oedipus that because of this oracle, the couple left their infant son on Mount Cithaeron, leaving him to die of exposure. The queen reasons that Laius's later death at the hands of highwaymen at a place where three roads met is conclusive proof that the oracle was false. Jocasta's soothing words upset Oedipus, who questions Jocasta intently about the detail of the crossroads. He now begins to fear that he may be the unintentional victim of his own curse. He explains to Jocasta the circumstances of his upbringing in Corinth as the child of King Polybus and Queen Merope. A comment made by a drunken man at a feast about Oedipus's legitimacy led Oedipus to question his parents and to harbor doubts about his origins. He set off to Delphi, where he received the frightening prophecy that he would slay his father and commit incest with his mother. To insure that the prophecy could not possibly come true, Oedipus then left Corinth for good. In his travels, Oedipus encountered a party of travelers at a place where three roads met. Provoked by a violent assault, Oedipus slew the old master and his servants. What if the old man should turn out to have been Laius?

Oedipus reasons that the only way to prove or disprove his new suspicions is to question the surviving eyewitness to the murder, whom Jocasta had sent to a remote region long ago. He commands the shepherd to be summoned as the scene closes.

PART 2

In Scene 3, Jocasta announces to the Thebans that she is conducting sacrifices to the gods. A messenger from Corinth enters to tell Jocasta and Oedipus that King Polybus is dead and that the Corinthians wish Oedipus to become their king. When Oedipus confirms that Polybus died of natural causes, he concludes that part of the oracle, at any rate, has been proved false. The messenger, however, overhears Oedipus's concern about the other part of the oracle: the prediction of incest with his mother. He interrupts to assure Oedipus that he need have no fear: Polybus and Merope were not his real parents. The messenger himself, many years ago, had been given the infant Oedipus on Mount Cithaeron, with his ankles pierced and tied together, by another shepherd who had found the baby. The Choragos suggests that this shepherd is the same shepherd with whom Oedipus has already resolved to interrogate. Jocasta breaks in to urge Oedipus not to pursue the matter further. Her distress mounts as Oedipus insists he cannot let the matter rest, now that he is so close to the truth about his own identity. Ironically, he interprets Jocasta's anxiety as fear that Oedipus may turn out to be lowborn.

Oedipus questions the shepherd intently. The shepherd tries to evade the queries with vague answers, but under the pressure of Oedipus's threats the awful truth is finally revealed. Oedipus was the child of Laius and Jocasta, left on Cithaeron to die as an infant. He now knows himself as the unwitting murderer of his father and the husband of his own mother. With a cry of anguish, he rushes offstage. The chorus laments the tragic misery of Oedipus's destiny.

In the Exodos, or final scene, a messenger describes to the Theban elders Jocasta's suicide by hanging and Oedipus's self-blinding with the brooches from her robes. Oedipus enters to lament his fate. Determined to leave Thebes for a wretched life of exile, Oedipus begs Creon to care for his children. The Choragos closes the play by reflecting on the frailty of humankind.

MORE ABOUT THE AUTHOR

Sophocles' seven extant plays span the last forty years or so of his long career. The three plays on the Oedipus legend—*Oedipus the King, Oedipus at Colonus,* and *Antigone*—are often said to comprise Sophocles' "Theban cycle." *Ajax* dramatizes the anguish and madness of the Greek hero Ajax when, after the death of Achilles at Troy, Achilles' arms were awarded to Odysseus rather than to him. In the *Women of Trachis,* Sophocles presents the story of Deianeira, the wife of Heracles, whose plan to recapture the love of her philandering husband caused his death instead. In *Electra,* Sophocles dramatizes another memorable heroine: the daughter of Agamemnon who avenged her father's death by joining with her brother Orestes to kill their mother Clytemnestra and her lover Aegisthus. Finally, Sophocles' *Philoctetes* dramatizes the efforts of Odysseus and Neoptolemus to persuade the wounded hero Philoctetes—who had been abandoned on an island on the way to Troy—to rejoin the Greek army and to participate in the Trojan War.

A CRITICAL COMMENT

"In the interplays of speaking out and reticence, of arbitrary interpretation and ironic hidden truths, of insight and blindness, the *Oedipus Tyrannus* offers a paradoxical paradigm of man and his knowledge that challenges not only fifth-century or modern claims for the rigor, certainty, and exhaustiveness of man's intellectual progress, but also the security of the reading process itself with its aim of finding, and delimiting, the precise, fixed and absolute sense of a text, a word. Athenian tragedy questions again and again the place and role of man in the order of things; and in its specific questioning of man's status with regard to the object and processes of knowledge and intellectual enquiry, the *Oedipus Tyrannus* instigates a critique relevant not only to the fifth-century enlightenment and its view of man's progress and achievement but also to the play's subsequent readings and readers. 'In some sense,' writes Dodds, 'Oedipus is every man and every man is potentially Oedipus.' He quotes Freud, who wrote 'Oedipus's fate moves us only because it might have been our own.' The model of Oedipus as interpreter of signs and solver of riddles, of Oedipus as the confident pursuer of knowledge through rational enquiry, of Oedipus as the searcher for insight, clarity, understanding, indeed provides a model for our institutions of criticism. It is as readers and writers that we fulfill the potential of Oedipus's paradigm of transgression."

—*from* Reading Greek Tragedy,
Simon Goldhill

FOR FURTHER READING

Edmunds, Lowell. *Oedipus: The Ancient Legend and Its Later Analogues.* Baltimore: Johns Hopkins University Press, 1985.

Edmunds, Lowell, and Alan Dundes. *Oedipus: A Folklore Casebook.* New York: Garland Publishing Inc., 1984.

Goldhill, Simon. *Reading Greek Tragedy.* Cambridge: Cambridge University Press, 1986.

Jones, John. *On Aristotle and Greek Tragedy.* London: Chatto and Windus, 1962.

Knox, Bernard M. W. *Oedipus at Thebes.* New Haven: Yale University Press, 1957.

Segal, Charles P. *Tragedy and Civilization: An Interpretation of Sophocles.* Cambridge: Harvard University Press, 1981.

Sophocles. *The Oedipus Cycle: An English Version.* Trans. Dudley Fitts and Robert Fitzgerald. San Diego: Harcourt Brace Jovanovich, 1977.

Taplin, Oliver. *Greek Tragedy in Action.* Berkeley: University of California Press, 1978.

Unit Introduction:
Roman Literature

After the death of Alexander the Great in 323 b.c., the center of power in the Mediterranean moved westward to Rome. With this shift, the Greek cultural legacy also passed into Roman hands. Early Latin literature relied heavily on Greek models for both style and content. But by the end of the Age of Augustus, writers such as Catullus, Virgil, Ovid, and Tacitus had carved out a Latin literature that could stand as a worthy inheritor of the Greek tradition.

BACKGROUND

THE HEIRS OF HELLAS

The Romans were the first inheritors of the Greek legacy. In fact, until Neoclassicism swept Europe in the late seventeenth and eighteenth centuries, the Romans were perhaps the most avid Grecophiles. They appropriated the Greeks' pantheon and weaved the tales of the Olympian gods together with their own native mythology. They copied Greek temple architecture, and Roman art collectors imported masterpieces of Greek pottery and sculpture and routinely commissioned copies. Roman aristocrats in the third and second centuries B.C. supported a system of Greek primary and secondary schools for the education of their sons, and Greek scholars were customarily invited to Rome to present lectures on rhetoric.

The Romans created their own literature mainly by reforging the genres developed by the Greeks. Toward the end of the third century B.C., for example, Livius Andronicus made the first translation of the *Odyssey* into Latin, adapting and Romanizing many of the characters and situations in Homer's epic. Not without stylistic flaws, Livius's rendering of Homer nevertheless became an influential model for succeeding Roman poets. Similarly, Roman playwrights, such as Plautus and Terence, Romanized the stock characters of Greek comedy, especially those of Menander's plays, which until archaeological discoveries in Egypt in this century were practically unknown.

Around the beginning of the second century B.C., another influential poet, Ennius, was translating the tragedies of Euripides and Aeschylus and writing his epic *Annales,* which traces Rome's beginning to the fall of Troy. Indebted to the Homeric models, Ennius's poem appropriately begins with the poet learning in a dream that he is the reincarnation of Homer. And so, by the time Virgil came to write the *Aeneid,* the supreme epic of Rome, Homer's models had already been thoroughly absorbed into the Roman literary tradition.

LATIN POETS, GREEK MODELS

As with the epic, in lyric poetry the Romans looked to the Greeks for thematic inspiration and for polished examples of versification. Catullus, for example, included translations of Sappho and Callimachus among his own poems, and Horace closely imitated the stanzaic forms of Archilochus, Alcaeus, Anacreon, and Pindar as well as Sappho in his *Epodes* and *Odes.* In comparison to Horace, who seems the embodiment of conservative Greco-Roman learning and stay-at-home moderation, Ovid strikes us at first as a genius who both courted the patronage of the mighty and exposed their flaws. A true cosmopolitan living at the hub of the empire before his exile, Ovid drew upon culturally diverse sources for his poetry. In the *Metamorphoses* especially, Ovid not only re-creates and reinvigorates the old Greek and Roman myths but also includes tales from other Mediterranean cultures. Scholars have also noted in the *Metamorphoses* Ovid's debt to Greek predecessors, such as Nicander, Parthenius, and Callimachus. In its themes, chronological development, and use of Homer's meter, the *Metamorphoses* assumes epic proportions without ever attempting to encroach on the nationalistic claims of Virgil's *Aeneid.* Nevertheless, each in its own distinctive way is a shining literary monument of Augustan Rome.

Roman historical writing, too, had its beginnings in the Greek tradition. In fact, the earliest Roman historians wrote in Greek in order to justify Rome's expansionist policies in the Hellenistic world. Other early Roman histories took the form of annals and *tabulae pontificum,* which recorded such events as triumphs, famines, and eclipses insofar as they related to priestly matters and ceremonies.

By the time of Sulla (c. 138–78 B.C.) and the waning years of the Republic, all the forms of Greek historical writing were firmly established in Rome, most notably the autobiography, biography, monograph, and military memoir. Of this last type, the most famous example is probably Julius Caesar's *Commentaries on the Gallic War*. With Julius Caesar, Sallust, Livy, and Cicero, the content of the historical writing is deeply tied to each author's personality and style.

THE WIT AND WISDOM OF TACITUS

Tacitus, writing roughly a century and a half after Sallust, was nevertheless greatly influenced by him. As any student who has attempted to translate Tacitus knows, his style is highly compressed and wholly his own. He rarely uses direct quotations, preferring to adapt what his characters were known to have said in order to give events his own spin. He can sum up a person's character in a single, well-turned phrase. High-minded, opinionated, at times bitingly ironic, Tacitus is, nevertheless, almost always a reliable reporter of facts and events he witnessed firsthand. His authoritative command of weighty subjects, his powerful style, and his nobility of purpose in such works as the *Annals, Histories,* and *Agricola* earn Tacitus his rank among the world's greatest historians.

UNIT PROJECTS

1. **Researching a Work of Fine Art.** Virgil's account in the *Aeneid* of the death of the Trojan priest Laocoon and of his two sons may have been partially inspired by a famous statue known as the Laocoon Group, now in the Vatican Museum. One of the most influential of all ancient sculptures, it had an enormous impact on Michelangelo and other artists after it was unearthed in 1506 in a Roman vineyard. Research the history of the Laocoon Group and prepare a written or oral report on its significance. Who created the sculpture, and what did the ancient Romans think of it? How did it affect Renaissance artists after its rediscovery? What is your opinion of this work? Does it deserve its fame?

2. **Researching Archaeological Evidence.** Did Troy actually exist? If so, was it destroyed in war as Virgil describes? Find out what archaeologists have discovered about the ancient site in Asia Minor that many scholars believe may be Troy. Prepare a display of maps, diagrams, and pictures with captions summarizing the archaeological evidence.

3. **Selecting Translations for an Anthology.** Working in a small group, do research in the library and assemble an anthology of Roman poetry. In addition to works by such major writers as Virgil, Catullus, Horace, and Ovid, consider including examples by Lucan, Lucretius, Propertius, Tibullus, Martial, and Juvenal. Select only those poems or excerpts from longer works that you think your classmates will enjoy reading. Organize your anthology chronologically or by theme and include brief biographies of the poets.

Design a cover and distribute copies of your anthology to the class.

4. **Preparing an Illustrated Glossary.** Roman historians, such as Julius Caesar, Livy, and Tacitus, often give detailed descriptions of military equipment and tactics in their accounts of battles. Working as part of a team, prepare an illustrated glossary of Roman military terms, such as *auxiliaries, centurion, chariot, cohort, legion, onager, phalanx, praetorian guard, triumph.* Include illustrations of different kinds of weapons and armament that Roman soldiers had at their disposal.

5. **Researching Roman Religion.** The Roman gods and goddesses—Jupiter, Juno, Mercury, Diana—were really Roman versions of the Greek pantheon. Still, there were some differences. Using various research materials, find out what you can about any of the following topics that relate to Roman religion: What was the native Roman religion like before the adoption of Greek models? What aspects of native Roman religion remained even after the appropriation of the Greek pantheon? What were some of the major mystery religions or religious cults in the Roman empire? Report your findings to the class using visual aids where appropriate.

6. **Drawing a Diagram.** By perfecting the use of the arch, the Romans were able to build bridges, aqueducts, and buildings on a monumental scale. So sturdy are some of these structures that they remain in use to this day. Learn how an arch works to distribute weight. Then draw a poster-sized diagram showing how the concept of the arch enabled the Romans to build engineering marvels. Display your diagram in class.

7. **Preparing an Oral Report.** Like President Thomas Jefferson, the Roman Emperor Hadrian was an architect. In fact, Jefferson based his design for the Rotunda at the University of Virginia on Hadrian's Pantheon, which still stands in Rome. Research to learn more about both of these buildings. What characteristics make them masterpieces of architectural design? How does each function today? How did Jefferson vary Emperor Hadrian's design? Prepare an oral report for the class.

8. **Illustrating Women's Fashions.** As in our day, Roman fashions changed with the times. Women's hairstyles in particular underwent dramatic changes between the time when Catullus was writing about Lesbia in the first century B.C. and when portraits of the wives of the emperors became sights on Roman coins in the second century A.D. Using coins, sculptures, and wall paintings as resources, draw up an illustrated chronology of women's hairstyles in ancient Rome.

9. **Dramatizing a Tale.** Ovid's *Metamorphoses*

includes dozens of tales about miraculous transformations. Find one transformation that you particularly enjoy and work with classmates to stage it for the class. Consider ways to make the metamorphosis especially dramatic and exciting. For example, you may devise a surprising costume change or use puppets instead of live actors.

10. **Writing an Editorial.** According to Tacitus, Nero shifted blame for the burning of Rome from himself onto the Christians. Tacitus, however, does not express outrage toward Nero's cruelty nor sympathy for the innocent scapegoats. In fact, he implies that the Christians were likely suspects since they were generally perceived as being guilty of "abominations" and of "horrible and shameful iniquity." Read more to learn about attitudes toward the early Christians in Rome. From the standpoint of a loyal Roman, what threat did Christianity pose to Roman authority in general and to the institution of the Roman emperor in particular? Write an editorial presenting the Roman government's case against the Christians.

---

from the AENEID
from Book 2: The Fall of Troy
Virgil ▼ Translated by Robert Fitzgerald ▼ (Textbook page 383)

SUMMARY

In Book 2 of the *Aeneid,* the hero Aeneas narrates the sack of Troy. He begins by recounting the Greek trick of the Trojan horse. Pretending to withdraw from Troy, the Greeks spread the rumor that they left behind the wooden horse as an offering to the gods for their safe return home. Actually, they concealed a band of warriors inside the horse. The priest Laocoon warned the Trojans not to bring the horse inside the city. When two monstrous snakes killed Laocoon and his sons, however, the Trojans concluded that the horse must be a sacred offering and brought it within their gates. That night, the Greek warriors concealed within the horse burst out into the darkened city and opened the gates to their fellow soldiers.

Aeneas then tells how the ghost of Hector appeared to him in a dream, warning him of Troy's imminent destruction and telling him to save himself through flight. Aeneas awoke, armed himself, and rushed into the streets, which were full of the turmoil of armed conflict and burning buildings. Together with a small group of comrades, Aeneas plunged into the fighting. During the melée, Coroebus was killed while trying to protect his beloved, the prophetess Cassandra.

Aeneas and his band overcame a detachment of Greek soldiers and disguised themselves by donning Greek armor and insignia. They were thus able to kill a number of the invaders, but their ruse backfired when they were attacked by their own men, who mistook them for the enemy.

Aeneas was drawn by a battle cry to Priam's castle. There he witnessed the fate of the king, who despite his age had buckled on his armor. Pyrrhus, the son of Achilles, slew Priam's son Polites before his father's eyes and then slaughtered the old king himself on the steps of an altar. Aeneas then saw Helen of Troy and felt a passionate urge to slay her in vengeance for the destruction of Troy. Aeneas's divine mother, Venus, intervened, however. She urged him to restrain himself and to accept destiny and the will of the gods.

Arriving at his house, Aeneas was at first unable to convince his father Anchises to leave the city with him. But when Jupiter sent the omens of a tongue of flame around the head of Iulus, Aeneas's little son, and a crack of thunder and a shooting star, Anchises agreed. Carrying his father on his shoulders and leading his son by the hand, Aeneas started to make his way out of the city. Amid the confusion, his wife Creusa disappeared. Sick with anxiety and fear, Aeneas turned back to search for her—too late, however, as she was killed in the tumult. The ghost of Creusa appeared to him, urging him to flee and to fulfill his destiny of founding a new city in Italy. Aeneas rejoined his family and friends, and the band of exiles set out for the mountains.

MORE ABOUT THE SELECTION

Virgil devotes Book 6 of the *Aeneid* to the hero's visit to the underworld. In this book, he illustrates Aeneas's reverential love for his father and confirms his purpose or mission: the founding of Rome. Anchises shows Aeneas a glorious panorama of future Roman greatness, culminating in Augustus' restoration of a new Golden Age. This vision of the future spurs on Aeneas to accomplish his destiny in Books 7–12. Book 6 is thus the structural climax, or turning point, of the epic as a whole.

Even while it stresses Roman glory, however, Aeneas's vision in the underworld simultaneously emphasizes the price of that glory: war, destruction, and human loss. Toward the end of Book 6, for example, the final figure in the pageant of future Romans is the young Marcellus (42–23 B.C.).

Marcellus, whom Augustus was grooming as his heir, was cut off in the prime of his life. It is said that when Virgil recited this passage to Augustus and the court, everyone present wept.

In other scenes and details in Book 6, Virgil employs the literary technique of ambiguity, in which the poet uses a single element such as an image, a figure of speech, or an event to suggest two conflicting meanings. A famous example occurs in the final lines of Book 6. In the tradition of great epic heroes, Aeneas has survived a dangerous journey to the land of the dead. In a passage modeled on Homer's *Odyssey,* Virgil tells us that there are two gates of Sleep: the gate of ivory and the gate of horn. He then suggests an undertone of sadness and mystery by having Aeneas exit from the underworld not through the gate of horn, by which true dreams pass, but rather through the ivory gate, the portal of *false* dreams. What can the poet be implying? That Aeneas was, on some level at least, deluded? That Roman glory was, to some degree, an illusion? Or that we can never know the true degree of suffering and loss that lies beneath the surface of even the most glorious achievements? Whatever the poet's theme, this passage at the turning point of the *Aeneid* is typically Virgilian in its wealth of implications and symbolic suggestiveness.

A CRITICAL COMMENT

"We hear two distinct voices in the *Aeneid,* a public voice of triumph, and a private voice of regret. The private voice, the personal emotions of a man, is never allowed to motivate action. But it is nonetheless everywhere present. For Aeneas, after all, is something more than an Odysseus manqué, or a prototype of Augustus and myriads of Roman leaders. He is man himself; not man as the brilliant free agent of Homer's world, but man of a later stage of civilization, man in a metropolitan and imperial world, man in a world where the State is supreme. He cannot resist the forces of history, or even deny them; but he can be capable of human suffering, and this is where the personal voice asserts itself. . . .

"Aeneas's tragedy is that he cannot be a hero, being in the service of an impersonal power. What saves him as a man is that all the glory of the solid achievement which he is serving, all the satisfaction of 'having arrived' in Italy means less to him than his own sense of personal loss. The *Aeneid* enforces the fine paradox that all the wonders of the most powerful institution the world has ever known are not necessarily of greater importance than the emptiness of human suffering."

—from "The Two Voices of Virgil's Aeneid,"
Adam Parry

FOR FURTHER READING

Cairns, Francis. *Virgil's Augustan Epic.* Cambridge: Cambridge University Press, 1989.

Camps, W. A. *An Introduction to Virgil's Aeneid.* Oxford: Oxford University Press, 1969.

Commager, Steele, ed. *Virgil: A Collection of Critical Essays.* Englewood Cliffs, N.J.: Prentice-Hall, 1966.

Eliot, T. S. "Virgil and the Christian World." *On Poetry and Poets.* New York: Farrar, Straus & Co., 1957.

Knight, W. F. Jackson. *Roman Vergil.* London: Faber & Faber, 1944.

Parry, Adam. "The Two Voices of Virgil's *Aeneid.*" *Modern Critical Views: Virgil.* Ed., Harold Bloom. New York: Chelsea House, 1986.

Virgil. *The Aeneid.* Trans. Robert Fitzgerald. New York: Random House, 1983.

LYRIC POEMS OF CATULLUS

Translated by Reney Myers, Robert J. Ormsby, and Peter Whigham ▾ (Textbook page 411)

SUMMARY

In "Wretched Catullus, Leave Off Playing the Fool," Catullus first addresses himself, urging himself to give up what is forever past—his love affair with Lesbia. He recalls the sunny days when his love flourished. But now he must harden his heart. He tells Lesbia not to expect to see him any more.

In "Lesbia Says She'ld Rather Marry Me," the speaker says that Lesbia has told him she would prefer him as her husband over anyone else—even Jupiter himself. The speaker wryly remarks, however, that the promises of women to their lovers are unreliable.

In "If Ever Anyone Anywhere," the speaker exults because Lesbia has restored herself to him. This unexpected, unlooked for event has made today a "white" (namely "lucky") day in the calendar. The speaker asks who can possibly be happier than he is.

In "I Hate and I Love," the speaker claims that he both hates and loves at the same time. He does not know how this is possible. He can only feel the anguishing conflict in his heart.

MORE ABOUT THE AUTHOR

Catullus's infatuation with Lesbia seems to have begun in the year he arrived in Rome, 62 B.C.— when the poet was about twenty-two years old and Lesbia was in her early thirties. In 59 B.C., Catullus's brother, to whom he seems to have been very close, died in Asia Minor. Catullus left Rome to visit his home in Verona for a while. When he returned to Rome, he found that Lesbia had abandoned him for Marcus Caelius Rufus, a friend of Cicero. This may have been a factor in Catullus's decision to leave Rome a second time in 57 B.C.— on this occasion as a staff assistant to Gaius Memmius, who was traveling to the province of Bithynia (in Asia Minor) to take up his post as governor. While he was in Asia Minor, Catullus visited the tomb of his brother, and that visit was the occasion of one of his most famous and eloquent lyrics. He returned by sea to Rome in 56 B.C. The following year, the affair with Lesbia seems to have ended forever. Catullus wrote her a bitter farewell.

A CRITICAL COMMENT

"It is just this quality, this clear and almost terrible simplicity, that puts Catullus in a place by himself among the Latin poets. Where others labor in the ore of thought and gradually forge it out into sustained expression, he sees with a single glance, and does not strike a second time. His imperious lucidity is perfectly unhesitating in its action: whether he is using it for the daintiest flower of sentiment . . . or for the expression of his vivid passions and hatreds in some flagrant obscenity or venomous insult, it is alike straight and reckless, with no scruple and no mincing of words."

—from Latin Literature,
J. W. Mackail

FOR FURTHER READING

Catullus. *Catullus: The Complete Poems for Modern Readers.* Trans. Reney Meyers and Robert J. Ormsby. New York: Routledge, 1972
—*The Poems of Catullus.* Trans. Peter Whigham. London: Penguin, 1966.
Quinn, Kenneth, ed. *Approaches to Catullus.* Cambridge: Cambridge University Press, 1972.
Ross, David O., Jr. *Style and Tradition in Catullus.* Cambridge: Harvard University Press, 1969.
Wheeler, A. L. *Catullus and the Traditions of Ancient Poetry.* Berkeley: University of California Press, 1934.

THE GOLDEN MEAN

Horace ▾ Translated by William Cowper ▾ (Textbook page 416)

CARPE DIEM

Horace ▾ Translated by Thomas Hawkins ▾ (Textbook page 417)

SUMMARY

In "The Golden Mean," Horace advises a friend to observe moderation in all things. Those who aim neither too high nor too low are likely to be the happiest people, since their expectations are not extreme. A philosophical outlook accepts both good and bad fortune with equanimity, since life's vicissitudes regularly involve both good and evil.

In "Carpe Diem," Horace warns his friend Leuconoe that it is fruitless to try to know the future. True wisdom consists in seizing the day and in enjoying the present moment, rather than in spending time worrying about the future.

MORE ABOUT THE AUTHOR

The influence of Horace on Western literature has been considerable—and nowhere more pronounced than in England. Horace's poetry was the model for at least four important genres of English verse: the ode, the verse epistle or letter, the verse satire, and the verse essay of literary criticism. Probably the most impressive English ode in the style of Horace was written by Andrew Marvell (1621–1678) to commemorate a public event: "An Horatian Ode Upon Cromwell's Return from Ireland" (published posthumously in 1681). Horace himself had written a number of public, ceremonial odes, in which he often praised Augustus.

Alexander Pope (1688–1744) used Horace's verse epistles as models for his verse letters in "Imitations of Horace." These epistles afford a wealth of detailed insights into English literary and cultural life in the early eighteenth century. Perhaps the best of these poems is the "Epistle to Dr. Arbuthnot" (1735), which Pope addressed to his friend who had been the personal physician to Queen Anne. The witty, gently mocking tone of Horace's satires also inspired Pope in his verse satires and in his famous mock epic, *The Rape of the Lock* (1714). Finally, the form and critical premises of Horace's *The Art of Poetry* strongly influenced Pope in the English poet's *Essay on Criticism* (1711).

A CRITICAL COMMENT

"There are many grounds for the attraction felt towards Horace by men differing in nationality, century, and time of life. Some have been drawn to his matter, others to his form, others to both combined. Certainly, one unfailing source of charm is his self-revelation. He makes his confessions, fears, musings, and judgments entertaining. No Latin author writes so openly and so winningly for the friendly reader. . . . In an easy rambling habit of discourse, he listens to his own humors, and with sincerity registers reflections, memories and fancies as they cross his mind. Here then is the autobiographic charm of Montaigne, who also had that mellowness of wisdom which led Sainte-Beuve to style him 'the French Horace.' So we are captured by everything that Horace chooses to unfold about himself. . . . So far from offending, Horace can never tell us too much. We cannot but remember his moods, his likes and dislikes, his feelings on life. We note his constant desire to avoid extravagance in thought or behavior, that preference for his own *aurea mediocritas* [golden mean] which saved him from excess. Amid banquets, wines, flowers, congenial company, peaceful seclusion, pleasures of nature, he enjoys life temperately. He advises others to do the same. Similar restraint underlies his detachment as a spectator of mankind. He touches human foibles for the most part gently and with a laugh. He can set himself in the place of others."

—*from* A Literary History of Rome,
J. Wight Duff

FOR FURTHER READING

Commager, Steele. *The Odes of Horace*. New Haven: Yale University Press, 1962.

Duff, J. Wright. *A Literary History of Rome*. Ed. A.M. Duff. New York: Barnes and Noble, 1960.

Fraenkel, Eduard. *Horace*. Oxford: Oxford University Press, 1957.

Reckford, Kenneth J. *Horace*. New York: Twayne, 1969.

from METAMORPHOSES

Ovid ▾ Translated by Rolfe Humphries ▾ (Textbook page 422)

SUMMARY

First declaring his intention to tell of transformations from the world's beginning to his own time, Ovid, in "The Creation," recounts the making of heaven and earth. At first, nature was in a state of chaos with all substance constantly changing and forever at war with itself. Then God, or perhaps Nature, brought order to the chaos, and the four elements of fire, earth, water, and air found their proper places. The globe of earth was molded and its features were formed. The stars shone from the heavens, the abode of the gods. All the various animals were given their proper places, and, finally, as the culminating touch of creation, humanity was created.

In "The Four Ages," Ovid tells first of the Golden Age, when life was peaceful and harmonious. Jove's defeat of Saturn ushered in the Age of Silver, during which humans sought shelter from the newly developed seasons and agriculture was invented. In the Age of Bronze, humans learned to be aggressive. People were quick to arm, but they still had some goodness in them. Finally, in the Age of Iron, all traces of goodness have fled from the earth. Humans in this stage know only hate and greed, murder and violence.

MORE ABOUT THE SELECTION

Ovid is true to his word in the opening lines of the *Metamorphoses*. He begins his poem in Book 1 with an account of the creation at the "world's beginning," and he ends it in Book 15 with a description of the transformation of the assassinated Julius Caesar into a star and a series of compliments to the emperor Augustus. On the surface, this is the last metamorphosis of the poem's numerous transformations, and Ovid has achieved his goal of bringing his narrative up to the present time.

But *is* Caesar's metamorphosis really the last one in the poem? In an epilogue, Ovid imitates a famous ode by Horace, boasting that he has completed a poem that will outlast time itself. The *Metamorphoses,* Ovid suggests, will make its creator immortal. Julius Caesar may have become a star, but Ovid, ever playfully immodest, says that *he* will be borne far beyond the stars (15.875–876). It is hard to resist the inference that the final metamorphosis Ovid describes is his own—the transformation of himself, through his own poetry, from an ordinary poet to an immortal bard.

A CRITICAL COMMENT

"Ovid's re-creation of myths as stories, within a theme of eternal change, liberated him from the necessity of following a Homeric precedent such as Virgil employed in the writing of his great Roman epic. Ovid used his loosely gathered romances and tales to exhibit his imaginative virtuosity. Within his large design, he incorporated stories from all reaches of the Mediterranean world, from Egypt as well as Crete, nor was his interest that of the anthropologist. It was rather that of one who could not resist the retelling of any story, provided it had color and enough action to hold attention. . . .

"The fifteen books of the *Metamorphoses* contain a number of repetitious details as men and women are turned into trees, birds, or stones. Ovid's battle scenes have an overflow of blood and destruction;

his fond listing of names is often tiresome; his flaws of taste are frequent, and his retelling of some Greek stories coarsens the clear lines of the originals. But having said this much in dispraise of Ovid's masterpiece, one feels that one has missed the reasons why it has survived. At his best no writer of this Golden Age in Roman literature has excelled him in the rapid unfolding of a narrative, nor has any surpassed him in the direct revelations of psychological detail. However far-fetched, melodramatic, or strained a few of his situations may seem to the twentieth-century reader, they never fail to create the illusion of life—in its mystery and irony, in its splendor or cruelty; in its affectionate humors and warmth of feeling, in its celebration of earthly beauty."

—*from the Introduction to* Metamorphoses, *translated by Horace Gregory*

FOR FURTHER READING

Galinksy, G. Karl. *Ovid's Metamorphoses: An Introduction to its Basic Aspects.* Berkeley: University of California Press, 1975.

Jones, A. H. M. *Augustus.* New York: W. W. Norton and Co., 1971.

Otis, Brooks. *Ovid as an Epic Poet.* 2nd ed. New York: Cambridge University Press, 1971.

Ovid. *Metamorphoses.* Trans. Rolphe Humphries. Bloomington: Indiana University Press, 1955.

Syme, Ronald. *History in Ovid.* New York: Oxford University Press, 1979.

Williams, Gordon. *Change and Decline: Roman Literature in the Early Empire.* Berkeley: University of California Press, 1978.

THE BURNING OF ROME
from The Annals

Tacitus ▼ Translated by George Gilbert Ramsay ▼ (Textbook page 430)

SUMMARY

The great fire at Rome broke out near the Circus and spread quickly as winds fanned the flames and few obstacles blocked its path. Nero, who was at the seaside town of Antium, returned to the city only when the fire was approaching his mansion. The fire was finally brought under control on the sixth day, but a second, more destructive fire soon broke out on property owned by Tigellinus, a friend of the emperor. Rumors spread that Nero had set the fire because he harbored an ambition to build a new city named after himself.

Rebuilding of Rome began and rituals and festivals were held to appease the gods. Nothing, however, could dispel the suspicion that the fire had been set by Nero's order. Nero found a scapegoat in the Christians, whom he cruelly persecuted. Many were arrested and condemned to horrible deaths, including being burned alive. Popular sympathy, however, turned against him, since people were disgusted by his tyrannical cruelty. Nero also ordered that Italy and other parts of the Roman Empire be ransacked for contributions to pay for the new building program.

MORE ABOUT THE AUTHOR

Tacitus' fascinating style has been the subject of very detailed analysis by experts. The historian's way of writing is rapid, concise, syntactically varied, and highly pictorial. His style is also full of allusions to many Roman authors and literary traditions. For example, here is the very first sentence of Tacitus' *Annals* in Latin, together with a literal translation:

Urbem	Romam	a	principio
The city	Rome	from	the beginning
	reges	habuere	
	kings	had (ruled)	

The first thing a Roman reading this sentence aloud (and that was how Romans probably read) would notice is that, even though Tacitus' narrative is in prose, the first sentence he wrote constitutes a perfect hexameter—the meter of early Roman historical "annals" or chronicles, and, of course, the meter of the Roman genre of epic, which had culminated in Virgil's *Aeneid.* The second unusual thing a Roman would notice in Tacitus' sentence is the archaic third-person plural perfect ending of the verb *habuere.* (In Tacitus' time, this word would normally be *habuerunt.*)

Why does Tacitus do this? His hexameter sentence creates a multitude of allusions and possible meanings. On one level, he is indirectly announcing in his very first words his allegiance to a poetic tradition whose splendors may lie in the past but whose literary "truth" and emotional pull Tacitus feels keenly. The archaic verb ending possibly hints at Tacitus' fierce independence and idiosyncratic choice of words. Possibly, as well, he chose it because the form and sound contributed just the right note of archaism to evoke that primitive, semi-legendary era of the founding of Rome and the first kings. When we realize that Tacitus' language in almost every sentence produces such complex, subtle overtones and emotional responses, we begin to appreciate why he has been acclaimed as perhaps the greatest prose stylist of Latin literature.

A CRITICAL COMMENT

"Still later over that city, with a capping intensity of detail that exceeds in both cruelty and visual extent the prior atrocities, there burn living torches, the Christians whom Nero has accused of the arson so as to throw suspicion off himself. . . .

"This intensity transfigures the partiality of Tacitus. An unnatural light, the raised bodies of so many victims, shines out when daylight has failed over the ruined city. This detail, which easily lends itself to metaphorical extension, etches its concreteness on the text. It comprises an implied contradiction: Nero sets a fire to a throng of the accused to demonstrate that he has not set the earlier fire. And it carries its own intensification: not buildings, but now bodies, are burning. The executions take place not secretly, as in Nero's two attempts on his mother, or rapidly, as after some corrupt judicial conviction, but with horribly protracted slowness, on high, in the open air. . . .

"This is not the first imaginative recasting of the fire of Rome that Nero has undertaken, since he pretends, in his insane sensitivity, that the fire furnishes a kind of literary spectacle by imitating the Fire of Troy, inciting him to play his lyre before it in another detail that has captured the imagination of the ages ("Nero fiddled while Rome burned"). He has made the catastrophe into a display, and the burning of the Christians is a further display. The visible and the psychological, imperial power and what for Tacitus is an exotic and suspicious religion, are set to run riot in this passage."

—from History/Writing, Albert Cook

FOR FURTHER READING

Benario, Herbert. *An Introduction to Tacitus.* Athens, Ga.: University of Georgia Press, 1975.

Dudley, D. R. *The World of Tacitus.* Boston: Little, Brown, and Co., 1968.

Luce, T. James. "Tacitus," in *Ancient Writers: Greece and Rome,* Volume 2. New York: Charles Scribner's Sons, 1982.

Tacitus. *The Annals of Tacitus: Books XI–XVI.* Trans. George Gilbert Ramsay. London: John Murray, 1909.

Walker, B. *The Annals of Tacitus.* Manchester: Ayer Co. Pub., 1952.

NOTES

Unit Introduction: Indian Literature

The traditional literature of India can be divided into two categories: Vedic and Classical. Vedic literature is named after the vedas, the sacred hymns and rituals that were composed and passed down orally from about 1500 B.C. until 700 B.C. The Upanishads and several other philosophical commentaries were also composed during this time. Vedic literature was eventually recorded in Sanskrit, which means "perfect speech" and was considered the language of the gods. The literature of the Classical period (700 B.C.– A.D. 1000) was also written in Sanskrit, which by 600 B.C. had become an unchanging, "frozen" literary language. Classic Indian literature includes the two great epics the Mahabharata and the Ramayana, as well as many collections of folk tales and fables such as the Panchatantra.

BACKGROUND

THE VEDAS

Veda means *knowledge* or *lore* in Sanskrit. The Vedas include hymns, descriptive myths, invocations, and extended liturgies representing the sacred wisdom of the ancient Aryans. The *Rig Veda* (literally, the "veda of praise") is the oldest and most important of the Vedas. The Vedas were transmitted orally with a high degree of fidelity over several hundred years by Brahmans, the priestly caste. Although the hymns are not expressions of an organized religious philosophy, they do represent the beginnings of the Hindu faith. Today, the Vedas are considered by most Hindus to be the most authoritative source of spiritual truths.

VEDIC INSIGHTS

From Vedic literature we can deduce some of the concerns and values of the ancient Aryans. In general, the people living in the Vedic era were inquisitive and appreciative of the natural world. Many of the hymns praise the beauty of the earth and the wonder of existence. The imagery of the Vedas is filled with an exuberant optimism. The Aryans often personified natural phenomena as gods (see "Night," page 456) in an attempt to understand and perhaps placate natural forces.

In addition to the hymns of praise, the *Rig Veda* contains mythic lore that helps to explain Vedic ideas about the order of the universe. This order revolves around the opposition of forces of good and evil. The good is represented by the gods, who are benevolent and provide light, rain, and other necessities to humans. The realm of evil is governed by demons, figures of darkness and cunning. In the *Rig Veda,* the god Indra leads a war against these demons. After the leader of the demons is slain, the gods institute a system of cosmic order called *rita.* The demons, however, oppose the system and periodically attempt to undermine it. One of these attempts is related in the later Hindu epic *Ramayana.*

THE UPANISHADS

By the sixth century B.C., there were many new religious and philosophical schools seeking answers to basic questions such as the meaning of the self, and the origin and order of the universe. The Upanishads, one of several commentaries composed by priests during the Vedic period, presents a new religious theory of great subtlety and sophistication. The basic principles revealed in the Upanishads include the idea that the individual self (*atman*) is also part of the universal self (*brahman*). Each person's soul undergoes an endless cycle (*samsara*) of rebirths, sufferings, and death, assuming a new physical form in each successive life depending on the ethical quality of actions (*karma*) undertaken in the preceding life.

The law of karma means that for every thought and act there is an inevitable consequence. Acts of hostility or aggression that harm other creatures negatively affect subsequent lives. In order to unite atman and brahman and thus attain spiritual release (*moksha*), a person must engage in various forms of *yoga*—physical and spiritual discipline.

The one hundred and eight selections of the Upanishads reveal the roots of traditional Hindu social and moral codes. Together with the Vedas and the sutras, they gave rise to the complex and varied religious beliefs and practices which comprise Hinduism.

HINDUISM

The Vedic period was one of religious synthesis and evolution. The ancestor and nature worship of the ancient Aryans was evolving complex rituals, sacrifices, and other practices. At the same time, concepts such as reincarnation (the transmigration of souls) were borrowed from the native peoples of the Indus Valley that the Aryans had conquered or displaced. The eventual product of such borrowings and development was the infinitely varied religious and social system known as Hinduism.

Hindu beliefs and practices are as varied as the Indian people themselves. However, to fully appreciate Indian literature, the reader must be familiar with at least a few of the basic concepts and beliefs shared by most Hindus. These include *varna* (the caste system), *karma* (one's actions and their cosmic consequences), and *dharma* (one's divinely ordained duty, according to one's caste).

THE CASTE SYSTEM

The Aryans recognized the functions of priests (Brahmans), warriors and rulers (Kshatriyas), and traders and farmers (Vaishyas). Later they created the caste of the Sudras, who were responsible for performing menial tasks. Eventually, the ancient Aryans came to believe that these four castes were divinely ordained. In addition, a fifth social division was developed by the Aryans. This was not so much a caste as an "outcaste." The people who belonged to this "outcaste" group are often referred to as "untouchables" because, until very recent times, contact between them and any other, higher caste was considered unclean and defiling. Today, there are approximately 3,000 identifiable castes and sub-castes in India, and although laws and increasing urbanization have undermined the caste system to some degree, this complicated social system remains largely intact.

KARMA AND DHARMA

The ancient Aryans believed that a person's soul progresses from body to body in successive lives until it is sufficiently purified to be reunited with Brahman. Leading a good life means that a person follows his or her dharma by faithfully carrying out the duties of the caste he or she was born into. This will lead to rebirth into a slightly higher caste. The life that is closest to union with Brahman is that of the priestly caste. If a person is unfaithful to the rules of his or her caste, he or she will be reborn into a lower caste or into the body of an animal or insect. The basic law of karma—whatever is done in one lifetime directly affects the next—binds humans to the cosmos in a cycle of birth and death that can end only when one is reunited with Brahman.

CULTS AND SECTS

The pantheon of nature gods in the *Rig Veda* gradually diminished in importance over time, but many of the deities continued to have local importance. Vishnu the Protector and Shiva the Destroyer became major deities and led to two major sects: Vaishnavism (worship of Vishnu), and Shaivism (worship of Shiva). Among Vishnu's nine incarnations are Krishna, who appears in the *Mahabharata;* Rama, the hero of the *Ramayana;* and the historical Buddha.

BUDDHISM AND JAINISM

Buddhism and Jainism are rooted in a religious movement that occurred about 600 B.C. The movement was in opposition to the sacrifice-oriented, caste-segmented culture of early Hinduism. Both religions rejected the religious authority of the Vedas and preached messages of salvation without regard for caste.

Jainism stresses extreme asceticism and strict nonviolence. The central tenet of Jainism is that an eternal soul, the *jiva*, exists in every living thing and must be freed by renouncing involvement in worldly affairs. Jain holy men and women wear masks over their faces, filter their water, and lightly sweep their paths as they walk so that they will not inadvertently kill any living thing. They own no possessions and beg for all their food. They do not even participate in agriculture, since various creatures are often killed while one plants, cultivates, and harvests crops.

Buddhism was inaugurated in the sixth century B.C. by Siddharta Gautama, called the Buddha. Buddha is said to have been born into a royal family of the warrior (Kshatriya) caste. He was reared in luxurious surroundings and did not venture beyond the palace walls until he was twenty-nine. After finally seeing the poverty and suffering of the outside world, he renounced his princely life and set off as a wandering ascetic in search of enlightenment. After six years of study, meditation, and fasting, he sat beneath a tree and came to see the eternal truths he had been seeking.

In his first sermon he outlined the Four Noble Truths that were to become the foundations of Buddhist teaching. These include: 1) life is suffering, 2) desire is the cause of suffering, 3) suffering can only be eliminated by extinguishing desire, and 4) desire can only be eliminated by the Eightfold Path to righteousness—right views, right intentions, right speech, right conduct, right livelihood, right effort, right mindfulness, and right meditation.

Although Buddhism never replaced Hinduism, which still includes about eighty percent of the

Indian population, it took hold in Tibet, China, Japan, and in many other parts of Asia. It also philosophically influenced many Western thinkers such as the nineteenth-century American Transcendentalist writers Ralph Waldo Emerson and Henry David Thoreau.

THE EPIC AS POPULAR SACRED TEXT

The two great epic poems of India are the *Mahabharata* and the *Ramayana*. The *Mahabharata* is the older of the two, dating from about 300 B.C. Although its main narrative is attributed to a sage called Vyasa, many other anonymous scribes added to the story, making the total work a compendium of treatises on theology, history, government, and ethics. Unlike the gods in the Vedas, the gods in the Hindu epics interact with humans in the same physical and intellectual sphere, making the works more accessible to the average person.

The *Mahabharata* provides a record of a distant war and details the human attempt to justify and explain the moral implications of the struggles of life. Some episodes, such as "Hundred Questions" (textbook page 461), delineate the ideas of the Upanishads in a more concrete way. One of the most famous sections of the *Mahabharata* is the *Bhagavad-Gita* (literally, the "song of the holy one"). It is an extended conversation between the warrior Arjuna and Krishna, who is an incarnation of the god Vishnu. During the conversation, details about how dharma and karma function in human lives are revealed.

The second epic poem, the *Ramayana,* is by far the most popular and widely known work in India. Based on an episode in the *Mahabharata,* the *Ramayana* tells the story of the prince Rama, a model of perfect nobility who is said to be the seventh incarnation of Vishnu. The story of Rama's adventures continues the concept of *rita* and the struggle between gods and demons first outlined in the *Rig Veda*. The *Ramayana* gives us an example of how the gods balance the forces of good and evil in the world, and it also establishes the prototype for the ideal Hindu husband and wife.

Together, these two great epics show the growing Brahmanic control over the immensely complex religious and social environment of the Aryans. Through the easily understandable medium of epic drama, the *Mahabharata* and the *Ramayana* inculcate the values of orthodox Hinduism.

DIDACTIC CLASSICAL LITERATURES

Two other important literary forms followed the heroic epics. The Puranas, a class of Sanskrit works giving legendary accounts of creation and genealogies of gods and kings, serve as secondary scriptures of Hinduism. The eighteen Great Puranas focus mainly on the gods Brahma, Vishnu, and Shiva. Love, altruisim, self-sacrifice, and the value of nature, science, and art are among the many

subjects of the Puranas.

The didactic purposes of the Puranas also appear in the Indian beast fables, which are among the most ancient in the world. One of the most significant achievements of the classical period was the gathering and anthologizing of these ancient fables and folk stories. The collections were given unity by a frame story and told in a consistent style and tone. For example, the introduction to the *Panchatantra* presents the frame-story of the education of a king's thick-witted sons. This frame turns the stories of the *Panchatantra* (textbook page 480) into a series of lessons in statecraft.

Collected folktales like the *Panchatantra* unveil some of the quandaries and values of the early Indians. While the Vedic material and epics embody overtly religious themes, the *Panchatantra* is an attempt to deal with morality through lay examples. The stories provide practical lessons for listeners who want advice on how to conduct their daily lives.

The language of Indian fables and folktales is generally simple and direct and the narratives are punctuated with brief, epigrammatic verses. Of all the literature of the classical period, these stories come closest to being popular literature and have been widely translated.

UNIT PROJECTS

1. **Composing a Song.** Write a song of praise to some element of nature such as dawn or dusk. Follow the form and length of "Night" from the *Rig Veda*. You may set your song to original or existing music and then make a recording of it or perform it live for your class, either by yourself or with other classmates.

2. **Dramatizing a Scene.** Write a one-act play based on one of the selections from the Indian epics. Assign parts to your classmates and rehearse the play. When you are ready, present the play to the class.

3. **Interviewing a Hero.** Choose a hero from one of the selections in this unit. Imagine you are a host for a television talk show and prepare a series of questions to ask your hero. The questions may concern the story you have read, or they may be more general. For example, you may ask Yudhistira of "Hundred Questions" about his experience with Yama and his thoughts about life in general. You could interview Arjuna as he prepares to battle against Bhishma and Drona. Choose a classmate to act as the hero you have chosen, and conduct the interview for the class.

4. **Building a Diorama.** Build a diorama of your favorite scene from a selection in this unit (the battle of Rama and Ravana, Yudhistira answering the yaksha's questions at the banks of the pond), or of a historical or geographical Indian scene that you find in a book or other source (a Hindu

temple; a rural scene near a river; the Taj Mahal). Use whatever materials you wish in your diorama, and display it for the class.

5. **Debating an Idea.** Prepare a debate based on the advice given by Lord Krishna: "Killing in the line of duty is acceptable if one is following one's dharma." With class members, debate both sides of the argument.

6. **Reporting an Event.** Imagine that you are an eyewitness to the action of one of the selections in this unit. For example, you may have witnessed the battle between Rama and Ravana. Using details from the selection, prepare a segment of a television newscast in which you report the incident to your audience.

7. **Researching Indian Art.** India boasts many beautiful art forms, notably architecture, sculpture, wall painting, and miniature painting. Research one of these major Indian art forms and report what you learn about its history and characteristics to the class in an oral report. Use audiovisual resources such as pictures in books, posters, slides, and whatever other pictorial references you can find to supplement your talk.

8. **Enacting a Fable.** Considering the theme of "Right-Mind and Wrong-Mind," write a contemporary skit developing the ideas presented in the framework story or in the internal fable. Choose classmates to help you dramatize your fable and present it to the class or videotape it for class viewing.

9. **Illustrating a Selection.** Create an illustration or a book cover for one of the selections in this unit. You might wish to incorporate aspects of Indian miniature painting in your design. Display your illustration to the class and respond to their comments and questions.

10. **Presenting a Report.** Choose one of the important concepts from this unit and go to your school or public library to gather information about it. Then write a report and deliver it to the class. For example, research Sanskrit, the language in which all the selections of this unit were written, or prepare a report on one of the basic Hindu concepts of varna, karma, or dharma. You could also research a topic about India's culture or history: the building of the Taj Mahal; Indian music; classical Indian court dramas; the Mogul Empire; the religious significance of the Ganges, and so on.

NIGHT
from the Rig Veda
Translated by Wendy Doniger O'Flaherty ▼ (Textbook page 456)

SUMMARY

Night is personified as a glorious goddess who draws near at the end of day. Night is a revered, powerful, beneficent goddess who pushes away her sister, the twilight, and provides a time of rest for people and animals. Although the speaker still calls on dawn to banish night, the hymn is offered to Night as a song of praise.

MORE ABOUT THE SELECTION

"Night" is the only hymn in the *Rig Veda* dedicated to the goddess of night. The Vedas present the various universal powers—fire, wind, water, night, and dawn—as gods and goddesses. These deities are not creators of the world, but they oversee the various processes of life.

Over several centuries seers, called *rishis,* related the hymns of the *Rig Veda.* That the original reciters of the *Rig Veda* are referred to as "seers" rather than as "authors" stresses the Hindu belief that the hymns are of divine origin. The Vedas are thought to have been revealed to rather than composed by the seers and they became the means by which the mysteries of the divine could be explored.

Although the *Rig Veda* provides the modern reader with the roots of Hinduism, it is not an all-inclusive document. Hinduism continued to develop, and the various deities continued to evolve. The deities worshiped in the Vedas are linked with natural phenomena: Indra is associated with the thunderstorm, Agni with fire, Dyaus with heaven, and Prthivi with earth. Vishnu is particularly significant in later Hindu literature. He is credited with separating the heavens and earth and figures significantly in the *Mahabharata,* where he takes the earthly form of Krishna. In the *Ramayana,* Vishnu is manifested as Rama.

A CRITICAL COMMENT

"The verses of the *Rig Veda,* the primary wisdom collection, vibrate with the energies of creation. Like all melodies, they convey and create far more than any associated conceptual meaning can suggest. Their melodious and rhythmic vibrations resonate with the reverberations of cosmos-creating energies. Participating in this creation, the seers found words, rhythms, and melodies with the power to open the human heart, mind, and feelings to these same vibrant world-creating energies. Through the liturgy of sacrificial celebration, these mantric sounds, melodies, and rhythms allowed the

Vedic people to join in the process of cosmic creation—particularly self-creation and the creation of community.

"Liturgy combines the joyous melodies of song and chant with the symbolic actions of ritual re-creation and sanctification. Vision of reality, vibrant sound of creation, and rhythm of human participation are all combined in the liturgical act. The liturgical nature of the Vedas cannot be overemphasized. These verses are intended to be recited, sung, and chanted, not read. We all know that a verse recited affects us more profoundly than does the same verse read and that a lyric sung has beauty and power that the same lyric read or recited cannot approach. Similarly, the liturgical combination of thought and action that unites feeling and understanding in the ritual re-enactment of primordial creation and sanctification has the power to transform our existence through participation in our own creation far beyond that of ordinary actions and words.

"The fact that the verses of the Vedas are poetic in form and liturgical in function warns us against trying to reduce them to strictly rational forms of literal meanings. This sacred wisdom goes far beyond mere intellectual knowledge; it is wisdom heard and felt in the hearts of the great seers and expressed by them in poem and song so that it might resound in the hearts of all people, awakening them to the tremendousness, mysteriousness, and joy of their own being as they participate in cosmic creation.

"The language that the poet-seers had to express what they heard in their hearts was ordinary language—language evolved to deal with the ordinary visible world. But they used this language in new ways that were poetic, musical, metaphorical, and highly symbolic, creating vehicles of sound that could carry the hearer into the heart of the creative process of human becoming.

"It is very difficult for us, sharing fully in neither the ordinary Vedic world-view nor the extraordinary vision of the seers, to understand this language and to feel its power. We must constantly remind ourselves that the Vedic myths and symbols have their own logic. When we approach them with the logic of linear rational thinking and attempt to force them into conceptual equivalents, we gain clarity and precision at an exorbitant price. The original integrity and richness is lost, and with that is lost also the power of these verses to transform life."

—*from* The Indian Way,
John M. Koller

FOR FURTHER READING

Bishop, Donald H., ed. *Indian Thought.* New York: John Wiley & Sons, 1975.

Le Mee, Jean, trans. *Hymns from the Rig Veda.* New York: Alfred A. Knopf, 1975.

O'Flaherty, Wendy Doniger, trans. *The Rig Veda: An Anthology.* London: Penguin, 1981.

Zaehner, R. C. *Hinduism.* London: Oxford University Press, 1975.

HUNDRED QUESTIONS
from the Mahabharata
Translated by R. K. Narayan ▾ (Textbook page 461)

SUMMARY

During the Pandava brothers' exile in the forest, they are exhorted by a Brahman to search the woods for the stolen staff and sticks he uses in his religious rituals. Believing that, as a warrior, his dharma demands he aid the priest, Yudhistira leads his brothers on the search.

From youngest to oldest, the first four brothers find a pond. When each attempts to drink from it, he is confronted by a voice that seems to come from a crane. The voice claims it owns the pond and insists that the brother answer his questions before he drinks. Nakula and Sahadeva ignore the warning and fall to the ground dead as soon as they drink the water. Arjuna and Bima unsuccessfully attack the source of the voice with arrows and a mace, respectively, and then drink from the pond and also fall dead to the ground.

The last and eldest brother, Yudhistira, comes to the pond. Seeing the bodies of his brothers,

Yudhistira adheres humbly and respectfully to the wishes of the voice, who reveals himself as a *yaksha,* or forest divinity. The spirit's hundred or more far-ranging questions concerning the beliefs of Hinduism come at Yudhistira like arrows in combat, but he answers them knowledgeably.

The yaksha, who is actually Yama, God of Justice and father of Yudhistira, then offers to reward Yudhistira for his answers with the life of one of his slain brothers. Yudhistira judiciously chooses the youngest, Nakula, one of his step-brothers, so that Madri, his second mother, may also have a living son. This choice so impresses Yama that he grants Yudhistira the lives of all four brothers and the gift that the brothers and their wife may go anywhere unrecognized.

MORE ABOUT THE SELECTION

Although the *Mahabharata* has many varied episodes, it also has one major plot—the story of the bloody battle for power between families of cousins, the Kauravas and the Pandavas. The blood relationships and mutual affections of the cousins add pathos to their inability to resolve their differences peacefully. After much hideous and unrestrained violence, the Pandavas are ultimately victorious. Their victory is at so bitter a cost, however, that it brings them little joy. Years later the warriors of both sides are reconciled in heaven.

The quarrel between the two families begins when the eldest Kaurava brother becomes jealous of his cousins after his father gives them a piece of his kingdom as their own. He then challenges the eldest of the Pandava brothers to a game of dice. The Pandava brother Yudhistira, proves unskilled at the game and loses first his wealth, then himself and his brothers, and finally their wife, all of which he has unwisely staked on the game. When the wife is lost, one of the Kaurava brothers insults her by trying to disrobe her before the whole court. This tasteless act brings down on him the terrible curse of Bhima, who vows to one day drink the Kaurava brother's blood.

The king restores the kingdom to the Pandavas, but another gambling match loses the land for them again. As a condition of the new bet, the Pandava brothers are required to spend twelve years in exile. "Hundred Questions" takes place near the end of this twelve-year exile.

A few centuries after it was written, the *Mahabharata* was translated from Sanskrit into other Indian languages and the languages of neighboring areas. Before long, the plot and morality of the epic became fodder for plays, ballads, sermons, political philosophies, and court festivals. As the Indian empire's trade expanded in the early Christian era, storytellers who followed the merchants found positions in royal courts and spread the tales of the *Mahabharata* and the *Ramayana* west to Europe and into southeast Asian areas, including Burma, Thailand, and Vietnam. Over time, the epic was translated into many local languages, fashioned to fit the needs of the people, and adopted into many cultures.

A Critical Comment

"Scholars have worked hard to identify the recensions, alterations, and additions [to the *Mahabharata*], and definitive editions are available indicating the changes from the original versions. It is a controversial field, but the main story is accepted on all hands and beyond all argument: once upon a time in ancient Hastinapura lived a royal family—with five brothers of divine origin on one side, and their one hundred cousins on the other, at war with each other. This framework is filled with details and lines of the finest poetic values in Sanskrit. . . .

"*The Mahabharata* consists of eighteen parvas (or parts), as many volumes by the present measure of production. Being a work dependent on oral report, there is naturally much repetition, perhaps for the benefit of a listener who might have missed a piece, as the narration goes on day after day. In this method of narrative a character reporting elsewhere on a situation which the reader already knows, gives again a complete account to his listener. The epic form is detailed and leisurely, and the technique of narration is different from what we are used to. There is an unhurrying quality about it which gives it stature. To point a moral, a complete, independent story of great length and detail may be included, a deviation from the mainstream which can run to several hundred pages. . . .

"Another factor which swells *The Mahabharata* is the philosophic discussion—discourses on life and conduct which one or another of the sages expounds—sometimes running to several hundred lines at a time. . . .

"Although this epic is a treasure house of varied interests, my own preference is the story. It is a great tale with well-defined characters who talk and act with robustness and zest—heroes and villains, saints and kings, women of beauty, all displaying great human qualities, super-human endurance, depths of sinister qualities as well as power, satanic hates and intrigues—all presented against an impressive background of ancient royal capitals, forests, and mountains.

"The actual physical quantum of the epic is staggering. If only a single word could be used to indicate the gist of each stanza, the total length of such a sampling would still run to one hundred thousand words. . . .

"For a modern reader in English, one has necessarily to select and condense. I have not attempted any translation, as it is impossible to convey in English the rhythm and depth of the original language. The very sound of Sanskrit has a hypnotic quality which is inevitably lost in translation. One has to feel content with a prose narrative story form."

—*from* The Mahabharata,
R. K. Narayan

For Further Reading

Buck, William. *Mahabharata: A Retelling*. Berkeley: University of California Press, 1973.

Carrière, Jean-Claude. *The Mahabharata: A Play*. Trans. Peter Brookk. New York: Harper & Row, 1987.

Kinsley, David R. *Hinduism*. Englewood Cliffs, NJ: Prentice-Hall, 1982.

Narayan, R.K. *The Mahabharata*. New Delhi: Vision 1987.

Organ, Troy W. *The Hindu Quest for the Perfection of Man*. Athens, OH: Ohio University Press, 1970.

PHILOSOPHY AND SPIRITUAL DISCIPLINE
from the Bhagavad-Gita
Translated by Barbara Stoler Miller ▾ (Textbook page 469)

SUMMARY

This ethical dialogue between the third Pandava brother, Arjuna, and his charioteer Krishna, a manifestation of the god Vishnu, is narrated by Sanjaya, an attendant to King Dhritarashtra.

On the eve of battle with the Kauravas, the branch of the family with whom the Pandavas are feuding, Arjuna questions Krishna on the ethics of killing his kinsmen, on what the desired outcome of the battle should be, and on how to deal with the pity he feels for his potential victims. Krishna responds by rejecting pity and grief as unnecessary. He explains that life is a cycle including temporary death that leads to another life. Since the immutable self never dies but is continually reborn, it is impossible to really kill anyone.

Krishna urges Arjuna to understand that a warrior's dharma, or duty according to his caste, is to participate in battle. Krishna emphasizes that a warrior shirking his duty would give the impression of cowardice and would result in shame, which is worse than any other fate. Arjuna then asks how to attain sure insight through contemplation. Krishna responds that when one can give up all desire and not be disturbed by the sensual, material world, then one will be content, or sure, within oneself. Krishna urges Arjuna to be impartial toward emotion and gain, to ignore empty rituals, to control his senses, and thus to gain discipline which will lead to serenity.

MORE ABOUT THE SELECTION

The most important text in the *Mahabharata,* the *Bhagavad-Gita* was probably written in the first century A.D. The text fuses together many divergent strands of speculative philosophy, cultic theism, and worldly social theory. Its principal message is that the supreme religious obligation of every person is to perform the duties of his or her own caste, his or her dharma.

The human struggle within Arjuna can be interpreted as representing the struggle between two apparently conflicting strains of Hinduism. An important sacred text, the Upanishads, suggests that the aim of humans is to unite with Brahman, the oversoul. One way to achieve this union is by purifying one's self of all material and physical burdens and withdrawing from a worldly life in favor of a meditative one. Yet, at the same time, every person must follow his or her dharma by fulfilling the duties associated with his or her caste. It is exactly this conflict Arjuna faces: if he fights, he fulfills his dharma as a military leader; if he seeks to unite himself with Brahman through asceticism, he must withdraw from an active life and thus abandon his dharma.

Krishna provides the solution to this dilemma. A charioteer and kinsman to Arjuna, Krishna is also his spiritual mentor and the earthly, incarnate representation of the god Vishnu. It is Vishnu's function to bring truth and enlightenment to humans in time of great conflict. In answer to Arjuna's dilemma, Krishna first tells him that he must accept his status as a warrior and follow the dharma his caste prescribes by fighting with skill and courage. He must not fight to gain riches or glory, but simply to fulfill his life role. In doing so, he will create favorable karma and will ultimately achieve union with Brahman. Krishna thus resolves both the overall Hindu conflict of following one's dharma versus leading a contemplative, ascetic life. Successful fulfillment of one's dharma is revealed to be a means of uniting with Brahman that is just as valid as the path of asceticism.

A CRITICAL COMMENT

"The *Bhagavad-Gita,* which is essentially a section of the great epic, is nonetheless probably an addition, and was not part of the original story. It seems to me possible that the author of it was attracted by the detached part Krishna played in the war, and thus found it very suitable to his character, and slotted it in a very dramatic point in the tale. Krishna's wisdom therefore, and his role as a teacher, is probably an accretion to his original role as warrior. It is rather as if King Arthur, who perhaps represents a much embellished memory of an actual person, had been given by a later writer a passage in the *Morte D'Arthur,* in which he lectured Sir Bedivere, on the merits of a holy life.

"While the conception of Krishna probably developed in this way, from a dim legendary warrior, to a teacher, to an exotic beguiler of hearts, the cult of Krishna must have followed the same progress. Thus at the time in which the epic *Mahabharata* was 'crystallising,' Krishna was considered to be a merely human hero; but by about the second century B.C., as we know from the account of the Seleucid ambassador Megasthenes, Krishna was looked on as an incarnation of Vishnu. This semi-divine quality of Krishna must have given rise to worship of him, and it was thus natural that when the additions were made to the *Mahabharata* around the second century A.D., the distillation of the sacred teachings of the time would have been put into his mouth.

"Krishna's role in the *Bhagavad-Gita* added greatly to his prowess, for this short book is a beautiful summary of Indian philosophy and religion. In it Krishna gives the teaching that one should seek to grasp the self: the very source of our consciousness, and having grasped it remain in the self throughout all one's actions. This is the essence of the great religious works which make up the most ancient part of Indian literature. But Krishna also teaches that if one places all one's love and faith in him, one will similarly attain the aim of human life. This looks forward to the cult of Krishna as a god of love.

"Just as Krishna himself is made up of numerous layers which embody different ideals, so the standing of Krishna today in India is a blend of all these things. Almost every sect of Hinduism—and Hinduism out of all religions is the most free and comprehensive—gives Krishna some veneration.

Even amongst the sternest and most unemotional Sankhya followers, or those who seek to find the self by rigorous intellectual inquiry, Krishna is venerated because of his teaching in the *Bhagavad-Gita*."

—from The Legend of Krishna,
Nigel Frith

FOR FURTHER READING

Easwaran, Eknath. *The Bhagavad Gita for Daily Living.* Berkeley: The Blue Mountain Center of Meditation, 1975.

Miller, Barbara Stoler, trans. *The Bhagavad-Gita: Krishna's Counsel in Time of War.* New York: Bantam, 1986.

Singer, Milton, ed. *Krishna: Myths, Rites, and Attitudes.* Chicago: The University of Chicago Press, 1971.

RIGHT-MIND AND WRONG-MIND
from the Panchatantra
Translated by Arthur William Ryder ▾ (Textbook page 480)

SUMMARY

"Right-Mind and Wrong-Mind" is a framework fable concerning the plight of two very different young men. Right-mind is generous and trusting, while Wrong-Mind is treacherous, greedy, and abusive.

While traveling abroad with Wrong-Mind, Right-Mind finds a cache of one thousand dinars, which he generously offers to share with his friend. Wrong-Mind suggests that each take only one hundred dinars and bury the rest. After spending the hundred dinars, Wrong-Mind suggests that they each take another hundred dinars. After spending this money, Wrong-Mind secretly digs up the remaining cache and later accuses Right-Mind of stealing it.

In court, the two men are ordered to undergo an ordeal, a painful and difficult test that is designed to determine guilt or innocence. To avoid the ordeal, Wrong-Mind insists that he has a witness, a forest goddess, who can testify to his innocence. Wrong-Mind then hides his father in a hollow tree. When the officials of the court come to the forest, the father's voice is heard proclaiming Right-Mind's guilt. The angry Right-Mind then takes justice into his own hands and burns the tree, revealing the father, who implicates his son, Wrong-Mind. Wrong-Mind is hanged for his theft and deception, and Right-Mind is rewarded with the king's favor.

Within this tale is an animal fable narrated by the protesting father of Wrong-Mind in an attempt to stop his son's deceit. The fable, "A Remedy Worse

Than the Disease," concerns a heron whose young have been eaten by a snake. The heron seeks the advice of a crab, his natural enemy. The cunning crab advises the heron to lure a mongoose to the tree where both the heron and snake live so that the mongoose will eat the snake. The heron follows this advice, but the mongoose eats not only the snake, but also the heron and his young,

MORE ABOUT THE SELECTION

Indian literature contains three major collections of folktales, the *Jataka,* the *Panchatantra,* and the *Katha Sarit Sagara.* Scholars think that the oldest collection is the *Jataka,* from which some tales have been traced to the third century B.C. The stories of the *Jataka,* like other Indian literature from the early periods, were originally passed down orally, and the exact period when the stories were gathered into a systematic form and written down is unknown. The collection eventually came to incorporate more than five hundred tales reportedly based on the enlightening experiences of the Buddha.

. The *Panchatantra* is the most famous of the Indian story cycles. Scholars believe the collection goes back to the beginning of the second century B.C. The stories are a combination of Sanskrit prose and poetry, with the prose used for telling the tales and poetry for summing up the morals. While earlier Indian works, including the *Jataka,* the *Vedas,* and the *Gita,* involve a religious element, the *Panchatantra* is a practical guide to surviving and thriving in the physical world.

The stories of the *Panchatantra* were first translated into Middle Persian in the sixth century A.D. Since then, many of the stories have become world classics. The *Panchatantra* has appeared in some two hundred versions in more than fifty different languages and has influenced the literatures of many lands. The fables of La Fontaine, for example, owe a clear debt to the *Panchatantra*.

Like many subsequent story collections, such as the *Thousand and One Nights,* Chaucer's *Canterbury Tales,* and Boccaccio's *Decameron,* the *Panchatantra* establishes its unity through a frame story, presented as the introduction. The frame story tells of a Brahman, a priest, who is attempting to teach within six months the art of statecraft to two rather stupid and spoiled princes.

A CRITICAL COMMENT

"One feature of the tales is the universality of their sentiment. We are constantly reminded that human nature has not changed very considerably during the past twenty, or twenty-five, centuries. The old faults and failings, hopes and fears, loves and hatreds, pleasures and disappointments, are continually recurring; and though much of the conversation is put into the mouths of beasts, it is genuine human thought and feeling that prompt the utterance. In the original we have page after page of shrewd observations, proverbs, and well-worn maxims. Vishnusharman, the first compiler of the work, aimed at nothing more than the teaching of worldly wisdom and rational human happiness. This was to be obtained by the exercise of the intelligence in securing a moderate fortune, personal safety, learning, and a wide circle of friends.

"Incidentally he dealt with many aspects of life, and touched on a diversity of themes: religion, polity, education, love and marriage, joy and sorrow, friendship and treachery, victory and defeat, making money and losing it, and everything else of ordinary interest. We have familiar discourse, noble sentiment, classic purity of style, and a vein of gentle humor. It is significant of all great literature that it never goes completely out of fashion, and its teaching is everywhere applicable. And this is the secret of the popularity of the *Panchatantra,* which makes a common appeal, for it deals with no particular class of society, but ranges over a wide field of diverse human experience."

—*from* Tales from the Panchatantra, *Alfred Williams*

FOR FURTHER READING

Campbell, Joseph. *Myths to Live By.* New York: Viking, 1972.

Dorson, Richard M., ed. *Folktales Told Around the World.* Chicago: The University of Chicago Press, 1975.

Garg, Ganga Ram. *An Encyclopedia of Indian Literature.* Atlantic Highlands, NJ: Humanities Press, 1983.

Ryder, Arthur William, trans. *The Panchatantra: Translated from the Sanskrit.* Chicago: University of Chicago Press, 1925.

RAMA AND RAVANA IN BATTLE
from the Ramayana
Translated by R. K. Narayan ▾ (Textbook page 486)

SUMMARY

This selection contains the rousing finale to the epic battle between Rama, an earthly incarnation of the god Vishnu, and Ravana, the many-headed king of the demons who has kidnapped Rama's wife Sita.

After Ravana loses his leading officers to the monkey hordes serving as Rama's soldiers, he vows to end the bloody war by confronting Rama man to man. To aid Rama, the gods send a chariot and Matali, the charioteer of the war-god, Indra. Rama first allows Ravana to take the lead, hoping Ravana will tire himself with his antics. The ensuing battle is fierce. For each attack, a successful and destructive counterattack is made. For instance, Ravana sends off a shower of arrows, but Rama's arrows meet and shatter Ravana's. Ravana then uses ten bows in his twenty arms, but Rama remains unscathed. At one point, Rama's arrows actually pierce Ravana's armor, causing him to wince. In retaliation Ravana uses an asthra, a weapon with supernatural power, which Rama counteracts with his own supernatural attack. Later, Ravana casts a flaming trident that Rama stops with a perfectly timed mantra (chant).

Finally, Rama sends out his fiercest weapon, the Brahmasthra, a weapon designed by Brahma, the Creator. Aiming at Ravana's heart, his one weak spot, Rama strikes home. The weapon burns away the ugly layers of anger, conceit, and other evils, revealing the pure side of the monster. Examining the dead body, Rama is concerned when he sees a scar on Ravana's back. Fearing he has shot his enemy in the back, Rama is relieved when Ravana's brother tells him the wound is an old scar from an elephant attack. Rama departs, allowing funeral rites for Ravana to commence.

MORE ABOUT THE SELECTION

The *Ramayana* is a compilation of popular tales about a legendary national hero. The sage Valmiki is said to have woven the tales together, uniting them with a framework story. However, for hundreds of years the epic remained a growing, living entity to which various episodes, asides, and changes were added by local storytellers, often to honor the resident lord or to include local geography, customs, or history.

In general, the *Ramayana* juxtaposes two extreme societies, the ideal good and the ultimate evil and reflects the basic Hindu tenets of reincarnation and karma. In traditional Hindu mythology, the gods and demons represent the two extremes of existence and carry on a continual struggle in the world. While good and evil are usually balanced, there are times when the scale dips in the direction of evil. At these times the god Vishnu, the preserver, intervenes by sending down to earth an avatar, or human incarnation of himself. Myths of Vishnu refer to nine such earthly avatars, most notably the eighth incarnation, Krishna of the *Mahabharata* and other tales, and the seventh incarnation, Rama of the *Ramayana*.

According to tradition, the evil demon king Ravana had upset the balance of good and evil on earth. Because Ravana had honored Brahma, the god had granted Ravana his wish that no god could ever destroy him. But since Ravana's pride had not permitted him to ask immunity from humans, Vishnu decided to send a human avatar to confront Ravana. Subsequently, Rama and three other sons were born to King Dasaratha. Rama received half of Vishnu's nature, the second son a quarter, and the other two an eighth each.

Rama emerges from the epic not as just a hero, but as a physical incorporation of all the Hindu virtues, especially truth. His superior powers are evidenced early—when courting Sita, an incarnation of Vishnu's wife, the goddess Lakshimi, Rama passes an epic test when he is able not only to bend Shiva's bow, but to break it. His superior honor is demonstrated when, after his father is tricked into sending him into exile, he refuses a summons to return to rule because he feels honor-bound to abide by his father's declaration. While he is in exile, his honor is further tested when the giantess Surpanakha tempts him to be unfaithful to his wife Sita. His refusal of Surpanakha's advances leads to the confrontation with her brother, the evil Ravana.

Sita, Rama's wife, bears comparison to Penelope, the loyal wife of another epic hero, Ulysses. Just as Rama is the perfect man, Sita is the perfect Indian woman, embodying the virtues of humbleness, duty, selflessness, and submissiveness. Her loyalty is demonstrated when she fends off the advances of her captor, Ravana, and remains loyal to her husband.

The *Ramayana* stands as a key Hindu text in that it is a devotional work leading people to worship Rama, an incarnation of Vishnu, while it also teaches people how to follow their dharma.

A CRITICAL COMMENT

"It [the *Ramayana*] is a work of exemplars, of models of good behavior which people in distress and frustration, when doubts assail them, can follow and imitate with beneficial results. We have Rama, the noble and virtuous prince whose supreme heroiesm lies not so much in the fact that he conquers his enemies, but in the fact that he stoically and dispassionately endures the greatest hardships, including rejection and calumny on the part of his nearest family.

"For many Indians, especially those who worship God as Vishnu, the *Ramayana* is mainly a religious poem describing the avatar (incarnation) of God on earth, his struggles with the powers of evil and his victory. The incarnation is often unaware of his divine role, but his actions are always noble, his regard of his fellowmen gracious and kind, his patience and forbearance of other people's slights exemplary—until he is faced with the embodiment of real wickedness, the devil incarnate. Then his righteous ire is aroused and his determination to eradicate and kill the evil powers cannot be stopped. For many in the audience listening to *Rama's Way,* that constitutes the essential story. But even those who are not particularly religiously oriented appreciate the *Ramayana* as a fascinating tale of adventure, heroism, exciting plots, and frightful monsters."

—*from* the Introduction to The Ramayana,
B. A. van Nooten

FOR FURTHER READING

Buck, William. *The Ramayana*. Berkeley: University of California Press, 1976.

Coomaraswamy, Ananda K., and Sister Nivedita. *Myths of the Hindus and Buddhists*. New York: Dover, 1967.

Ions, Veronica. *Indian Mythology*. New York: Peter Berick, 1983.

Narayan, R.K. *The Ramayana: A Shortened Modern Prose Version of the Indian Epic*. New York: Penguin, 1972.

UNIT 6: CHINESE AND JAPANESE LITERATURES

Unit Introduction: The Literature of China

Writing and literature have been an important part of Chinese culture for thousands of years; some examples of early writing date as far back as 1500 B.C. The accumulation of writing over the centuries makes for the most voluminous literary heritage in the world. By the time of the T'ang dynasty (A.D. 618– 906), literature was a vital part of civic life. In fact, every applicant for a position in the civil service had to demonstrate a thorough knowledge of literature by reciting from **The Book of Songs** *and composing original verse.*

BACKGROUND

POETS AS POLITICIANS

Poetry is the most revered literary form of ancient China. To the ancient Chinese, poetry was an exercise in contemplation, the translating of a particular moment into a complex form with precise, evocative, and sometimes symbolic language. Nature is the primary subject of Chinese poetry, which is used both to evoke a feeling or mood and to suggest the connection between humanity and nature. The ancient Chinese appreciated the concise beauty and form of poetry and understood its usefulness in diplomatic and political situations. As a result, for nearly 1,300 years a thorough familiarity with the 305 poems in *The Book of Songs* as well as other poetry collections was a core component in any examination for a position in the civil service. Knowledge and appreciation of poetry was no doubt a guarantee of eloquence and careful wit on the part of the civil servant.

Several themes and philosophies crop up again and again in ancient Chinese poetry. Many poems dwell on personal relationships, particularly familial ones. China's ancient poets frequently lament their fear and loneliness due to war or exile from family and homeland. Poetry was also used as means of moral instruction. *The Book of Songs,* in fact, was later used by Confucius to teach the basic tenets of his philosophy.

CHINESE PHILOSOPHIES

Confucianism is considered both a religion and a philosophy, as it deals with the material world more than with spiritual concerns and provides its followers with a definitive guide to life. Confucius

(551–479 B.C.) had entered the civil service but was forced into political exile for thirteen years, during which he served as a teacher. Since the seventh century B.C., traveling teachers had taught what are known as the Six Classics, that is, six classic texts that covered everything from history to religion to music to literature. Confucius not only taught these classics but also commented on them and offered new interpretations. Soon Confucius' ideas and philosophies became a school of thought, which, after his death, was taught by his disciples.

Confucianism embodies three ideas: *yi,* or righteousness; *ming,* or destiny, the will of Heaven; and *Chung Yung,* or moderation, the Chinese equivalent of the Golden Mean. Confucius taught his followers to live modestly and harmoniously and to take responsibility for personal action. The teacher based his social morality on Chinese society during the earlier part of the Chou dynasty, which Confucius regarded as a "Golden Age." A return to the morality of this earlier era, when people lived the most harmonious and creative lives, would assure a stable society in which every individual would function in contented harmony with others.

Another influential philosophy is Taoism, set down in the *Tao Te Ching.* The book is attributed to the writer Lao-tzu, whose name is the honorific title "Old Master." Lao-tzu was a contemporary of Confucius, but his philosophy was very different. Unlike Confucianism with its analects and precise definitions of a good, moral life, Tao, or "The Way" is not easily defined or described. The point of Taoism is to identify and harmonize oneself with the workings of the universe and nature. Meditation, inactivity, and withdrawal from society are necessary to obtain a sense of oneness with the forces of the universe. "The Way" is not something to strive for energetically; it is something that must be allowed to happen gradually.

Buddhism, and later Zen Buddhism, were also religions popular among followers of both Confucianism and Taoism. Introduced to China from India, Buddhism operates on the principle that humans suffer because of their desires and selfishness, and that with the renunciation of desire will come perfect peace and enlightenment. Buddhism is like Taoism in its rejection of the outside world and its peaceful, but alert preparation for sudden but complete enlightenment.

ANECDOTES AND OTHER PROSE

The principles or beliefs of Confucianism and Taoism in China have long been taught with the aid of pithy prose narratives: Confucius's *Analects* and the anecdotes of famed Tao masters. The Confucian *Analects* is essentially a collection of sayings, often disjointed and cryptic, attributed to the great teacher but written down long after his death. Like the *Analects*, Taoist anecdotes are brief and to the point; they focus on a single event, told with little narrative detail. Often amusing or satirical, their purpose is to enlighten the listener.

Despite the important role that the *Analects* and Taoist anecdotes played in Chinese culture, Chinese narrative prose was not encouraged the way poetry was. Narrative tales were not written until the eleventh century; the first recognized Chinese novel, *Dream of the Red Chamber,* was written seven centuries later in the eighteenth century. And although Ssu-ma Ch'ien's historical narrative was admired for its style, because of its political subject matter, it was considered controversial, and some sections were censored.

UNIT PROJECTS

1. **Researching Chinese Pictographs.** A pictograph is a picture used as a symbol of an idea. Research the pictographs of China. Write a brief report on the system of Chinese pictography—how it works, how it has changed over the centuries, what it looks like. Present your report to the class with illustrations.

2. **Writing and Delivering a Persuasive Speech.** Nature was a major subject of ancient Chinese poetry. What can we in Western culture learn from this fact? Write a persuasive piece in which you explain the difference between Chinese and Western perspectives on nature. In your conclusion, present some realistic steps for improving our own "relationship" with nature based on the Chinese model.

3. **Debating Philosophies.** Work with a partner and write a script in which Confucius and Lao-Tzu debate the relative merits of their philosophies or ways of looking at life. You should each take the role of one of the sages. Present your debate to the class.

4. **Writing a Taoist Anecdote.** Imagine that you are an early Taoist and are forming the concept known as "The Way." In two or three paragraphs, write an anecdote that reveals what "The Way" is for you. As a guide to the art of living, your anecdote should focus on how humans relate to nature and to each other. Read your anecdote to the class.

5. **Creating a Catalog of Li Ch'ing-chao's Art Collection.** Imagine that the lost art collection of Li Ch'ing-chao has been recovered and that it is your job to catalog it. Put together a catalog of ten of the most important pieces (watercolor paintings, sculpture, and so on) in the collection. You will need to do some research on the art that would have been available or appropriate for Li Ch'ing-chao's collection. Present your catalog with illustrations and details of each piece to the class.

6. **Reporting on the Great Wall of China.** The Great Wall of China is the longest human structure ever built. Write a research report on the Great Wall that explains its history, purpose, and construction. Consider also how it has survived the centuries. Present your research to the class, with illustrations.

7. **Researching Chinese Women Poets.** Li Ch'ing-ch'ao was not the only woman among the ancient Chinese poets. After doing some research, write a report on other ancient Chinese women poets. Choose two poems that you like best from their work and present them to the class. How is it like or unlike the works of the male poets Li Po and Tu Fu, for example?

8. **Creating a Time Line.** With a partner, research the history of China's dynasties and create a time line that depicts each dynasty, the years of its power, and the major accomplishments of the period. Illustrate your time line with pictures of some of the buildings, art forms, or other creations associated with each dynasty.

9. **Researching the *I Ching*.** One of the Six Classics associated with Confucius is a three–thousand–year–old book that is still used, even by Westerners, as a source of wisdom and divination, or prophecy: the *I Ching* or *Book of Changes.* The *I Ching* uses illustrations, called hexagrams, to convey philosophical meanings. People who use the *I Ching* interpret these hexagrams in order to gain insight or figure out appropriate actions to take. Many translations of the *I Ching*—as well as commentaries on the book—are available today. With one or more partners, research the *I Ching* and prepare a lecture to deliver to the class. Be prepared to explain the history of the *I Ching*, how it is used, and what the various hexagrams and

commentaries mean. You could also give the class a demonstration of the coin method of divination. You may wish to prepare handouts to help your classmates follow your lecture.

from THE BOOK OF SONGS
Translated by Arthur Waley ▼ (Textbook page 515)

SUMMARY

Song 103 expresses a woman's longing to return to her own land and people. In Song 130 a soldier who has been uprooted from his home in order to defend the empire expresses both sorrow and anger at the injustice of the peasant-soldier's life.

MORE ABOUT THE SELECTIONS

The Book of Songs is the earliest extant poetic anthology in East Asia. Compiled between 1000 and 700 B.C., *The Book of Songs* is intended as tribute to the Chou dynasty's King Wen. The original Chinese title, *Shih* ("song-words"), is the Chinese word for poetry. After 500 B.C., when Confucius reinterpreted the songs as moral teachings, *The Book of Songs* was called *Shih Ching* ("song-word scripture"). Since that time, *The Book of Songs* has been one of the Six Classics that were basic to Confucian teaching. At one time, it was thought that Confucius had authored the entire collection, but now it is believed that he perhaps selected the 305 poems from as many as 1,000 poems written between 1000 and 700 B.C. Confucius held these poems in the highest esteem, and he taught that one could not enter heaven without knowledge of them.

While the poems serve as a teaching tool of Confucianism, they also present a portrait of a historical period. During the Chou dynasty, a feudal society replaced the slave-owning society of the Shang dynasty (1766–1122 B.C.). As in Europe during the Middle Ages (A.D. 1000–1500), peasants worked for lords who had been granted land by the emperor. In times of peace, the peasants farmed the land. In wartime, the men served as soldiers when their lord went to battle. It is clear from the two songs that at the time they were written, the world was still an unpredictable and dangerous place, and that closeness to loved ones was important but not always possible.

A CRITICAL COMMENT

"The preservation of the *Songs* is due to the fact that they were used for a variety of social and educational purposes which had nothing to do with their original intention. Confucius, for example, tells us that a knowledge of the *Songs* enables us to incite other men to desirable courses, helps us to observe accurately their inmost feelings and to express our own discontents, to do our duty both to parent and prince, and finally 'to widen our acquaintance with the names of birds, beasts, plants, and trees.' In anecdote after anecdote of the Tso Chuan chronicle . . . we can see the Songs in actual use as 'incitements,' as diplomatic 'feelers,' as a veiled means of displaying one's own intentions or sounding those of a fellow-diplomatist. For example, when the Duke of Lu in 544 B.C. has taken refuge in a foreign land, owing to the menaces of the Chi family, and hesitates to return, his Minister 'incites' him by intoning No. 122, with its refrain 'let us go back.' The emotional effect of the familiar poem is greater than that of any direct appeal. . . . In public life a man who does not know the *Songs* is 'as one whose face is turned towards the wall.' An envoy sent from Sung to Lu in 530 B.C. fails to recognize the allusion in a song recited on his arrival, and is at a loss how to reply. His mission is completely discredited, and it is predicted that he will come to speedy ruin. This may seem to us bizarre; but much the same fate would have befallen an eighteenth-century Member of Parliament who failed to understand an allusive quotation from Vergil."

—*from the Preface to* The Book of Songs,
Arthur Waley

FOR FURTHER READING

Liu, Wu-chi, and Irving Yucheng Lo, eds. *Sunflower Splendor: Three Thousand Years of Chinese Poetry*. New York: Doubleday, 1975.

Waley, Arthur, trans. and ed. *The Book of Songs*. 2nd ed. New York: Grove Press, 1960.

Watson, Burton, trans. and ed. *The Columbia Book of Chinese Poetry*. New York: Columbia University Press, 1984.

Wu, K. C. *The Chinese Heritage*. New York: Crown, 1982.

POEMS OF LI PO

Translated by Arthur Cooper ▼ (Textbook page 520)

SUMMARY

QUIET NIGHT THOUGHTS

This poem epitomizes the terse, four-line form that was Li Po's forte and was very popular at the time. It is a wistful poem in which the speaker describes the illusions of frost created by the moonlight and dreams of home.

LETTER TO HIS TWO SMALL CHILDREN

The speaker imagines how time has passed at his home in the three years since he left. He is made terribly homesick by these thoughts and has scribbled this poem in a quick letter.

MORE ABOUT THE AUTHOR

Li Po was born at a time when Confucianism was overshadowed by both Buddhism and Taosim, and Li Po studied all three philosophies. Taoism best fit his character and poetry: Li Po was unconventional and spirited, blithely traveling through life, following his inner, poetic drive, exploring mysticism, and enjoying the beauties of nature. His life was dedicated to poetry, friendships, and merrymaking.

He lived during one of China's finest periods of civilization, the prosperous T'ang dynasty. With the borders protected from outside invaders, peace and a benevolent emperor reigned for the first forty years of Li Po's life. Dubbed the "Golden Age," this was a period in which literature and art thrived. Li Po was well known for his poetry during his lifetime. He was also charming and interesting, and he easily found hospitable friends, relatives, and supporters, many of whom were well established in government positions. He spent his life traveling, studying, meditating, and writing poetry. At the age of fourteen he wrote his first *fu,* which used a style combining poetry and prose. Toward the middle of his life, both the golden age and Li Po's fortunes began to decline. The atmosphere in the court was characterized by intrigues, plots and counterplots, treachery, and rumors of rebellion. Wars and famine reduced the population by thirty-six million. A friend of Li Po was accused of a conspiracy to overthrow the emperor and was executed. Because Li Po never took the government exams, which was extremely unusual for a qualified candidate, he never secured a position that would have provided financial security and prestige. Instead, Li Po spent the last years of his life—marked by rebellions and anarchy—in exile. He died as he lived, more concerned with his poetry than with politics.

A CRITICAL COMMENT

"Li Po is one of the early Chinese poets about whose life we know most, and we might easily slip into regarding him as typical at any rate of the more Bohemian sort of literary man in T'ang times. But if we compare his career with those of other poets who lived at about the same period we find that in one important aspect it was unique. He is the only well-known writer who neither went in for the Literary Examinations (the normal method of entry into the Civil Service) nor ever held any regular official post. . . .

"The poems, then, are those of a man who in the eyes of a society largely dominated by bureaucratic values had completely failed in his career or rather had failed to have a career at all. There were poets who had lost their jobs and poets who after a time had returned voluntarily to private life. But that a great poet should never have had a job at all was almost unprecedented. Some people no doubt thought that such a situation was highly discreditable to the Government. . . .

"Moreover his status as a 'banished Immortal,' though it helped to account for his genius, did not appear to facilitate his Taoist endeavors. His career as an alchemist was abortive; he grew old and grey before his time. But despite all his failures his poems, unlike those of Tu Fu, do not seem ever to have been written under the stress of actual deprivation. Prices after A.D. 755 rose by more than 300 per cent; but Li Po never refers to any difficulty in getting enough to eat and drink. He seems indeed (apart from the few weeks spent in prison) to have got through the revolution with very little personal discomfort. To the sufferings of less privileged people he was, it would seem, almost wholly indifferent, and this has tended to estrange him from the present generation of Chinese."

—*from* The Poetry and Career of Li Po,
Arthur Waley

FOR FURTHER READING

Cooper, Arthur. *Li Po and Tu Fu.* New York: Penguin, 1965.

Obata, Shigeyoshi, trans. *The Works of Li Po.* New York: Paragon Reprint, 1965.

Waley, Arthur. *The Poetry and Career of Li Po.* London: George Allen and Unwin, 1950.

Whincup, Greg. *The Heart of Chinese Poetry.* New York: Doubleday, 1987.

POEMS OF TU FU

Translated by Arthur Cooper and Kenneth Rexroth ▾ (Textbook page 528)

SUMMARY

FOR WEI PA, IN RETIREMENT

A middle-aged man meets with his boyhood friend after twenty years of separation. They lament the passing of many acquaintances and find it difficult to believe the years could have passed so quickly.

NIGHT THOUGHTS AFLOAT

The speaker in this poem tells of his loneliness at night.

JADE FLOWER PALACE

The speaker describes the ruins of a once great castle and ponders the decaying effects of the passage of time.

MORE ABOUT THE AUTHOR

Along with Li Po, Tu Fu is considered one of China's greatest poets. The two were contemporaries and friends, and their lives share many similarities. They both began writing poetry at the age of fourteen and left their homes in their late teens to travel extensively through China. They were from upper-class families with royal lineage and were well educated. Both poets lived the later years of their lives in exile, avoiding the tumultuous decline of the T'ang dynasty. Tu Fu was thirty-two when he met Li Po, eleven years his senior and already a well-known poet. The attraction was immediate and Li Po composed two poems celebrating their friendship; Tu Fu wrote over a dozen.

The two poets differ considerably in their writing styles, however. Li Po has been described as the "people's poet," while Tu Fu has been called a "poet's poet" because of his technical expertise. Tu Fu was noted for his mastery of a difficult form of poetry called *lu-shih,* especially in his later years. With its many stylistic restrictions, earlier poets relegated *lu-shih,* to simpler themes. Tu Fu was more innovative; his realistic subjects ranged from everyday, familial matters to the social ramifications of current events. Notably, Tu Fu also broke with past poetic tradition by expressing more than one mood in a poem and exploring previously unmentionable subject matter.

Largely a family man, Tu Fu pursued government positions to provide for his children and to fulfill the Confucian ideal of the scholar's responsibility to the emperor. Ironically, he failed the civil service exams through which all the major poets of that time, except Li Po, secured government positions. Like Li Po, Tu spent his later years wandering, disillusioned with his life and lack of recognition. Weak and ailing, he died on a journey home. Forty-three years later his grandson brought his body home for reburial in a family plot.

A CRITICAL COMMENT

"One dimension of Tu Fu's range is an objective realism unheard of in earlier poetry. He brought every aspect of public and private experience into the domain of poetry, including life's more unpleasant aspects, which traditional decorum had frowned upon. And the spirit of Tu's engagement with this unexplored terrain was profound in its implications: he conceived experience in the precise terms of concrete detail. As a result, the very texture of his poetry is an act of praise for existence itself. . . .

". . . In addition to a new world of objective clarities, Tu Fu's realism opened up new depths of subjectivity, not only in terms of subject matter, but formally as well. During his later years of wandering, Tu's writing focused more and more on the solitary self cast against the elemental sweep of the universe, and that new subject matter was reflected in Tu's innovative language. While the discontinuous organization continued to give his poems a kind of intuitive complexity, Tu Fu's highly refined language extended richness to the extreme, and beyond. It became so distilled and distorted as to be nearly unintelligible at times, while his imagery often approached the surreal. . . .

"Nevertheless, there is at the heart of Tu Fu's sensibility a profound detachment from things, himself included. Rather than offering freedom from the mundane world, Tu's detachment is hopelessly complicated by a deep love for all things. While it allows his empathy to surpass the bounds of personal response, it also graces him with an exquisite sense of humor, one capable of subtly bringing a geologic perspective to even the most trying of his own circumstances."

—*from* The Selected Poems of Tu Fu,
David Hinton

FOR FURTHER READING

Hawkes, David. *A Little Primer of Tu Fu.* Oxford: Clarendon Press, 1967.

Hinton, David, trans. *The Selected Poems of Tu Fu.* New York: New Directions, 1988.

Hung, William. *Tu Fu: China's Greatest Poet.* Cambridge, MA: Harvard University Press, 1969.

PEONIES

Li Ch'ing-chao ▾ Translated by Kenneth Rexroth and Ling Chung ▾ (Textbook page 534)

SUMMARY

The speaker admires the flowerlike beauty and innocence of a young woman grooming herself on a balcony. With the passage of time, beauty will wilt and turn to dust—a time the speaker does not welcome.

MORE ABOUT THE AUTHOR

The constantly changing nature of the Sung court in twelfth-century China and the foreign invasions threatening it directly affected Li Ch'ing-chao's life. Her father and her husband's father were both government officials. Shortly after her marriage, her father and father-in-law supported opposing factions at court. Her father favored the status quo, and as the reformists became more influential, he was banished from the court and exiled. Her father-in-law excelled within the new structure at first, but was later accused of accepting bribes. The dishonored family was powerless and held no government posts for years.

As a result, Li Ch'ing-chao and her husband returned to their country home and were able to devote themselves to their many cultural and intellectual interests. Contrary to general practice, Li Ch'ing-chao was well educated, for her family had encouraged her to pursue her studies of antiquity and to exercise her many talents. She and her husband spent years collecting and cataloging their art treasures. Together they wrote an extensive treatise on the subject of ancient writings, with a particular emphasis on inscriptions from monuments.

While her husband traveled in search of artifacts for their collection, Ch'ing-chao wrote poetry, much of which reflects her loneliness and deep feelings for her husband. Her excellence in the *tz'u* form, as well as in other styles, established her as one of China's greatest women poets. *Tz'u* is more flexible than the formal, restrictive *lu-shih* that Tu Fu used. Poets turned to the *tz'u* when they wished to describe personal emotions and feelings. The form reached its height of popularity with Li Ch'ing-chao's poetry during the Sung dynasty.

Ch'ing-chao spent the later years of her life fleeing from foreign invaders. Devastated by the death of her husband, the poet retreated further south to the new capital and never returned home. She maintained her interests in art and politics and continued to write poetry during the remainder of her life.

A CRITICAL COMMENT

"As Ch'ing-chao grew older, her *tz'u* poems lost their former vitality and color, but were permeated with a growing sense of reconciliation. Although she had experienced much hardship and many shocks, she was still able to celebrate the beautiful and the artistic, no matter how humble and minute they were. . . .

"But her love for the lost homeland was as strong as ever:
I send blood-stained tears to the mountains and rivers of home,
And sprinkle a cup of earth on East Mountain.

"Here her tears were turned into a libation for the downfall of her family, her nation, and for the suffering of the people. The scope was sweeping, the pathos all-embracing. In her younger days, her tears were shed for her personal feelings of loneliness. . . .

"Ch'ing-chao is a master of employing imagery in diverse styles. She was the only Chinese woman author who mastered a great variety of styles and excelled in both the writing of *shih* and *tz'u* poetry. . . .

"Very little is recorded about her remaining years. She probably stayed with the family of her younger brother. She traveled to Chechiang Province when she was fifty-two, because of an alarm over an attack from the Tatars. She composed several poems there. . . . Apparently old age did not diminish her devotion to art."

—*from* Li Ch'ing-Chao: Complete Poems,
Ling Chung

FOR FURTHER READING

Hu, Pin-chang. *Li Ch'ing-chao*. New York: Twayne, 1966.

Li Ch'ing-chao. *Li Ch'ing-chao: Complete Poems.* Eds. and trans. Kenneth Rexroth and Ling Chung. New York: New Directions, 1979.

Rexroth, Kenneth, and Ling Chung, trans. and eds. *The Orchid Boat: Women Poets of China.* New York: McGraw-Hill, 1973.

from the ANALECTS

Confucius ▼ Translated by Arthur Waley ▼ (Textbook page 538)

SUMMARY

The *Analects* consists partly of sayings and partly of dialogues between Confucius, "the Master," and his disciples. Nowhere is Confucius quoted directly; generally, he is paraphrased as he comments on a particular situation or presents a solution to a problem. The selected *Analects* give a good overview of the tenets of Confucianism: selflessness, modesty, goodness, inner strength, and social responsibility.

MORE ABOUT THE AUTHOR

Confucius lived from 551 to 479 B.C., during the last half of the Chou dynasty (1122–256 B.C.) when China was an empire of states ruled by feudal lords and surrounded by hostile peoples. Within the empire, the populace lived in fear, not only of foreign invasion, but also of the constant warring between the states. This was a time of interstate aggressions, powerless kings, deadly rivalries, and assassinations.

Confucius' main concern was a return to the stability and orderliness of the early Chou dynasty and the responsible leadership of the ancients. The rulers of antiquity were guided by a "mandate of heaven": If they were fair and just rulers, they would continue to rule; but should they become evil and corrupt, the heavenly powers would replace them with others. This had proven true throughout history as negligent rulers were eventually deposed. These ideas are incorporated into Confucian thought: The capable and virtuous should rule, and the past provides answers for the present and future.

In an attempt to put his theories into practice, Confucius spent many years traveling from state to state trying to interest rulers in his doctrines. He had little success with the entrenched sovereigns. Consequently, he returned to his home to teach the art of statecraft and excellent government to those who wished to enter or advance in government service. Statesmanship was his curriculum and conversation was his principal method of teaching. His efforts spawned a number of disciples who formed their own schools, promulgating Confucius' teachings among generations of Chinese youth, even though Confucius left no written works.

The early Confucian canon consisted of the "Six Classics," the basic texts for generations of Chinese. Traditionalists believe that Confucius wrote all six. Most scholars, however, agree that he authored "Spring and Summer Annals," an official record of historical events in the state of Lu, and was a commentator on the *I Ching,* or the "Book of Changes." Confucius reworked the "Book of Rituals" and the "Book of Music" and is believed to have edited the "Book of History" and the "Book of Songs" (see textbook page 514). The considerable legacy of Confucianism pervades classical literature, philosophy, and the very history of China.

The *Analects* focus on the concept of proper conduct, the "Way of Goodness." Comprised of twenty books containing 497 analects, they are not categorized, nor is there any particular arrangement. The *Analects* could be considered an elementary textbook for Chinese children since it has been a basic component of education in Asia for over two thousand years.

A CRITICAL COMMENT

"Before they were able even to comprehend the difficult, archaic language of the *Analects,* much less its ideas, children were obliged to commit the text to memory. There it remained, stored in their minds, to be gradually illumined by later study and experience. Having mastered the words of the text, they could spend the rest of their lives, if they were so disposed, pondering and savoring its meaning and finding ways in which its words were applicable to their own situation. . . .

"Since there is so little context or explanation included in the *Analects* itself, [the reader] may proceed to construct his own explanations of what the passage means to him and how it tallies with his own experience. Some passages dealing with specific details of the life of ancient China may never have anything more than historical interest for the modern reader. Some passages may come to life only when he has read farther in Confucian thought and seen how the hint given in the *Analects* has been elaborated and expanded by later writers. Some passages can perhaps not be fully appreciated until the reader himself has undergone experiences similar to those referred to in the text. But, if Chinese and Japanese scholars are to be believed, the meager sayings of the *Analects,* when so studied and contemplated over the years, will take on deeper and deeper meaning the older one grows. As one's own experience broadens to match that of Confucius and his disciples, the pronouncements of the *Analects* will one by one light up with the light of personal recognition. Once this has happened, the words of the *Analects* will become for him the most succinct and poignant summation of that particular idea or experience, and he will understand to some degree why they have been regarded with such reverence."

—*from* Early Chinese Literature, *Burton Watson*

FOR FURTHER READING

Chai, Ch'u, and Winberg Chai, trans. and eds. *The Sacred Books of Confucius and Other Confucian Classics*. New York: Fawcett Premier, 1972.

Lin, Yutang, trans. and ed. *The Wisdom of Confucius*. New York: Modern Library, 1943.

Waley, Arthur, trans. *Three Ways of Thought in Ancient China*. New York: Doubleday, 1956.

———. *The Analects of Confucius*. New York: Vintage, 1938.

from the TAO TE CHING

Lao-tzu ▾ Translated by Stephen Mitchell ▾ (Textbook page 543)

SUMMARY

There are eighty-one passages in the Tao Te Ching, which is usually divided into two parts: Tao (the "Way") and Te ("Virtue"). The selected passages are from the Tao part of the work.

Passage 2 describes the natural balance and order of things in the universe and the wise teacher's response to them.

The first section of Passage 8 characterizes the supreme good as like water that is comfortable at any level. The following two sections describe the best way to live.

Like Passage 2, Passage 29 comments on the natural order and balance in the world and the best way to exist in it.

MORE ABOUT THE SELECTION

There is little reliable information about the life of Lao-tzu (also spelled Laotse, Lao-tse, Lao Tan, and Laozi). The historian Ssu-ma Ch'ien wrote that Lao-tzu's original name was Li Erh, and he was Keeper of the Imperial Archives at Loyang, the new capital of the Chou empire. Lao-tzu, like other intellectuals of his time, pondered the meaning of life, which seemed more evil and tragic than ever before. He apparently enjoyed discussing his ideas with his friends, but did not write them down. According to legend, when he was ready to leave China and cross the boundary into heaven, the guard would not let him pass until he wrote the passages that became the *Tao Te Ching*. It is more likely that the followers of Lao-tzu collected his sayings. Critics doubt the authenticity of certain passages, but the overall consistency of the work indicates that it is the work of a single, highly original thinker. However, the first known manuscript of the *Tao Te Ching* dates from one thousand years after the death of Lao-tzu.

Some translators believe that the *Tao Te Ching* was basically a political treatise on laissez-faire government. In urging humility, serene acceptance, and inaction, it was a response to both Confucianism's emphasis on statecraft and the unrestrained exercise of political power that was typical of the period. Others see the *Tao Te Ching* as a religious text preaching peace between humanity and nature. In any event, the *Tao Te Ching* was the basis of the philosophy and religion called Taoism.

Taoism in ancient China took several different forms. Lao-tzu had scorned the idea of gods, but adherents of some Tao sects worshiped Lao-tzu as well as many gods. Some Taoists emphasized techniques for achieving the long life and immortality that were thought to flow from the Tao. They sometimes withdrew from society and spent their lives in meditation. Others attempted to achieve immortality by means of certain dietary, breathing, sexual, or magical practices.

The basic philosophy of Taoism advises a quiet, calm, and simple life, close to nature, detached from as many desires as possible. It is anti-ritual, anti-government, and anti-war. Taoist philosophy has had a lasting influence on Chinese literature, art, calligraphy, and music. Acupuncture, Taoist yoga, and the t'ai chi ch'uan system of exercise are all based on Taoist beliefs. Many Taoist attitudes were later incorporated into Zen philosophy.

As a folk religion, Taoism appealed greatly to the peasant masses of China. Taoist priests treated the sick with rituals and magic charms. A complicated moral code evolved from the *Tao Te Ching,* and elaborate temples were built. After the Communists gained power in China in the mid-twentieth century, religious practices of Taoism were officially banned. But Taoist thought so permeates Chinese culture that its influence continues to be noted.

A CRITICAL COMMENT

"To Lao-tse [Lao-tzu], the harmony that naturally existed between heaven and earth from the very beginning could be found by anyone at any time, but not by following the rules of Confucius. As he stated in his *Tao Te Ching* . . . earth was in essence a reflection of heaven, run by the same laws, not by the laws of men. These laws affected not only the spinning of the distant planets, but the activities of the birds in the forest and the fish in the sea. According to Lao-tse, the more man interfered with the natural balance produced and governed by the universal laws, the further away the harmony retreated into the distance. The more forcing, the more trouble. Whether heavy or light, wet or dry, fast or slow, everything had its own nature already within it, which could not be violated without causing difficulties. When abstract and arbitrary rules were imposed from the outside, struggle was inevitable. Only then did life become sour.

"To Lao-tse, the world was not a setter of traps but a teacher of valuable lessons. Its lessons needed to be learned, just as its laws needed to be followed; then all would go well. Rather than turn away from "the world of dust," Lao-tse advised others to "join the dust of the world." What he saw operating behind everything in heaven and earth he called Tao, "the Way." A basic principle of Lao-tse's teaching was that this Way of the Universe could not be adequately described in words, and that it would be insulting both to its unlimited power and to the intelligent human mind to attempt to do so. Still, its nature could be understood, and those who cared the most about it, and the life from which it was inseparable, understood it best.

"Over the centuries Lao-tse's classic teachings were developed and divided into philosophical, monastic, and folk religious forms. All of these could be included under the general heading of Taoism. But the basic Taoism that we are concerned with here is simply a particular way of appreciating, learning from, and working with whatever happens in everyday life. From the Taoist point of view, the natural result of this harmonious way of living is happiness. You might say that happy serenity is the most noticeable characteristic of the Taoist personality, and a subtle sense of humor is apparent even in the most profound Taoist writings. . . ."

—*from* The Tao of Pooh, *Benjamin Hoff*

FOR FURTHER READING

Bynner, Witter. *The Chinese Translations*. Ed. James Kraft. New York: Farrar Straus, 1978.

Chen, Ellen M. *The Tao Te Ching*. New York: Paragon House, 1989.

Deng, Ming-Dao. *The Wandering Taoist*. New York: Harper & Row, 1983.

Henricks, Robert, trans. *Lao-Tzu: Te-Tao Ching*. New York: Ballantine Books, 1989.

Hoff, Benjamin. *The Tao of Pooh*. New York: E.P. Dutton, 1982.

Lao Tzu. *Tao Te Ching*. Trans. Stephen Mitchell. New York: Harper & Row, 1988.

TAOIST ANECDOTES

Chuang Tzu, Lieh Tzu, Lui An ▾ Translated by Moss Roberts ▾ (Textbook page 548)

SUMMARY

The selected anecdotes were written by three Taoists who hoped to convey the messages of Taoism through brief tales.

WAGGING MY TAIL IN THE MUD

When Chuang Tzu was serving as a minor clerk in his district, an officer asked him if he would consider a royal position. Chuang Tzu tells them he's heard that the king has a dead tortoise in his hall. He asks if the tortoise would be happier having its shell honored, or happier wagging its tail in the mud. Like the turtle, Chuang Tzu prefers to keep wagging his tail in the mud.

THE BUTTERFLY

Chuang Tzu tells of a dream in which he was one with a butterfly. But he wonders if he could be the butterfly dreaming that it is Chuang Tzu.

GOLD, GOLD

Lieh Tzu tells of a man who loves gold so much that he steals some in front of a crowd of people. He tells the guards who catch him that he saw only the gold, not the people.

THE MISSING AXE

Lieh Tzu tells of a man whose axe was stolen. Because he suspects his neighbor's son, everything about the boy confirms the bad opinion he has of the boy. When the man finds his axe, he sees that the boy is no different from other children .

THE LOST HORSE

Lui An tells of a man whose horse runs away. Sadness is replaced by joy when the horse returns with a stallion. The son's lameness after a fall from the horse becomes fortunate when it prevents him from service in the army.

MORE ABOUT THE AUTHORS
CHUANG TZU

Chuang Tzu (also spelled Chuangtse) was born in east-central China approximately 365 B.C. His family name was Chou, so he is sometimes called Chuang Chou. Chuang means "peaceful" or "calm," qualities that characterize his writing, although he can also be caustic and angry. Sometimes called the co-founder (with Lao-tzu) of Taoism, Chuang Tzu's book, *Chuang Tzu,* is considered more definitive of Taoist thought than the *Tao Te Ching,* even though Lao-tzu's work is more famous. Chuang Tzu is said to have worked as a minor official, but he spent many years living as a hermit. The historian Ssu-ma Ch'ien wrote that Chuang Tzu had a "sparkling wit," but no king or prince could make use of him because he had no respect for anyone.

Chuang Tzu's doctrines were a reaction against Confucianism, which had become the "establishment" philosophy. He presents many of his ideas in the form of dialogues between one philosopher and another—Lao Tzu and Confucius, for example. Chuang Tzu does not, however, deal with questions of politics. Unlike Lao Tzu, he gives no advice to rulers. He is instead concerned primarily with the freedom of the individual.

The *Chuang Tzu* includes real historical figures, but he also writes about fantastic creatures, such as talking insects and flying dragons. He also refers to a wonderful land inhabited by gods and superhumans who are models of behavior for Taoists who aspire to perfection. Later Taoism based its mystical practices on his allusions to different ways (such as breathing exercises, meditation, and fasting) of freeing the spirit from physical constraints.

Critics consider Chuang Tzu to be the greatest prose writer of the Chou Dynasty. His vivid imagery, wit, and imagination combined with a vigorous style to create a work that Burton Watson describes as "incisive" and "brilliant."

LIEH TZU

The Taoist Lieh Tzu (also called Lieh Yuk'ou) is mentioned several times in *Chuang Tzu*. Both Lieh Tzu and Chuang Tzu were given the title *Chen-Jen,* which means "immortal person." According to legend, Lieh Tzu was so holy that he could ride the wind. The Taoist ideas in his book, the *Lieh Tzu* are very similar to those in *Tao Te Ching* and *Chuang Tzu*. Both Chuang Tzu and Lieh Tzu believed that the perfect person could become one spiritually with any other creature. They also taught compassion towards all living things. Critics consider Lieh Tzu's writing to be simpler and somewhat less original than Chuang Tzu's.

LUI AN

Lui An, a prince of the Han dynasty, was particularly interested in promoting the art of writing *fu,* a poem with a highly complex structure. He attracted the leading writers of *fu* to his court, and wrote eighty-two *fu* himself. His major work is the *Huai-nan Tzu,* which contains an almanac of government activities as well as Taoist doctrines, anecdotes, and legends. The downfall of this highly cultured and talented prince was caused by his desire to avenge the death of his father. The emperor, who was Lui An's cousin, had accused Lui An's father of treason and had sent him into exile where he starved to death. Lui An's adherence to the teachings of Taoism made him unwilling to take direct action. He wanted to have the emperor assassinated, but postponed the coup until it was found out. Lui An then felt that his only honorable choice was to end his own life.

A CRITICAL COMMENT

"The central theme of the *Chuang Tzu* may be summed up in a single word: freedom. Essentially, all the philosophers of ancient China addressed themselves to the same problem: how is man to live in a world dominated by chaos, suffering, and absurdity? Nearly all of them answered with some concrete plan of action designed to reform the individual, to reform society, and eventually to free the world from its ills. . . . Chuang Tzu's answer . . . is grounded upon a wholly different type of thinking. It is the answer of a mystic. . . . Chuang Tzu's answer to the question is: free yourself from the world. . . .

"He saw the man-made ills of war, poverty, and injustice. He saw the natural ills of disease and death. But he believed that they were ills only because man recognized them as such. If man would once forsake his habit of labeling things good or bad, desirable or undesirable, then the man-made ills, which are the product of man's purposeful and value-ridden actions, would disappear and the natural ills that remain would no longer be seen as ills, but as an inevitable part of the course of life. Thus, in Chuang Tzu's eyes, man is the author of his own suffering and bondage, and all his fears spring from the web of values created by himself alone. . . .

". . . Chuang Tzu employs every resource of rhetoric in his efforts to awaken the reader to the essential meaninglessness of conventional values and to free him from their bondage. One device he uses to great effect is the pointed or paradoxical anecdote, the *non sequitur* or apparently nonsensical remark that jolts the mind into awareness of a truth outside the pale of ordinary logic—a device familiar to Western readers of Chinese and Japanese Zen literature. . . .

"Finally, Chuang Tzu uses throughout his writings that deadliest of weapons against all that is pompous, staid, and holy: humor. Most Chinese philosophers employ humor sparingly—a wise decision, no doubt, in view of the serious tone they seek to maintain—and some of them seem never to have heard of it at all. Chuang Tzu, on the contrary, makes it the very core of his style, for he appears to have known that one good laugh would do more than ten pages of harangue to shake the reader's confidence in the validity of his pat assumptions."

—*from* The Complete Works of Chuang Tzu,
Burton Watson

FOR FURTHER READING

Kaltenmark, Max. *Lao Tzu and Taoism*. Stanford, CA.: Stanford University Press, 1969.

Lin Yutang. *The Wisdom of China and India*. New York: Random House, 1942.

Roberts, Moss, trans. and ed. *Chinese Fairy Tales and Fantasies*. New York: Pantheon, 1979.

Waley, Arthur. *Three Ways of Thought in Ancient China*. London: George Allen & Unwin, 1939.

Watson, Burton, trans. *The Complete Works of Chuang Tzu*. New York: Columbia University Press, 1968.

NIEH CHENG
from RECORDS OF THE HISTORIAN
Ssu-ma Ch'ien ▾ Translated by Burton Watson ▾ (Textbook page 553)

SUMMARY

The story of Nieh Cheng comes from the biographical section of the *Records of the Historian*. After killing a man, Nieh Cheng has escaped with his mother and sister to another state where he works as a butcher. Later, Yen Chung-tzu, an official in the service of the ruler of Han, has a dispute with the prime minister. Fearing for his life, Yen Chung-tzu flees the state. Learning of Nieh Cheng's past, Yen Chung-tzu finds him and asks him to assassinate the prime minister. Nieh Cheng says he can neither accept the money nor promise to serve anyone as long as his mother is alive.

After his mother dies, Nieh Cheng recalls Yen Chung-tzu's appreciation of him and his offer of friendship. He goes to Yen Chung-tzu and asks his permission to take revenge on Yen Chung-tzu's enemy. Nieh Cheng works alone and kills not only the prime minister, but many of his guards. Then, after mutilating his face so he could not be recognized, he kills himself.

The ruler of Han posts a reward of a thousand gold pieces for anyone who can identify the assassin. Suspecting that her brother might have committed the murders, Nieh Cheng's older sister, Jung, travels to the marketplace of Han where the assassin's body is displayed. Passersby scold her for mourning her brother, but Jung sorrowfully says that her brother had been willing to die for Yen Chung-tzu because Yen Chung-tzu had recognized his worth and had been kind to him. She then dies of grief by her brother's side.

MORE ABOUT THE AUTHOR

Ssu-ma Ch'ien's father, Ssu-ma T'an, was a scholar whose offical duties as historian of the imperial court consisted mostly of keeping astrological records. Ssu-ma T'an began gathering information for a history of the Han dynasty. Before he died, he asked his only son, Ssu-ma Ch'ien (sometimes spelled "Szuma Chien"), to finish his work. Following his appointment as court historian, Ssu-ma Ch'ien began to travel around China collecting information and writing a history not only of the Han dynasty and China, but of all the world and people known at his time. But, Ssu-ma Ch'ien made a terrible political error. Although he and a General named Li Ling were not friends, Ssu-ma Ch'ien admired the military man's bravery. In 99 B.C., after many victories over the invading Huns, Li Ling suffered an overwhelming defeat and surrendered. Li Ling's enemies spread the rumor that he was giving military secrets to the Huns. When Emperor

Wu asked Ssu-ma Ch'ien for advice, Ssu-ma Ch'ien defended the general and compared him to the heroes of the past. His defense angered the emperor. Ssu-ma Ch'ien was tried for and found guilty of misleading the emperor. The punishment was castration or a large fine, which Ssu-ma Ch'ien could not afford to pay. His desire to finish his historical record was greater than any shame over his punishment and kept him from committing suicide, which his contemporaries considered a more honorable end than castration.

After Ssu-ma Ch'ien had been imprisoned for three years, the emperor discovered that General Li had not betrayed him, and Ssu-ma Ch'ien was released from jail at age fifty. The emperor appointed him his confidential secretary and liaison between the emperor and his prime minister, as well as the job of official historian. Ssu-ma Ch'ien completed his monumental *Records of the Historian* after five years and died shortly thereafter.

Ssu-ma Ch'ien's strong convictions about right and wrong caused him to write frankly about the ugly conduct of the Chinese emperors. He described in detail the cruelty, arrogance, superstition, and vulgarity of several rulers. No one knows what he wrote about Emperor Wu, who had punished him, because that part of the *Records of the Historian* was banned and destroyed immediately after it was published.

Records of the Historian is considered not only a great history but also a literary classic. The *Records* contains five parts: the annual records of the rulers of the Han dynasty; tables of important dates and events; essays on topics such as rivers, persuasive speech, and music; histories of the feudal states; and biographies of famous people. The last chapter is an autobiography of the historian himself. Ssu-ma Ch'ien's descriptive skills bring characters and events to life, and he was one of the first writers to include realistic dialogue. Many later Chinese writers took their material from *Records of the Historian*. Even today, many storytellers, playwrights, and writers of Chinese opera base their stories on the work of Ssu-ma Ch'ien.

A CRITICAL COMMENT

"Like earlier historical works, Ssu-ma Ch'ien's narrative is almost always focused on the life and deeds of the individual. He gives far more attention than his predecessors to the influence of geography, climate, economic factors, customs, and institutions upon the course of history. . . . But when all other factors have been noted, it is still primarily the will of the individual which, in his opinion, directs the course of history. . . .

"Ssu-ma Ch'ien has a great deal to say in the way of personal comment upon the events he describes and the lives of the men he is dealing with. Many of these sections of personal comment add new material to the narrative, discuss its reliability, attempt to trace the cause of events, or describe the historian's own experiences as they relate to the subject. Many of them are given up to subjective moral judgments . . . or to expressions of admiration, censure, or pity. These passages are among the most interesting and lively in the *Shih chi*, and show Ssu-ma Ch'ien as a very human writer, deeply, often passionately involved in his subject. . . .

"One expects to find rulers, statesmen, and military leaders figuring prominently in a history. But who but Ssu-ma Ch'ien would include chapters on the lives of fortune-tellers, . . . famous assassins (some of whom bungled the job at the crucial moment), humorists, big businessmen, or local bosses? In a way he seems to have been aiming at something like the modern social historian's 'picture of an age.' The core of his narrative is political history, since politics, in his view, was the highest among human activities. He is interested in individuals, not social classes as a whole. . . . But the range of individuals he is interested in and feels is worth writing about is far broader than in earlier works. He created for posterity not only a new form for the ordering and presentation of historical material, but a new concept of the breadth and complexity of history."

—*from* Early Chinese Literature, *Burton Watson*

FOR FURTHER READING

Szuma Chien (Ssu-ma Ch'ien), *Records of the Historian.* Trans. Yang Hsien-yi and Gladys Yang. Hong Kong: Commercial Press, 1974.

Wang, Zhongshu. *Han Civilization.* Trans. K. C. Chang, et al. New Haven: Yale University Press, 1982.

Watson, Burton. *Early Chinese Literature.* New York: Columbia University Press, 1962.

Watson, Burton, trans. *Records of the Grand Historian of China.* New York: Columbia University Press, 1962.

Unit Introduction: The Literature of Japan

(Textbook page 558)

The development of a distinctively Japanese culture came about from the mixing of indigenous elements with recognized foreign importations, chiefly from Japan's neighbors in China and Korea. The periodic sealing off of the islands from outside influences—sometimes for a hundred or more years—enabled Japan to absorb influences from mainland Asia and then transform these influences into a form uniquely Japanese.

BACKGROUND

EARLY HISTORY

Before reading the poetry and prose in this unit, it is important to acknowledge the influence of Chinese culture on Japanese literary history. This influence began during the late sixth and early seventh centuries A.D., when the Japanese Yamato clan unified the numerous warring groups of the country and introduced elements of Chinese culture to the Japanese people. The leader of the Yamato clan, Prince Shotoku, adopted the Chinese system of government, with an emperor, a capital city, and governors assigned to oversee particular regions of the country. He then incorporated Chinese philosophy, religion, literature, and the Chinese method of writing into Japan's newly formed royal court. Like the impact of Greek culture on Europe, Chinese culture deeply affected the developing Japanese culture. The Japanese absorbed the influences of China and adapted them to fit the different interests, temperaments, and needs of the Japanese people.

Beginning in the eighth century, the poetry of Japan clearly reflects the impact of Chinese culture. During this time, Japanese poetry was written by the educated aristocratic court poets. These poets felt that a sophisticated and civilized literary style must be steeped in Chinese philosophy and religion, and that it must be recorded in the Chinese writing system. While some Japanese court poets focused on the distinctly Japanese landscape, most followed the poetic forms of the Chinese, wrote in the Chinese language, and incorporated the Buddhist doctrine into their work.

THE EMERGENCE OF WOMEN WRITERS AND LOVE POETRY

The Chinese method of writing affected the evolving Japanese literary tradition in two important ways. It opened the fields of poetry and prose to women writers, and it introduced love as a serious subject in Japanese literature. Ironically, these developments occurred in a somewhat roundabout way. During the Heian era, aristocratic courtiers, both male and female, often passed the time by writing. Many of the gentlemen of the court scorned the Japanese writing script and insisted upon reading and composing poems in the Chinese language. However, since the women of the court in this period were rarely educated in Chinese, they began to use the new Japanese script, *kana,* meaning "borrowed names." These women soon created a remarkable body of prose and poetry in their native language. Among the striking literary accomplishments of this period are Sei Shōnagon's witty and vividly descriptive *Pillow Book* and Lady Murasaki Shikibu's *The Tale of Genji,* which is considered by many scholars to be the first novel in the history of literature.

While the elitist men of the court insisted on using the Chinese language for religious, political, and literary subjects, they had to use *kana,* the only script taught to women, when they engaged in courtship rituals. These rituals involved the exchange of tanka between the men and women of the court, and it was through these tanka that love became a prominent and respected poetic expression in the evolving literary tradition of Japan. Tanka that expressed passion and longing were celebrated and published in the Heian imperial anthology, the *Kokinshū,* and poets such as Ono Komachi became legendary through stories, poems, and plays in the following centuries. Thus, the inaccessibility of the Chinese writing system to women in Japan prompted the development of a unique Japanese literature.

BUDDHISM AND SHINTOISM

In a more direct manner, the influence of Buddhism is evident in nearly every element of Japanese culture, including literature, painting, architecture, and even gardening. Buddhism came into the mainstream of Japanese life after intermingling with Shinto, "The Way of the Gods." Shinto is generally regarded as Japan's native religion. However, the derivation of the term itself—from the Chinese *shin,* "god," and *tao,* "way"—suggests Shinto's close ties to China's Taoism.

In early times, Shintoism saw all objects and phenomena as possessed by good or evil spirits to be pleased or propitiated. When Buddhism was first introduced to Japan from Korea in A.D. 522, Shinto zealots felt the "national gods" were being threatened. The new religion was ousted, but the eventual incursion could not be stopped. Buddhism came to live with Shintoism in relative harmony. For most Westerners, the idea of adhering to two religions at once is alien. Indeed, Western visitors to Japan are often puzzled to find that many of the great Buddhist temples in Japan have small, unassuming Shinto shrines clustered about them. But just as it was in India and China, Buddhism in Japan was able to adapt itself to local circumstances.

The study of Buddhism became the focus of the intellectual aristocracy during the Heian Age, and the influences of the religion are apparent throughout the poetry and prose of the period. Combined with Shintoism, Buddhism helped to form the Japanese aesthetic, emphasizing concepts such as temporality, simplicity, and suggestion. These concepts, which focus on the imagination and the acceptance of change, are evident in the tanka of the *Kokinshū,* Sei Shōnagon's *Pillow Book,* and Lady Murasaki Shikibu's novel, *The Tale of Genji.* Shintoism then combined with the Buddhist sect of Zen to form the philosophical force behind the Noh dramas of the fourteenth and fifteenth centuries, the Zen parables of the fifteenth century, and the haiku of the seventeenth century.

CONFUCIANISM AND THE JAPANESE WARRIOR CODE

An interesting and uniquely Japanese philosophy developed from the melding of Shinto with Confucian thought in the seventeenth century. Shinto ideas were joined to the Confucian doctrine of ethical social action to define what came to be known as *bushidō,* "the way of the warrior." *Bushidō* prescribed a way of life for the samurai, the warrior in feudal service to his lord. It called for the samurai to serve his lord with unwavering loyalty and with selfless devotion to moral principle. *Bushidō* provided for the well-known act of harakiri, or ritualistic suicide, when the warrior had failed in his feudal duty or had lost in battle.

JAPAN TRANSFORMED

Japan's move from a warring state filled with battling clans to a unified country was roughly concurrent with the introduction of influences from China and Korea. Japan ultimately used these influences to form its own distinct literary history. The new centralized government included a court that placed great value on cultural enrichment and literary expression, rewarding poetic accomplishment and sponsoring the development of the Noh drama. Writers such as Sei Shōnagon vividly captured the life within the imperial court,

while later poets such as Issa and Bashō composed haiku that reflected the experience of everyday people. The poetry and prose of Japan reflect the social and political history of the country. The selections in this unit provide readers with observations, descriptions, and experiences that dissolve the boundaries of foreign cultures and distant centuries.

UNIT PROJECTS

1. **Writing a Love Song.** Write a love song based on one of the tanka you have read. You may incorporate the actual lines from a tanka into the song or base the lyrics on your personal associations to particular images in the tanka. Compose music to accompany the lyrics and then perform your song in class.

2. **Making a Collage out of Poetic Images.** Research the seasonal references used in Japanese tanka and haiku, finding out what each season is like in Japan. Then make a collage of each of the four seasons, using photographs, drawings, and found objects that represent each season. When you have finished your collage, share it with your classmates.

3. **Researching a Poet/Artist.** Research the paintings of Taniguchi (Yosa) Buson, who is recognized as one of the greatest painters of his time (see illustration, page 613), in addition to being one of Japan's finest haiku poets. As you study Buson's paintings, compare the similarity between the visual imagery of the paintings and the imagery in his haiku. Bring photocopies or art books from the library showing what you have researched to share with the class.

4. **Investigating the Lives of Women in Medieval Japan.** Sei Shōnagon and Lady Murasaki Shikibu provide modern readers with valuable information about the lives of women of the court in Japan's Heian era. Using the library, research the lifestyles of women in medieval Japan, both aristocrats and ordinary people. Decide which kind of lifestyle you would prefer to lead if you were a Japanese woman at that time, and include your preference in your presentation.

5. **Researching the Music of Japan.** Listen to records, tapes, or compact discs and put together a sampling of classical and/or contemporary Japanese music to share with your classmates. When listening to the music, make a list of the differences between Eastern and Western music.

6. **Writing a Fictional Journal.** Write a series of journal entries based on Tetsugen's journey as he traveled through Japan collecting contributions for the publication of the Zen sutras. Use information from the Zen Parable "Publishing the Sutras" to make the journal

entries seem real and believable. To describe Tetsugen's travels and observations with concrete detail, you might also want to look at photographs of the Japanese mountains, villages, and countryside.

7. **Writing a Noh Skit.** With a few classmates, write and perform a skit in the Noh tradition. You can base your skit on an important personal, historical, or literary event. Like Seami Motokiyo, create characters that are flat and symbolic. You can also use a chorus that expresses the characters' thoughts and observations. Costumes can be based on current clothing

trends or the stylized costumes that are used in Seami's plays. As in Noh drama, you can also emphasize the tone of your skit by incorporating music into the action and dialogue. When your skit is ready, perform it for your class.

8. **Creating a Noh Mask.** Create a mask for Seami Motokiyo's character Atsumori. To begin, think of how you want to depict Atsumori in the Noh style. You may want to start by sketching the expression you want to show on the mask. Then, using heavy paper or papier-mâché, form the mask and paint it. When you have finished, display your mask in class.

TANKA POEMS

Translated by Geoffrey Bownas and Anthony Thwaite ▼ (Textbook page 569)

SUMMARY

Written between the seventh and twelfth centuries, the five poems shown here reflect the traditional tanka themes of love, nostalgia, and impermanence. Tanka belongs to a type of verse called *waka*, that is, any Japanese poem consisting of alternating five- and seven-syllable lines. Each tanka includes the characteristic seasonal reference while juxtaposing emotional images with images from nature. By placing concrete imagery next to abstract imagery, tanka requires readers to associate their own experiences and feelings with the content of the poems. In this way, each tanka will have a different meaning for every reader.

MORE ABOUT THE AUTHORS

PRINCESS NUKADA

Very little is known about Princess Nukada, the earliest of the five poets represented in this section. She lived during the seventh century and is noted as one of its most accomplished poets, as well as the favorite of the court in which she lived. All we know of her character, however, is what her passionate verse reveals.

OSHIKOCHI MITSUNE

One of the outstanding poets of the Heian period, Oshikochi was active during the ninth century. Although he held only minor posts in the government, tales told about him paint the portrait of an imperial favorite at court. He is known to have excelled in poetic competitions of the day and is particularly noteworthy for composing poems for screens. In addition, he was an editor of the *Kokinshū* (see below), in which some two hundred of his poems have been preserved.

KI TSURAYUKI

A close friend of Oshikochi, Ki Tsurayuki was the main compiler of the *Kokinshū*, the famous poetic anthology commissioned by the emperor. The volume was comprised of twenty chapters and a preface written by Tsurayuki that became the first piece of criticism actually written in the newly adapted Japanese alphabet. He later went on to produce another anthology of poetry selected from the best of the *Kokinshū* and the prose work *Tosa nikki,* a famous journal which describes his own journey to the capital. Because he preferred to write in Japanese, the diary was produced under the pen name of a woman. Tsurayuki achieved popularity as a poet and a high rank at court during his lifetime.

ONO KOMACHI

With seventeen of her poems printed in the *Kokinshū*—the only ones written by a woman—Ono Komachi is described by Tsurayuki as one of its six geniuses. Little is known about her life except that she was as famous for her impressive physical beauty as for her poetry during her earlier years. Legend details her rejection of marriage in hopes of becoming the consort of the emperor and her subsequent fall into poverty and loneliness.

SAIGYO

In contrast to the other poets represented here, Saigyo as a poet did not flourish at court. Instead he left the emperor's service during his twenties to become a Buddhist priest. Best described as a traveling poet, Saigyo wandered about the Japanese countryside composing poetry deeply committed to nature. In his later years, he circulated among the literary at the capital and finally settled in Ise where he taught poetry and conducted contests in its composition.

A CRITICAL COMMENT

"Love poetry was in fact virtually the only kind of poetry written in Japanese during the ninth century, the dark age of waka, when courtiers who usually expressed their thoughts in Chinese verse wrote waka mainly for presentation to women, who normally did not learn Chinese. Love poetry came to occupy an extremely prominent place in Japanese literature, second only to poetry describing the seasons. In this respect Japanese poetry differs from Chinese poetry, in which few works by the major poets were devoted to love. Poems on friendship, so common in Chinese literature, are virtually nonexistent in Japan, but poems on love were so central an element in the Japanese tradition that even persons for whom the composition of love poetry was inappropriate often wrote poems on topics like parting the morning after a meeting. Writing this kind of poetry demonstrated that a given priest or an aged courtier, whatever the realities of his life, was not insensitive to the most moving of human experiences. . . . "
—*from* The Pleasures of Japanese Literature, *Donald Keene*

FOR FURTHER READING

Bownas, Geoffrey, and Anthony Thwaite, trans. *The Penguin Book of Japanese Verse*. New York: Penguin, 1964.

Keene, Donald. *The Pleasures of Japanese Literature*. New York: Columbia University Press, 1988.

Miner, Earl. *The Japanese Tradition in British and American Literature*. Princeton, NJ: Princeton University Press, 1966.

Miner, Earl, Robert E. Morrell, and Hiroko Odagiri. *The Princeton Companion to Classical Japanese Literature*. Princeton, NJ: Princeton University Press, 1985.

HAIKU

Translated by Harold G. Henderson, Peter Beilenson, and Harry Behn ▾ (Textbook page 576)

SUMMARY

The six haiku included here were written by four of the great Japanese haiku poets. The poems reflect the essential haiku themes of change and permanence, and they include references to seasons, a mandatory ingredient in all haiku. The three-line, seventeen-syllable haiku offer readers an image, or moment of truth, and then demand that readers complete the poems by associating their own experiences and emotions with the images.

MORE ABOUT THE AUTHORS

MATSUO BASHŌ

Suggesting that he was like a bat, Bashō contended that he was somewhere between priest and layman, or bird and rat. Although Bashō was a member of the samurai class, he renounced his privileges in favor of a wandering life. On his travels through Japan, Bashō taught the rich and poor, the farmers and the samurai. He was greatly loved and admired during his lifetime and wherever he wandered on his journeys, people welcomed him and asked for his poetic guidance. Many of his greatest haiku were written during his travels.

Bashō's school of poetry, *Shofu,* placed emphasis on the concepts of change, permanence, and *sabi,* an intense feeling of quiet or desolate yet beautiful loneliness. The concepts of change and permanence greatly distinguish Bashō from other poets of his time, who measured the success of a poem by its references to the poetry of earlier periods; Bashō believed that poems should change frequently to ensure freshness.

UEJIMA ONITSURA

Onitsura followed the example of Bashō in abandoning samurai service for poetry and life among the common folk. In addition to his critical verse, he is known for his critical study of the *haikai*—a verse form that evolved from the tanka and from which the haiku form developed. Many haiku scholars regard Onitsura as one of the most interesting and individual of the haiku poets; his work is at once exuberant and profoundly philosophical.

TANIGUCHI BUSON

Along with Bashō and Issa, Buson is one of the traditional "triumvirate" of haiku masters. Also known as Yosa Buson, he was both a poet and a painter. His verse, which is marked by vivid visual imagery, has an affinity with some of the great Chinese poets. Buson's verse records a variety of responses to similar situations and phenomena, which makes the reader aware of a highly complex personality. Taken together, his scores of poems on rain, for example, make for a vision of variegated colors.

KOBAYASHI ISSA

Perhaps because of periods of impoverishment in his own life, Issa always aligned himself with the poor and neglected. Where the more deeply philosophical Bashō is probably the most highly regarded of all Japanese poets, Issa is the most widely loved. Not only is he recognized as the

A CRITICAL COMMENT

"The central vision of a Dante or a Dostoevsky posits the existence of some point of anchorage in the endless, shifting sea of life, some stable point of reference to which life's vagaries can be related. The very lack of this in Pushkin accounts for a great deal. Pushkin's was a pragmatic mind, concerned primarily with the immediacy of life on earth. At the same time Pushkin became and remained intensely aware of Death, to which, indeed, he at times seemed irresistibly drawn. It is Pushkin's feeling for Death that provides a key to many of his feelings for the experiences of life. Lacking a "central vision"—specifically a Christian central vision—he could not feel Death as a prelude to some continued existence or life hereafter; for him Death simply rang down the curtain on the final act of life here below. And this almost pagan view of Death's inevitability and finality imbues with added poignancy what he wrote about our earthly existence—which is indeed his sole concern. Life's unrelenting ebb, the irretrievable passage of time, the unpredictability of Fate—the vulnerability of man's destiny, a metaphysical despair—these are some of the preoccupations and moods which go hand in hand with and accentuate the more dynamic sides of Pushkin's passionate nature: his zest for life, his wit and humor, his pursuit of love, his intense feeling for beauty in many forms. There is in much of Pushkin's work an exuberant, uncomplicated, almost sunlight quality. But his view of the world is, in the final analysis, somewhat bleak and tragic."

—*from* Alexander Pushkin, *Walter N. Vickery*

champion of the common folk, but his use of colloquial speech has made him seem truly one with ordinary people. Many critics, however, find his work uneven and claim that many of his seventeen-syllable poems cannot be called true haiku.

A CRITICAL COMMENT

The following excerpt is taken from Matsuo Bashō's *The Rustic Gate*. It expresses the poet's parting words to one of his favorite students, Morikawa Kyoroku. Within these words, Bashō reveals his thoughts on the purpose and value of poetry.

"It was just in the autumn of last year that, quite by chance, I met him and already I am lamenting deeply our separation. One day, when the time of parting approached, he knocked at the door of my thatched hut, and we spent the whole day in quiet conversation.

"Talented as he is, he loves both painting and *haikai* poetry. I asked him once as a test why he liked painting, and he said it was because of poetry. 'And why do you love poetry?' 'Because of painting.' Two things he studied for one purpose. Indeed, since it is said that it is shameful for a gentleman to have many accomplishments, it is admirable that he makes one use of the two arts.

"In painting he was my teacher; in poetry I taught him and he was my disciple. My teacher's paintings are imbued with such profundity of spirit and executed with such a marvelous dexterity that I could never approach their mysterious depths.

"I said to him as we parted, 'My poetry is like a stove in the summer or a fan in winter. It runs

against the popular tastes and has no practical use. But there is much that is affecting even in the poems of Toshinari and Saigyo that were lightly tossed off. Did not the retired Emperor Go Toba say of their poetry that it contained truth tinged with sorrow? Take strength from his words and follow unswervingly the narrow thread of the Way of Poetry. Do not seek to follow in the footsteps of the men of old; seek what they sought. That is what Kūkai wrote, and it is true of *haikai* poetry as well.' Saying these words I lifted my lantern and showed him outside the rustic gate, where we parted."
—*from* The Rustic Gate, *Matsuo Bashō*

FOR FURTHER READING

Bownas, Geoffrey, and Anthony Thwaite, trans. *The Penguin Book of Japanese Verse.* New York: Penguin, 1964.

Beilensen, Peter, and Harry Behn, trans. *Haiku Harvest.* Mount Vernon, NY: Peter Pauper Press, 1962.

Keene, Donald. *Japanese Literature: An Introduction for Western Readers.* New York: Grove Press, 1955.

Henderson, Harold. *An Introduction to Haiku.* New York: Doubleday, 1958.

Sato, Hiroaki, and Burton Watson, trans. *From the Country of Eight Islands: An Anthology of Japanese Poetry.* New York: Morningside-Columbia University Press, 1986.

---

from THE PILLOW BOOK

Sei Shōnagon ▾ Translated by Ivan Morris ▾ (Textbook page 581)

SUMMARY

"In Spring It Is the Dawn," the first entry in *The Pillow Book*, is a brief account of the author's favorite time of day for each of the four seasons, and the natural occurrences that endear each to her.

"Hateful Things" devotes a paragraph to each of four situations the author finds distasteful, such as a chatty visitor who overstays his/her welcome.

"Things That Cannot Be Compared" highlights occurrences that are opposite in nature and also discusses the subtle distinctions between relative events, such as youth and age.

"Embarrassing Things" includes descriptions such as one's love getting drunk and becoming a bore, and an ignoramus talking knowingly to a learned person. Shōnagon's attitude toward the lower classes is particularly notable here.

"Masahiro Really Is a Laughing-Stock" details

several accounts of a fool of the court displaying his folly with misspoken idioms and deeds that provide entertainment for the rest of the court.

And finishing the set, "Pleasing Things" lists mundane occurrences which bring Shōnagon pleasure. Most are intellectual in nature, and many have to do with writing.

MORE ABOUT THE AUTHOR

Compared to the wealth of information that Sei Shōnagon left us, exceedingly little biographical data is available for her. *Sei* refers to her family name (Kiyowara), while *Shōnagon* is a court title meaning "Minor Counselor." Recent study suggests, however, that her real name may have been Nagiko. It is speculated that she was born into an upper-class and cultured family (both her father and her great-grandfather were poets), and that she received a respectable education in Chinese and

Japanese literature. It appears also that she may have married once, perhaps twice, and possibly bore a son and later a daughter. After approximately ten years of service, she left court following the fall of her empress, and there are stories both that she died in obscure poverty and that she joined a convent.

In addition to her prose work, Shōnagon is also well regarded for her poetry. There are some thirty poems in *The Pillow Book* itself, and others by her may be found in several anthologies of the day. There is no doubt, however, that Shōnagon's genius comes to us in the form of this diary, which is respected as the precursor to the *Zuihitsu* ("random" or "miscellaneous notes") form, for which classical Japanese literature is famous.

A Critical Comment

"Part diary, part essay, part miscellany, *The Pillow Book* of Sei Shōnagon, written in the early eleventh century, is as difficult to characterize as its witty and perceptive author. . . . Neither the life of the author nor the date of her work can be precisely ascertained, yet there is nothing whatsoever vague about her clever, clear-minded, and always eloquent account of her life at the court of Heian Japan.

"Because of her panache, Sei Shōnagon became the subject of a number of legends and observations, one of which was that her wit made up for her lack of beauty, another that her quick mind cut through any foolishness and pretense on the part of others. Indeed, later reputation considered her the very epitome of the cultivated, amusing, and brilliant woman who was more than a match in wit for any man. . . .

"If *The Pillow Book (Makura no soshi)* cannot now be classified or domesticated into a particular and comfortable literary genre, its combination of

observation and reflection nevertheless served as a model, directly or indirectly, for many later works that are themselves among the greatest of the Japanese traditional classics. . . . In the visual arts, Sei Shōnagon came to play a role as well. *The Pillow Book Scroll,* created in the fourteenth century, put many of Shōnagon's incidents into visual form, where they came to gain a new and expanded currency.

"The reader who begins *The Pillow Book* from the first entry in Ivan Morris's complete translation will notice what appears to be a haphazard arrangement of the various topics on which Shōnagon has chosen to comment. Memories of court ceremonies jostle with lists of things enjoyed or despised; introspective responses to the beauties of the seasons rub up against information on details of court life so accurately recorded that modern cultural historians continue to pore over them for clues on the life of the period. In that sense, indeed, *The Pillow Book* serves as a sourcebook as well as a work of what we might loosely term literature. So sure is Shōnagon's instinct, and so skillful her ability to make choices, that the smallest objective detail she records takes on an energy that can attract and hold the attention of any modern reader."

—*from* A Reader's Guide to Japanese Literature, *J. Thomas Rimer*

For Further Reading

Keene, Donald, ed. *Anthology of Japanese Literature.* New York: Grove Press, 1955.

Rimer, J. Thomas. *A Reader's Guide to Japanese Literature.* Tokyo: Kodansha International, 1988.

Sei Shōnagon. *The Pillow Book of Sei* Shōnagon. Ed. and trans. Ivan Morris. New York: Columbia University Press, 1967.

ZEN PARABLES

Translated by Paul Reps ▼ (Textbook page 591)

Summary

Muddy Road

A monk helps a girl by carrying her across a muddy road. Later his traveling companion says he should not have helped the girl because monks are not supposed to touch females. The monks says he left the girl behind, and asks if his companion is still carrying her.

A Parable

Running from a tiger, a man grabs a vine and swings himself over a precipice. As he hangs from the vine, one tiger stands above him, another tiger waits

below him, and two mice begin to chew the vine. Seeing a strawberry, he picks it, and it tastes wonderfully sweet.

Publishing the Sutras

After Tetsugen decides to publish the Buddhist sutras in Japanese, he spends twenty years collecting money to finance his undertaking. The first two times he has enough money, famine and epidemic threaten the lives of the people and he gives the money away to help the suffering. The third time he collects donations, he is finally able to publish the sutras. However, the first two sets of "invisible" sutras are considered even more valuable than the third one.

The Thief Who Became a Disciple

A thief enters Shichiri Kojun's home while the latter is reciting the sutras. Shichiri directs the thief to his money and asks the thief to leave enough money for Shichiri to pay his taxes. He then tells the thief to thank him for the gift. Later, when Shichiri is asked to testify against the thief in court, he explains that the man is not a thief because Shichiri offered him the money, and the man thanked him for it. After his prison sentence, the thief goes to Shichiri and becomes his disciple.

The Taste of Banzo's Sword

Matajuro Yagyu requests an apprenticeship with the great swordsman Banzo. The more impatience Matajuro reveals, the longer Banzo tells him his studies will take. When Matajuro recognizes why Banzo rejects his impatience, he begins his apprenticeship, cooking, cleaning, and gardening for the master. After Matajuro's three years of servitude, Banzo finally sneaks up and hits Matajuro with a wooden sword. From that moment on, Matajuro must constantly defend himself from Banzo's sword. Matajuro learns his skills so rapidly that he becomes the finest swordsman in the country.

More About Zen

The Zen parables reflect the values emphasized in Zen training and life. Zen parables are both humorous and serious in tone. Because laughter can accompany Zen enlightenment, humor is an important component of Zen teachings. The Zen scholar R.H. Blyth describes the positive effect of humor in Zen teachings by saying that laughter knocks down "the intellectual barrier; at the moment of laughing something is understood. . . . Laughter is . . . an infinite and timeless expansion of one's nevertheless inalienable being."

Zen teachers use *koans,* or conundrums, and entertaining parables to instruct students. The purpose of the parables and conundrums is to invite a sudden state of awareness that cannot be acquired through philosophizing. In *The Spirit of Zen,* scholar Alan W. Watts explains: ". . . to chase after Zen is like chasing one's own shadow, and all the time one is running away from the sun." With the vanishing of the shadow, enlightenment, or awareness, occurs.

Zen parables attempt to lead readers to a moment when the shadows vanish. Traditionally, the parables are intended to be contemplated, not discussed. They offer readers an essence of Zen without preaching its virtues. Through the serious and comic circumstances presented in these parables, students can begin to understand Zen values as well as the suggestive method of Zen instruction.

A Critical Comment

"The Zen habit of self-searching through meditation to realize one's true nature, with disregard of formalism, with insistence on self-discipline and simplicity of living, ultimately won the support of the nobility and ruling classes in Japan and the profound respect of all levels of philosophical thought in the Orient.

" . . . Zen spirit has come to mean not only peace and understanding, but devotion to art and to work, the rich enfoldment of contentment, opening the door to insight, the expression of innate beauty, the intangible charm of incompleteness. Zen carries many meanings, none of them entirely definable. If they are defined, they are not Zen.

"It has been said that if you have Zen in your life, you have no fear, no doubt, no unnecessary craving, no extreme emotion. Neither illiberal attitudes nor egotistical actions trouble you. You serve humanity humbly, fulfilling your presence in this world with loving-kindness and observing your passing as a petal falling from a flower. Serene, you enjoy life in blissful tranquility. Such is the sprit of Zen, whose vesture is thousands of temples in China and Japan, priests and monks, wealth and prestige, and often the very formalism it would itself transcend.

"To study Zen, the flowering of one's nature, is no easy task in any age or civilization. Many teachers, true and false, have purposed to assist others in this accomplishment. It is from innumerable and actual adventures in Zen that these stories have evolved."

—from Zen Flesh, Zen Bones: A Collection of Zen and Pre-Zen Writings, *Paul Reps*

For Further Reading

Blyth, R.H. *Zen in English Literature and Oriental Classics.* New York: E. P. Dutton, 1960.

Reps, Paul, ed. *Zen Flesh, Zen Bones: A Collection of Zen and Pre-Zen Writings.* Garden City, NY: Anchor- Doubleday, 1961.

Stryk, Lucien, and Takashi Ikemoto, eds. and trans. *Zen: Poems, Prayers, Sermons, Anecdotes, Interviews.* Garden City, NY: Doubleday, 1965.

Watts, Alan W. *The Way of Zen.* New York: Random House, 1965.

ATSUMORI

Seami Motokiyo ▾ Translated by Arthur Waley ▾ (Textbook page 600)

SUMMARY

Atsumori tells the story of the priest Rensei, a former warrior, who travels to Ichi no tani to pray for the soul of Atsumori, a young man whom he killed in battle many years earlier. When Rensei arrives at Ichi no tani, he hears two Reapers playing the flute. The Reapers tell the story of their journey and their sorrow, and Rensei speaks to them about the music they play. One of the Reapers asks Rensei to pray the Ten Prayers for him. Rensei says he will pray if the Reaper identifies himself. When the Reaper says he is a member of the clan of Atsumori, Rensei expresses his happiness to meet a member of Atsumori's family, and he begins to pray for the Reaper.

As Rensei prays, the Chorus expresses the gratitude of Atsumori, and the ghost of the young warrior appears and greets the priest. The story of Atsumori's death is then told through the voices of the Chorus and Atsumori. Using images from nature, the young warrior describes the travels of his clan, their stay on the shore of Suma, and his father's decision to fight the Taira clan. Rensei remembers the sound of the flute the night before the battle, and Atsumori tells him it was the music from his own bamboo flute that the priest heard.

The Chorus and Atsumori describe the departure of Atsumori's clan and his abandonment on the shoreline. The Chorus describes Rensei's pursuit of the young warrior and Atsumori's brave fight among the waves and surf. As the Chorus tells of Atsumori's death, the young warrior's ghost rises and moves toward Rensei to kill him. Rensei continues to pray to Buddha for Atsumori's salvation, and Atsumori's ghost recognizes that through his prayers the priest has shown that he is no longer his enemy. The play ends with the Chorus expressing Atsumori's desire for Rensei to pray for him again.

MORE ABOUT THE AUTHOR

We know surprisingly little about the life of the artist who is credited with elevating Noh drama to the fine and demanding art that it became. Seami (a name he took on later in priesthood and often spelled Zeami) Motokiyo (1363–1443) was the son of one of the great Noh actors of his own time, Kanami. A part-time critic who wrote three treatises helping to define the still-nebulous dramatic form called Noh, Kanami was also a teacher and ran a school for actors. From the early age of seven or eight, Seami studied under his father's tutelage. When the boy was near the age of ten, his father won the patronage of the shogun Ashikaga Yoshimitsu, and both father and son were rewarded with an invitation to live at the court.

When Seami reached his early twenties, his father died, but Seami had trained hard and was ready to take on the stage himself. He strove for perfection in his art, bringing in older forms of music and dancing to complete the drama. Seami reached his height as an actor in the year 1408, at the age of forty-five, when his benefactor Yoshimitsu died. Ignored by the new shogun but undeterred, Seami went on to write several critical works and one hundred and fifty plays. His treatises on the quality and form of Noh drama are considered particularly essential to the development of Noh theories.

Approaching sixty, Seami handed his work in the theater over to his son and entered the priesthood. Shortly after this, his family's standing took an unfortunate turn, and Seami, although an old man, was supposedly exiled. He was apparently allowed to return to the capital where he died in about 1443.

A CRITICAL COMMENT

"Noh creates a dramatic atmosphere of unresolved tension, or unresolved longings, or irresolution in the dramatic sense—and then this dramatic situation is resolved by a kind of aesthetic realization which evolves from the dramatic situation as its own archetype. This resolution takes the form of a dance, which can best be compared to a crystal of sugar dropping into a supersaturated solution. All the sugar that is held in solution will crystallize around the introduced crystal and form rock sugar until the solution is no longer saturated.

"What eventuates is not a sense of resolved climax, but a sense of realized significance. This is a different thing—not the Aristotelian pattern of tragic drama as we have known it in the West. . . . You are dealing with human experience reduced to pure archetypes, the sort of thing that people called deities and demigods and heroes. . . .

"This is what makes major writing major—the ability to project human experience against a heroic background, to pour human thought and motivation and life into figures which exemplify the universal tragic situation of all [people] everywhere. . . . All works of great art have this in common—the ability to realize human experience in its most archetypical and ideal forms."

—*from* Bird in the Bush, *Kenneth Rexroth*

FOR FURTHER READING

De Barry, William Theodore, Donald Keene, and Tsunoda Ryusaku, comps. *Sources of Japanese Tradition.* New York: Columbia University Press, 1964.

Keene, Donald, ed. *Twenty Plays of the Nō Theatre.*
New York: Columbia University Press, 1970.
Keene, Donald. *Nō, the Classical Theatre of Japan.*
Tokyo: Kodansha International, 1966.
Waley, Arthur. *The Nō Plays of Japan.* New York:
Grove Press, 1950.

NOTES

UNIT 7: PERSIAN AND ARABIC LITERATURES (Textbook page 619)

Unit Introduction: Persian and Arabic Literatures

Until the rise of Islam, Persian and Arabic cultures had little interaction. With the founding of the Islamic religion in A.D. 651, the Arab culture dominated the region. Most Persians converted to Islam, but they also retained a large measure of cultural autonomy. This fusion of the Arabic and the Persian cultures produced the mystical poetic and prose writings of Sufism and a Persian national epic, the **Shahname.**

BACKGROUND

GEOGRAPHICAL AND HISTORICAL PERSPECTIVES

Persian and Arabic literatures represent two cultural heritages that differ in many ways. However, these literatures are often grouped together because of the geographical and historical links between them. The ancient Persian homeland included the mountains and plains north and east of the body of water known today as the Persian Gulf, while the ancient Arabs occupied the desert peninsula just southwest of the Gulf. The two groups were traditionally neither allies nor enemies. The early Persians' main foes were the Babylonians and Greeks to the west and, later, the Turks to the north, while the early Arabs' chief conflicts were mostly inter tribal. Not until the emergence of Islam did the Persian and Arab peoples enter into a union, and even after Persia was subsumed by the Islamic empire, the two cultures retained significant differences. The contact between the two groups, however, was ultimately to provide far-reaching benefits, not only for the Persian and Arabic cultures, but for the rest of the world as well.

THE EARLY PERSIANS

During the reigns of Cyrus, Darius, and their successors (from around 500 B.C.), people of the Persian Empire enjoyed the benefits of a prosperous and long-established city culture. The official religion was Zoroastrianism, founded by Zoroaster (Zarathustra) in the seventh century B.C. This religion held that an evil god and a good god were engaged in an enduring battle. Ultimately, the good god, Ahura Mazda, would triumph, but the evil god, Ahriman, also had power in the universe and must not be ignored or discounted.

In accordance with certain precepts of Zoroastrianism, Persian society was grouped into four castes. The king's officers and other government leaders came from the highest caste, that of the Zoroastrian priests or Magi (singular form: Magus). The Magian governmental system was hierarchical and elitist. Its hierarchies were illustriously efficient; in later years, after the coming of Islam, the Magian system was adopted with great success by the Abbasid Caliphate in Baghdad and, later, by the Samanid Dynasty of Iran. The Persian culture was well enough established that Persian literature and other arts retained their integrity and continued to develop even after the empire fell to Alexander the Great in 331 B.C.

The ancient Persians were enriched by the cultures of the many groups with whom they interacted. The arts, philosophies, music, crafts, and sciences of Mesopotamia, the Near East, Egypt, Greece, and India all offered advances that Persians readily accepted. For example, for their monuments and inscriptions, Persian artisans customarily used the "classical" cuneiform script of the ancient Sumerians. To facilitate commerce within their huge empire, Persian scribes recorded many documents on Egyptian papyrus, using the widely understood Aramaic language of the ancient Hebrews. The Magi valued literature and ensured that major cities had libraries, collecting not only Persian writings but also the writings of neighboring cultures.

At the same time, distinctly Persian cultural elements also figured prominently in people's daily lives. For example, standard dress for men of the empire included trousers, a Persian invention; and the two major holidays were the Zoroastrian festivals celebrating the coming of spring and fall.

The empire's literature, as well, was uniquely Persian in form and themes. The earliest significant written literature of Persia was the *Avesta,* the Zoroastrian scriptures, dating from the sixth century B.C. These consisted of prose portions, which detailed religious rituals, and poetic portions or hymns, known as *gathas.* There was also a much older Persian oral tradition, which came to include maxims, animal fables, hero tales, histories, legends, and a minstrel poetry that was syllabic and accentual rather than rhymed and metrical. Some scholars have hypothesized a relationship between early Persian animal fables and similar fables in the *Panchatantra* of India.

EARLY ARABIAN CULTURES

As early as the tenth century B.C., prosperous agricultural and mercantile kingdoms flourished in the Arabian peninsula, near Yemen. But for reasons that are unclear, these kingdoms fell into decline. By the fourth century B.C., Arab society had become largely nomadic and tribal. Arabs lived in individual clans with no centralized power. Southern Arabs, in the area of modern Yemen, had a more settled lifestyle; northern Arabs wandered the deserts. Only a few major cities existed on the Arabian peninsula, and each was locally governed, independent of the others. Most Arabs lived nomadic lives outside the cities, loading their tents onto camels to follow their cattle herds, arranging alliances and settling disputes within the patriarchal organizations of their extended clans, much as modern Bedouins still do today.

The early nomads prized honor, cunning, daring, generosity, and eloquence. The Arab nomads were skilled equestrians and sword wielders, holding clan competitions and, especially in lean times, raiding other groups or robbing passing caravans. These caravans, which followed trade routes connecting China and sub-Saharan Africa, India and the Mediterranean, gave early nomads on the Arabian peninsula one thing in common with the early Persians: a fairly extensive knowledge of other cultures. Arabs were pantheistic, worshiping various local and familial gods. Shrines were tended by select families, the duties being passed down from parents to children. Prominent throughout Arabia was a belief in *jinn,* (also called genies), supernatural creatures who could assume any shape and work miracles.

Poets were highly regarded among the early Arabs for several reasons. Not only did they compose literature, but, like the griots of West Africa, they learned by heart much of the traditional oral literature and historical material of their clans. They were respected for their knowledge as well as for their eloquence. A clan's poets were traditionally ranked at one of four levels. At specified times, poets participated in marathon literary contests, composing and reciting verses, sometimes accompanied by flutes or tambourines. The highest-ranked poets might also occupy clan or tribal leadership positions or assume certain priestly duties.

Arabic literature before Islam was exclusively oral. Writing was known from early times—one funerary inscription commemorating a great leader dates from A.D. 328, and many clans left names or brief statements on stones and potsherds throughout the Arabian peninsula. Writing was also used for business transactions, it was not until the eighth century A.D. that poetry and literary prose began to be routinely recorded in writing. Arabic poetry was marked by complex and varied rhyme schemes and metrical forms. Two major poetic genres were the short lyric and the longer ode. An ode could be used as a praise poem, a poem of ridicule, a love poem, a metaphorical description, or an elegy. One famous collection of seven odes by various poets, dating from the century preceding Islam, is the *Ma'allaqat,* or *Golden Odes.* The elegies of al-Khansa (textbook page 631), bridging the pre-Islamic and Islamic periods, are also well known. Pre-Islamic prose forms included aphorisms, speeches, histories, legends, and adventure tales such as those later collected in writing in *The Thousand and One Nights* (page 640).

LITERATURE IN THE ISLAMIC EMPIRE

The birth of Islam galvanized both Arabic and Persian literature. The language of the Koran (textbook page 635), rhythmic and elaborate, set a new standard for Arabic prose. An extensive new genre, that of Koranic commentary, arose. Perhaps most significantly, the tradition of recording literature in writing took root.

In the seventh century, Islamic Arabs annexed Persia. Persian Zoroastrians gradually converted to Islam and adopted Arabic as the language of both commerce and literature. Yet the deep differences between Persians and Arabs were reflected in the fact that, over the years, most Arabs belonged to the Sunni, or traditionalist, sect, whereas most Persians embraced Shiite, or Shi'a, Islam, a rival faction. In addition, as the centuries passed, Persian Muslims developed the mystical branch of Islam called Sufism, in which some scholars see remnants of Zoroastrian beliefs.

These religious developments had significant effects on Persian literature, for the influences of the Arabic language and Islamic thought were considerable, and many later Persian writings, such as the works of Hafiz, Rumi (textbook page 663), and Saadi (page 667), emerged from Sufi teachings. Some critics also find strong Sufi influences in the *Rubáiyát* of Omar Khayyám (page 656).

Political events within the new empire also affected the development of literature. When Mohammed died in 632, he left no heir and no provisions for continued leadership of the Islamic movement. A committee of Islamic leaders at Medina, seeking to preserve the movement, decided to appoint the head of one of the larger Arab clans as Mohammed's caliph (successor), so that leadership could be passed down along predictable family lines, reducing the chance of power struggles. The leader of the chosen clan moved the caliphate from Medina to Damascus, sparking a profound cultural change as his tribe and other followers, former nomads, settled into city life. Damascus had earlier been a center of Greek and Roman culture, and the literary traditions of the ancient Greeks and Romans brought invigorating new influences to bear on Arabic literature. However, disagreement arose among Muslims over whether the chosen clan really deserved the caliphate. This disagreement precipitated the schism between Shiite and Sunni Muslims and, a century later, led to the establishment of the Abbasid Caliphate.

THE ABBASID CALIPHATE

The movement to install Abbas, a distant relative of Mohammed, as caliph was fueled by a revolt in Khorasan, a northeastern province of Persia which was traditionally a seat of Persian nationalism. In 750, Abbas's Persian supporters killed many leaders of the Damascus-based ruling caliphate, which was seen as oppressive and had grown unpopular in Iran. Abbas then seized power and moved the caliphate to Baghdad. In gratitude for the Persians' aid, he gave high offices to many Persians, who gradually reinstated the old Magian cultural traditions and systems of government. This merging of the Arab and Persian cultures produced a flowering of literature and other arts. One far-reaching result was the appearance of literary translations of Persian works into Arabic. These translations brought Persian influences—ranging from animal fables to stylized etiquette handbooks—into Arabic literature. The translations into Arabic also ensured the survival of the Persian literary tradition, for the Arabic language was to remain dominant, eclipsing Persian, for several centuries. One of the most important Persian works translated into Arabic was the collection of legends and historical tales on which Ferdowsi, in the tenth century, drew for his epic *Shahname* (page 649).

In 751, just as Abbas was coming to power, the Chinese attacked the northeastern Islamic outpost of Samarkand. The Chinese attack and their subsequent defeat brought yet another significant change to Persian and Arabic literatures when Chinese captives introduced the art of paper-making to the Islamic Empire. As paper replaced the more cumbersome papyrus and vellum that had previously been used for books, written literature became more widespread and readily available throughout the empire.

Meanwhile, the surviving members of the Damascus caliphate, which had conquered Spain in 711, had fled to Cordoba. There, in 929, their descendants established a new caliphate whose cultural achievements rivaled those of the Abbasids. The Cordoba caliphate brought an infusion of scientific and cultural developments to medieval Europe, and in turn was enriched by European literary influences (notably the songs of the troubadours), giving rise to outstanding lyric poets, including the Moorish authors Ibn Sara and Al-Thurthusi.

THE WANING OF THE EMPIRE

Over the years, Abbasid power eroded. By 874, a dynasty of local rulers, the Samanids, had established itself in Iran. Under the Samanids (875–999), national feeling ran high, and Iranian writers returned to the use of the Persian language for literature. As it turned out, the language had been greatly enriched by the influx of Arabic words and literary forms. Persian poetry was especially affected; the earlier Persian minstrel songs, employing assonance rather than rhyme or meter, had by the time of the Samanids been replaced by a number of poetic structures involving complex and varied meters and rhyme schemes. The Samanid princes fostered Persian arts and literature, commissioning writings and artworks, offering patronages to poets and artists, and showcasing their work. The epic *Shahname* of Ferdowsi (textbook page 649), is generally considered the stellar literary achievement of Samanid patronage.

After 1050, a series of major invasions weakened and ultimately destroyed the Islamic empire. The first invaders were the Seljuk Turks who, in 1055, descended from the north to take Baghdad and pressed on to the borders of Byzantium in the east. When the Byzantine emperor asked European kings for help against the Turks, his request triggered a European invasion of the Islamic empire: the Crusades. The armies of the Crusades first captured Jerusalem in 1099 and did not finally withdraw until 1192. In 1258, a third invasion, that of the Mongols under Genghis Khan and his clan, swept Persia. The Mongols converted to Islam and essentially ruled Persia until the fourteenth century. Thus the people of the Islamic Empire experienced several centuries marked by calamitous invasions, punctuated by periods of relative calm under foreign rule.

Yet, through all the years of invasion and political instability, Persian and Arabic literature continued to thrive. Arabic works included both erotic and satiric poetry, histories, prose commentaries on the Koran, and the *Hadith* genre of writings about the life and thought of Mohammed. Persian literature also evolved in a growing multitude of poetic and prose forms, including *rubáiyát,* or quatrains, such as those of Omar Khayyám (textbook page 656); *masnavi,* or longer lyrics, such as those of Rumi (textbook page 663); *ghazals,* or sonnet-like lyric odes, such as those of Hafiz and Saadi; and a new prose style of understated elegance best exemplified in works also composed by Saadi (textbook page 667).

CULTURAL CROSSROADS

In many ways, the ancient Persian and Arabic literary heritage benefited from, and contributed to, other cultures of both the East and the West. Because of the positions of Persia and Arabia as cultural crossroads, significant aspects of the thought and literature of many groups have been preserved and elaborated within the Persian and Arabic literary traditions. Still, both Persian and Arabic literatures retained their own integrity, forms, and themes. They serve as testaments to the vigor and enduring achievements of two unique peoples.

UNIT PROJECTS

1. **Collaborating on an Investigative Report.** Collaborate with classmates to research the many scientific and cultural benefits that Europeans gained from contact with the Persian and Arab cultures during the Moorish occupation of Spain and later during the Crusade. Present your findings in a panel discussion.

2. **Creating a Board Game.** Create a board game based on the adventures of Sindbad the sailor. You might begin by locating *The Thousand and One Nights* and reading more Sindbad tales. Then, perhaps working with classmates, design a game board that lets players compete to follow one of the hero's routes. Include the perils and the wonders that the hero encounters along the way, and come up with an appropriate goal for your game. Devise and write rules for your game, and teach classmates to play it.

3. **Creating and Presenting an Art Exhibit.** Create a group of illustrations, collages, or sculptures based on one or more of the poems in the unit. You might consult art books to get an idea of art forms dating from the time period(s) of the poem(s) you have chosen, and incorporate some aspects of those art forms in your work. Write a brochure to accompany your work, explaining what inspired your art and what you feel it expresses. Exhibit your artwork and post your brochure for classmates.

4. **Producing a News Report.** Plan and direct a television news program in which you and classmates "report" on events mentioned in the unit. These may be either historical events mentioned in the unit introduction and literary background information, or fictional events from one or more of the literary works. Research the events you have chosen, gathering details for your news broadcast. Write scripts for all newscasters, and present your news program.

5. **Writing and Directing a Dramatic Scene.** Script two or more episodes from works in this unit, turning the episodes into scenes that can be acted out. Decide on appropriate stage directions, props, costumes, dialogue, sound effects, and background music to accompany each scene. Direct classmates in acting out your scenes. Then discuss how dramatizing them changes their effects.

6. **Making a Model.** Design and build a model of an astrolabe or another scientific instrument developed by early Persians or Arabs. Or, explain and demonstrate a technique or concept that Europeans learned from contact with the Persian or Arabian culture, such as a precept of astronomy, mathematics, or medicine, or a technique used in the weaving of rugs or textiles or in the painting of miniatures. Present your work to the class, explaining the sources of your information.

7. **Creating a Diorama.** With classmates, create a diorama showing a scene from one of the works in the unit. Choose a work with specific descriptive information. Then research the culture and the time period of the scene you have chosen. Using specifics from the work and facts from your research, make your diorama as detailed and as accurate as possible. When you have finished it, display it to the class.

8. **Discussing Sufi Teaching Tales.** The Sufis use tales and anecdotes, both humorous and serious, to convey truths about life. These "teaching tales" are an important aspect of Sufi thought. At the library find books that contain Sufi teaching tales (a good place to start is with Idries Shah's books *Tales of the Dervishes, The Way of the Sufi*, and his various Mulla Nasrudin books). Choose one of these tales and read it aloud to the class. Then lead a discussion in which you and the other class members ponder the various levels of meaning in the tale. What truths about life does the story reveal?

9. **Producing a Video.** Create a video that relates to one of the briefer selections in the unit. You might, for example, make a video elegy similar to al-Khansa's elegiac poem, or you might make a video based on the ideas expressed in Rumi's "Unmarked Boxes." Choose and edit your shots and audio track carefully. Write a brief postscript to accompany your video, explaining why you chose the images, sounds, and sequences you did.

10. **Collaborating on a "Living Museum" Exhibit.** With a group of classmates, research the clothing styles, foods, furnishings, and/or types of music that were common during the time period covered by one or more of the works in the unit. Then collaborate to recreate an evening of "living history," showing a Persian or Arabian home from a past age. Prepare foods and create costumes,

furnishings, and possibly music that reflect the customs of the time. Either stage your exhibit in the classroom, or videotape it to show to your teacher and classmates.

ON HER BROTHER

al-Khansa ▼ Translated by Willis Barnstone ▼ (Textbook page 631)

SUMMARY

In this brief elegy, al-Khansa recalls with pride and sorrow her brother—a courageous soldier who died in battle at an early age.

MORE ABOUT THE AUTHOR

Al-Khansa's full name was Tumadir bint Amr. She was born about A.D. 575 and grew up in the tribal family of the Sharid, a branch of the Banu Sulaim. The Banu Sulaim lived in the desert near other tribes. As was the custom then, these tribes engaged in raiding and counterraiding for plunder.

Al-Khansa's family was well respected. Al-Khansa grew up with her full brother Mu'awiya and her half brother Sakhr. Both were excellent horsemen and raiders. However, Sakhr, the younger one, was a man of exceptional character who eventually became the head of the Banu Sulaim. When his brother was killed after a raid, Sakhr avenged his death. Later, Sakhr himself died after receiving a wound during a raid. Most of al-Khansa's poems are elegies for her brother Sakhr.

Al-Khansa was a cultured, independent, and dignified woman. She refused her first marriage proposal to an elderly man. Later, she married three times. Four of her sons died fighting for the cause of Islam, and the remaining son and daughter became poets. Al-khansa became blind in her old age and died around A.D. 644.

A CRITICAL COMMENT

"The hero of [al-Khansa's] poetry is Sakhr. She mourns him, praises him and adores him. She nurses his memory passionately and sheds copious tears on his loss. He is an obsession to her. Every season of the year, every portion of the day and the night, every aspect of life, every demonstration of generosity, courage, and nobility and every sight of distress reminds her of Sakhr and works up a storm of grief in her mind. Sakhr was her half brother while Mu'awiya was the full one, yet she has neither such intense love nor so great a regard for the latter as for the former. Moreover, she had even closer and more intimate relations than the two— her sons, daughters and husbands, but she laments none of them with such devotion, zeal and emotion as she laments Sakhr. In her latest *diwan* of about a thousand verses, over nine hundred are devoted exclusively to the lamentation of the commendable deeds and pleasing qualities of Sakhr. The most striking, and to some extent, puzzling side of al-Khansa's character is this one-sided abnormality of her love. It appears from her poetry as if she had none in the world except her brother Sakhr, for she bemoans the loss of none of her sons or daughters or husbands except that of Mirdas, her last and only meritorious husband, whom she immortalizes in a more laudatory than elegiac poem of eleven lines. Her father never becomes individually the subject of her elegy; Mu'awiya is usually lamented in combination with Sakhr, and in the few poems which exclusively refer to him the elegy is not so enthusiastic or earnest or glorious.

"Counting mainly on what she has said of Sakhr in her elegiac poetry, we may declare his personality to be the paramount cause of her extraordinary attachment to him. Two more contributory factors may have completed and sublimated this love. The first was a deep sense of obligation on her part to Sakhr, who had given her ungrudging support in all moments of need and distress in her life—a support without which she might have suffered heavily. We are told that, except for Mirdas, her husbands were a constant drain on her resources—wasteful, unaspiring and gambling people. For a number of times, she had approached Sakhr in her need and he had given half his wealth to her. . . .

"The second contributory factor may have been the filial love which he bore her and the implicit obedience which he extended to her. Evidence of this is available from al-Khansa's confession to the Mother of the Faithful, when the latter asked her about Sakhr's behavior towards her, that he was kind, considerate and respectful to her. These two factors alone could have been sufficient to install his love in that corner of her heart where the love of husbands (symbols of support) and that of sons (symbols of obedience and filial regard) reside, and the consciousness of which makes her cry out in agony: 'He was my chosen one from amongst all relatives and now that he is dead, I find no purpose in life.'"

—*from* History of Arabic Literature, *K. A. Fariq*

FOR FURTHER READING

Barnstone, Willis and Aliki Barnstone, eds. *A Book of Women Poets from Antiquity to Now*. New York: Schocken, 1980.

Beeston, A. F. L., T. M Johnstone, R. B. Serjeant, and G. R. Smith, eds. *Arabic Literature to the End of the Umayyad Period*. Cambridge: Cambridge University Press, 1983.

Fariq, K. A. *History of Arabic Literature*. Delhi: Vikas, 1972.

Nicholson, Reynold A. *A Literary History of the Arabs*. Cambridge: Cambridge University Press, 1966.

from the KORAN

Translated by N. J. Dawood ▾ Textbook page 634

SUMMARY

The four surahs, or chapters, are from the Koran, the book of the Muslim God Allah. All but one of the surahs begins with the invocation to Allah: "In the name of Allah, the Merciful and Compassionate." All the chapters included in the text, except for "The Cessation" serve as a praise of and call to worship of Allah. "Daylight" also reminds worshipers to treat others with the same compassion Allah has shown to them. "The Cessation" is a warning of the end of the world and an admonition to follow the straight path, which is possible only by the will of Allah.

MORE ABOUT THE SELECTION

According to Muslims, the Koran is the infallible word of God as it was revealed to the Prophet Mohammed by the Angel Gabriel. Mohammed was born in Mecca some time between A.D. 570 and A.D. 571. His family belonged to the Quraysh tribe. His father, Abdallah, died just before Mohammed was born, and his mother, Aminah, died when he was about six years old. While he was an infant, Mohammed lived in a foster home. Later, he went to live with his paternal grandfather, Abd al-Muttalib, who died two years later and entrusted Mohammed to another of his sons, Abu Talib. According to some biographers, Mohammed traveled with his uncle with the trade caravans from Mecca to Syria.

At the time, the Arabs were practicing polytheism. Some admirers of the monotheism of Judaism and Christianity, known as *hanifs,* eventually rejected the idolatry of their people and formed their own religion. Mohammed was influenced by the *hanifs* and took to prayer and meditation in solitude at a cave outside Mecca. There, one night, around A.D. 610, according to Muslim tradition, the Angel Gabriel came to Mohammed and told him to recite in the name of the Lord. What Mohammed heard from Gabriel, and what he then recited to his followers, was a direct revelation of the word of God.

Mohammed's revelations were at first memorized by his followers. Later, they were written down on whatever writing materials were available—stones, palm leaves, and the like. The revelations were all gathered during the reign of Umar, the second caliphate. The version put together during the next caliphate—of Uthman—was and is considered the authorized version.

A CRITICAL COMMENT

"The Koran admittedly occupies an important position among the great religious books of the world. Though the youngest of the epoch-making works belonging to this class of literature, it yields to hardly any in the wonderful effect which it has produced on large masses of men. It has created an all but new phase of human thought and a fresh type of character. It first transformed a number of heterogeneous desert tribes of the Arabian peninsula into a nation of heroes, and then proceeded to create the vast politico-religious organizations of the Muhammedan world which are one of the great forces with which Europe and the East have to reckon today."

—*from the Introduction to* The Koran,
G. Margoliouth

FOR FURTHER READING

Arberry, A. J., trans. *The Koran Interpreted*. New York: Collier, 1955.

Dawood, N. J., trans. *The Koran*. New York: Viking, 1990.

Khan, Muhammad Zafrulla, trans. *The Quran*. London: Curzon Press, 1975.

Rodwell, J. M., trans. *The Koran*. London: J. M. Dent & Sons, 1983.

from THE THIRD VOYAGE OF SINDBAD THE SAILOR
from The Thousand and One Nights
Translated by N. J. Dawood ▾ (Textbook page 639)

SUMMARY

The ship carrying Sindbad, his sailors, and some merchants goes off course and heads for the Isle of Zughb, where apelike dwarves dwell. The dwarves overtake the ship, haul the sailors to shore, and then set sail in the ship. On the island, the sailors find in the courtyard of an enormous palace bones, an open oven, a bench, pots and pans, and iron spits for roasting. They spend the night there, but in the morning, a giant who lives at the palace returns. He sees the men and chooses the captain to roast and eat. While the giant sleeps, the men search for a hiding place, but find none. That night, the monster roasts and eats another man. The merchants then decide on a plan to kill the giant. They build a raft and leave it ready on the shore. That night, after the monster roasts and eats yet another man, the men plunge red-hot iron rods into his eyes to blind him. They board their raft and set sail, but the blinded giant and a giantess hurl boulders at them, killing all but Sindbad and two merchants who manage to escape.

MORE ABOUT THE SELECTION

The Thousand and One Nights had its origins in India, Persia, Turkey, and Arabia. Some of the stories first circulated orally for centuries until they were written down. Collections of these stories existed as early as the ninth century. One such collection was a Persian storybook, now lost, called *Hazar Afsana* (A Thousand Legends). *Hazar Afsana* provided the title and the idea of the frame story for *The Thousand and One Nights*.

Many manuscript versions of *The Thousand and One Nights* existed. Europeans first enjoyed the tales through an early eighteenth-century French translation by Antoine Galland. At this time, Islamic scholars did not feel that the tales had any high cultural value since they lacked profound moral lessons and were meant solely to entertain. But Europeans—the general public and scholars alike—were delighted with the stories. Galland's translation sparked a Middle and Far East craze in Europe, and it led to a number of translations of Eastern works into European languages. Galland's *Arabian Nights* also inspired the "Oriental tale" in European literature—eighteenth- and nineteenth-century poems and stories set in highly romanticized Eastern locales.

The version of *The Thousand and One Nights* that we read today was compiled by an unknown Egyptian publisher in the late eighteenth century. Scholars believe that the Sindbad stories come from the Arabic oral tradition and that they are among the oldest stories in the collection.

A CRITICAL COMMENT

"The work consists of four categories of folk tales—fables, fairy tales, romances, and comic as well as historical anecdotes, the last two often merging into one category. They are divided into nights, in sections of various lengths, a division that, although it follows no particular plan, serves a dual purpose: it keeps Shahrayar and us in suspense and brings the action to a more familiar level of reality. The essential quality of these tales lies in their success in interweaving the unusual, the extraordinary, the marvelous, and the supernatural into the fabric of everyday life. Animals discourse and give lessons in moral philosophy; normal men and women consort or struggle with demons and, like them, change themselves or anyone else into any form they please; and humble people lead a life full of accidents and surprises. . . . Yet both the unusual incidents and the extraordinary coincidences are nothing but the web and weft of Divine Providence, in a world in which people often suffer but come out all right at the end. They are enriched by the pleasure of a marvelous adventure and a sense of wonder, which makes life possible. As for the readers, their pleasure is vicarious and aesthetic, derived from the escape into an exotic world of wish fulfillment and from the underlying act of transformation and the consequent pleasure, which may be best defined in Freudian terms as the sudden overcoming of an obstacle.

"Such an effect, which is contingent on merging the supernatural and the natural and securing a willing suspension of disbelief, the storyteller of the *Nights* produces by the precise and concrete detail that he uses in a matter-of-fact way in description, narration, and conversation, bridging the gap between the natural and supernatural situations. It is this quality, by the way, that explains the appeal of these tales to the romantic imagination. . . . Thus the phantasmagoric is based on the concrete, the supernatural grounded in the natural."
—*from the Introduction to* The Arabian Nights, *Husain Haddawy*

FOR FURTHER READING

Dawood, N. J., trans. *The Penguin Tales from the Thousand and One Nights.* Hammondsworth, England: Penguin, 1973.

Haddawy, Husain, trans. *The Arabian Nights*. New York: W. W. Norton, 1990.

Muhsin, Jassim Ali. *Scheherazade in England*. Washington, D.C.: Three Continents Press, 1981.

from THE TRAGEDY OF SOHRÁB AND ROSTÁM
from the Shahname

Ferdowsi ▾ Translated by Jerome W. Clinton ▾ (Textbook page 648)

SUMMARY

This selection from the *Shahname* relates the final encounter between Rostám, the Iranian hero, and his son, Sohráb, a young warrior from Turan, who grew up without knowing his father.

Rostám and Sohráb grapple in hand-to-hand combat. In the end, Rostám throws Sohráb down and mortally wounds him with a stab to the heart. Sohráb tells Rostám that he accepts death as his fate. He does express sorrow, however, at not finding his father. Sohráb shows Rostám the seal Rostám had given Sohráb's mother as proof of his paternity. Realizing that he has killed his own son, Rostám nearly faints. Sohráb begs his father not to grieve and to persuade the Iranians to allow the Turks to return home in peace. Filled with grief, Rostám returns to his army. His army, having lost hope of seeing him again, rejoices. Rostám tells his men not to pursue the war with the Turks.

MORE ABOUT THE AUTHOR

Ferdowsi is considered one of the seven outstanding writers of Persian literature. His life's work, the *Shahname,* or *Book of Kings,* recounts, in metrical and rhymed verse, the history of the Iranian nation from the creation of the world to the defeat of Iran's last king, Yazdigard III. The first half of Ferdowsi's poem is based on ancient myths and legends; the second half chronicles the dynasties of the shahs.

Ferdowsi was born in Tus, an area in the province of Khorasan. His family owned land, which they themselves cultivated. He and his family belonged to the Dehgan class, a class which was known for preserving the country's traditions and for educating its sons.

Ferdowsi began writing the *Shahname* in his middle age, continuing the work of Dakiki of Tus. Dakiki was murdered in A.D. 980, leaving the *Shahname* unfinished, with only one thousand lines written. The poem took Ferdowsi thirty-five years to complete.

A CRITICAL COMMENT

"The western reader of the *Shah-nama [Shahname]* will learn much—and may gain in enjoyment—by some comparison of its similarities and differences with the *Iliad.* Although Ferdowsi works with a number of written and even 'literate' sources, at least in the first half of the *Shah-nama,* as in the *Iliad,* the roots of oral tradition are close to the surface. Both poems employ a simple, facile meter and their rhyme schemes are suited to the long narrative and aid in memorizing. The heroes in both epics are affixed with appropriate epithets and are easily recognizable even without mention of their names. Both poems make use of a certain amount of repetition to assist recapitulation. Episodes of battle and heroism are modulated by sequences of chase, ostentatious banquets and idyllic revels, and ceremonious councils and parleys. Semi-independent sub-episodes are interspersed to vary the mood and relieve the tedium of the narrative. . . . Both poets lavish masterful attention upon the details of the martial life—the description of armors and weapons, the personal and near magical love of the heroes for their mounts and their armor, etc.—that breed and sustain a sense of epic involvement. Both poems abound in little warm human touches that evoke pathos and enhance the evolving drama.

"Transcending these more or less formal similarities are the fundamental parallels of human behavior under similar relationships and social conditions and recognizable range of human types in the *Iliad* and the *Shah-nama.* The affinities of the indispensable hero Rostám with Achilles [is only one] of the evocative suggestions of artistic kinship between the two epics. . . .

"The *Shah-nama* is inordinately longer than the *Iliad.* Essentially it is made in two segments: the mythical first half and the 'historical' second half. The psychological and artistic seam cannot be concealed. The fundamental affinities with the *Iliad* are primarily true of the first half. But even there the unity of theme, the limitation of action and time, the rapid devolution of the 'plot,' the resolution of the conflict and the uncanny proportions of the *Iliad* are missing. Ferdowsi's 'historical' mission undoubtedly scatters the artistic impact of the *Shah-nama* and diffuses the focus of its aesthetic concept. But the 'wrath of Achilles,' after all, is not the sole catalyst of Homer's art. The validity and viability of the *Iliad* rests in its general relevance to the human situation. In this sense the artistic 'flaw' of the *Shah-nama* is more than made up by, and perhaps makes for, its greater universality."

—*from the Prologue to* The Epic of Kings, *Armin Banani*

FOR FURTHER READING

Banani, Armin. Prologue. *The Epic of Kings*. Ferdowsi. Trans. Reuben Levy. Chicago: University of Chicago Press, 1967.

Ferdowsi. *The Tragedy of Sohráb and Rostám*. Trans. Jerome W. Clinton. Seattle: University of Washington Press, 1987.

Levy, Reuben, trans. *An Introduction to Persian Literature*. New York and London: Columbia University Press, 1969.

from the RUBÁIYÁT

Omar Khayyám ▼ Translated by Edward FitzGerald ▼ (Textbook page 656)

SUMMARY

Khayyám's rubáiyát are at once brief, bittersweet poems about the enjoyment of youth and the passing of life, and a series of metaphors for religious principles and experiences. Translator Edward FitzGerald adapted the fragments attributed to Omar Khayyám and arranged them in a frame that suggests the passage of a single day from sunrise to sunset.

MORE ABOUT THE TRANSLATION

Edward FitzGerald's liberal translation of Omar Khayyám's *Rubáiyát* was published in 1859. It was not well received by readers, however, until it was taken up by the artist/poet Dante Gabriel Rossetti and poet Algernon Charles Swinburne. Rossetti was a founder of the Pre-Raphaelite Brotherhood, a small group of artists and writers who felt an affinity and nostalgia for the simplicity of early Italian Renaissance art. The Pre-Raphaelites were Romantics by nature, appreciative of the bonds between humans and the relation between humans and nature. Their work often had a moralistic intent as well. It is no surprise, then, that Khayyám's wistful call to youthful, often idyllic pleasure would be attractive to them. Swinburne, unlike Rossetti, was a member of the Decadent poets. He lived a bohemian lifestyle and celebrated the sensual experience in life as well as in art, until his breakdown in 1879. Afterwards, his poetry had a distinctly morbid cast. Both these characteristics are visible in Khayyám's work.

The interest in Khayyám continued into the late nineteenth century and early twentieth century in Britain. Despite the strict Victorian morality that it preached, the British upper class had spoiled itself on its power over much of the world. As a result, many wealthy young readers were jaded, desirous of living life fully if briefly. This notion of *carpe diem,* of seizing the day, that Khayyám describes in part fueled the kind of romanticism that led up to and was perpetuated in the early years of the First World War.

A CRITICAL COMMENT

"Khayyám's thoughts, poured out in his simple and extremely beautiful rubá'is, were those of a philosophic and searching mind. He was puzzled by the mysteries of existence and lamented inconstancy and death. He did not believe in resurrection, and the deaths of the young and of beautiful women in particular filled him with pain, and the sufferings of man saddened him. He pondered man's origins and his rapid departure. He never stopped asking why men have come into this world and where they are to go when they die. Why were they placed in a world of pain and confusion? Umar [Omar] knew too well the finality of death and confessed that he was at a loss to discern God's purpose. Yet he was strongly aware of the beauty of nature and the loveliness of youth. He wished to take advantage of the fleeting time and spend it merrily. What is thought of as his Epicureanism was not of the simple 'eat, drink, and be merry' variety. Rather it was intended as an antidote for the sorrows of the world. Khayyám was a man of admirable moral standards. His unusual independence of mind was accompanied by a remarkable loftiness of attitude. He neither flattered nor preached. His rubá'is [rubáiyát], free of the heaviness of advice, offer instead gentle suggestion.

"His thoughts on the uncertainty of the world, his praise of wine, and his insistence on seizing time and enjoying life can also be seen in the works of some of the other Persian poets, among them *Shah-Nama [Shahname]* of Ferdausi [Ferdowsi]. . . .

"Umar's epigrammatic and rich quatrains are timeless. The pain and wonder which they voice are such as many in every generation of mankind have experienced, and the agony of his soul reflects those of all sensitive and thinking individuals. His worries, his fear, his dark despairs are such as every man of perception must at times feel. It is not surprising if many later poets, moved by the sad reality of his poetry, have echoed his thoughts."

—*from the Introduction to*
The Rubā'īyāt of 'Umar Khayyām,
Parichehr Kasra

FOR FURTHER READING

Arberry, Arthur J. *Omar Khayyám.* London: John Murray Publishers Ltd., 1959.

Arberry, Arthur J. *The Romance of the Rubáiyát.* New York: The Macmillan Company, 1959.

Dashti, Ali. *In Search of Omar Khayyám.* New York:

Columbia University Press, 1971.

Khayyám, Omar. *Rubáiyát of Omar Khayyám.* Trans. Edward Fitz Gerald. New York: Grosset & Dunlap, 1946

Kasra, Parichehr, translator and editor. *The Rubā'īyāt of 'Umar Khayyám.* New York: Scholars' Facsimiles & Reprints, Inc., 1975.

UNMARKED BOXES

Rumi ▾ Translated by John Moyne and Coleman Barks ▾ (Textbook page 663)

SUMMARY

The speaker reminds us not to grieve for lost pleasures; no pleasure is ever lost without being replaced by a different one. Everything is a changeable expression or embodiment of God's joy, including one's self.

MORE ABOUT THE AUTHOR

Sufis believe the sufism has always existed, and that the various organized religions of the world are all potential "vehicles" for a Sufi understanding of reality. However, most non-Sufis agree that Sufism began to flourish after the coming of Islam to Persia. A mystical religion, Sufism teaches that one can make contact with the divine, attaining an intimate knowledge of God, through rigorous exercises in self-development, including meditation.

Rumi was one of the most influential sufi masters and the founder of the Order of Whirling Dervishes. According to the noted Sufi scholar Idries Shah, Rumi explained the development of Sufi belief in this way: humans go through three stages of spiritual development. In the first stage, humans worship anything from rocks to money. Next, humans decide either that they accept or reject God, meaning the God presented to them by theologians. In the final stage, the Sufi stage, humans no longer say they accept or reject God: the Sufi concept of God is one that is personally experienced; once it is experienced it can hardly be accepted *or* rejected. Rumi instructed his Seekers—those who sought contact with the divine—to abandon the systems of seeking knowledge that had been taught to them from birth. He believed that to embrace a system that has been force-fed by others, even logic, was supremely illogical. Only through self–development could the Seeker attain fulfillment. To this end, Rumi led his Seekers in a range of mind and body activities from movement and meditation to work and play, all aimed at reaching self-knowledge and knowledge of the divine.

Rumi's reputation spread well beyond his circle of fellow Sufis. Chaucer referred to Rumi in his writings, and, centuries later, Dr. Johnson admired the sage's writings. Rumi's *Masnavi* (Spiritual Couplets), from which "Unmarked Boxes" comes, is influential among all Moslems, and even some members of the Shi'ite sect of Islam refer to the *Masnavi* as the Persian Koran. The *Masnavi* contains jokes, conversations, fables, instructions, and lyric poetry. Its organization is classically Sufi: the total impact of its seemingly scattered genres is to inundate the reader in the Sufi message.

A CRITICAL COMMENT

"The inequalities of [Rumi's] lyrical outbursts have long been recognized. Of him it may well be literally true that he never blotted a single line; composing as he did spontaneously, he could not be expected to have a meticulous regard for niceties of style, nor to be always alive to the desirability of not repeating himself. It must also be conceded that his range of topics is somewhat circumscribed; he sang as a Sufi, and 'Sufism,' as R. A. Nicholson wrote in 1898, 'has few ideas, but an inexhaustible wealth and variety of illustration. Among a thousand fluttering masks the interpreter is required to identify each old familiar face.' This poverty of themes is naturally not confined to mystical poetry; profane verse in the languages of Islam was also condemned from the start, because of a strict classical canon of recognized subjects, to an endless repetition of threadbare tropes and worn-out conceits. But it is precisely in this context that Rumi's genius may be most clearly discerned. Whereas other Persian poets were content to resign themselves to convention, and to restrict their creative impulse to elaborating fresh (but not always so very fresh) variations on given themes, Rumi seemingly originated an extensive range of new subjects and new illustrations. The stock-in-trade of Sufi quietism, piety, austerity, passion, theosophy had already been exploited . . . ; Rumi invented the whirling dance to the song of the reed-pipe, and with it set the entire universe of emotion, thought and language spinning to a fresh and exhilarating rhythm. New similes, new metaphors, new images poured from his enraptured soul, as he struggled to give expression to ecstatic experiences of unquestionable power and authenticity."

—from *Classical Persian Literature,*
A. J. Arberry

FOR FURTHER READING

Arberry, A. J. *Classical Persian Literature.* London: George Allen & Unwin Ltd., 1967.

Rumi. *Mystical Poems of Rumi.* Trans. A. J. Arberry. Chicago: University of Chicago Press, 1974.

Rumi. *Night and Sleep.* Trans. Coleman Barks, and Robert Bly. Cambridge, MA: Yellow Moon, 1981.

Rumi. *Open Secret: Versions of Rumi.* Trans. John Moyne, and Coleman Barks. Putney, VT: Threshold Books, 1984.

Rumi. *Unseen Rain: Quatrains of Rumi.* Trans. John Moyne, and Coleman Barks. Putney, VT: Threshold Books, 1986.

ANECDOTES AND SAYINGS OF SAADI

Translated by Idries Shah ▼ (Textbook page 667)

SUMMARY

The sayings and anecdotes of Saadi express Sufi beliefs, such as the renunciation of material things, the pursuit of a spiritual unity with God, self-discipline, and selflessness.

MORE ABOUT THE AUTHOR

Much of what is known about Saadi (also spelled Sa'di) is based on rumor and facts extrapolated from his writings. He was born Mosleh al-Din 'Abdallah in Shiraz, around 1210. It is said that he lived to be more than one hundred years old, but more likely he lived to be eighty, dying around 1290. Saadi lived during a turbulent time when the Middle East was under constant assault by Mongolians from the east and European Christian crusaders from the west. One story in the *Gulistan* suggests that Saadi was taken prisoner by crusaders and later ransomed. Nevertheless, Saadi received an excellent education and traveled a great deal. His journeys led him to India and on several pilgrimages to Mecca. Saadi was a devout Sufi and lived an ascetic life; his writings reflect Sufi spiritualism and search for truth.

Saadi took up writing upon his return to Shiraz from his travels. The *Gulistan* (Rose Garden), his best known work, is a collection of moral tales, some original and some from traditional sources. Saadi's stories are at once entertaining and moralistic. The anecdotes in this text, which are taken from the *Gulistan,* are brief and direct, though some, like "The Pearl" and "Relative" are distinctly metaphorical, much like the parables of the New Testament. The anecdotes are often sobering comments on the hypocrisy of the world and the joy of simple devotion. The tone of the anecdotes is at once wise and practical.

The *Gulistan* was first translated into Latin and introduced to the West in 1651. It was admired by rationalist writer Voltaire. It was not translated into English, however, until the nineteenth century, when the British first established colleges for teaching languages of the East, particularly the languages of the British colonies. The *Gulistan* served as an excellent primer for English speakers learning Persian and becoming acquainted with other cultures in the Near East.

A CRITICAL COMMENT

"It is the privilege of genius to play its game indifferently with few as with many pieces, as Nature draws all her opulence out of a few elements. Saadi exhibits perpetual variety of situation and incident, and an equal depth of experience with Cardinal de Retz in Paris, of Doctor Johnson in London. He finds room on his narrow canvas for the extremes of lot, the play of motives, the rule of destiny, the lessons of morals, and the portraits of great men. He has furnished the originals of a multitude of tales and proverbs which are current in our mouths, and attributed by us to recent writers. . . .

"When once the works of these poets are made accessible, they must draw the curiosity of good readers. It is provincial to ignore them. . . . Saadi, though he has not the lyric flights of Hafiz, has wit, practical sense, and just moral sentiments. He has the instinct to teach, and from every occurrence must draw the moral, like Franklin. He is the poet of friendship, love, self-devotion, and serenity. There is a uniform force in his page, and, conspicuously, a tone of cheerfulness, which has almost made his name a synonym for this grace. The word *Saadi* means *fortunate.* In him the trait is no result of levity, much less of convivial habit, but first of a happy nature, to which victory is habitual, easily shedding mishaps, with sensibility to pleasure, and with resources against pain. But it also results from the habitual perception of the beneficent laws that control the world. He inspires in the reader a good hope. What a contrast between the cynical tone of Byron and the benevolent wisdom of Saadi! . . . I find in him a pure theism. He asserts the universality of moral laws, and the perpetual retributions. He celebrates the omnipotence of a virtuous soul. A certain intimate and avowed piety, obviously in sympathy with the feeling of his nation, is habitual to him. All the forms of courtesy and of business in daily life take a religious tinge, as did those of Europe in the Middle Age. . . . The Persians have been called 'the French of Asia,' and their superior intelligence, their esteem for men of learning, their welcome to Western travelers . . . would seem to derive from the rich culture of this great choir of poets, perpetually reinforced through five hundred years, which again and again has enabled the Persians to refine and civilize their conquerors, and to preserve a national identity."

—from a preface to the Gulistan
Ralph Waldo Emerson

FOR FURTHER READING

Arberry, A. J. *Classical Persian Literature.* London: George Allen & Unwin Ltd., 1967.

Bowen, John Charles Edward. *Poems from the Persian.* London: The Unicorn Press, 1964.

Levy, Reuben, trans. *An Introduction to Persian Literature.* New York and London: Columbia University Press, 1969.

Sa'di. *The Gulistan of Sa'di.* Ed. W G. Archer. New York: Capricorn Books, 1964.

Shah, Idries. *The Way of the Sufi.* New York: E.P. Dutton, 1968/1970.

Wickens, G. M., trans. *Morals Pointed and Tales Adorned.* Canada: University of Toronto Press, 1974.

Yarshater, Eshan, ed. *Persian Literature.* New York: Bibliotheca Persica, 1988.

NOTES

Unit Introduction:
The Middle Ages

Because most people during the Middle Ages could not read, most popular literature was transmitted orally. Epics like the Nibelungenlied and Song of Roland were passed on orally for generations before being written down sometime around the twelfth century. While most literature before the twelfth century was written in Latin, literature written in vernacular languages began to emerge during the late Middle Ages. Medieval writers such as Dante and Chaucer wrote their classic verses in vernacular languages, reflecting the growing secularization of the European world as it began to enter the Renaissance.

BACKGROUND

A DYNAMIC ERA

The historical period referred to as the Middle Ages spans a millenium linking the collapse of the Western Roman Empire to the dawn of a new period of empire-building in the New World. Such a vast time frame, of course, is artificial, a convenience for the historians who invented it. It cannot be stressed enough that the medieval period was not static, that the political and cultural landscape was continuously changing and growing.

Another point to remember in any study of the Middle Ages, especially as a literary period, is that the term is customarily restricted geographically to western Europe—or more precisely northwestern Europe—thereby excluding the Byzantines to the southeast, the Moors to the southwest, and the Slavs to the east, all of whom contributed to world literature at various stages of the period. In most respects, medieval literature is not as representative of Mediterranean culture as are the literatures of ancient Greece and Rome. The regions that gave rise to the *Prose Edda* and to the *Nibelungenlied* were wet and wintry, far more environmentally hostile than were most of the lands that formed the Roman Empire.

As an illustration of the dynamic nature of the period, consider first what the region was like in the early Middle Ages—the years before A.D. 1000, which historians used to call the Dark Ages. There were no great cities; forests covered all but a few cultivated areas; Christian missionaries were still hard at work converting pagans; most buildings and churches were constructed of wood; war was a primitive matter of swords and arrows; and politically the region was a patchwork of petty kingdoms ruled by illiterates. *Beowulf* is an example of the literature that emerged from this historical context.

In contrast, by the end of the Middle Ages, many great cities had arisen and become the hubs of commerce; the "universal" Church was struggling to suppress dissension from within; great stone buildings and cathedrals were commonplace; gunpowder, cannons, and the crossbow had changed the face of war; and powerful, often well-educated princes, like René of Anjou, were expected to be as proficient in the fine arts as in statecraft. In the interim, feudalism, along with the ideals of knighthood, chivalry, and courtly love, had begun to wane, surviving more in literature than in reality and eventually becoming the object of parody by the likes of Cervantes (page 823). Amidst the dynamism and apparent chaos of the Middle Ages, feudalism and the Church are the two institutions that provided some stability during the period and gave the literature its distinctive character.

FEUDALISM: ONE PILLAR OF MEDIEVAL SOCIETY

Feudalism provided an inexpensive yet effective system of military defense by subordinating various petty lords and their militias under the control of a more powerful but often financially-strapped overlord. In return for their allegiance, the lord usually granted each of his vassals a fief, a portion of land along with its peasant population. Thus the vassal's castle with its surrounding villages became a unit in a larger network of political alliances. The feudal system may have developed from the Germanic institution of the *comitatus,* which Tacitus mentions. These were a band of warriors who swore absolute loyalty to a war chief. Charlemagne's Twelve Peers mentioned at the beginning of the excerpt from the *Song of Roland* (page 694) suggest an ancient *comitatus.*

Between the vassals and the peasants, a seignorial system developed, which possibly evolved from the master/slave system of Roman estates, which the Germanic kings inherited after the collapse of the Western Roman Empire. The seignorial system essentially provided a means for the "nonproductive" nobles to be supported by those classes of society that produced the goods and services—the tenant farmers and craftspeople of the village. In return for labor (tenants often gave three days per week in direct service to their landlords), for rents, and for a portion of their own crops and cattle, the villagers were granted the lord's protection in times of turmoil.

Though the nobles had great wealth, power, and freedom in comparison to the lower classes, life in a typical castle was not comfortable by today's standards. The household section of a castle usually consisted of only two main rooms: a great hall and a bedchamber. The hall was reserved for conducting business, hosting banquets, and housing knights in time of war. In the bed chamber, the lord and lady would share their great bed with any dignitary visiting them at the time; children and relatives would occupy smaller, portable beds nearby; and the household servants would sleep scattered about on the floor. Because castles were generally cold and damp, their inhabitants wore many layers of clothes in all but the warmest weather—even to bed if necessary. Only the richest nobles could afford to heat their castles sufficiently in winter, and then the chambers would be smoke-filled. If arranged marriages hampered romantic love among the upper classes, so did their living arrangements. Knowing this, we get a better understanding of the context for Marie de France's passionately romantic *lais*—even if, as some scholars believe, she lived within the somewhat grander surroundings of the English court as the half sister of King Henry II. A modern film like *The Lion in Winter,* about King Henry II, in many ways gives us an accurate picture of the relative squalor in feudal times; however, only by reading the literature of the period can we fully appreciate the ideals and aspirations by which people hoped to govern their lives.

THE CHURCH IN THE "AGE OF FAITH"

The second great pillar of medieval society, the Church, gave a semblance of unity to the squabbling feudal kingdoms with their shifting alliances. The Church, provided a faith for nobles and commoners alike and a single spiritual leader in the Pope. It also provided an efficient administrative hierarchy that transcended political boundaries and a code of canon law that operated in counterpoint to the laws of the secular sphere. Finally, the Church gave the multilingual hodgepodge of European states a common diplomatic language: Latin. Even after vernacular languages replaced Latin in the writing of secular literature, Latin long remained the official language of church and government documents.

The Church also controlled education within medieval society and was responsible for the gradual revival of learning and literacy at the top levels of society. In addition to religious training, the Church curriculum included the seven traditional liberal arts of grammar, rhetoric, and logic (the trivium), as well as arithmetic, geometry, astronomy, and music (the quadrivium). Schools functioned within small parishes but also on a larger scale at monasteries and cathedrals. With Latin as their common language, it was easy for scholars to travel from one seat of learning to another. By the end of the twelfth century, great universities had emerged, such as those at Paris, Bologna, Cologne, Oxford, and Salamanca.

The universities encouraged ever wider exchanges of scholarship and thus fostered a renewed study of classical literature. For example, through contacts with Muslim scholars—most notably Averroës of Córdoba in Spain (1126–1198), whose numerous philosophical commentaries were translated into Latin—the texts of Aristotle were recovered. These translations and "discoveries" in turn spurred a European interest in the classics—Greek and Roman philosophy, mythology (especially as transmitted through Ovid), medicine, and poetry—that influenced not only medieval religious writers like Thomas Aquinas but also secular writers like Dante Alighieri. In Canto 4, lines 131–144, of the *Inferno,* Dante assigns Aristotle preeminence among the other Greek philosophers by referring to him as "the master of those who know," and he acknowledges his indebtedness to Averroës' commentary on Aristotle's works.

Students need only scan the footnotes that accompany Dante's *Inferno* or Chaucer's "The Wife of Bath's Tale" in the textbook to begin to understand how the new learning led to a synthesis of ideas drawn from religious, classical, and contemporary secular sources. Such modes of thinking in the late Middle Ages transcended political and ethnic boundaries, measured traditional beliefs against other systems of thought, and ultimately led to the birth of classical humanism in the Renaissance.

UNIT PROJECTS

1. **Devising a Code of Chivalry.** Imagine that you are instituting a modern order of knighthood. What rules of conduct would you want your knights to uphold? Think of a name for your

order and draw up a formal code of chivalry. Illustrate your code with an appropriate coat of arms and insignia and display it in class.

2. **Exploring Medieval Music.** Much of the music from the Middle Ages was used in religious services, but a great body of it reflected the literary concerns of the period, such as saints' lives, epic heroes, and courtly love. Listen to several recordings of medieval music, especially (if possible) by such composers as Hildegard von Bingen (1098–1179) and Philippe the Chancellor (1165–1236). Prepare a representative sampling of both religious and secular music to play for the class. Introduce each selection and supply helpful background information, especially about the musical instruments of the period.

3. **Selecting Illustrations.** Imagine that you are part of a team in the art department of a publisher preparing an edition of the *Song of Roland*. You have been asked to illustrate specific lines from the poem with examples of medieval art. Begin by selecting three or four short passages from the poem that have strong visual appeal. Then, using books of medieval art, find appropriate illustrations for each passage.

4. **Drawing a Comic Strip.** Working with a partner, adapt the encounter between Thor and Loki from the *Prose Edda* as a comic strip. First make a rough plan of how many frames you think you will need to convey the story of their contest. Then write the copy and edit it down so that it will fit in each frame. Finally, draw the frames; color them if you wish. Either display the finished original of your comic strip in class, or reproduce it for distribution in comic-book form.

5. **Illuminating a Manuscript.** Before the invention of the printing press, books were copied out by hand and sometimes illuminated, or lavishly decorated, with painted scenes and intricate borders. In the library, look at modern facsimiles of famous illuminated manuscripts, such as *The Hours of Catherine of Cleves*. Then fashion a passage from one of the selections from this unit, such as Marie de France's "Chevrefoil" or Chaucer's "The Wife of Bath's Tale," as it might have appeared in a medieval illuminated manuscript. Consider decorating the border of your page and using an intricate initial letter.

6. **Designing a Rose Window.** The large, roselike, stained-glass windows found in Gothic cathedrals symbolize the orderly perfection of God. After consulting art books, design a modern rose window based on a medieval model. Construct your window from colored paper or old cloth, and display it in class.

7. **Designing a Castle.** Prepare a "blueprint" or a series of sketches of the Fisher King's castle visited by Perceval. Give your plan authenticity by doing research to learn about the standard features of medieval castles. (A good source book is David Macaulay's *Castle*.) If you wish, construct a three-dimensional model based on your plan.

8. **Preparing a Performance.** With a group of classmates, adapt "How Siegfried Was Slain" as a drama. If necessary, one performer may serve as a narrator. Consider using music (such as passages from Richard Wagner's opera *Siegfried*) to add power to your drama.

9. **Comparing Images of Afterlife.** Although Dante's vision of Hell, Purgatory, and Heaven in his *Divine Comedy* is unique, it reflects the influence of Christian tradition in which he lived. Working alone or with a small group, gather images or descriptions of the afterlife from other cultures (such as Egyptian and Native American) and other religious traditions (such as Islam, Hinduism, and Buddhism). Present your findings to the class and discuss the similarities and differences among the various beliefs.

10. **Creating a Travel Brochure.** The storytellers in Chaucer's *Canterbury Tales* are engaged in a pilgrimage to worship at the tomb of St. Thomas á Becket in Canterbury Cathedral. What other sites were popular as destinations of pilgrimages during the Middle Ages? What did pilgrims typically hope to see and accomplish on their journeys? How did they travel, and where did they stay along the way? After gathering some background information, create a travel brochure advertising a pilgrimage to a spot that might have appealed to pilgrims in medieval times.

---

from the SONG OF ROLAND

Translated by Frederick Goldin ▾ (Textbook page 694)

SUMMARY

Lai 110: Led by Oliver, Roland, and the Archbishop, the French fight furiously, slaying thousands of pagans. But French losses are heavy, and out of France comes a terrific rain and hailstorm and an earthquake, terrifying everyone. It is not Judgment Day, but the world grieving for the death of Roland (yet to come).

Lai 130: Roland finally decides to sound his horn (olifant) to call for Charlemagne's help. Oliver scolds Roland for not sounding the horn sooner and says he will prevent a reunion of Roland and his fiancée, Oliver's sister, Aude.

Lai 131: Oliver says that many French have died because of Roland's wildness. Roland and Oliver will die before the day ends.

Lai 132: Archbishop Turpin urges the two men to stop quarreling. Roland should sound the horn; then Charles (Charlemagne) can avenge and bury the French dead.

Lai 133: Roland sounds the horn. Charles hears it and realizes that the French are in battle. Ganelon disagrees.

Lai 134: As Roland sounds the horn, he hemorrhages from his mouth and in his head. Charles realizes that the French need assistance, but Ganelon reminds the king of Roland's pride and says that he is just strutting and bragging. Ganelon advises Charles to return to France.

Lai 168: Roland's brain hemorrhages. Feeling near death, he walks toward Spain, climbs a hill, and faints.

Lai 169: A Saracen rushes over to take Roland's sword.

Lai 170: Roland revives and shatters the Saracen's skull with the olifant, smashing the horn to pieces.

Lai 171: Now blind, Roland strikes a dark rock ten times with his sword, Durendal. He prays for help to the Virgin Mary, recalls battles that he has won with the sword, and predicts that its next owner will not be as great as he.

Lai 173: The dark rock breaks, but Durendal will not break. Roland names the saints' relics in Durendal's handle and hopes that the sword will never fall into pagan hands.

Lai 174: Roland lays the horn and the sword under his body as he lies facing the Saracens so that Charles will say that he died a conqueror. He confesses his sins and offers his glove to God.

Lai 176: As Roland dies, he remembers the battles he has fought, his comrades, and Charles. He confesses his sins, prays for mercy. The angels Gabriel and Michael bear his soul to Paradise.

More About the Selection

Although the selection concludes with the death of Roland, the remaining half of the epic recounts Charlemagne's revenge for the death of his nephew, who had delayed sounding the horn for so long because he did not want to compromise his pride and honor by calling for help. After Charlemagne defeats the Saracens, Ganelon's treachery is realized, and his body is tied to four horses, then ripped apart. When Aude hears of Roland's death, she dies of a broken heart at Charlemagne's feet. When Turpin dies, Charlemagne arranges for his

heart, and those of Oliver and Roland, to be preserved in urns.

While to modern readers Roland may come across primarily as a naive and rather pig-headed brute, these same characteristics were viewed by contemporary audiences not as flaws but as indicators of the guilelessness and pride befitting a medieval epic hero. The values of the hero of a *chanson de geste* like *Song of Roland* reflected the pre-eminence of both feudalism and the Church in eleventh-century Europe: Roland's devotion to both Charlemagne and God drive him to daring feats of military prowess. The later Middle Ages would see a shift of these values, evident in chivalric romances such as *Perceval.* Unlike the earlier medieval hero, the romance hero's devotion is more often directed toward a lady than a feudal lord, and his religious devotion is more likely to express itself in humbling acts of penitence or chastity than in the pursuit of military glory.

A Critical Comment

"*The Song of Roland* is a *chanson de geste,* an Old French epic poem about the exploits (Latin *gesta*) of a great vassal in the service of his lord (or, as in certain later poems, in revolt against his lord.) The lord that Roland serves is depicted as the Emperor of Christendom; Charlemagne, in turn, is in the service of the supreme Lord of heaven, and so the feudal pyramid rises above the world to end in the Author of all existence. The close relation between the epic genre of this poem, the feudal society it depicts, and the religious war that comprises nearly all of its action is the principle of its unity, and many errors of interpretation occur when one forgets what holds the poem together.

Paien unt tort e chrestiens unt dreit, says Roland, rallying his men (line 1015); *Nos avum dreit, mais cish glutun unt tort,* he says again, in the midst of the battle: pagans are wrong and Christians are right; we are right and these swine are wrong. Nowadays, of course, nobody has the right to talk like that, and so this famous exhortation is often condemned as a soldier's mindless partisanship. But in fact Roland is stating a major theme of the poem: the life of the feudal vassal can have no value unless it is sanctified by service to God. The pagan vassals are exact doubles of Christian vassals—they are brave, meticulously hierarchized, faithful to their lords; they wear the same armor, they have their councils, their battle-cries, their twelve peers, their famous swords, and their men of wisdom—and so the one radical difference between the two sides in this poem is exactly what Roland says it is, the fact that Christians are right and pagans are wrong. The pagans have devoted all of their virtues and their vast feudality to the worship of false gods; and so the greater their nobility, the greater their crimes and treasons. The pagans are loyal, but their loyalty is obstinacy, because they are against God and steadfast in their refusal to worship Him. The Christians are savage in battle, but their savagery is sanctified, transformed into the zeal of martyrdom, because they are justified by God. The poet goes to great pains to show how the Saracen structure reflects the Christian at every point; it is because they are the enemies of God and worship Mahumet [Mohammed] that the pagans can never be more than reflections. Roland's famous utterance therefore means exactly the opposite of what it is often taken to mean. It is the warrior's expression of humility, his understanding that without the belief in God we are all *glutun*. Roland is a Christian vassal and knows that without the grace of God his great qualities

would lead him to perdition.

"One must always be mindful of the Christian inspiration of *The Song of Roland.*"

from the Introduction to The Song of Roland, *Frederick Goldin*

FOR FURTHER READING

Goldin, Frederick, trans. *The Song of Roland*. With an introduction by the translator. New York: W. W. Norton & Company, 1978.

Hollier, Denis. *A New History of French Literature.* Cambridge: Harvard University Press, 1989.

Vance, Eugene. *Reading The Song of Roland.* Englewood Cliffs, N.J.: Prentice Hall, 1970.

THOR AND LOKI IN GIANTLAND
from the Prose Edda
Snorri Sturluson ▼ Translated by Jean I. Young ▼ (Textbook page 706)

SUMMARY

The gods Thor and Loki and their goats spend a night at a farmer's house. Thor cooks the goats, and he and Loki invite the farmer's family to share the meal. Thor directs the family members to throw the bones onto the goatskins, but the farmer's son, Thjalfi, breaks one of the bones to get the marrow. The next morning, Thor consecrates the goatskins, and the goats stand up, but because of Thjalfi's deed one is lame in the hind leg. The family begs for mercy, and Thor takes the son and the daughter, Roskva, as servants in compensation.

Leaving the goats behind, the four set off for Giantland. At nightfall they come to an enormous hall and settle in. At daybreak Thor discovers the giant Skrymir. Thor realizes that the hall he and the others had slept in was, in fact, Skrymir's glove. Thor agrees to accompany Skrymir, who carries all their provisions in his own bag. When Skrymir goes to sleep, Thor tries to open the bag and is enraged that he can't. Thor smites the giant twice on the head with his hammer, Mjollnir. After each blow the giant wakes, but returns to sleep uninjured. Just before dawn Thor strikes Skrymir again, with the same result. The giant suggests that Thor travel on to the stronghold called Utgard, where he will find even bigger giants.

At Utgard, Thor and his companions squeeze through the bars of the gate and greet the king, Utgard-Loki, who tells them they cannot stay unless they perform a great feat. The god Loki proposes to eat faster than any giant in the stronghold, but the giant Logi defeats him. Thjalfi proposes to run faster than any giant, and Hugi defeats him twice. Thor proposes to out-drink any of the giants, but unable to drain the horn with his second and third drafts, he gives up. Utgard-Loki then challenges Thor to lift

his gray cat up from the ground, but Thor is only able to raise one paw. Now angry, Thor proposes to wrestle with any giant in the stronghold. Utgard-Loki calls his foster mother, Elli, to be Thor's opponent. She defeats Thor, and he and his companions are then shown great hospitality, despite the shame Thor feels.

The next morning, Utgard-Loki then explains how he used spells to deceive Thor and his companions. Utgard-Loki is actually the giant Skrymir who had protected his head from Thor's blows with a hill. His tricks included pitting Thjalfi against the speed of thought and daring Thor to drink the entire sea and wrestle with the power of old age. Angered, Thor grips his hammer to strike Skrymir yet again, but the giant and the stronghold disappear.

MORE ABOUT THE AUTHOR

Snorri Sturluson began his education at the age of two at the farm of Jón Loptsson, a very wealthy and cultivated Icelandic chieftain. Under the tutelage of Loptsson, Snorri learned the lore of Iceland and developed a broad point of view that was genuinely European.

At the age of twenty, Snorri married a wealthy woman, Herdís Bersadóttir, and began to acquire real estate and influence. In recognition of Snorri's increasing power, King Haakon IV invited him to Norway, where he stayed for two years, mediating commercial disputes between the two countries and becoming a follower of Haakon, who wanted ultimately to control Iceland.

Snorri returned to Iceland with many gifts from Haakon, who had persuaded Snorri to serve as his representative there. Because his countrymen did not appreciate his efforts for the foreign king, Snorri desisted from his duties to Haakon. When Snorri betrayed Haakon by becoming president of Iceland's high court, Haakon had him assassinated by Snorri's own son-in-law.

Like Chaucer and Dante, Snorri combined two careers: politics and literature. In addition to the *Prose Edda,* with its entertaining mythology and its discussions of poetic tradition and technique, Snorri wrote *Heimskringla,* a history of Norwegian kings including a long biography of Saint Olaf, who as king unified and Christianized the nation.

A CRITICAL COMMENT

"It is a matter of common knowledge that the richest and purest source extant for the ideas and attitude to life of the early Germanic peoples is the literature of Iceland during the twelfth and thirteenth centuries. This ancient inheritance is usually regarded as having been slowly destroyed by the impact of Christianity and other foreign influences during the period between the conversion of Iceland (in 1000) and about 1400. This is true enough as far as its beginning and end are concerned, but is far from being the whole story of Old Icelandic literature. Attack and resistance alternate. The literature of thirteenth-century Iceland is much more Icelandic than that of the twelfth, and when Snorri Sturluson's work is considered—and he played the greatest part in this change—it becomes clear that it is not only a question of defense but also of counter-attack. . . .

"During Snorri's lifetime (1179–1241) the ancient art of Icelandic poetry was threatened on two sides. In the first place a narrow-minded clergy, in their desire to obliterate every trace of heathenism, had gone so far as to banish the names of the old gods from those of the days of the week (in Icelandic, Tuesday, Wednesday, Thursday and Friday are called Third Day, Mid-week-day, Fifth Day and Fast Day respectively). It was no wonder that they considered it sinful for poetry to incorporate all the ancient mythological kennings which were incomprehensible without some knowledge of the myths of the Aesir. . . .

"It was a customary belief in the Middle Ages, evident from the legendary sagas of the kings of Norway previously mentioned, that the ancient gods, particularly Thor and Odin, did really exist: that they were devils and evil spirits that might appear in many shapes to tempt men and do them various injuries. By denouncing these superstitions Snorri, at one and the same time, administered a rebuke to the clergy, whilst safeguarding himself from any attack on the grounds that he was preaching heathenism to young poets. . . . Snorri has finally ensured himself complete liberty to say all he wants. He can now tell the "Saga" of the world and the gods all the way from Ymir to Ragnarok, interspersing it with his own reflections (concerning, for example, the origin of life) and setting it forth in all its splendor and power, its comic and its tragic aspects. And while the scholar and poet in him are relating this instructive and entertaining tale, it is as if he were glancing over his shoulder at the clergy and asking, 'What reason can there be for hating and despising a faith which, after all, served our forefathers as a guide to a life of courage and achievement?'"

—from the introduction to
The Prose Edda of Snorri Sturluson,
Sigurdur Nordal

FOR FURTHER READING

Crossley-Holland, Kevin. *The Norse Myths.* New York: Pantheon, 1980.
Einarsson, Stefan. *A History of Icelandic Literature.* New York: The Johns Hopkins Press for the American-Scandinavian Foundation, 1957.
Snorri Sturluson. *The Prose Edda of Snorri Sturluson.* Introduction by Sigurdur Nordal. Trans. Jean I. Young. Berkeley: University of California Press, 1964.

CHEVREFOIL

Marie de France ▼ Translated by Robert Hanning and Joan Ferrante ▼ (Textbook page 717)

SUMMARY

The audiences of the time would have been familiar with the tale of Tristan's exile from the court of King Mark due to Tristan's love for the queen, Iseult, brought about by the accidental drinking of a love potion. In this particular *lai* (in English, *lay*), Tristan has returned to Cornwall from his exile in South Wales in order to be nearer his love Iseult. Knowing that he can see Iseult on her way to Mark's court for the Pentecostal holiday, Tristan cuts his name into a hazel tree. Iseult, of course, recognizes the sign, orders the knights who ride with her to stop, and goes off to find Tristan in the woods. She assures Tristan that King Mark is sorry about the exile and will reconcile with Tristan. While waiting for Mark to send for him, Tristan, upon instructions from Iseult, composes a new *lai* about the honeysuckle and the hazel tree, the symbol of their profound love, as these two plants, once entwined, cannot survive without the other.

MORE ABOUT THE SELECTION

Marie de France's audience already knew the story and hence the names of the characters. Marie's telling, however, reflects the social conditions of the twelfth-century aristocracy living under the code of chivalry. By referring to Iseult as "the queen," she emphasizes the great social and political distance between the lovers. For although he is one of Arthur's knights, Tristan is not of royal lineage. The social chasm between them enhances the poignancy of the lovers' plight. The conditions under which Tristan and "the queen" must meet belies the closely monitered life and lack of bodily freedom that a woman of Iseult's status had to endure. Yet, like many of Marie's heroines, the queen creatively transcends the strictures of her life by suggesting that Tristan compose a *lai* to commemorate their rendezvous. The queen's invocation of poetry to overcome the worldly constraints on her life also serves to endow Marie's art with a meaning and purpose beyond mere entertainment.

An interesting point concerning the legend of Tristan and Iseult is that Tristan had *two* lovers, both with the same name. One Iseult was French, the daughter of the Duke of Brittany, and was Tristan's wife. But the Iseult he loved was the daughter of an Irish king and married to King Mark of Cornwall. The two Iseults are both crucial to Tristan's fate. At one point in the story, Queen Iseult cures Tristan of a wound. Later, in France, Tristan sends for Queen Iseult to heal another wound. Tristan's wife, the French Iseult, tells him that his lover is not coming, and he dies of a broken heart. When Queen Iseult arrives too late, she kills herself.

A CRITICAL COMMENT

"Marie de France was perhaps the greatest woman author of the Middle Ages and certainly the creator of the finest medieval short fiction before Boccaccio and Chaucer. Her best work, the *Lais* . . . is a major achievement of the first age of French literature and of the 'Renaissance of the Twelfth Century,' that remarkable efflorescence of Western European culture that signaled the end of the 'Dark Ages' and the beginning of many ideas and institutions basic to modern civilization. One of the twelfth century's most significant innovations was its rediscovery of love as a literary subject—a subject that it depicted, anatomized, celebrated, and mocked in a series of masterpieces, almost all of which were written in lucid French verse. Among these pioneering love

texts, which would soon be adapted and imitated in all the vernaculars of Europe, none better stands the test of time than Marie's *Lais*. The combination of variety, virtuosity, and economy of means that characterizes the twelve short stories of fulfilled or frustrated passion . . . gives ample and constant evidence of Marie's mastery of plot, characterization, and diction, while the woman's point of view she brings to her material further distinguishes the *Lais* from the longer narratives of love and adventure composed by her male contemporaries. . . .

"Perhaps the most recognizable 'signature' of her work is the symbolic creature or artifact around which a *lai* is organized for maximum intensity and suggestiveness within the least possible narrative duration. The nightingale in *Laüstic*, the hazel tree wound about with honeysuckle in *Chevrefoil*, the hungry swan in *Milun*—all provide valuable insight into the nature of love in their respective narratives, insight that might otherwise require development through thousands of lines of poetry. Marie carefully places her symbols in the context of character revelation and tersely expressed dramatic irony, which prompts the reader to draw separate conclusions about the worth of the lovers and their love in a given *lai*. Accordingly, symbols and situations frequently parallel each other in two or more *lais*, yet the denouements, and the judgments we pass on their justice or injustice, will vary widely from one *lai* to another. The result of this process of 'paired contrasts' is that, as we read on, our experience of each narrative is reinforced and complicated by resonances, often ironic, of its predecessors."

from the Introduction to The Lais of Marie de France, *Robert Hanning and Joan Ferrante*

FOR FURTHER READING

Capellanus, Andreas. *The Art of Courtly Love*. Trans. John Jay Parry. New York: Oxford University Press, 1944.

Ewart, Alfred, ed. *Marie de France, Lais*. New York: Oxford University Press, 1947; reprinted 1965.

Marie de France. *The Lais of Marie de France*. Trans. Robert Hanning and Joan Ferrante. New York: E. P. Dutton, 1978.

Mickel, E. J., Jr. *Marie de France*. New York: Twayne, 1974.

THE GRAIL, *from* PERCEVAL

Chrétien de Troyes ▼ Translated by Ruth Harwood Cline ▼ (Textbook page 722)

SUMMARY

During his search for his mother, Perceval meets a fisherman who tells Perceval that there is no bridge or boat that he can use to cross the river. He directs the youth to his own manor house for a night's rest. But when Perceval follows the fisherman's directions, no house appears. Believing that he has been tricked, the knight cries out against his deceiver. When a square, gray, stone tower appears, Perceval praises the fisherman.

Inside the tower he meets a nobleman, the mysterious Fisher King, who, though ill, greets him hospitably. As they talk, a squire brings a unique sword to the nobleman, a gift from his niece. The nobleman gives the sword to Perceval, who admires its rich craftsmanship. Next a squire passes by carrying a white lance dripping with blood. Perceval does not ask about the lance because he has been warned against asking questions and seeming impolite. Two more squires enter with candelabra, and a maiden enters bearing a bejeweled grail, which casts a brilliant light and makes the candles grow pale. Yet again, Perceval remains silent. Finally, servants carry the ailing nobleman to his bedroom, and Perceval remains in the hall to sleep peacefully. He awakes the next morning to find the hall deserted. After searching the castle in vain for the others, Perceval mounts his horse and rides through the gate and over the drawbridge. As he does so, the bridge begins to rise, and only a great leap by the horse saves them both from injury. Perceval calls for information, but no one responds.

More About the Selection

Like the life of Marie de France, that of Chrétien de Troyes must be inferred from his literary works. Obviously well educated, he knew classical and contemporary literary works. He may have been in religious orders, and he probably visited England.

Chrétien is best known for the six long narrative poems that he composed between 1160 and 1180, which dramatize the idealism, chivalry, and elevated matters of the court of King Arthur. *Perceval* is the poem still read most widely today. Interestingly, it is not until five years after the episode at the mysterious castle that Perceval learns the purpose of the grail. On Good Friday, Perceval meets his uncle, a hermit, who explains that the grail contained wafers for the Fisher King's father, who lived on them only. The hermit says that the grail is holy. Perceval repents of his sins and takes holy communion, thus formally converting to Christianity.

The significance of the bleeding lance is never explained in the poem. Scholars have suggested several possibilities. A legendary Celtic lance once dripped blood. Another lance, in the *Metamorphoses* of Ovid, would, when thrown, return dripping blood. A third lance story, probably known by Chrétien, tells how Longinus, a blind Roman centurion, pushed his lance into the side of the crucified Jesus. Blood ran down the lance onto Longinus's hand. When he ran this hand across his eyes, his sight was restored. Interesting as these lance prototypes are, the poem itself offers no direct statement of the meaning of the lance paraded past Perceval. Either Chrétien died before he could compose an explanation or, more likely, he wished to leave the lance an object of mystery.

A Critical Comment

The following critic believes that the key to the puzzle of the lance and the grail in *Perceval* lies in Welsh folklore.

"Too few in their recondite researches have noticed certain elementary facts. Perceval was a knight from Wales; the Welsh ate from *'scutellis latis et amplis,'* 'wide and capacious dishes,' whereas the word grail was defined soon after Chrétien's time as *'scutella lata et aliquantulum profunda,'* 'a wide and rather deep dish'; Welsh medieval tradition records a dish which, like the Grail in several romances, miraculously provided whatever food one desired; the *Mabinogion* presents us with a King Bran, who held court in North Wales, was famous for his feasts, and was wounded with a lance in the foot in battle, whereas the French romances tell us that the Fisher King was named Bron and describe his sumptuous hospitality, and Chrétien himself informs us that he was wounded in battle with a javelin through the thighs.

"There are numerous other links between the Grail legend and Wales, and the elements which we cannot find in early Welsh literature can be recognized in Irish sagas of the Dark Ages. . . . In them we find venerable hosts, miraculous vessels of plenty, and a young hostess, who in other stories appears as a monstrous hag, like Chrétien's Loathly Damsel.

"What, then, of the . . . Grail? For the answer one must turn back again to Wales and to King Bran, so noted for his hospitality. He possessed a horn which produced whatever drink or food one desired—a counterpart to the dish of plenty. Translated into French, the horn in the nominative case would be *corz* or *cors,* and since drinking horns were not common in France, it would suggest *cors,* 'body.' The Corpus Christi, the Body of Christ, was credited in Chrétien's time with miraculous nutritive powers. Once miraculous dish and miraculous wafer were associated, no wonder that one became a receptacle for the other, even in defiance of ecclesiastical ordinance and good sense.

"This natural interpretation of the word *cors,* which Chrétien presumably took over from his source, was repeated in one form or another by successive romancers and led to the gradual Christianization of the legend, to the misconception of the Grail as a chalice, to the identification of the bleeding lance with the lance of Longinus, which pierced the side of Christ, and to the substitution of the virgin Galahad for the amorous Perceval as the hero of the Grail quest. Seldom, if ever, has a misconception inspired a literature so vast, so beautiful, so strange; and Chrétien's poem, the first example of that literature, though it puzzles one as a consequence of that misconception, enthralls one by its strange beauty."

—*from* Medieval Romances, *Roger Sherman Loomis*

FOR FURTHER READING

Chrétien de Troyes. *Perceval or the Story of the Grail.* Trans. Ruth Harwood Cline. Athens, GA: The University of Georgia Press, 1985.

Frappier, Jean. *Chrétien de Troyes: The Man and His Work.* Trans. Raymond J. Cormier. Athens, OH: Ohio University Press, 1982.

Holmes, Urban T., Jr., and M. Amelia Klenke. *Chrétien, Troyes, and the Grail.* Chapel Hill, NC: University of North Carolina Press, 1959.

Loomis, Roger S. *Arthurian Tradition and Chrétien de Troyes.* New York: Columbia University Press, 1949.

Staines, David, trans. *The Complete Romances of Chrétien de Troyes.* Bloomington, IN: Indiana University Press, 1990.

HOW SIEGFRIED WAS SLAIN
from the Nibelungenlied
Translated by A. T. Hatto ▼ (Textbook page 733)

SUMMARY

Preparing for a hunt, Siegfried kisses his wife Kriemhild, who tells him of her two ominous dreams and urges him not to go. Siegfried assures Kriemhild that he knows of no enemies, and he leaves for the hunt. At the hunt, Siegfried kills every beast his hound starts, outshining every other hunter. As the hunters prepare to leave the forest, their noise starts a fierce bear that Siegfried pursues, captures, and brings back to the campfire tied to his saddle. When the bear escapes, Siegfried pursues and slays it with his sword.

At the feast, Siegfried is thirsty and wants wine, but there is none, so he challenges Hagen to race to a spring. Although he arrives first, he courteously waits for King Gunther to drink first. As Siegfried finally stoops for a drink, Hagen throws a spear at the sign of the cross on Siegfried's tunic, piercing Siegfried's heart. Full of rage, Siegfried pursues Hagen and sends him reeling from a blow with his shield, and then collapses. Dying, he rebukes those who plotted his murder. The knights lay Siegfried on a golden shield and plot to conceal Hagen's guilt. Not caring whether Kriemhild learns of the murder, Hagen says that he will take Siegfried home.

MORE ABOUT THE SELECTION

Many of the events of the *Nibelungenlied* roughly parallel actual historical events in Europe. During the fifth and sixth centuries, as the Roman Empire was falling into decline and Germanic tribes wandered through Europe, the Burgundian tribe was in fact decimated by Huns. Siegfried himself was likely a Merovingian noble. Various sagas about the events of this time period were passed down orally for centuries, including stories about Siegfried's life and death, the demise of the Burgundians, and the death of Attila the Hun (whom, according to legend, Kriemhild wed following Siegfried's death). It was not until the twelfth century that one author wove these various legends, inconsistencies and all, into the unified epic we read today.

That the epic is the end product of a number of sagas from the oral tradition is apparent in the shifts in tone that occur throughout the narrative. For example, the radical change in the character of Kriemhild, a demure, chivalric maiden in the first half of the epic who metamorphoses into a ruthless avenger in the second half, indicates more than one oral source for the written work. And while some parts of the epic present a grim and violent view of life consistent with the rough-and-tumble heroic epic tradition in which the sagas were forged, others celebrate the more refined and chivalric values being promoted in the anonymous author's own twelfth-century culture. It is in the presentation of all of these values, however contradictory they may appear, that the *Nibelungenlied* is truly a national epic, one that reflects both the historical and the timeless traditions of a culture.

A CRITICAL COMMENT

"The *Nibelungenlied* has often been called the *Iliad* of the Germans, and the comparison . . . is suggestive. The German poem represents at once an earlier and a later stage of epic development than the Homeric epic. On the one hand, in story and motive it is cruder and more primitive; its feelings and passions are simple and fundamental. Siegfried and Hagen, Brünhild and Kriemhild, are without the subtler attributes of Homer's heroes; their motives are always naïvely transparent. On the other hand, in literary art and beauty of language, in wealth of poetic imagery, in balance and proportion, the *Nibelungenlied* belongs to a less advanced stage of epic poetry than the *Iliad*. But its development has, as it were, proceeded further than that of the Greek epic; and the course of that development is more apparent, for the German poem is at the same time a Christian epic and epic of chivalry, while the events and personages it describes belong to an age alike ignorant of Christianity and chivalry.

"The *Nibelungenlied* is the national epic of the German people of the Middle Ages; it is representative in so far as it mirrors not the ideas of a single poet, but of the entire race. Its theme was a common possession; its ideas of loyalty, of nobility, of kingly virtue, its scorn of treason and deceit and its firm faith in the implacableness of rightful vengeance—all this is flesh and blood of its time and people. The *Nibelungenlied* may in such respects be primitive, but it is not barbaric; nor is it, as we have seen, without pathos and lyric beauty. . . . And like all great national epics, the *Nibelungenlied* is built up upon a simple and fundamental thought, of which the poet never loses sight: 'nâch liebe leit'—'after joy sorrow.' This idea, the retribution which follows on the heels of all earthly happiness, sounds like a deep organ note through the *Nibelungenlied* from its opening words to its close."

—*from* A History of German Literature,
J. G. Robertson

FOR FURTHER READING

Hatto, A. T., trans. *The Nibelungenlied*. Harmondsworth, England: Penguin Books, Ltd., 1965, reprinted 1969 and 1970.

Mowatt, D. G., and Hugh Sacker. *The Nibelungenlied: An Interpretative Commentary*. Toronto: Toronto University Press; Oxford: Clarendon Press, 1967.

Robertson, J. G. *A History of German Literature*. Ed. Edna Purdie, W. I. Lucas, and M. O'C. Walshe. 5th rev. ed. Edinburgh: William Blackwood & Sons, 1966.

Schoenberner, Franz. *The Nibelungenlied*. Trans. Margaret Amour. New York: The Heritage Press, 1961.

from the INFERNO

Dante Alighieri ▼ Translated by John Ciardi ▼ (Textbook page 747)

SUMMARY

Canto 1: As Dante wanders in a dark wood, having strayed from the straight road, he meets a leopard, a great lion, and a she-wolf, all of which block his way up a hill and discourage his spirit. Sliding down the hill back into the wood, he meets the poet Virgil, who promises to lead him through the place where damned souls suffer.

Canto 3: Virgil explains that the inscription above the gate to Hell means that Dante must be brave as he passes among the damned. The first set of tormented souls they encounter, crying and wailing in a black haze, are those humans whose lives were worthy of neither praise nor blame, as well as the fallen angels who took no sides in Satan's rebellion against God. Many run naked while being stung by wasps and hornets. Next Dante and Virgil see a throng of souls waiting on the beach of a wide river for Charon to ferry them across. Charon refuses to ferry the living Dante with other shades despite Virgil's orders. Virgil explains to Dante that the damned have died in God's wrath and have, in fact, willed their own destruction by choosing to live sinfully. Terrified by the sights and sounds of Hell, Dante faints.

Canto 5: With the damned moaning like animals, Dante and Virgil descend to the second circle of Hell and encounter the grotesque judge Minos who assigns each soul to its punishment. Dante sees the whirling and battering torments of carnal sinners who on earth abandoned their reason to satisfy their appetites. The shade of Francesca tells of her love for Paolo and of their deaths. Overcome with pity, Dante once again faints.

Canto 33: Dante and Virgil observe Count Ugolino gnawing at the head and neck of Archbishop Ruggieri. Ugolino and Ruggieri were political allies, but the Archbishop betrayed Ugolino by imprisoning him, his sons, and his grandson, starving them to death. Virgil and Dante move on to a frozen place where those who sinned against hospitality suffer. It is so cold that their tears of pain and grief freeze in their eyes. Friar Alberigo begs the two visitors to relieve his pain. He tells them that some souls, such as he and Branca D'Oria, fall into Hell while their bodies continue to live on earth. The canto closes with a bitter apostrophe to Genoa.

Canto 34: Dante and Virgil find Satan at the center of Hell. His constantly beating wings stir up an icy wind that blows over the souls of the worst sinners, those who betrayed their masters. They lie in grotesque positions, completely frozen in ice. Satan's mountainous upper chest and arms jut above the ice. His head has three hideous faces, and his six eyes weep tears of blood and pus. Each mouth chews eternally the three worst traitors in history: Judas Iscariot, Brutus, and Cassius.

Having completed the tour of Hell, Virgil carries Dante on his back and climbs with him down the shaggy body of Satan and out of Hell. As they emerge, Dante looks up and sees Satan's legs rising high into the air. Virgil explains that Lucifer's fall from heaven landed him in Hell, where he now reigns as Satan, upside down. Crossing the river

Lethe, the two climb out of the cavern and emerge beneath the stars on Easter morning.

MORE ABOUT THE AUTHOR

Dante was born into a family whose means, though modest, enabled him to become well educated and to make friends among the leading citizens of Florence. As a young man of twenty-four, Dante fought in a battle intended to preserve the independence of Florence from control by the Church or a centralized national government. In 1291, Dante married and had two sons and one daughter. In 1292 or 1293, Dante published his first collection of poems, *La Vita Nuovo* (*The New Life*), in honor of Beatrice, a woman whom he had loved from afar since the age of nine.

Dante then immersed himself in Florentine politics. Many of his activities opposed the efforts of Pope Boniface VIII to acquire power over Tuscany, the region of Italy in which Florence is located. Boniface called Dante to Rome, and in his absence, his political enemies triumphed in Florence and condemned Dante to exile and to death if he ever returned to Florence.

Dante traveled widely during his exile, often performing secretarial or political duties for rulers of various Italian city states. His literary output during the exile consisted of incomplete prose works on philosophy and linguistics. When Henry VII, the Holy Roman Emperor, invaded Italy, Dante welcomed him, hoping that he would bring peace and unity to Italy. Dante wrote *De Monarchia* (*On Monarchy*) to explain his belief that God willed the Holy Roman Emperor to rule in the secular world, just as God willed the Pope to rule in the religious world. However, Henry's efforts failed, and he soon died. Dante's hopes for a peaceful and unified Italy were permanently extinguished. Dante then threw himself into the completion of the *Divine Comedy* (of which the *Inferno* is but one section), finishing it shortly before he died at Ravenna in September 1321. Like his follower and admirer, Chaucer, Dante was politically active, championed the vernacular as a vehicle for poetry, and wrote his greatest poem on the theme of a pilgrimage.

A CRITICAL COMMENT

"[The *Divine Comedy*] is a narrative poem whose greatest strength lies in the fact that it does not so much narrate as dramatize its episodes. Dante had doubtless learned from experience how soporific a long narrative could be. He also firmly believed that the senses were the avenues to the mind and that sight was the most powerful ('noblest' he would have said) of these. Hence his art is predominantly visual. He believed also that the mind must be moved in order to grasp what the senses present to it; therefore he combines sight, sound, hearing, smell and touch with fear, pity, anger, horror and other appropriate emotions to involve his reader to the point of seeming actually to experience his situations and not merely to read about them. It is really a three dimensional art.

"The *Divine Comedy* is also an allegory. But it is fortunately that special type of allegory wherein every element must first correspond to a literal reality, every episode must exist coherently in itself. Allegoric interpretation does not detract from the story as told but is rather an added significance which one may take or leave. Many readers, indeed, have been thrilled by the *Inferno*'s power with hardly an awareness of further meanings. Dante represents mankind, he represents the 'Noble Soul,' but first and always he is Dante Alighieri, born in thirteenth-century Florence; Virgil represents human reason, but only after he has been accepted as the poet of ancient Rome. The whole poem purports to be a vision of the three realms of the Catholic otherworld, Hell, Purgatory and Paradise, and a description of 'the state of the soul after death'; yet it is peopled with Dante's contemporaries and, particularly in the materialistic realism of the *Inferno*, it is torn by issues and feuds of the day, political, religious and personal. It treats of the most universal values—good and evil, man's responsibility, free will and predestination; yet it is intensely personal and political, for it was written out of the anguish of a man who saw his life blighted by the injustice and corruption of his times."

—from the Introduction to the Inferno, *Archibald T. MacAllister*

FOR FURTHER READING

Barbi, Michael. *Life of Dante*. Trans. and ed. Paul G. Ruggiers. Berkeley, CA: University of California Press, 1954.

Dante Alighieri. *The Inferno*. Trans. John Ciardi. New York: Mentor—New American Library, 1954.

Holmes, George. *Dante*. New York: Hill and Wang, 1980.

THE WIFE OF BATH'S TALE
from The Canterbury Tales
Geoffrey Chaucer ▾ Translated by Nevill Coghill ▾ (Textbook page 774)

SUMMARY

Long ago in the days of King Arthur, a knight rapes a maiden. Although Arthur condemns the knight to death, the queen pleads for his life, and Arthur places the knight's fate in her hands. She tells the knight that she will spare his life if, within a year, he can discover what women desire most. The knight searches widely but after a year has found no one answer that women will agree upon. On his way home, he meets a foul-looking old woman who promises to tell him the right answer if he will swear to do whatever she asks of him. The knight agrees, upon his honor.

At court the knight tells the queen that women want most to have mastery over their husbands. All of the women in the court agree that this answer is true. The old woman now demands that the knight marry her, and despite his disgust at the idea, he must comply. In bed that night, he is miserable and tells his new wife that she is old, plain, poor, and of low birth. She argues that his complaints lack wisdom and charity, and then offers him a choice: either to have her old and ugly but faithful; or young and pretty and unfaithful.

The knight leaves the choice to her. Certain now that she can rule as she sees fit, she becomes a lovely woman and promises to be both fair and faithful. They live out their lives in bliss.

MORE ABOUT THE AUTHOR

Chaucer's political career began early. He may have been as young as eleven when he became a page to the wife of Lionel, a son of King Edward III. Two years later he was in France with the English army, where he was taken prisoner. It is believed that funds from the royal treasury paid his ransom. Later, as a diplomat, he returned to France and, indeed, traveled widely on the European continent. Other noble positions he held included controller of customs in the port of London, knight of the shire in Kent, and deputy forester of a royal forest in Somerset. When he died in 1400, he was buried in the poet's corner in Westminster Abbey.

Chaucer was thoroughly a man of the world: husband, father, soldier, diplomat, and administrator, widely observant of manners and morals. He poured his observations and his vast learning into *Troilus and Creyseyde,* a tragedy of true love turned false; into his translation of Boetheus's *The Consolation of Philosophy;* and into *The Canterbury Tales.* As a churchman, Chaucer wrote with both scorn and humor about ecclesiastical officers such as friars and pardoners whose hypocrisy damaged the faith; but he also wrote with admiration of the Nun's Priest, the Clerk, and the Parson, whose intelligence, learning, and kind gentleness embodied genuine Christian virtue.

Chaucer was very interested in science. *The Canterbury Tales* contains many allusions to medieval medicine (especially in the portrait of the Physician in the General Prologue, and in "The Nun's Priest's Tale"), astrology, and alchemy ("The Canon's Yeoman's Tale"). Chaucer's contribution to medieval astronomy is his significant prose work *Treatise on the Astrolabe.*

Chaucer was in his fifties when he composed *The Canterbury Tales.* To this poem he brought his rich maturity, his ripe wisdom, his delightful comic spirit, his narrative gift, and his profound love for the English vernacular.

A CRITICAL COMMENT

The following comment refers to the character of the Wife of Bath herself, as revealed in the prologue to the tale she "narrates."

"In the General Prologue we became aware of the many husbands and pilgrimages of the Wife of Bath; of her gay clothing, her fair, bold, red face, her large hips, her laughter, and joking; and her knowledge of the 'olde daunce' of the art of love. These, however, are only hints of what is to come when she reveals herself in the prologue to her tale. . . . She must love, and she must wield the whip; she must dominate, and she must succumb. She was born under the influence of Venus, and also under Mars. Venus gave the Wife lecherousness, but Mars gave her sturdy hardiness. The complexity of her character, and its contradictions, give her an added dimension of reality. . . .

"Still more of Alice's character is revealed by the tale she tells, and even by the little sermon on gentilesse, poverty, beauty, and old age which she permits her fairy-tale heroine to preach before the denouement in order to teach the hero all he needs to know. Further touches are added to the portrait of the Wife of Bath by her contacts with other pilgrims during various links and tales. . . . Thus she seems to have belonged to the vivid milieu of the poet and his audience as well as to *The Tales,* where her ideas stir up such a variety of comments on marriage, 'sovereynete,' 'gentillesse,' and related problems. Here, in short, is a figure involved in dramatic clashes of speech and action and principle. Her extensive travels and experience give the impression of a woman living in a wide world. The story of her life, with its glimpses of earlier years, and its hints and promises for her future, has the effect of giving her an extension in time as well as in space. Her essential mystery deepens as we are made aware of the cosmic background of the planets; and when she tells her tale, successive shadowy alter egos loom behind her in deepening perspective; old Alice on the Canterbury road, the young Alice in her memory and in the fields; the 'olde wyf' of the tale, the heroine transformed to be young and fair, and the 'elf-queene' who 'daunced full ofte in many a grene mede.' Chaucer has gone beyond all precedent in endowing the Wife of Bath with humanity, and with life, and in his presentation of the golden splendor of her personality, wherein Venus, and Mars, and the 'Queene of Fayerye' contend for 'sovereynetee.'"

—from the Introduction to The Tales of Canterbury, Robert A. Pratt

FOR FURTHER READING

Bowden, Muriel. A Reader's Guide to Geoffrey Chaucer. New York: Ferrar, 1964.

Brewer, Derek. Chaucer and His World. New York: Dodd, Mead, 1977.

Chaucer, Geoffrey. The Canterbury Tales. Trans. Nevill Coghill. London: Penguin Books, 1951.

Gardner, John Champlin. The Life and Times of Chaucer. New York: Knopf, 1976.

Quinn, Esther C. "Chaucer's Arthurian Romance." Chaucer Review 18 (1984): 211–20.

NOTES

_____

_____

_____

_____

_____

_____

_____

_____

_____

_____

_____

_____

_____

_____

_____

_____

_____

_____

_____

_____

_____

_____

UNIT 9: FROM THE RENAISSANCE TO THE ENLIGHTENMENT (Textbook page 796)

Unit Introduction: Renaissance Literature

The Renaissance was a bustling and exciting time that pushed ideas, arts, and institutions into a tremendous state of flux. Drawing on the values and aesthetics of the ancient Greeks and Romans, Renaissance humanists developed a new world view that revolved around human thoughts, values, and creativity. At the heart of Renaissance philosophy was an assertion of the value and dignity of the individual.

BACKGROUND

A TIME OF TRANSITION

From the years of the Black Death in the mid-fourteenth century until the early seventeenth century, great changes occurred throughout Europe. Feudal, agricultural, church-dominated states gave way to free trade, expansionism, and more secular city-states. A new view of humanity and the world was transforming Europe. Secularism and individualism led to the expansion of scientific and philosophical horizons and a burst of creativity in the fine arts. All of these changes facilitated the creation of new social, political, and economic institutions. The period called the Renaissance can thus be seen as a transition from medieval Europe to pre-industrial Europe.

HUMANISM

The Renaissance emphasis on human learning rather than on the teachings of the Church led to a movement called humanism. The movement took its name from the *studia humanitatis,* the fields of study such as grammar, rhetoric, poetry, history, and philosophy. Renaissance scholars believed that, in order to become fully-realized human beings, people had to master these fields of knowledge. Classical Greek and Roman writers were particularly revered, since they had excelled in such studies and their works were thought to contain the wisdom that would show the modern individual how to live.

The revival of interest in Greek and Roman civilization led many scholars to search for lost manuscripts, sculptures, medallions, coins, and other artifacts of classical antiquity. The goal of the search was not merely the artifacts themselves, but the information that would allow Renaissance leaders to incorporate classical precepts and ideals into current educational, political and social structures, as well as into the creation of works of art and literature.

The new value placed on individual learning and achievement led to the concept of the "Renaissance man"—a person with a broad range of knowledge. The epitome of the Renaissance man may have been Leonardo da Vinci, who excelled in the fields of art, philosophy, and science.

THE ITALIAN RENAISSANCE

The energy and creativity of the Renaissance were first seen in Italy—largely due to the new trade routes to Africa and the East that had brought much wealth to the Italian city-states. This wealth helped to break down the old feudal order and allowed many merchants to become patrons of the arts. These patrons supported countless artists.

In Italy, the forerunners of the literary Renaissance were Petrarch, Boccaccio, and others who valued the learning and art of the ancient Greeks and Romans. Petrarch rediscovered Cicero's letters and stimulated a renewed appreciation of the ideas of Plato and Aristotle. Both Petrarch and Boccaccio were among the first to write in the vernacular Italian, rather than in Latin, the literary language of the day.

From Italy, the Renaissance spread north to France, England, the Netherlands, Germany, and Spain. By the time it arrived in the north, however, its purely cultural aims had given way to the needs of the Reformation.

THE REFORMATION

One of the goals of the humanists was to free people's minds from the dogma of the medieval Church. Their emphasis on free inquiry and secular learning challenged traditional Christian teachings and advanced a new respect for the pre-Christian classics. This intellectual challenge came at a time when other forces were already eroding the power of the Church.

With the rise of world trade, a wealthy merchant class and a new middle class had emerged. These two classes rejected the traditional ascetic values of the Church and instead sought profit and material wealth. This lust for luxury soon affected the clergy as well as the laity, and the Church was revealed to be an institution as vulnerable to corruption as any other. It was not long before the general populace began to question the authority of the Church and condemn its vast wealth.

During the late Middle Ages, critics began to appear and demand that the Church reform itself. The Reformation officially began in 1517 when an Augustinian monk named Martin Luther tacked his protests to the door of a church in Wittenberg. When the Church responded by persecuting him, Luther broke from it and established a national German church. His example inspired reformist leaders in Switzerland and the Netherlands. Quarrels between Henry VIII of England and the Roman Pope led to another major break and the establishment of the Church of England. Thus, some countries of northern Europe became strongholds of Protestantism, while France, Italy, and Spain remained largely loyal to the Catholic Church. This division led to ideological and political ferment, which frequently erupted into violence and war.

POLITICS AND SOCIETY

While the Renaissance is usually remembered as a time of great artistic and literary creativity, it was also a time of brutal hardships—poverty, disease, and famine. With the growth of commerce, many agricultural workers were forced to seek employment in the cities, where they often led wretched lives. Urban growth exacerbated the breakdown of the feudal system and promoted the consolidation of cities and states under single powerful rulers.

As national monarchies arose, there was a scramble for power among the wealthy. The breakup of the feudal stability of the Middle Ages and the rivalries created by new trade opportunities gave greater importance to these national powers. At the same time, a sense of national identity was replacing medieval ties to the Church.

These conditions shook the political structures of Europe. Reacting to the anarchy and turmoil caused by new conditions and hoping to bring a better world out of this period of change, many people began to question the conduct and responsibilities of rulers and of the individual. One result of such questioning was Niccolò Machiavelli's pragmatic advice to rulers in The Prince.

LITERATURE OF THE RENAISSANCE

Renaissance literature was inspired by the renewed interest in the classics and by the far-ranging intellectual ferment of the period. The literature of the period had a larger audience than ever before due to two new developments—the invention of mass printing and the spread of education. The professional writer emerged as a new phenomenon, and fiction and drama in particular were enriched by the influences of popular culture.

Poetry, however, remained the most important of the literary arts during the Renaissance. In most schools, students wrote poetry in Latin based on classical models and translated classical Latin poetry into the vernacular. This training led to a great number of very competent poets and a few great ones, including Francesco Petrarch and William Shakespeare, both of whom became masters of the new sonnet form.

Prose fiction in the Renaissance was moving toward the novel form. Characters and settings were presented with realistic detail that was new to literary storytelling. Boccaccio's stories and Cervantes's Don Quixote reveal their authors' skills in developing the sort of complex narrative that is lacking in even the best of the medieval tales and romances.

The Renaissance also ushered in a great revival of drama. In England, this tradition came into the hands of young writers such as Shakespeare, Christopher Marlowe, and Ben Jonson, all of whom had read the ancient Greek and Roman dramas. Their plays were often based on classical plots or ancient legends, but they dealt with the current social problems and the external struggles of the human spirit.

UNIT PROJECTS

1. **Researching Renaissance Art.** The Renaissance is famous for its works of fine art—painting, engraving, sculpture, and architecture—as well as for the literature represented in this unit. Choose one of the four categories of art listed above, and at a local or school library, research Renaissance art works from your chosen category. You may want to narrow your topic further by focusing on a particular style or on leading figures. Prepare an oral report using art reproductions to illustrate your points.

2. **Writing a Love Letter.** Much Renaissance literature centers around love relationships. Choose a love relationship from one of the selections in this unit and write a love letter from one partner to the other.

3. **Reporting on a "Renaissance Person."** Leonardo da Vinci has been described as the ultimate "Renaissance man." Conduct research

to find out about another "Renaissance person" from the Renaissance. After gathering information about this person from library reference books, write a report telling why this person deserves to be called a Renaissance man or woman.

4. **Creating a Time Line.** Draw a time line that details a few Renaissance figures, their most famous achievements, and any political or social events that affected them. Use the unit time line on pages 794–795 as a model. Work broadly across many countries or pick a particular country such as Italy, Holland, or France to concentrate on.

5. **Researching Advances in the Renaissance.** The Renaissance was a time of great advances in many fields: exploration, the arts, medicine, printing, mechanics, human anatomy, astronomy, and other sciences. Select one of the fields listed above and research a major discovery or advance that was made in that field during the Renaissance. Here are some suggestions for research: Andreas Vesalius' researches in human anatomy; Nicolaus Copernicus' discoveries in astronomy; the painter Giotto's advances in perspective and the rendering of lifelike scenes; advances made in printing and publishing; revolutionary approaches in music, the visual arts, or education, and so on. Develop your research into an oral report. Support your report with visual references, if possible: slides, book illustrations, and the like.

6. **Writing a Quixotic Short Story.** Cervantes's character Don Quixote has become so well known that his name has become an adjective: *quixotic* (kwiks'•ät'ik) means excessively idealistic or chivalrous, like Don Quixote. Write your own quixotic adventure story. You may want to invent a character and situation, or cast yourself as the idealistic hero, narrating an exaggerated version of a real-life incident. Share your story with the class.

7. **Writing a Journal Entry.** Choose one of the characters from *The Tempest* and write a journal entry in which the character discusses his or her early impressions of the island. Include the person's hopes, fears, and plans for the future.

8. **Designing a Costume.** Design a costume for one of the characters in *The Tempest* and execute your design either in a detailed, colored drawing or as a real garment.

9. **Creating a Map.** Create a detailed map of one of the following: Italy during the Renaissance; the world as it was visualized during the Renaissance; Don Quixote's Spain; or even the imaginary Prospero's island. (Be sure to locate important areas from *The Tempest* such as Prospero's home, the site of the shipwreck, and Caliban's cave.) You will want to look at reproductions of sixteenth-century world maps as inspiration for your own.

10. **Researching Important Renaissance Figures.** The Renaissance was full of influential people whose achievements and deeds affected the Western world for years to come. Research the life and works of one of the following figures, or another of your choice: Niccolò Machiavelli, Desiderius Erasmus; Saint Thomas More; Lorenzo dé Medici; the Borgia family; Michel de Montaigne; Lope de Vega; Michelangelo; Christopher Columbus. Present your findings to the class in an oral report.

SONNET 61

Francesco Petrarch ▾ Translated by Joseph Auslander ▾ (Textbook page 808)

SUMMARY

The speaker uses half of the octave to bless the time and place where he first saw his beloved. The second half of the octave introduces the suffering that "Love" has caused. The sestet explores the paradox of the speaker's feelings: Love has wounded him with "sweet pain," yet he blesses that pain—the sighs, tears, and despair of love. In the last two lines of the sonnet, the speaker blesses his beloved not because she is the source of his fame, but because she is so worthy of a blessing.

TO HÉLÈNE

Pierre de Ronsard ▾ Translated by Robert Hollander ▾ (Textbook page 809)

SUMMARY

The speaker addresses a young woman who has rejected him. In the octave he tells her that when she is old she will recall Ronsard's poems of praise for her, and she will regret not having been more receptive to him. The last two lines implore Hélène to seize the moment, cast off her disdain for the speaker, and enjoy what is offered to her before it disappears.

SONNET 29

William Shakespeare ▾ (Textbook page 810)

SUMMARY

The speaker recounts the blessings of love when he faces misfortune. In lines 1–4, the speaker describes his feelings of loneliness and self-pity when he falls on hard times. In the second quatrain, he says that when he is feeling down he envies other men—wishing he were more attractive and so on. At these times, he says in the third quatrain, his thoughts turn to his lover and suddenly his dark mood lifts. In the closing couplet, the speaker declares that just thinking of his love makes him feel so wealthy and fortunate that he would not change places with a king.

SONNET 64

William Shakespeare ▾ (Textbook page 810)

SUMMARY

Exploring the theme of transience and mortality, the speaker begins by saying that he has seen time destroy things that seemed everlasting. The second quatrain depicts cyclical change—the ocean becomes land and vice versa. In the third quatrain, the speaker says that each time he sees similar rises and ruins in the state, he ponders that time will ultimately come and take his love away. The final couplet states the speaker's paradoxical situation: Because he will ultimately lose his love (to death), he weeps to have her now.

MORE ABOUT THE AUTHORS

FRANCESCO PETRARCH (1304–1374)

Along with Dante and Boccaccio, Petrarch is one of the three great pillars of Italian Renaissance literature. Although he studied law at the University of Bologna, he only practiced it for a short time. After receiving an inheritance, Petrarch was free to devote himself to his true love, the study of the ancient writers and their legacy of humanism.

Petrarch wrote many poems—some addressed to friends, others dealing with contemporary people and affairs, and still others on religious themes. But the dominant subject of his work is Laura, a woman whose beauty obsessed the poet. Scholars have debated the identity, and even the existence, of Laura. Most conclude that she was Laura de Noves, the wife of Hugues de Sade. From the moment Petrarch saw her in 1327, she highlighted every aspect of his life, and he wrote about three hundred poems to her.

Petrarch has had an immense influence on the literature of England. Chaucer used Petrarch's Latin translation of the Griselda story of the *Decameron* for his "Clerk's Tale," and Thomas Wyatt and the Earl of Surrey used his work to introduce the sonnet to England.

PIERRE DE RONSARD (1524–1585)

As a child, Ronsard had intended to become a courtier or a soldier. When he was sixteen, however, he became very ill and suffered a permanent hearing loss, which ended his hopes of a career in the court. Three years later, Ronsard's father died. With his inheritance, Ronsard began to study ancient Greek and Latin, and to use the concepts and styles of classical literature in his own work.

Spurred by his friends, Ronsard started the group "Brigade," whose mission was to revitalize French literature by incorporating elements of humanism found in the classics. Within a short time, the seven-member group changed its name to "Pleiade," after the seven-star constellation.

Ronsard's first work, the *Odes* (1550), was modeled after the work of Horace and Pindar. In 1574, Ronsard wrote his epic poem the *Franciade,* modeled after the *Iliad,* which deals with Francus, the legendary founder of Paris. Late in life, Ronsard retired to the country where he continued to write nature poetry and love poems to Hélène de Surgéres. The *Folâtries, Mélanges, Odes,* and *Amours de Marie* are simple, sensual, love poems that celebrate rustic pleasures and evoke the gentle atmosphere of the French countryside.

WILLIAM SHAKESPEARE (1564–1616)

In the late sixteenth century, sonnet sequences were very fashionable, and many great writers, including Wyatt, Surrey, Sidney, and Spenser, were writing them. Shakespeare's work in the sonnet form, however, surpasses that of all his fellow English sonneteers. All of Shakespeare's 154 sonnets are tenderly human and warmly intimate. The first 126 sonnets are addressed to a beloved friend, a handsome and noble young man. Sonnets 127–154 are written to a cruel but fascinating "Dark Lady," whom the speaker loves in spite of himself. Themes that recur throughout the sonnets are the inevitable decay brought about by time and the immortality love and beauty achieve in poetry.

Shakespeare's sonnets were probably composed between 1593 and 1601, but they were not published until 1609. Even then, they were published without Shakespeare's consent. It is believed that until their publication they were circulated privately among Shakespeare's friends, a common practice of the time.

A CRITICAL COMMENT

"To Petrarca [Petrarch] belongs the honorable, but in some measure thankless, part of the pioneer. Living as he did before the shining of the earliest ray of the Renaissance, to him may be applied the Eastern epithet, *Subh-i-Kazib*, the dawn before the dawn—that first faint light which is obliterated and forgotten as soon as the daylight has visited us. Yet the *Subh-i-Kazib* truly heralds the dawn, and the dawn is not without it.

"Petrarca had something new to say to his own age, and the eternal truth of his message is attested by the fact that it is no less important to ours. Like every pioneer, he made mistakes—even fatal ones—but he hewed out the road along which future generations have marched in triumph. From that time to this, great acquisitions in knowledge have been made, there has been much progress, much achievement, but the literary standard unfolded by Petrarca remains with us. Turning to the classics as the source from which all inspiration is to be drawn, he was saturated with the idea that it is a folly to stop short of perfection: he engaged men to the worship and the pursuit of what was highest in art and purest in taste, and hence it is that his ideal abides with us, and that our generation, no less than his own, has to acknowledge itself intellectually his debtor.

"Petrarca has been called 'the first modern man,' and indeed, there is about him a sense of freedom and emancipation; he gives the impression of one who is peculiarly conscious of his own individuality and who has conquered a world for himself. His many-sidedness, too, is intensely modern; poet, scholar, musician, letter-writer, collector, copyist, traveler, botanist, politician, solitary and man of society, nature-worshipper and art-lover. Apart from his genius, one hardly knows which to admire most, his versatile interest or his enormous industry; the mind whose first need was solitude, or the heart that could not live without friendship. This very complexity of character should make him a study particularly sympathetic to our time, when all literature demonstrates that, like Browning, we feel that little else but the development of a soul is worth studying."

—*from* Francesco Petrarca,
Maud F. Jerrold

FOR FURTHER READING

Armstrong, Elizabeth. *Ronsard and the Age of Gold*. Cambridge: Cambridge University Press, 1968.

Auslander, Joseph, trans. *The Sonnets of Petrarch*. New York: Longmans, Green, 1931.

Mann, Nicholas. *Petrarch*. Oxford: Oxford University Press, 1984.

Martin, Philip. *Shakespeare's Sonnets: Self, Love and Art*. Cambridge: Cambridge University Press, 1972.

Shakespeare, William. *The Complete Works of William Shakespeare*. Eds. William George Clark and William Aldis Wright. Macmillan, 1934.

Wait, R. J. C. *The Background of Shakespeare's Sonnets*. New York: Schocken, 1972.

THE TALE OF THE FALCON
from the Decameron

Giovanni Boccaccio ▾ Translated by Mark Musa and Peter Bondanella ▾ (Textbook page 815)

SUMMARY

Federigo is deeply in love with Monna Giovanna. He wantonly spends his fortune trying to gain her love, but she refuses him. Having used all his money, he retires to a modest home in the country where he has only one extravagance, his falcon. Monna Giovanna has a country estate nearby, and after the death of her husband, she and her little boy go there for the traditional year of mourning.

Monna Giovanna's son and Federigo become friends, and the boy especially likes Federigo's falcon. Later, when the boy becomes ill, he tells his mother that if he were to have the falcon he would get better. Monna Giovanna is hesitant, but since her love for her son is greater than her embarrassment in seeking Federigo out, she visits the latter. Having nothing suitable to feed his guest, Federigo has the falcon prepared as the main course of their meal.

After they have eaten, Monna Giovanna states her mission, and Federigo weeps, explaining what he has done. Inwardly, Monna Giovanna is touched by his generosity. She returns home and her son dies soon after. Following another period of mourning, her brothers urge her to remarry, and she chooses the poor but noble Federigo.

MORE ABOUT THE AUTHOR

An admirer of Dante and Petrarch, Boccaccio was an advocate of the new kind of literature and learning that they heralded. His first work, however, the long romantic novel *Filocolo,* was written in the conventionally florid style of the day. It was a commercial success, as was the epic poem, *Teseida,* also written in an elaborate style. Boccaccio's next book, *Filostrato,* was less elaborate and is considered Boccaccio's breakthrough to a more natural style. His next work, *Amorosa Visione,* is a witty battle of the sexes. Throughout these early works, Boccaccio was developing his own style; he finally found his voice in the *Decameron.*

In 1348, the Black Death struck Florence. Three out of every five people died, and life came to such a standstill that grass grew in the streets. This calamity provided the setting for the *Decameron,* as ten young Florentines who have fled to a country villa in the hills above Florence tell stories to pass the time as the plague rages in the city. The stories of the *Decameron* range from short anecdotes to complex tales involving many episodes. The themes of the stories cover a variety of human experiences and worldly problems, but the dominant themes are love and the misdeeds of monks and friars.

A CRITICAL COMMENT

"Most readers would agree that the most moving item of the fifth day is the ninth story, contributed by Fiammetta; it is the tale of [Sir] Federigo and his falcon, sacrificed in the service of his lady. It is all but unique among the stories of the *Decameron* in that the focus is not on guile or fortune but on true chivalric gentleness; even the note of carnal eroticism is absent. It is small wonder that Tennyson and Longfellow found the tale to their taste; it has an authentic nineteenth-century flavor, compounded of nobility, tenderness, and sad irony. . . .

"The substance of the *Decameron,* for all its variety of action, is surprisingly consistent in its depiction of the contemporary world—a world . . . that has put idealism aside. It is, in fact, a world where individuals are motivated by hedonism, self-interest, and an honest respect for the forces of nature and the legitimate claims of human sentiments. Yet for all that, it is a world that accepts conventional social usages, condemns pretentiousness and arrogance, and has nothing against the practice of virtue so long as it doesn't interfere with the pursuit of happiness. It is a rational world, a common-sense world, compassionate at least if not altruistic. It is such a world as we live in today and one may suspect not different from the marketplace world of all ages. If the contemplation of the activities of its citizens often arouses laughter (as was surely the author's intention), the *Decameron* likewise, through its humanity and realism, wins our understanding and compels our interest. It has its own truth. And both for its scope and its art, its creative magic and the wealth of its substance it has every right to stand on our shelves beside the *Divine Comedy.*"

—*from* Boccaccio,
Thomas G. Bergin

FOR FURTHER READING

Boccaccio, Giovanni. *The Decameron.* Trans. Mark Musa and Peter Bondanella. New York: W.W. Norton, 1977.

Deligiorgis, Stavros. *Narrative Selection in* The Decameron. Iowa City: University of Iowa Press, 1975.

Mazzotto, Giuseppe. *The World at Play in Boccaccio's* The Decameron. Princeton, NJ: Princeton University Press, 1986.

Potter, Joy H. *Five Frames for* The Decameron. Princeton, NJ: Princeton University Press, 1982.

---

from DON QUIXOTE

Miguel de Cervantes ▼ Translated by Samuel Putnam ▼ (Textbook page 823)

SUMMARY

CHAPTER 1

Don Quixote is a middle-aged gentleman of La Mancha. Unlike most gentlemen, he no longer hunts or attends to his property, but spends all of his time reading books about chivalry. Because of his constant preoccupation with these fanciful tales, he goes mad.

With his mind full of images of adventure and enchantment from his books, Don Quixote decides to become a knight-errant and go forth in search of adventure. He takes down the family armor, fashions the accoutrements that go with it, and names his bony old nag Rocinante. He knows that as a knight-errant, he must also have a fair lady to whom he may dedicate his dangerous battles and noble deeds. He chooses a country girl whom he hardly knows, Aldonza Lorenzo, and renames her Dulcinea del Tobosor.

from CHAPTER 2

Don Quixote sets forth one morning to right all the injustices of the world, but he soon realizes that he has never been formally dubbed a knight. He resolves to have himself knighted by the first person he meets.

In the intervening text, not included in the student book, Don Quixote later finds an innkeeper who "knights" him. Before his adventures can begin, however, his family and friends trick him into returning home. They treat him as a lunatic and refuse to let him read the books that led him into his madness.

from CHAPTER 7

Back in his home village, Don Quixote meets a poor farmer named Sancho Panza whom he convinces to serve as his squire, promising him the governorship of an island or a province. Don Quixote sells many of his possessions to raise money for his journey and sends Sancho out to buy the things they will need. One night, Don Quixote and Sancho secretly ride out and begin their adventures.

from CHAPTER 8

Don Quixote and Sancho catch sight of thirty or forty windmills, which Don Quixote mistakes for giants. Sancho corrects him, but his master pays no attention. When Don Quixote attempts to do battle with one of the windmills, he and Rocinante are thrown to the ground. The knight feels it is the work of the magician Freston, who he also believes was responsible for depriving Don Quixote of his library. As a result of his fall, Don Quixote loses his lance and becomes depressed.

Recalling an old tale, Don Quixote tears off a "withered bough" to serve as his lance. While his trusty squire sleeps, Don Quixote spends the night thinking of his lady Dulcinea. The next morning, the two continue on their journey and Don Quixote makes Sancho promise not to defend him if they are attacked. Sancho promptly promises to obey.

MORE ABOUT THE AUTHOR

Together with three other great Spanish writers—Lope de Vega (1562–1635), Tirso de Molina (1583–1648), and Pedro Calderón de la Barca (1600–1681), Cervantes wrote during Spain's Golden Age. His three contemporaries were playwrights, as was Cervantes in his early years. Although his plays received little recognition, we can see his theatrical flair as Don Quixote assumes the trappings of the knight-errant, much as an actor prepares for a role. And just as a dramatist causes our distinctions between reality and illusion to blur, so does Cervantes create a character who cannot distinguish fact from fantasy. Don Quixote's inability to separate the real and the unreal is one of the most compelling aspects of his character.

Although Cervantes also dabbled in romances and short stories, it is his comic epic *The Ingenious Gentleman Don Quixote of La Mancha* for which he is renowned. *Don Quixote* is a parody of the chivalric romances that were quite popular at the time. Cervantes probably used many of the adversities of his own life as raw material for Don Quixote's adventures. Cervantes may also have modeled Don Quixote after a madman named Rodrigo Pacheo.

Although *Don Quixote* was meant as a social critique of the romantic literary movement, the book has been thoroughly enjoyed by countless readers. This is probably because we generally find at least a little bit of Quixote in ourselves. We stumble along like the main character and are sometimes laughed at for our efforts. Nevertheless, we sense the compassion with which Cervantes treats our idealistic hero, even though the books that Don Quixote admires are silly and the adventures that he undertakes all end comically. There is a pathos here as we are forced to acknowledge the frailty of humankind. It is Cervantes's masterful blend of humor and pathos that makes his novel a landmark in the development of literature.

A CRITICAL COMMENT

Not all hearts are warmed by reading *Don Quixote*—a testament, perhaps, to its complexity. As the noted critic and novelist Vladimir Nabokov sees it, Cervantes' novel offers anything *but* a compassionate view of humanity.

"Both parts of *Don Quixote* form a veritable encyclopedia of cruelty. From that viewpoint it is one of the most bitter and barbarous books ever penned. And its cruelty is artistic. The extraordinary commentators who talk through their academic caps or birettas of the humorous and humane mellowly Christian atmosphere of the book, of a happy world where 'all is sweetened by the humanities of love and good fellowship,'. . . —these gushing experts have probably been reading some other book or are looking through some rosy gauze at the brutal world of Cervantes' novel. There is a legend that one sunny morning King Philip the Third of Spain (a freak in his own right, who had succeeded in 1598 his father, the gloomy and fish-cold Philip the Second) upon looking from the balcony of his palace was struck by the singular behavior of a young student who was sitting on a bench in the shade of a cork oak . . . with a book and frantically clapping his thigh and giving vent to wild shrieks of laughter. The king remarked that the fellow was either crazy or was reading *Don Quixote*. A rapid courtier ran out to find the answer. The fellow, as you have guessed, was reading *Don Quixote*.

"What exactly provoked this outburst of wild merriment in the gloomy world of the Philips? I have listed a whole set of jollities for the merry young student to choose from. . . . So we start in

Chapter 3 with the innkeeper who allows a haggard madman to stay at his inn just in order to laugh at him and have his guests laugh at him. We go on with a shriek of hilarity to the half-naked lad flogged with a belt by a hefty farmer (Chapter 4). We are convulsed with laughter again in Chapter 4 when a mule driver pounds the helpless Don Quixote like wheat in a mill. In Chapter 8 another belly laugh is given unto us by the servants of some traveling monks, who pull every hair from Sancho's beard and kick him mercilessly. What a riot, what a panic! Some carriers in Chapter 15 beat Rocinante so hard that she drops to the ground half-dead. . . .

"... Attitudes of excruciating pain such as that of Sancho Panza in the same Chapter 15 provoke another moan of mirth. By this time Don Quixote has lost half an ear—and nothing can be funnier than losing half an ear except of course losing three-quarters of an ear—and now, please, notice the blows he received during one day and one night: (1) wallops with packstaves, (2) a punch on the jaw at the inn, (3) sundry blows in the dark, (4) a bang on the pate with an iron lantern. And the next day is nicely started by his losing most of his teeth when he is stoned by some shepherds. The fun becomes positively rollicking by Chapter 17, when in the famous blanket-tossing scene, some artisans—woolcombers and needlemakers, described as 'merry fellows all of them, well intentioned, mischievous, and playful'—amuse themselves at Sancho's expense by tossing him in a blanket as men do with dogs at Shrovetide—a casual allusion to humane and humorous customs."

—*from* "The Brutal World of Don Quixote,"
Vladimir Nabokov

FOR FURTHER READING

Bloom, Harold, ed. *Miguel de Cervantes*. New York: Chelsea House, 1987.

Cervantes Saavedra, Miguel. *The Ingenious Gentleman Don Quixote de la Mancha*. Trans. Samuel Putnam. London: Cassell, 1953.

Efron, Arthur. *Don Quixote and the Dulcineated World*. Austin, TX: University of Texas Press, 1971.

El Saffar, Ruth. *Critical Essays on Cervantes*. Boston: G.K. Hall, 1986.

Nabokov, Vladimir. *Lectures on Don Quixote*. New York: Harcourt Brace Jovanovich, 1983.

THE TEMPEST

William Shakespeare ▼ (Textbook page 845)

SUMMARY

Summaries of each scene can be found in the Pupil's Edition and in the Annotated Teacher's Edition.

MORE ABOUT THE ELIZABETHAN THEATER

The theater of Shakespeare's time offered an audience a vastly different experience from that of modern theater. The atmosphere at an Elizabethan theater was more like a lively summer picnic, with people eating, drinking, socializing, and perhaps getting boisterous and belligerent. Such an atmosphere naturally affected Shakespeare's craft. Actors had to be well-trained in all aspects of their trade, and scenes had to be loud and entertaining in order to keep the attention of the audience.

Most of Shakespeare's plays were produced at the Globe, a theater built on the Thames River in 1599. But in all likelihood, *The Tempest* was performed at a more intimate theater, the Blackfriars. With its higher cost of admission, the Blackfriars catered to a higher-class audience. Also, the theater was fully roofed and could be used at night and during the winter. Because it was enclosed, it could also accommodate greater special effects. For example, in the shipwreck scene in Act 1 of *The Tempest,* the Blackfriars stage crew could provide a blackout and flashes of lightning. Such a special effect would have been impossible in the daylight of the Globe. In addition, the delicacy of the poetry and the ephemeral nature of some of the characters in *The Tempest* would have been much easier to convey in the Blackfriars.

The Tempest has often been viewed as a summing up of Shakespeare's attitudes toward art and human nature, reflecting a mood of generosity and philosophical reflection. More than one critic has seen in the character of Prospero a self-portrait of Shakespeare himself, since both are magicians of sorts and in control of microcosmic worlds. The play has been called Shakespeare's valediction, in which he bids farewell to the theater, the city, and court life before retiring with his family to Stratford.

A CRITICAL COMMENT

"*The Tempest* is more haunted by the passing of time than any other play I know: I suspect that even its name is the Latin *tempestas,* meaning time as well as tempest, like its French descendant *temps,* which means both time and weather. This is partly because Prospero, as a magician, has to be a close watcher of time: his knowledge of the stars tells him when it's time to tell Miranda about her past ("The very minute bids thee ope thine ear"), and he also says to Miranda that his lucky star is in the ascendant, and unless he acts now he's lost his chance forever. All through the play he keeps reminding Ariel of the time, and Ariel himself, of course, is longing for his freedom, even "before the time be out." The right moment can also be associated with tragic or evil actions: we remember Pompey in *Antony and Cleopatra,* missing his chance for the murders that would have made him master of the world. The evil right moment for Antonio and Sebastian comes when Alonso and Gonzalo drop off to sleep, and Antonio's speeches urging Sebastian to murder them are full of the imagery of time. The proverb that time and tide wait for no man is constantly in the background: even though this is a Mediterranean island, there is much talk about tides and their movements. Tragic or evil time presents a moment for, so to speak, cutting into the flow of time. Antonio and Sebastian have no idea how they are to get off the island after they've murdered Alonso, but that doesn't matter: they must seize the moment. Comic time is more leisurely, because it's adapted to nature's own rhythms, but in a comedy everything mysterious comes to light in time. . . .

"Comic time can be leisurely, but it can also be very concentrated: Ferdinand and Miranda are united for life even though, as Alonso says, they can't have known each other more than three hours. . . . Unless things are done in the proper time and rhythm, everything will go wrong. The play is full of stopped action, like the charming of Ferdinand's and Antonio's swords; the Court Party, Ariel says to Prospero "cannot budge till your release." The theme of release spreads over all the characters in the final recognition scene, including the release of Ariel into the elements, and carries on into Prospero's Epilogue, when he asks the audience to release him by applause."

—from Northrop Frye on Shakespeare,
Northrop Frye

FOR FURTHER READING

Frye, Northrop. *Northrop Frye on Shakespeare*. Ed. Robert Sandher. New Haven, CT: Yale University Press, 1986.

Frye, Roland Mushat. *Shakespeare: The Art of the Dramatist*. London: George Allen & Unwin, 1982.

Palmer, D. J., ed. The Tempest, *A Casebook.* Nashville: Aurora, 1970.

Shakespeare, William. *The Tempest.* Folger Shakespeare Library Edition. New York: Washington Square Press, 1961.

Slater, Ann Pasternak. *Shakespeare, The Director.* Totowa, N.J.: Barnes & Noble, 1982.

NOTES

Unit Introduction:
Literature of the Enlightenment (Textbook page 934)

The Enlightenment, a time of great optimism and faith in human reason, grew directly out of the humanism of the Renaissance. During this period, science continued to make great strides, and writers and philosophers used the scientific tools of logic, reason, and skepticism to write thoughtful, often satirical, essays and works of fiction. Most political and social systems of modern times are founded on the ideas formulated by the great writer-philosophers of the Enlightenment, such as Descartes, Locke, and Voltaire.

BACKGROUND

RATIONALISM

A philosophy called rationalism dominated the Enlightenment. Working from the theories of Aristotle and Saint Thomas Aquinas, the rationalists believed that the truth about any matter could be determined through rigorous intellectual inquiry. One of the main proponents of rationalism, René Descartes, wrote that we should never accept any idea as true until we have established its truth beyond a doubt. This skepticism and demand for intense scrutiny became a major theme of the Enlightenment.

THE RISE OF DEISM

Rationalism complicated the religious turbulence of the post-Reformation centuries and had a profound effect on theology and on religious institutions. Many church officials and others felt compelled to reinterpret traditional theology to prove that Christianity was rational. This notion gave rise to Deism, a doctrine that asserts that God created a rational, mechanistic universe, set it in motion, and then, in effect, walked away. The Deists also asserted that God implanted certain ethical and moral laws in every person. This meant that there was no need for the ceremonies or teachings of a church, since every person had the innate capacity to know right from wrong. The Deists' concept of an aloof, intellectual God was fundamentally different from the traditional Christian concept of a loving, fatherly God.

The German mathematician and philosopher Gottfried Wilhelm von Leibnitz took Deism one step further and argued that in the rational universe created by a rational God, everything has a place and purpose, even evil. Not everyone agreed. Voltaire, for example, lampooned this facile optimism in *Candide*.

THE IMPACT OF SCIENCE

The enthusiasm for scientific investigation that had begun in the Renaissance fully dominated the Enlightenment and provided the inspiration for most of the philosophical and political activity of the age. Diderot's *Thoughts on the Interpretation of Nature* (1754), which advocates intellectual freedom, encourages young men to engage in scientific experimentation. Scientific research was also spurred by the invention of new instruments such as the microscope, telescope, and thermometer.

Of all the scientific developments of the period, however, the most important may have been that of mathematical science. The most influential work of the period was Sir Isaac Newton's masterpiece, *The Mathematical Principles of Natural Philosophy* (1687), which describes the universe as a kind of mathematical machine that is orderly, logical, and governed by absolute laws that can be discovered by human reason and described mathematically. Newton's theories were the chief authority for the idea that order could be discovered in all fields— religion, politics, literature, and even morality.

PHILOSOPHERS OF THE ENLIGHTENMENT

Not since the fifth and fourth centuries B.C. in Athens had philosophers played so great a role in a society. The philosopher-author Voltaire dominated the Enlightenment. In his works, he sought to purge his age of superstition, dogmatism, tyranny, and sentimentality. His *Essay Upon Morals* (1756), for example, claimed that in spite of superstition, prejudice, zealotry, and all the other stumbling blocks that humankind has created for itself, people have been able to progress through their powers of reason.

Jean Jacques Rousseau, another French philosopher, claimed that man is naturally good and innocent and becomes corrupted only because of the vices of his environment. In *The Social Contract* (1762), Rousseau argues that the rights and responsibilities of an individual derive from an agreement, or social contract, between the individual and his or her ruler.

The English philosopher John Locke similarly championed the idea that people had certain natural rights that a ruler was obliged to observe and protect, or suffer popular overthrow. Locke's ideas influenced many people, notably Thomas Paine, Thomas Jefferson, and Benjamin Franklin. In *An Essay on Human Understanding* (1690), Locke argued against the Deists, asserting that at birth the mind is like a blank slate and that all our ideas come from personal experience.

The debate among Europe's intellectuals during the Enlightenment eventually moved to society at large. The middle classes, enriched by world trade, began to demand more power. The resulting social discontent eventually led to the English civil wars. The American and French revolutions were in many ways echoes of these wars.

WRITERS AND REFORMERS

The rationalism of the Enlightenment made many writers turn their talents to more practical ends, applying reason to religion, politics, morality, and society. Voltaire, Diderot, and many others wrote treatises on the natural sciences, astronomy, law, travel, philosophy, politics, and education. Intensely aware of their dependency upon classical culture, these writers clarified, sifted, and developed this heritage.

Although some rationalists saw human history as a story of progress and looked forward to a future in which all people would be free and equal, most people realized that there were currently great social inequities. The aristocrats of the time enjoyed a life of unparalleled richness and luxury. In the capitals of Europe, ladies and gentlemen dressed in silks and powdered wigs and were carried in ornamented sedan chairs through the squalid streets.

Many writers of the Enlightenment used satire to target the pretentiousness, hypocrisy, and materialism of the wealthy bourgeoisie. Outstanding examples include Voltaire's *Candide,* Jonathan Swift's *Gulliver's Travels,* John Dryden's *Absalom and Achitophel,* and Alexander Pope's *The Dunciad.* The fables of Jean de La Fontaine and the plays of Molière also ridiculed human foibles.

UNIT PROJECTS

1. **Interviewing a Historical Figure.** You are a reporter for a newspaper of the seventeenth or eighteenth century. With a partner, choose one of the major scientists, mathematicians, or philosophers discussed in the introduction to this unit. Then gather information about this person from library reference books and write out a series of questions and the person's likely answers. Perform this as a sketch for the class.

2. **Designing a Book Cover.** Design the cover for a book of La Fontaine's *Fables* or Voltaire's *Candide.* Execute your design in any medium you choose: markers, pastels, or paints.

3. **Writing a Modern Fable.** Fables are moral tales that often use animal characters. Using a modern story and setting, write and illustrate a fable for our times, perhaps one that addresses a social problem. Begin with the moral you wish to relate in your tale. Present your tale to the class.

4. **Giving a Musical Presentation.** Obtain a copy of Leonard Bernstein's score for the musical version of *Candide.* After listening to the entire score, choose songs that are relevant to parts of the work that you have read. Using school audio equipment, replay these sections for your classmates, explaining to which part of *Candide* you feel this music relates.

5. **Dramatizing a Scene.** With one or more classmates, act out one of the scenes from *Candide* or from one of La Fontaine's fables.

6. **Reading a Play.** Molière was one of the most important dramatists of the Enlightenment. In his **comedies of manners,** he satirizes the habits, dress, speech—in short, the values—of the middle and upper classes. Richard Wilbur's English translations capture much of the wit and elegance of Molière's original French. Obtain a copy of one of Molière's plays—*Tartuffe* and *The Misanthrope* are entertaining examples—from your school library. Read it, and present a report on your reading to the class.

THE COUNCIL HELD BY THE RATS
from Fables

Jean de La Fontaine ▾ Translated by Elizur Wright, Jr. ▾ (Textbook page 942)

SUMMARY

Rodilard is a cat who has been stalking and killing so many rats that the entire rat community is terrorized. Few rats are brave or foolish enough to leave their holes, even though they are going hungry. One day, while the cat is away, the rats hold a meeting to figure out how to rid themselves of the menace. The dean of the rats suggests that they put a bell around Rodilard's neck so that they will always be warned of his approach. All of the rats are pleased with this idea, but not one of them volunteers to perform the dangerous task. For many will discuss action, but few will undertake it.

THE COCK AND THE FOX
from Fables

Jean de La Fontaine ▾ Translated by Elizur Wright, Jr. ▾ (Textbook page 943)

SUMMARY

A clever cock is up in a tree guarding his flock when a fox approaches him and announces that the whole animal kingdom is now living in peace. The fox encourages the cock to come down and embrace him in brotherly celebration. The cock replies that he is elated to hear this news. Then he tells the fox that he sees two greyhounds in the distance that seem to be hurrying in the fox's direction—perhaps with the same glad tidings. The cock says he'll wait until the greyhounds come and then all of them can celebrate. The fox, however, quickly departs, saying he will return another day to rejoice. At this, the cock laughs, revelling in his deception of the deceiver.

MORE ABOUT THE AUTHOR

Jean de La Fontaine was a prolific writer, producing many comedies, lyrics, elegies, ballads, and tales. He is best known, however, for his use of the ancient form of the beast fable. In these light satires, Fontaine used the words and actions of his animal characters to comment on the follies of human behavior.

At the age of twenty-six, La Fontaine entered into an arranged marriage with Marie Héricart, who was then only fourteen. After La Fontaine had squandered her fortune, they were legally separated. Soon after, he depleted his own resources and for most of the rest of his life was dependent upon wealthy benefactors.

La Fontaine wrote in the era called *le grand classicisme* (approximately 1661–1685)—the time during which King Louis XIV had his greatest influence. Many critics have found lightly veiled criticisms of Louis XIV's court in La Fontaine's fables. Many of the fables' morals, for example, imply that the monarchy should have given the people greater freedom of expression. These subtle attacks were probably not appreciated by the court, for both La Fontaine and his great friend the playwright Moliére fell out of favor with the king. Fortunately, La Fontaine had many other rich and powerful friends, and he was able to move from one patron to another throughout his productive literary career.

Although La Fontaine was often extravagant and absent-minded, he was a careful and persistent writer. He composed the 238 tales that comprise the *Fables* over a period of twenty years. Among his other works are two short novels, *Adonis* and *The Loves of Cupid and Psyche*.

A CRITICAL COMMENT

"The popular origin of the traditional fable accounts for conventions which must be accepted if one is to enjoy it: the improbable assumption that animals can talk, the gratuitous assimilation of our own behavior to that of animals, incredible behavior at that. When used solely as an illustration for the purpose of elementary moral teaching, the original fable requires little adaptation: its simplicity enhances its didactic value. However, to turn it into a poetic genre and a work of art was a more difficult undertaking, the refined French readers to which it would be addressed being more skeptical than either the very young or the rustic public of the traditional fable. Yet La Fontaine did not attempt to alter these conventions: in his *Fables,* animals behave as they do only in the world of fables, where foxes feed on grapes, and cows, goats and ewes associate with lions to trap stags.

"It is in tone and style, rarely in invention, that La Fontaine shows originality. On the one hand, as we have already remarked, the poet accepts all the conventions of the popular fable and even stresses its naive and rustic aspects; on the other, he stands apart from the subject and makes his readers perceive a whole texture of far more sophisticated elements beneath the apparent simplicity of the genre. . . . In fact, the poet, following his natural inclination and the contemporary taste for subtlety, was to include the ingredient of humor in his particular kind of *gaieté*. The naive apologues, the rich composite language, the popular and familiar tone of the *Fables* did not necessarily imply the addition of a touch of humor; indeed, the didactic connotations of the genre seemed to preclude it. Yet the presence of these elements and the impression of informality which they gave created the most suitable conditions for a humorous treatment. . . . [T]he Fables can be understood and enjoyed on distinct levels: that of moral apologues relieved by a tone of light-hearted familiarity and that of a collection of poems distinguished by an ingenious and witty use of all the resources of a complex choice of words, a smooth combination of seemingly irreconcilable styles and humorous literary allusions. Thus the *Fables,* like most of La Fontaine's other works, do not cause laughter but rather a series of knowing smiles."

—*from* The Style of La Fontaine's Fables,
Jean Dominique Baird

FOR FURTHER READING

Baird, Jean Dominique. *The Style of La Fontaine's Fables*. New York: Barnes and Noble, 1966.

Hamel, Frank. *Jean de La Fontaine*. Port Washington, NY: Kennikat Press, 1970.

La Fontaine, Jean de. *Fables of La Fontaine*. Trans. Elizur Wright, Jr. Boston: 1861.

Mackay, Agnes E. *La Fontaine and His Friends*. New York: Braziller, 1973.

Tyler, J. Allen and Stephen M. Parrish, eds. *A Concordance to the Fables and Tales of Jean de La Fontaine*. Ithaca, NY: Cornell University Press, 1974.

from CANDIDE

François-Marie Arouet de Voltaire ▾ Translated by Richard Aldington ▾ (Textbook page 947)

SUMMARY

CHAPTER 1

The innocent young Candide lives in the castle of the powerful Baron Thunder-ten-tronckh in Westphalia. The servants suspect that Candide is the son of the Baron's sister and some unknown man. The other residents of the castle include the Baroness, who weighs 350 pounds; the Baroness's daughter Cunegonde, a rosy-cheeked girl of seventeen; and Dr. Pangloss, the tutor who believes that this is "the best of all possible worlds." One day when Cunegonde is out walking, she comes upon Dr. Pangloss giving a lesson to her mother's waiting maid. Their illicit lovemaking excites her, and the next day she and Candide engage in a similar experiment behind a screen. The Baron discovers them and expels Candide from the castle.

CHAPTER 2

Candide spends a terrible night in a snow-covered field. The next morning, he struggles to a nearby town where two men in uniform give him dinner and money and then force him to join a regiment. His training starts immediately and includes many beatings, and so he decides to walk away from the camp. He is soon caught and severely beaten. At the last minute, however, the King of the Bulgarians passes by and pardons Candide. Three weeks later, his health regained, Candide goes off to fight the French.

Between Chapters 2 and 17, Candide lives through the Seven Years' War, and escapes to Holland, where he encounters Pangloss. The doctor informs Candide that Cunegonde has been kidnapped by the Bulgarians, and that the rest of the family has been murdered. Pangloss and Candide head for Portugal, where Candide, but not Pangloss, escapes the Inquisition. Eventually Candide is reunited with Cunegonde, and the two sail for South America. Here Candide again loses his love, this time to the governor of Buenos Aires. Candide and his new servant Cacambo are compelled to flee once more.

CHAPTER 17

After their many hardships, Cacambo suggests that he and Candide return to Europe. Candide replies that he does not want to leave the part of the world where Cunegonde is held. They decide to go to Cayenne. During their perilous journey, their horses die and their canoe is smashed on the rocks, forcing them to travel on foot.

At last Candide and Cacambo arrive in a village filled with gold, emeralds, and rubies, which are deemed worthless by the people living there. The villagers invite them to a fabulous meal and then laugh uproariously when the two guests attempt to pay for the meal with gold they had picked up earlier. Their host explains that the government pays for everything, and Candide concludes that *this* must be the best of all possible worlds.

CHAPTER 18

Cacambo, who knows the native language, translates the many questions that Candide has for the host. Not knowing all the answers, the host sends them to an old courtier, who explains that the country is called Eldorado. After a long conversation on many topics, the old man orders a carriage, twelve servants, and six sheep to accompany Candide and Cacambo to the king. After a gracious welcome from the king, Candide and Cacambo tour the impressive city and later dine at the palace. They enjoy the king's hospitality for a month, but Candide is determined to continue his search for Cunegonde. Although it is nearly impossible to leave Eldorado, the king puts three thousand scientists to work and they build a machine that will hoist Candide and Cacambo out of the kingdom. The king gives the two men dozens of sheep laden with gold and jewels and sends them on their way.

CHAPTER 19

As Candide and Cacambo travel on, they lose everything but their sheep. Near the town of Surinam, they find a black man in rags, his left leg and right hand missing. When he explains that this is common treatment for slaves, Candide is horrified and says that he will renounce optimism since it is clear that the world is in a wretched condition.

Candide and Cacambo meet a Spanish sea captain who agrees to take them to Buenos Aires until he finds out that Candide intends to rescue Cunegonde. He explains that Cunegonde is the favorite mistress of the governor, and anyone who tries to take her will be hanged.

Candide sends Cacambo to try to rescue Cunegonde, and the three plan to meet in Venice. In trying to get passage to Italy, the guileless Candide loses nearly all of his money to a greedy ship owner. When he complains to a judge, he is further fined for disturbing the peace. Looking for a new companion to go with him to Venice, Candide advertises for the most unfortunate man in the province. Many applicants show up, and Candide listens to each miserable tale. At last he chooses Martin, a man of letters.

Eventually Candide is reunited with Cacambo, Dr. Pangloss, the old woman, and Cunegonde, whom he marries. The five retire to a small farm where they cultivate a garden in the hope of making life bearable.

More About the Author

Voltaire is the pen name of François-Marie Arouet. The author of *Candide* may have chosen this name because of its approximation to his adolescent nickname, *le volontaire,* which translates roughly as "the obstinate or headstrong one." Supremely self-confident, Voltaire loved high spirits, controversy, and absolute philosophical and moral truths.

A brilliant but unwilling student of law, a field he entered at his father's insistence, Voltaire instead set his heart on reforming humankind through literature. He published many treatises (some anonymously), which violently denounced the cases of intolerance and injustice that came to his attention. Shortly after the publication of *Candide* in 1759, Voltaire learned of the death of the son of Jean Calas, a cloth merchant. The son was found hanged and the father was accused and executed for the murder. After discovering the story of the son's suicide, Voltaire became convinced that a great injustice had been done. For three years, he worked tirelessly to clear the name of Jean Calas and to help his grieving family. Finally Voltaire succeeded in establishing Calas's innocence. Voltaire's work for the Calas family resulted in his *Treatise on Tolerance* (1763), a work that awakened much of the French public to the many sins that had been committed in the name of religion. Voltaire's struggle for the Calas family and the literary piece born from the effort, as well as his extensive

philosophical writings, earned him the title of the "conscience of Europe."

Although Voltaire was a sickly child who was not expected to live beyond the age of five, he lived to the age of eighty-three and left behind a legacy of philosophical treatises, tales, poetry, and dramatic literature that has survived for two hundred years.

A Critical Comment

"In its broadest sense, the subject of *Candide* is innocent man's experience of a mad and evil world, his struggle to survive in that world, and, eventually to come to terms with it and create his own existence within it. . . . The superiority of *Candide* lies in its universality, in its epic proportions.

"Basically, it has two things to say: the reality is bad; but the denial of that reality is even worse. If the world is wicked, let us at least not pretend that it is good, for that will not help us to cope with it. In *Candide* Voltaire shows us a world filled with catastrophes, sometimes natural but mostly man-made, and contrasts it with a philosophy that maintains, against all evidence, that all is well and could not, in fact, be better. The philosophy in this case is Leibniz's postulation that all is for the best in the best of all possible worlds, a metaphysical optimism summed up in Pope's famous aphorism, 'Whatever is, is right.'

"Neither Voltaire's experience nor circumstances inclined him to support such a view. He was wary of philosophical systems in general because they dealt in abstractions and did not, therefore, correspond to the reality of life—the only thing that concerned him. In 1758 a philosophy of optimism was the last thing that could appeal to him: he still smarted from the treatment received at the hands of both Louis XV and Frederick: the horror of the Lisbon earthquake was indelibly imprinted on his mind; and all around him he saw Europe being ravaged by a senseless and bloody war. Seizing therefore upon the German philosopher's metaphysical speculation, which he embodied in the character of Dr. Pangloss, he held it up to the light of experience and there exposed it in all its cruel absurdity."

—*from* Voltaire,
Peyton Richter and Ilona Ricardo

For Further Reading

Aldridge, A. O. *Voltaire and the Century of Light.* Princeton, NJ: Princeton University Press, 1975.
Mason, Haydn. *Voltaire: A Biography.* Baltimore: Johns Hopkins University Press, 1981.
Richter, Peyton and Ilona Ricardo. *Voltaire.* Boston: Twayne Publishers, 1980.
Voltaire, François-Marie Arouet. *Candide or Optimism.* Trans. Richard Aldington. New York: Nonesuch Press, 1940.

UNIT 10: THE NINETEENTH CENTURY: ROMANTICISM TO REALISM (Textbook page 976)

Unit Introduction: The Nineteenth Century

European literature of the nineteenth century was in many ways propelled by the dramatic political events, social conditions, and scientific discoveries that the era produced. The main movements of literary and artistic imagination in the nineteenth century fall into the categories of Romanticism and Realism.

BACKGROUND

RATIONALISM AND REVOLUTION

The political climate of Europe in the early nineteenth century was both a legacy of eighteenth-century rationalism and an outgrowth of current economic realities. Rationalism celebrated the individual's ability to use reason to resolve intellectual and political conflicts. Through their political treatises, rationalists had promoted both an awareness of social injustice and a resentment toward the monarchs and clerics responsible for such injustice. The Industrial Revolution that had begun in the mid-eighteenth century had resulted in a landless labor class that barely eked out a living; power and wealth were still distributed mainly among the landed aristocracy. The rationalists' message was not lost on the European labor class, whose miserable living conditions had pushed them to the edge of desperation. As a result, the late eighteenth and early nineteenth centuries were dominated by revolutionary activity throughout Europe, most notably the French Revolution in 1789.

The French Revolution began with the assembly of the States-General in May of 1789 and the storming of the Bastille to free political prisoners on July 14 (regarded now as the quintessential Romantic act). Initially, the Revolution attempted simply to reform the abuses of the monarchy, and won international support from liberals and radicals. English intellectuals such as William Wordsworth and Samuel Taylor Coleridge supported the Revolution until the Jacobin extremists came to power. The Jacobins, led by Maximilien Robespierre—himself a dedicated rationalist—soon turned the Revolution into a bloodbath now called the Reign of Terror. After several years of political chaos, Napoleon Bonaparte seized power in 1799 and crowned himself emperor of France in 1804.

Though Napoleon used the language of the rationalists to justify his acts and was initially hailed as a hero of the republic, it soon became evident that he was merely a despotic replacement for the deposed monarchy.

ROMANTICS AND THE "REAL WORLD"

In the light of rationalism's dramatic failure in France, the Romantic movement flourished. In England and France, Romanticism reacted against the balanced, analytical, and self-contained mood of rationalism. Some Romantics, like Wordsworth, believed that reality could not be understood analytically but must instead be experienced simply and naively—in the way that they liked to believe the "common people" experienced reality. These Romantics stressed the oneness of the individual with nature, and often felt that their melancholy, joy, and uncertainty were reflected by their environment.

A glorification of the common individual and the ordinary events and situations of an individual's life was a key issue for the early Romantics of France and England. Novels such as Victor Hugo's *Les Misérables*—regarded by some as the masterpiece of the Romantic movement in literature—often dealt with simple, working-class people. In Great Britain, poets such as Wordsworth and Robert Burns elevated humble, rustic people into poetic subjects and incorporated the everyday language of peasants into the language of poetry.

Some later Romantic writers in England and France, however, objected to the notion that the poet, a cultivated individual after all, should have anything to do with everyday people. They viewed the poet as a different kind of person entirely, far from innocent and splendid in self-imposed isolation. This defiant strain of Romanticism, to which Lord Byron, Percy Bysshe Shelley, and Charles Baudelaire belonged, was called "Satanic" or "Decadent" by its detractors, who felt the younger Romantics were egocentric, even evil. The Decadent school in France managed to survive, however, until the late nineteenth century. The Symbolist poets Paul Verlaine and Arthur Rimbaud, like Baudelaire, sought extremes of experience, flouted the conventions of proper society, and explored new forms, rhythms, and subject matters in their poetry.

The Romantic movement in Germany was greatly influenced by the Pietist movement of the Lutheran Church. The Pietists rejected religious orthodoxy and favored inquiry and observation of the self. In their movement to return to a "simpler faith," the Pietists were strongly opposed to rationalist skepticism. Another impulse toward Romanticism in Germany was rooted in the writings of Swiss-born philosopher Jean-Jacques Rousseau, who advocated the freedom, intuition, and emotions of the individual, and was an outspoken opponent of rationalism. Rousseau's ideas gave rise to a Romantic movement called Sturm und Drang (Storm and Stress). Named after the play by Maximilian Klinger, Sturm und Drang was characterized by emotionalism and turbulence.

Johann Wolfgang von Goethe was influenced by both Pietism and the Sturm und Drang movement. He eventually tempered his writings, however, with a neoclassical sophistication evident in *Faust, Part I*. The tension in Goethe's work between "classical" ideals of clarity and precision and "Romantic" ideals of freedom and emotionalism would come to characterize much of the art and literature of the nineteenth century.

TWO EXTREMES: GERMAN AND RUSSIAN ROMANTICISM

Unlike the English and French Romantic movements, the height of German Romanticism, which took place during and immediately after the Napoleonic wars, featured a highly nationalistic focus on German folklore and ballads. The first decades of the nineteenth century saw the publication of collections of songs and fairy tales, such as Jacob and Wilhelm Grimm's *Kinder- und Hausmärchen* (1812–1814) (textbook page 52). Heinrich Heine later adapted this nationalistic tradition in his *Book of Songs* (1827) by blending it with notes of Realism. German nationalism was not limited to literature, incidentally. As the century progressed, nationalist sentiments combined with xenophobia (fear of foreigners) and a narrow form of socialism that led ultimately to Nazism in the twentieth century.

Romanticism in Russia involved a less dramatic reaction against the previous era. In fact, the poets of this Romantic or "Golden" age of poetry in Russia resisted the French form of Romanticism, at least initially. In the early stages of the movement,

the poetic issues were purely technical, not ideological. The Russian poets of this time employed formal, classical versification and aimed for technical perfection. In their work, we find neither excesses of emotion nor a "return to nature." The works of Pushkin and others came to monopolize the book market and predominate literary opinion. The movement was distinctly a "gentlemen's" movement, and Pushkin's success marked the high point of the gentry's literary dominance in Russia.

But the Romantic movement in Russia was shaken up in late 1825 and early 1826 by Nicholas I's brutal repression of the Decembrist Revolt. Political strife disrupted the stable atmosphere of society and of literary endeavor, and a younger, more radical generation introduced German idealism. Progressive, plebeian-class journalists took control of the press and rose in public favor. French notions of Romanticism began to take precedence, and Russia in the 1830s and 1840s saw the rise of the novel and the plebeian class, and the decline of poetry and the aristocracy.

THE REALIST RESPONSE: SCIENCE INTO ART

In the mid-nineteenth century, European society found new concerns in the effects of industrialization and advancing science, which eventually spawned the Realist movement. Increasingly, European culture centered around urban economies based on manufacturing and trade. This technological "Age of Progress" brought satisfaction and gain to the rising capitalist middle class. But it also continued the merciless exploitation of the poorer classes employed in mines and sweatshops—both children and adults worked between fourteen and sixteen hours a day, often for less than subsistence wages. Social reform efforts were launched in various parts of Europe. In England, the attempts were liberal and centered on policy-making; on the Continent, the efforts were radical and revolutionary.

The expansion of industry was in some ways a result of the advance of science. Science in general made great strides during the second half of the nineteenth century and came to assume an unprecedented prestige. The prominence of science was assured by Charles Darwin's two scientific treatises, *The Origin of Species* (1859) and *The Descent of Man* (1871), which led Western society to rethink the relation of the individual to society and the world.

Scientific progress eventually made an impact on literature as well, affecting both the style and content of writing in the second half of the century. For example, French poets of the mid- to late nineteenth century, such as Baudelaire, Verlaine, and Rimbaud, paralleled the laboratory methods of science by departing from traditional conventions of theme and technique and experimenting with new kinds of prosody. In addition, they avoided the rich, decorative language found in Romantic poetry and instead aimed for precise, distilled, evocative images. In content, however, the Symbolists, like their Romantic precursors, railed against the increasingly urban and industrial course that society was taking.

A more dramatic parallel to society's preoccupation with science was evident in the prose of the Realist movement. Influenced by current scientific methodology and by a distrust of religion and the arts for their failure to provide accurate facts, European writers sought to reproduce scrupulously every aspect of life, however unappealing. Like the early Romantics, the Realists styled their language after the rhythms of everyday speech and chose everyday people as their subjects. But rather than glorify nature and the lifestyles of the common people, the Realists believed literature should "objectively" mirror reality. They sought to rid their fiction of the sentimentality and bias that they believed distorted the truth. Gustave Flaubert's *Madame Bovary* is considered the hallmark of French Realism.

French Realism's heavy emphasis on depicting the baser details of life led to a submovement called Naturalism. Whereas the Realists were subtly influenced by the scientific atmosphere of the age, the Naturalists drew an explicit (and false) analogy between the writer and the scientist. Under the influence of Émile Zola, Naturalist fiction and drama depicted brutal, pathological behavior, based on the assumption that viciousness is the necessary outcome of human heredity and the nineteenth-century environment. Yet not all of the writers of the Naturalist school were so extreme in this deterministic outlook. The irony of Guy de Maupassant and the social criticism of Norwegian playwright Henrik Ibsen are examples of the great achievements of Naturalism.

THE REALIST NOVEL IN RUSSIA

The Realist novel was an important form in Russia as well. In fact, it dominated Russian literature from 1845 to 1905 and is now considered Russia's most important contribution to world literature. In the 1850s and 1860s, the form was influenced by the earlier works of the Russian writer Nikolai Gogol, who had challenged certain taboos and made accessible to writers the baser aspects of life. There was, indeed, a journalistic feel to the movement, partly because prose was not censored as heavily as other genres. Within the movement, there was also a certain civic responsibility—writers were supposed to react to the current life of the nation.

Each of the great Realist writers of Russian literature had a distinct style. The earlier works of Leo Tolstoy were sprawling novels made up of loosely constructed, vividly detailed scenes, while his later works are much more simply constructed and make much more direct social statements.

Fyodor Dostoevsky's novels focused on the psychological turmoil of neurotic and disturbed individuals. Less dramatically than Dostoevsky, the plays and short stories of Anton Chekhov were also concerned with the emotional situation of his characters, but he is more noted for his evocation of characters' moods than for the violence and passion found in the works of his two predecessors. However different their approaches, these authors all used the novel and short story to present contemporary Russian life, with all its privations and sorrow.

Ultimately, the nineteenth century was one that saw the rise of many ideas—the value of the individual, of common people, of social justice for all—and the occurrence of many events—political revolts and restorations, and scientific advances—that have proven to be an important legacy for our contemporary society. These movements have also been the source of innumerable conflicts, both in the previous century and in our own. The corresponding advances in the literary world of the nineteenth century—explorations in style, content, and form—also continue to be an influence on the literature of our century.

UNIT PROJECTS

1. **Designing a Set.** Because *Faust* is not often performed on stage, and because *A Doll's House* is so often performed, each play offers challenges to a set designer. Design a miniature set for one of the scenes from *Faust* presented in this anthology, or one miniature set for *A Doll's House*. Present your models to the class, and explain how your design is effective for a stage production of the play.

2. **Writing a Nature Poem.** Wordsworth's "The World Is Too Much with Us" and Pushkin's "I Have Visited Again" both reflect an emotional identification with nature. Reread both of these poems. Then write your own poem, using aspects of nature and the natural world to reflect your emotional or physical needs, your ways of thinking, and so forth. You might want to go to some special place, such as your favorite park or beach, in order to encourage your writing. Present your poem to the class.

3. **Setting a Poem to Music.** Set "The Lorelei" to music. You can simply sing the poem to a tune of your own creation, or you can add instrumentation. You may also use an existing melody that you adapt. Perform your song for the class and explain how you created your tune for the poem.

4. **Writing a Poem About a Hero or Heroine.** Although Victor Hugo's "Russia 1812" focuses on a tragic defeat of Napoleon's involving the loss of hundreds of thousands of lives, the poet was actually a great admirer of the French general. Write a poem about your hero or

heroine; in your poem, include images that help convey those things about this person that you admire.

5. **Creating a Book Cover.** Reread "Invitation to the Voyage," "The Sky Is Just Beyond the Roof," and "The Sleeper of the Valley," and then paint or draw a book cover to accompany one of the poems. Your artwork can be either representational, depicting the actual setting of the poem, or it can be more conceptual, portraying the mood or feeling of the poem—the point is to focus on the various kinds of images evoked by the work. Display your work in class.

6. **Portraying a Poet.** Many of the poets of the nineteenth century, from early Romantics like Wordsworth to the "decadent" Symbolists, led colorful, even tragic lives. Choose one of these poets from this unit or another nineteenth-century poet—England's Elizabeth Barrett Browning or Spain's Rosalia de Castro, for example—as the subject for intensive biographical research. Armed with your information, assume the character of your poet and present the class with a brief synopsis of your life. Then field questions from the class about your beliefs and adventures.

7. **Preparing a Report.** In "The Jewels," Maupassant suggests a great deal about the woman Monsieur Lantin marries, without actually giving many explicit details about her. Using resource materials at the library, prepare a report for your class on the lifestyle of a middle-class French woman of the late nineteenth century. Research the kinds of clothing, jewelry, social activities, and so forth that such a woman might indulge in. What kind of education, legal rights, and social restrictions could such a woman expect?

8. **Fictionalizing a News Story.** Reread either "How Much Land Does a Man Need?" or "A Problem," paying close attention to the writer's style and technique. Then choose a news story from the paper or television and fictionalize it— write it as a short story, providing the kind of details and character motivation that the Realist writers would have done. Present your story to the class.

9. **Interviewing Fictional Characters.** With two other classmates, arrange a talk-show-style interview of Nora and Torvald Helmer of *A Doll's House*, in which they discuss their marriage, their outlooks on life, their past experiences, and what the future may hold for them. One student should play the interviewer, the other two should play Nora and Torvald. Either videotape the interview or present it to your class live.

10. **Creating a Collage.** Make a collage of images representative of the nineteenth century, focusing on the events and ideas of the era that have been revealed or expressed by the literary works in this unit. Use materials you have readily at hand, such as magazines, comic books, newspaper advertisements, and the like.

---

from FAUST, PART I

Johann Wolfgang von Goethe ▾ Translated by Louis MacNiece ▾ (Textbook page 988)

SUMMARY

The three archangels and a choir of angels proclaim the natural elements such as the sun and seas to be grand, incomprehensible creations of the Lord. Mephistopheles comes forward and says that he does not notice the Lord's noble creations; all he sees is man, who does not use his ability to reason and is lower than the beasts. The Lord mentions Faust, whom Mephistopheles describes as a driven madman. The Lord maintains that he will show Faust how to serve him, but Mephistopheles wagers that he can lead Faust astray.

Mephistopheles goes and offers Faust magical arts to aid him in his quest for experience of the universe, if Faust will agree to serve him in the hereafter. Faust agrees to become his servant, but only if he can ever offer Faust a temptation that makes him relax in his search for truth and meaning. The devil asks for a written declaration of this, with Faust's signature in blood. Faust is anxious to begin but, Mephistopheles warns that no human can achieve full experience of the universe. He then sends Faust to get ready for the journey, and, alone, describes how he will torment Faust with temptation.

MORE ABOUT THE AUTHOR

The work that launched Goethe's literary career was *Gotz von Berlichingen mit der eisernen Hand* (1773), a play about a sixteenth-century robber knight that some say founded modern German literature. Critics appreciated the strength of its noble hero, who rejected aesthetic, meek codes of behavior. The wider reading public enjoyed its features of castles, dungeons, and other Romantic attributes. Goethe established a reputation as a genius and made an even bigger impact on society with his story *The Sorrows of Young Werther* (1774). This epistolary novel of a young man who commits suicide because he cannot have the woman he loves sparked an enormous response in various parts of Europe for decades, affecting fashions and behavior. Young men even committed Werther-like suicides. When Napoleon Bonaparte met Goethe, he told the writer he had read the novel seven times.

With *Gotz* and *Werther,* his two early successes, Goethe became the leader of the Sturm und Drang (Storm and Stress) movement founded earlier by dramatist Maximilian Klinger. Goethe composed operettas and songs in this style, which was characterized by excitement, passion, and uproar. But the greatest literary success of Goethe's life, *Faust,* sixty years in the making, was influenced as much by events later in his life, such as his travels in Italy where he was exposed to the neoclassical ideas, as by the high Romanticism of the Sturm und Drang movement.

Like his character Faust, Goethe had a need for experience and understanding of life. Goethe considered himself a pagan and thought that art and science should take the place of religion. However, the methods through which Goethe probed for answers were sometimes scientifically unsound. Influenced by Johann Lavater's practice of "physiognomics," or divination of a person's character through his or her physical attributes, Goethe spent a great deal of time studying anatomy through human and animal skulls. Later, in the early 1790s, Goethe became interested in mathematics and physics. After making defective experiments, he was convinced that he had exposed Sir Isaac Newton as a fraud. He published some of his studies and findings in *Zur Farbenlehre* (1810), which he had worked on for eighteen years. Goethe's own need for continual inquiry and striving is portrayed dramatically in *Faust,* completed in 1831, the year before Goethe's death.

A CRITICAL COMMENT

"Goethe's definition of man's nature and needs as lying in activity rather than enjoyment comments on new assumptions that arose in his time and have largely governed Western society since. Acquisitiveness no doubt always was a prominent feature of man; but the new forces of industrial expansion were beginning to concentrate the mind and energies of Europe more and more exclusively on the production and consumption of material goods. The processes involved might seem dynamic enough—the harnessing of the required mechanical power, the multiplying of manufactured objects; and certainly they reached out with their effects far beyond the European continent. But the idea they implied that human fulfillment need only consist in accumulation or repetitive consumption was static and stultifying, and equivalent of the satiety which was all the Faust of legend could achieve, with the Industrial Revolution now playing the role of Mephisto [Mephistopheles] and a seemingly inexhaustible world of natural resources at its command. It would have been an inadequate idea of fulfillment even if the material means to it had been more widely and justly distributed.

"Against it Goethe sets his image of man as impatiently transcending gratification, pursuing instead goals which recede and change as he moves and which, if they were ever to afford satisfaction, would somehow have to preserve—as Faust's last vision does—the feel of the pursuit itself. For the pursuit *is* the goal, man is defined by movement. This goes further than the old Aristotelean definition of happiness as lying in the pursuit of worthwhile goals, and singles out the element of continual striving as the source of value in that process. It provides the ultimate term of comparison for Hegel's and Marx's concepts of alienation; and it remains relevant and thought-provoking now that industrial processes need less and less of the human energies they once monopolized, so that people may yet be free, in a rethought society, to follow activities that will be ends in themselves and to achieve growth of more than just the economic kind."

—from Goethe, T. J. Reed

FOR FURTHER READING

Amrine, Frederick, Francis J. Zucker, and Harvey Wheeler, eds. *Goethe and the Sciences: A Reappraisal.* Boston: D. Reidel, 1987.

Boyle, Nicholas. *Goethe: The Poet and the Age,* Vol. I. New York: Oxford University Press, 1991.

Goethe, Johann Wolfgang von. *Goethe's Faust, Parts I and II.* Trans. Louis MacNiece. New York: Oxford University Press, 1960.

Reed, T. J. *Goethe.* New York: Oxford University Press, 1984.

Weinberg, Kurt. *The Figure of Faust in Valery and Goethe: An Exegesis of Mon Faust.* Princeton, NJ: Princeton University Press, 1976.

THE WORLD IS TOO MUCH WITH US

William Wordsworth ▾ (Textbook page 1004)

SUMMARY

In this modified Petrarchan sonnet, Wordsworth asserts that we have lost our spiritual connection with nature. We have become so worldly, wasting our ability in fruitless efforts, that we are unmoved by its elements, such as the sea and the wind. If he were a pagan, at least he might have visions from nature—perhaps a god rising from the sea—that would ease his melancholy.

MORE ABOUT THE AUTHOR

Wordsworth's early adulthood was filled with an enthusiasm for and a love of nature that imbued all his writing. His writing in the 1790s and early 1800s was marked by the freshness and love of liberty that typified the Lake District poets. During this time, he and his close friend Samuel Taylor Coleridge published *Lyrical Ballads.* In 1805, he completed *The Prelude,* a long autobiographical poem that describes the development of a poet's mind. Two years later, the celebrated poems "Resolution and Independence" and "Intimations of Immortality from Recollections of Early Childhood" appeared in *Poems in Two Volumes,* along with many well-known lyrics. Wordsworth's creative genius in these early years was assisted in important ways by his sister Dorothy and his wife Mary. These women not only provided domestic comfort but also acted as personal assistants, recording his words and transcribing his writing. Wordsworth also frequently referred to Dorothy's journals to help focus his recollections of the places and events that he wrote about in his poetry.

During his forties, Wordsworth's writing lost much of the freshness and vigor of his earlier works. *The Excursion,* published in 1814, was a poem that Wordsworth considered an epic of the same proportions as Milton's *Paradise Lost.* His peers, however, found it a disappointment, and some critics actually ridiculed this work and others. In addition, the fact that Robert Southey was made Poet Laureate in 1813 and that Wordsworth's inspirational friendship with Coleridge had deteriorated may have exhausted and depleted Wordsworth's imagination and creative enthusiasm.

In spite of this decline in his popularity and creativity, Wordsworth received the attention and fame due to a distinguished poet when he was older. Tourists and friends came to visit him at his home at Rydal Mount in the 1830s. During his visits to London, he was lionized by high society. In 1838, the University of Durham conferred upon him the degree of Doctor of Civil Laws, as did Oxford in 1839. And finally, in 1843, he became England's Poet Laureate.

A CRITICAL COMMENT

"What is a Poet? To whom does he address himself? And what language is to be expected from him? He is a man speaking to men: a man, it is true, endued with more lively sensibility, more enthusiasm and tenderness, who has a greater knowledge of human nature, and a more comprehensive soul, than are supposed to be common among mankind; a man pleased with his own passions and volitions, and who rejoices more than other men in the spirit of life that is in him; delighting to contemplate similar volitions and passions as manifested in the goings-on of the Universe, and habitually impelled to create them where he does not find them. To these qualities he has added a disposition to be affected more than other men by absent things as if they were present; an ability of conjuring up in himself passions, which are indeed far from being the same as those produced by real events, yet (especially in those parts of the general sympathy which are pleasing and delightful) do more nearly resemble the passions produced by real events, than anything which, from the motions of their own minds merely, other men are accustomed to feel in themselves; whence, and from practice, he has acquired a greater readiness and power in expressing what he thinks and feels, and especially those thoughts and feelings which, by his own choice, or from the structure of his own mind, arise in him without immediate external excitement."

—*from the 1802 Preface to* Lyrical Ballads, *William Wordsworth*

FOR FURTHER READING

Gill, Stephen. *William Wordsworth: A Life.* New York: Oxford University Press, 1989.

Hartman, Geoffrey H. *Wordsworth's Poetry, 1787–1814.* Cambridge, MA: Harvard University Press, 1971.

Newlyn, Lucy. *Coleridge, Wordsworth, and the Language of Allusion.* New York: Oxford University Press, 1986.

Pinion, F. B. *A Wordsworth Companion: Survey and Assessment.* London: Macmillan, 1984.

Wordsworth, William. *The Complete Poetical Works of William Wordsworth.* Ed. Andrew Jackson George. Boston: Houghton Mifflin, 1932.

I HAVE VISITED AGAIN

Alexander Pushkin ▾ Translated by D. M. Thomas ▾ (Textbook page 1008)

SUMMARY

The speaker describes a visit to his ancestral home, a place where he once resided in exile for two years. In the intervening ten years much has changed, but during his visit he recalls the past and looks to the future.

His hard-working nurse is dead, her cottage in

disrepair. By the lake where he used to sit, the windmill is now badly warped and hardly turns in the breeze. And three pine trees—two together, one off by itself—whose rustling branches often greeted him, are unchanged, except that young trees are now growing up around the two adjacent trees. When these young trees have outgrown the older ones he will be dead, but he hopes his grandson will hear their rustling branches and think of him.

MORE ABOUT THE AUTHOR

Alexander Pushkin, a national hero in Russia, first came to the public eye in his mid-teens when he published "Recollections of Tsarskoye Selo." This political poem celebrating Russia's defeat of Napoleon launched Pushkin's career. At eighteen, he was assigned to a post in the foreign ministry. This led to a spree of debauchery in St. Petersburg, where he contracted a venereal disease, fought duels, and attacked the ultraconservative government of Czar Alexander through his poetry. Pushkin was exiled from St. Petersburg in 1820 for his subversive writings and sent to serve in Kishinev, in southern Russia. Shortly before he left, he published *Ruslan and Ludmila,* a Romantic epic poem. Critics severely disapproved of Pushkin's revival of old Russian legends in this work; they also felt that he dealt with prosaic, rather than poetic, material. While serving in southern Russia, Pushkin began his verse narrative *Eugene Onegin,* a novel in verse that is considered one of his masterpieces.

In spite of his growing literary reputation, Pushkin was watched carefully by the secret police. In 1824, because of political conditions and his atheistic writings, Pushkin was dismissed from the civil service and sequestered in his parents' estate. It is to this exile that he refers in "I Have Visited Again." Here he completed several important works, including his great play *Boris Godunov,* which was poorly received by the critics. In December of 1825, several of Pushkin's friends from school participated in an ill-fated rebellion against Czar Nicholas. Though Pushkin sympathized with the Decembrists, he managed to extract from the Czar a pardon from his own ongoing exile. For some time afterward, Nicholas kept watch over the tone and content of Pushkin's writings.

During his subsequent engagement to Natalya Goncharova, Pushkin wrote prolifically. He completed several dramatic works, including, in 1831, *Eugene Onegin.* Pushkin's later works include *The Bronze Horseman* (1833), a poem that combines history and fantasy as a statue of Peter the Great chases the clerk Eugene around St. Petersburg. His novel *The Captain's Daughter* would later influence Tolstoy's *War and Peace.* Nikolai Gogol said of this work, "Not only is it reality; it is even better."

A CRITICAL COMMENT

"The central vision of a Dante or a Dostoevsky posits the existence of some point of anchorage in the endless, shifting sea of life, some stable point of reference to which life's vagaries can be related. The very lack of this in Pushkin accounts for a great deal. Pushkin's was a pragmatic mind, concerned primarily with the immediacy of life on earth. At the same time Pushkin became and remained intensely aware of Death, to which, indeed, he at times seemed irresistibly drawn. It is Pushkin's feeling for Death that provides a key to many of his feelings for the experiences of life. Lacking a "central vision"—specifically a Christian central vision—he could not feel Death as a prelude to some continued existence or life hereafter; for him Death simply rang down the curtain on the final act of life here below. And this almost pagan view of Death's inevitability and finality imbues with added poignancy what he wrote about our earthly existence—which is indeed his sole concern. Life's unrelenting ebb, the irretrievable passage of time, the unpredictability of Fate—the vulnerability of man's destiny, a metaphysical despair—these are some of the preoccupations and moods which go hand in hand with and accentuate the more dynamic sides of Pushkin's passionate nature: his zest for life, his wit and humor, his pursuit of love, his intense feeling for beauty in many forms. There is in much of Pushkin's work an exuberant, uncomplicated, almost sunlight quality. But his view of the world is, in the final analysis, somewhat bleak and tragic."

—*from* Alexander Pushkin, *Walter N. Vickery*

FOR FURTHER READING

Mirsky, D. S. *Pushkin.* New York: Haskell House, 1974.

Pushkin, Alexander. *The Bronze Horseman: Selected Poems of Alexander Pushkin.* Trans. D. M. Thomas. New York: Viking, 1982.

Sandler, Stephanie. *Distant Pleasures: Alexander Pushkin and the Writing of Exile.* Stanford: Stanford University Press, 1989.

Vickery, Walter N. *Alexander Pushkin.* Boston: Twayne, 1970.

THE LORELEI

Heinrich Heine ▼ Translated by Louis Untermeyer ▼ (Textbook page 1013)

SUMMARY

In the first stanza, the speaker says he is inexplicably disturbed by an ancient legend, which he goes on to describe. It is twilight at the Rhine river; a mountain above catches some of the last rays of sunshine that illuminate a young woman among the rocks, dreamily combing her golden hair with a golden comb. She sings an ancient, magical song. A boatman below hears the song and becomes spellbound, ignoring the reefs in the river which destroy him, leaving only silence.

MORE ABOUT THE AUTHOR

As a young man, Heinrich Heine went to Bonn—ostensibly to study law. His studies would frequently be interrupted by his growing interest in writing poetry. At Bonn, Heine met August Schlegel, a translator of Shakespeare and lecturer on literature and prosody. Influenced by Schlegel, Heine adopted the style of the English poets and wrote sonnets, not the lyrics for which he later became famous. Many of these poems were published in magazines. After Heine learned of his beloved cousin Amalie's marriage, he entered a period of promiscuity during which he contracted the syphilis that later killed him. In 1821, Heine moved to Berlin and became involved in literary salons. He was influenced by the lectures of Hegel, whose thought signaled the end of the Romantic spirit and the approach of the Realist movement. Heine's canon, with its mixture of traditional lyrics and more contemporaneous irony, similarly reflects this shift.

In 1823, Heine published the well-received "Lyrical Intermezzo." In 1825, the poet, who was of Jewish descent, was reluctantly baptized. In order to be a successful candidate for the law degree he had to present himself to the faculty as a Christian and not as a Jew. That same year he received his Doctor of Law degree. In 1826, he completed "The North Sea," a poem that prefigures contemporary free verse, and *Travel Pictures,* satirical travel sketches in verse and prose. With the publication of this work he abandoned any idea of practicing law and decided to write exclusively.

Heine's famous *Book of Songs* (1827), in which "The Lorelei" appeared, won him some admirers, but most critics did not then fully appreciate the import of its fusion of the Romantic and the realistic. In 1831, Heine left Germany for Paris, not realizing then that he would be an expatriate for the rest of his life. There he continued to write, though his health and motivation deteriorated. Near the end of his life he was again inspired to write, in spite of the physical torment brought on by complications of syphilis, by a mysterious woman he called "La Mouche." He wrote love poems to her and worked on his "Memoirs," though he completed only a fragment before he died.

A CRITICAL COMMENT

"In its thirteenth edition at the time of the author's death, *Buch der Lieder* [Book of Songs] became the most widely read book of poetry in world literature, establishing the fame of its author and the wealth of its publisher, to whom Heine had sold it for a pittance. Indeed, so great was the popularity of *Buch der Lieder* that it overshadowed Heine's other, more mature and superior work, or at least delayed its appreciation. The broad public which the poet of *Buch der Lieder* so successfully wooed would have been shocked and repelled by the views that Heine actually held, while many of those who might have appreciated the more problematic and sophisticated "other" Heine turned away from the poet whose name was synonymous with *Buch der Lieder.*

"The format, tone, and style of *Buch der Lieder* is that of the folksong. Despite—or because of—his adherence to the simple forms and metric lines of the conventional four-line stanza, Heine achieved a distinctive voice surprisingly early. For, by and large, Heine's poetry owes much of its unique appeal to the subtle tension and interaction between the seemingly natural, homespun format and the flashes of his agile, sophisticated mind. Still, modern readers of the *Buch der Lieder* may well wonder what captivated the imagination of readers for a century. They will find in it much that seems mannered and derivative—especially in the early sections—and throughout, they will encounter verses that are flawed and weak, glib and trivial, and many that seem unbearably sentimental. The thought of facing 240 poems of which all but a handful deal with unrequited love may lead us to ask with Heine, albeit in a different context than he had in mind:

> Anfangs wollt ich fast verzagen,
> Und ich glaubt, ich trug es nie;
> Und ich hab es doch getragen—
> Aber fragt mich nur nicht, wie? (1:38)

(At first I almost despaired and thought I could not bear it; yet I did—but do not ask me how.)

Yet when we pause to scrutinize these lines, glib and facile as they seem, like an entry for an album which, in fact, they originally were, we find that even they tell us something about Heine's craft. . . . [T]his poem achieves a certain poignancy, as the penultimate of nine songs and the only one compressed into one stanza within a cycle that tells the usual bittersweet tale. Heine had a knack for arranging his independently conceived poems so that they complemented and enhanced each other in content, rhythm, and mood, to form a larger whole."

—from Heinrich Heine, *Hanna Spencer*

FOR FURTHER READING

Fairley, Barker. *Heinrich Heine: An Interpretation.* London: Oxford University Press, 1954.

Spencer, Hanna. *Heinrich Heine.* Boston: Twayne, 1982.

Untermeyer, Louis. *Heinrich Heine, Paradox and Poet.* New York: Harcourt, Brace, 1937.

RUSSIA 1812, *from* THE EXPIATION

Victor Hugo ▾ Translated by Robert Lowell ▾ (Textbook page 1017)

SUMMARY

This excerpt portrays Napoleon's first defeat, the retreat of the French army from Moscow. The opening lines describe the devastation to the ranks because of the blizzard: Injured men take shelter in horse carcasses and caissons, the guard and the soldiers freeze to death where they stand, hungry soldiers march dazed and barefoot in the snow. Lines 25–33 emphasize the private, lonely battle of each man against the elements; the weather conditions of the North are a more fearsome opponent than the Russian troops. Lines 41–48 describe the devastating attacks on the French by the Cossacks. Line 49 begins a second stanza that describes Napoleon himself, watching the routing of his men and the diminishing of his glories. The faith of the surviving soldiers in their leader is mingled with bitterness at their disaster. Napoleon despairs and realizes that this defeat is the atonement for his previous conquests.

MORE ABOUT THE AUTHOR

The prolific Victor Hugo believed that effort and concentration were the source of literary inspiration; he himself labored intensively at his writing throughout his life, despite political and personal conflicts.

In his early twenties, Hugo became close to his father, from whom he learned to appreciate the now-exiled Napoleon Bonaparte's political, military, and diplomatic abilities and his defense of the personal freedoms won during the French Revolution. He also learned to be suspicious of the reactionary rule of the Bourbons. This shift in sympathies is evident in his subsequent writing.

For the time being, however, Hugo was a favorite of the court. By his early twenties, he was already a writer of some renown. He was patronized by the Emperor Louis XVIII and befriended by the acclaimed author Alexander Dumas. In 1831, after the publication of two collections of poetry and the production of two plays, Hugo's novel *Notre-Dame de Paris (The Hunchback of Notre Dame),* written in only four months, was released. The novel's success was so tremendous that it prompted a revival of medieval architecture and caused the public to imitate Hugo's style of dress. The drama and literature critic Gautier described Hugo as "the greatest of living French poets, dramatists, and novelists."

Not satisfied with his highly successful literary career, Hugo decided to enter the political arena. By 1848, he was elected to the National Assembly. Hugo's interest in reform in labor and education led to his support for Louis-Napoleon in his successful campaign for the presidency. However, Louis-Napoleon's reactionary administration harrassed the presses, including one operated by Hugo and his sons. Hugo himself was eventually exiled and fled to the Channel Isles, where he wrote the Realist novel *Les Misérables* (1862). Also while in exile, Hugo publicly supported international seekers of freedom, such as the American abolitionist John Brown, whose attempted slave insurrection at Harper's Ferry, Virginia failed; and the Italian revolutionary Garibaldi, who attempted to liberate and unify Italy.

A CRITICAL COMMENT

"As for love, war, family pleasures, the sorrows of the poor, national splendors, all that which is peculiar to man and which constitutes the domain of the genre painter and of the history painter, what have we seen that is richer and more concrete than the lyrical poetry of Victor Hugo? If space allowed, this would doubtless be the occasion to analyze the moral atmosphere which hovers and moves through his poems and which derives very obviously from the author's own temperament. It seems to me that it is unmistakably characterized by a love which makes no distinction between what is very strong and what is very weak, and that the attraction exercised over the poet by these two extremes stems from a single source, which is the very strength, the primordial vigor with which he is endowed. Strength delights and intoxicates him; he approaches it as if it were a brother: fraternal affection. Thus he is irresistibly attracted to every symbol of the infinite, the sea, the sky; to all the ancient representatives of strength, Homeric or Biblical giants, paladins, knights; to enormous and fearful beasts. He makes child's play of fondling what would frighten weaker hands; he moves about in immensity without vertigo. On the other hand, but through a different tendency, whose source is, however, the same, the poet always shows warm compassion for all that is weak, lonely, sorrowful, for all that is fatherless: a paternal attraction. The man of strength, who senses a brother in all that is strong, sees his children in all that has need of protection or consolation. It is from strength itself and from the certainty that it gives to one who possesses it that the spirit of justice and of charity is derived. Thus in the poems of Victor Hugo there constantly occur those notes of love for fallen women, for the poor who are crushed in the cogwheels of society, for the animals that are martyrs of our gluttony and despotism. Few people have noticed the magic charm which kindness adds to strength and which is so frequently seen in the works of our poet. A smile and a tear on the face of a colossus is an almost divine form of originality. Even in his short poems devoted to sensual love, in those verses so voluptuous and so melodious in their melancholy, may be heard, like the continuous accompaniment of an orchestra, the deep voice of charity. Beneath the lover one senses a father and a protector. It is not a matter here of that sermonizing morality which, with its pedantic air and its didactic tone, can spoil the most beautiful piece of poetry but of an implicit morality which slips unnoticed into poetic matter like imponderable fluids into the machinery of the world. Morality does not enter into this art as its avowed purpose; it is intermingled with it and lost sight of, as in life itself. The poet is unintentionally a moralist through the abundance and plenitude of nature."

—from "Victor Hugo," Charles Baudelaire

FOR FURTHER READING

Baudelaire, Charles. "Victor Hugo." *Baudelaire as a Literary Critic.* Eds. and trans. Lois Boe Hyslop and Francis E. Hyslop, Jr. University Park, PA: Pennsylvania State University Press, 1964.

Bloom, Harold, ed. *Victor Hugo.* New York: Chelsea House, 1988.

Houston, John Porter. *Victor Hugo.* Boston: Twayne, 1988.

Hugo, Victor. *The Distance, the Shadows.* Trans. Harry Guest. London: Longwood, 1981.

Richardson, Joanna. *Victor Hugo.* New York: St. Martin's Press, 1976.

INVITATION TO THE VOYAGE

Charles Baudelaire ▼ Translated by Richard Wilbur ▼ (Textbook page 1023)

SUMMARY

Using luxurious, sensuous images of comfort and peace, the speaker invites a woman to live and love with him in a tranquil land: a land of glimmering skies, voluptuous flowers, luxuriant furnishings, and golden sunsets. The refrain, two lines at the end of each stanza, summarizes the speaker's imagined world as one of peace, luxury, and pleasure.

MORE ABOUT THE AUTHOR

As a young man, Baudelaire was a dandy and a rebel against authority. He was only a mediocre student, and while at school he contracted a venereal disease that would plague him for the rest of his life. In the late 1830s, his fondness for popular novels and journalism and his lack of a vocation spurred him to style himself as an insolent, witty man of letters. When he returned to Paris after an abortive trip to the East, he inherited his father's wealth, moved to the Latin Quarter, and squandered his legacy. To his very great humiliation, his appalled family sought a legally appointed financial administrator for his estate.

Baudelaire's flamboyant habits earned him a reputation as a writer and eccentric. In his early twenties, he was a member of the Club des Haschischins, a circle of writers and artists who met to partake of hashish. His *Les Paradis artificiels* gives an account of his experiences with the drug, condemning the illusory pleasures it offers.

In 1857, his *Les Fleurs du Mal,* a collection of poetry dealing with the antagonism between good and evil, was brought to trial on religious and public morality charges. The blasphemy charge was eventually dismissed, but Baudelaire and his publishers were found guilty of the public morality charge. They each had to pay a fine and lost certain civic rights. Though the trial resulted in the censorship of his work, the scandal brought him more fame; Baudelaire was now considered the leader of the new generation of poets. His 1861 edition of *Les Fleurs du Mal,* which offered a reordered and augmented collection, was considered even more noteworthy than the original. However, his health and debts continued to worsen, his interest in writing deteriorated, and he died in Paris in September of 1867.

A CRITICAL COMMENT

"Baudelaire was convinced that the age in which he lived was a decadence, and we who know it not only by his own passionate protest against it, but by Balzac's romantic anatomy of its corruption, must acquiesce in his conviction. The old aristocratic order had fallen; there was no new democratic order to supply its place: in the interval arose, like a growth of weeds on the site of a demolished building, as the sole principle of spiritual and social order, that reverence for wealth for its own sake which distinguished nineteenth century France. Guizot's "Enrichissez-vous" marked a social nadir. It was the age of rampant industrialism and violent and abortive revolution; of the hideous and uncontrolled eruption of the great cities; of all the squalor of a victorious and hypocritical materialism. Against this tyranny Baudelaire conceived it his duty to protest, not merely by the poetic utterances of cries of revolt but by the actual conduct of his life. The French romantic movement as a whole was animated to some extent by a spirit of protest against the sordidness of the age; but Baudelaire belonged to a curious section of the movement which had very little in common with romanticism as we generally conceive it now. His affinities were with the disciplined and contemptuous romanticism of Stendhal and Mérimée. This romanticism was rather

a kind of sublimated realism, based upon an almost morbid 'horreur d'etre dupe'—romantic in its aspiration away from the bourgeois society which it loathed, realistic in its determination to accept the facts as they were. . . ."
—from "Baudelaire," John Middleton Murry

FOR FURTHER READING

Baudelaire, Pierre Charles. *The Flowers of Evil*. Trans. Marthiel Matthews and Jackson Matthews. New York: New Directions, 1962.

Peyre, Henri, ed. *Baudelaire: A Collection of Critical Essays*. Englewood Cliffs, NJ: Prentice-Hall, 1962.

Pichois, Claude. *Baudelaire*. New York: Viking Penguin, 1989.

Starkie, Enid. *Baudelaire*. New York: Paragon House, 1988.

Turnell, Martin. *Baudelaire: A Study of His Poetry*. New York: New Directions, 1972.

THE SKY IS JUST BEYOND THE ROOF

Paul Verlaine ▾ Translated by Bergen Applegate ▾ (Textbook page 1029)

SUMMARY

Confined indoors, probably in prison, the speaker looks out at a calm, blue sky, a ringing bell, and a singing bird. He asserts that life can be found "there," outdoors, and emphasizes that the peaceful sounds he hears come from the outside. Finally, he addresses himself, asking what he has done with his lost youth.

THE SLEEPER OF THE VALLEY

Arthur Rimbaud ▾ Translated by Ludwig Lewisohn ▾ (Textbook page 1030)

SUMMARY

The speaker describes an idyllic scene: a river in a valley, a sunlit mountain, flowers, and deep, green grass. In this setting is a young soldier who seems to be sleeping peacefully—but who is actually dead, with two bullet wounds in his side.

MORE ABOUT THE AUTHORS

Verlaine, an important figure in the Symbolist and Decadent movements, has been recognized as a poetic genius mostly by later generations. He believed that verse should be musical, rhythmical, and evocative—unfettered by rhyme and regularity. He first became interested in writing poetry when he read Baudelaire's *Les Fleurs du Mal* while at school. He associated with a group of other writers that established a serialized anthology of poetry named *Le Parnasse contemporain*. The poetic theory of the Parnassiens, as this group became known, was an almost scientific reaction against Romanticism; they believed that poetry should be objective and impersonal, unlike the lyrical and self-revelatory poetry of the Romantics. The anthology published several poems by Verlaine, bringing him recognition.

Shortly after his marriage to Mathilde in 1871, Verlaine received a letter from Arthur Rimbaud asking him to read several enclosed poems. Greatly impressed, Verlaine invited Rimbaud to Paris and acted as the younger poet's literary mentor. Rimbaud's youth, surliness, and unkemptness diminished Verlaine's respectability; they were both eventually ostracized from literary society. Soon, Verlaine left his wife, and he and Rimbaud traveled to other parts of Europe together, apparently as lovers. Conflicts in their relationship led to Verlaine's shooting of Rimbaud in Brussels; he was prosecuted not for the shooting, but for suspected homosexuality. During his year in prison, he continued to write poetry. His collection *Romance sans paroles* was published in 1874, to almost no critical notice; however, it is now considered the first major Symbolist work. Following the deaths of Mathilde and his son, Verlaine worked further on his poetry and gradually regained some stature in Paris.

Rimbaud's own literary career began and ended in his youth. During that short time, he managed to become an influence on French poetry and, indeed, on all modern poetry. Like Verlaine, he is a prominent figure of the Symbolist movement.

As a schoolboy in Charleville, France, Rimbaud was already writing poetry, and he even submitted a poem to *Le Parnasse contemporain* in Paris. (The poem was rejected.) At the outbreak of the Franco-Prussian war, the fifteen-year-old Rimbaud ran away to Paris, inflamed with revolutionary fervor. He was soon sent back to Charleville, but some critics feel that Rimbaud must have had a traumatic experience during this foray that contributed to the violence and blasphemy of the poetry written soon after his return. Over the course of a few months, however, Rimbaud's poems became more spiritual and mystical. He developed an aesthetic doctrine that asserted the poet is a seer and a sufferer who must develop his art through self-induced delirium.

When Rimbaud returned to Paris as a young man and established himself with Verlaine, he wrote his best-known literature, including the collections *Les Illuminations* and *Une Saison en enfer*. After years of vagabonding, he died in Marseilles in 1891.

A CRITICAL COMMENT

"A dissatisfaction with materialism was at the root of *fin-de-siècle:* artists endeavored to assert the significance of their personal dreams, poses or symbols. The door to dreams and nightmares was opened on images of suggestive power. Artists tried to clothe ideas in forms accessible to the senses, or they withdrew into elaborate or exotic environments, or they became dandies, or indeed some remained in their respectable posts in government offices. Whatever the individual case, imagination was recognized in Baudelaire's phrase as 'queen of faculties.' The individual fruits of the imagination were as varied as were the forms of dissatisfaction with the materialism of the day. *Fin-de-siècle* was less a movement than an atmosphere.

Within it both 'Decadent' and 'Symbolist' artists revolted against a material viewpoint; 'One is entitled . . . to prefer the defeat of Athens to the triumph of the violent Macedonian,' was how the situation was summed up in 1881.

"The 'Decadents' were primarily a French manifestation of a malaise in evidence throughout Europe. They viewed with grave misgivings and pessimism the vigorous optimism and deadening comforts of materialism. They did not see their own age as in decline—indeed they were only too aware of its robust health. . . .

"The Symbolist was perhaps more dynamic in his reaction against materialism than was his pessimistic contemporary. He sought escape from the banal in an art that was expressive of ideas and emotions. In itself this did not mean that his art could not also reveal decadent characteristics. . . .

"The Symbolist placed great emphasis upon his means. Both the poem and (later) the painting gained in expressive power through an emphasis upon sounds, rhythms or colors employed, over and above what was represented.

"Artists whose works coincided with the ideas of either Symbolists or Decadents were often championed or patronized by writers and poets. The search by Symbolist and Decadent intellectuals for the pictorial ratification of their ideas produced an art movement that was among the most intellectual in the nineteenth century."

—*from* Symbolists and Decadents, *John Milner*

FOR FURTHER READING

Carter, A. E. *Paul Verlaine.* New York: Twayne, 1971.

Lewisohn, Ludwig, ed. and trans. *The Poets of Modern France.* New York: B. W. Huebsch, 1919.

Milner, John. *Symbolists and Decadents.* New York: E. P. Dutton, 1971.

Richardson, Joanna. *Verlaine.* New York: Viking, 1971.

Rimbaud, Arthur. *Complete Works.* Trans. Paul Schmidt. New York: Harper and Row, 1975.

Starkie, Enid. *Arthur Rimbaud.* London: Hamish Hamilton, 1947.

Verlaine, Paul. *Selected Poems.* Trans. Carlyle Ferren MacIntyre. Berkeley: University of California Press, 1970.

THE JEWELS

Guy de Maupassant ▾ Translated by Roger Colet ▾ (Textbook page 1034)

SUMMARY

The story tells of Monsieur Lantin, a clerk at the Ministry of the Interior in Paris. He meets and falls in love with a poor but beautiful young woman who seems the ideal, virtuous wife. They marry, and for six years she cares for him lavishly and makes a very comfortable home for him. His only complaint is her love for the theater, which spawns her love for gaudy, imitation jewelry. After going to the opera one night, she catches pneumonia and dies. Lantin is grief-stricken and soon finds himself unable to provide for himself materially as his wife did. In debt, he decides to sell one of his wife's necklaces. When the piece is appraised for far more than he expected, he realizes that his wife's "imitation" jewels are actually expensive presents from someone unknown to him. Though Lantin is humiliated by his wife's evident lack of virtue and by the jeweler's apprehension of this, he has all the jewelry appraised and realizes that the sale will make him quite wealthy. He quits his job and begins to live extravagantly. Six months later, he marries a virtuous woman who makes him very unhappy.

MORE ABOUT THE AUTHOR

Guy de Maupassant's parents separated when he was eleven. His apparently mild-mannered father had little impact on his life; however, his mother and her longtime friend Gustave Flaubert encouraged his writing throughout their lives.

In 1875, Maupassant joined a literary group called Les Soirées de Medin; this group developed the Naturalist movement of which Émile Zola and Maupassant were to become the leaders. Before this group, Maupassant read his story "Boule de suif" ("Ball of Fat"); his first success, it was published in the group's anthology in 1880. That same year, Maupassant was threatened with prosecution for immorality because of his racy poem "Au Bord de l'eau." Flaubert, who had suffered similar consequences for his novel *Madame Bovary,* wrote letters successfully interceding on his protege's behalf.

In 1881, Maupassant published his story *La Maisson tellier,* which is set in a brothel. Though sales were very good, some critics attacked him for depicting a low subject matter. At the age of thirty-four, Maupassant finished his famous short story "La Parure" ("The Necklace"), which was praised highly by Henry James. His well known novella, *Le Horla,* with its elements of insanity and the supernatural, demonstrates the influence of Paris's contemporary fascination with Charcot's experiments with mentally ill women at Salpetriere.

Toward the end of his life, Maupassant continued to write, despite the fact that his health and mental condition were impaired because of syphilis. The year 1888 saw the publication of the novel *Pierre et Jean,* considered one of his finest works, and *Le Roman,* an essay on Realist and Naturalist novels. Afflicted with migraine headaches and delusions, Maupassant died in 1893.

A CRITICAL COMMENT

"Guy de Maupassant's life was . . . highly representative of the changes in France in the latter half of the last century and of the greatness and the weakness of the society he lived in; both became too self-indulgent and introverted to pay attention to the corrosive force undermining them. If his life is representative of his age, his work has a universal value; his characters, though belonging by their dress, habits and way of life to their age, live on by the timeless features of their behavior and by the fact that it is on these that Maupassant concentrates for the motive of his stories. It is, moreover, his detached discriminating concision in presenting so succinctly and yet so convincingly what is essential for the reader's interest in and understanding of a story, and for the comments on human behavior to be inferred from it, that have given him the great reputation and constant appeal he has. In these qualities lies the originality of his talents as a *conteur.* In addition, in adapting a literary expertise, not seen in the short story since Mérimée, to his journalistic needs, Maupassant succeeded in bringing the genre to a much wider modern public. Readers today still appreciate his succinctness and the lucid and rapid flow of narrative it provides just as Tolstoy, Chekhov, Henry James and Somerset Maugham did in the past. It was indeed largely because of the brevity and brisk pace of his work that Maupassant was so easily translated and became so popular outside France. Only those more concerned with the academic criticism of his style rather than the clear presentation and readability of his work complain of his allegiance to what is partly a journalistic technique rather than an exercise in literary preciosity. As a freelance writer Maupassant could not afford to write for just a literary elite and needed to exploit his talents to live; he wrote in the manner and form he did for the newspapers and periodicals who paid him and their readers. In so doing, he virtually resuscitated the short story and gave it both a worthy literary form and a new popularity. The fact that his stories and novels are today as exciting, provoking or amusing as they were when they first appeared shows that, while his life is representative of his age, his work belongs to the timeless realm of classic literature."

—*from* Maupassant, *Michael G. Lerner*

FOR FURTHER READING

Donaldson-Evans, Mary. *A Woman's Revenge: The Chronology of Dispossession in Maupassant's Fiction.* Lexington, KY: French Forum, 1986.

Dugan, John Raymond. *Illusion and Reality: A Study of Descriptive Techniques in the Works of Guy de Maupassant.* The Hague: Mouton & Co. N. V., 1973.

Lerner, Michael G. *Maupassant.* New York: George Braziller, 1975.

MacNamara, Matthew. *Style and Vision in Maupassant's Nouvelles.* New York: P. Lang, 1986.

Maupassant, Guy de. *Selected Short Stories.* Trans. Roger Colet. New York: Penguin, 1971.

HOW MUCH LAND DOES A MAN NEED?

Leo Tolstoy ▾ Translated by Louise and Aylmer Maude ▾ (Textbook page 1045)

SUMMARY

Pahom, a peasant farmer, overhears his wife and her wealthier sister, who lives in town, each defending her lifestyle. Pahom's wife points out that the Devil offers more temptations in town. Pahom thinks that peasants like himself are too busy to be tempted; if only he had more land, he wouldn't fear even the Devil. The Devil decides to accept this challenge and resolves to trap Pahom by helping him to acquire land. As Pahom becomes more wealthy, he starts becoming more covetous and unneighborly; he taxes trespassing peasants, as do other landowners. Learning of a land opportunity beyond the Volga River, he moves his family to this area and does well raising crops. Still unsatisfied, he travels with a servant to the distant lands of the Bashkirs, in hopes of acquiring some of their vast land. The Bashkirs agree to his request, allotting him as much land as he can step off in a day. The night before the deed is drawn up, Pahom has a prophetic dream of his own death before a laughing demon. He walks all the next day and covers a great deal of ground. Upon reaching the finishing point, however, he dies from exhaustion, and is buried by his servant in six feet of land, all the land a man ultimately needs.

MORE ABOUT THE AUTHOR

Tolstoy's life demonstrates a conflict between his spiritual, intellectual needs and more earthly drives. His military experiences had instilled in him a desire to reform the world; he resolved to use his writing for moral purposes. In 1855 and 1856, he published *Sevastopol Sketches.* The book was an unromantic, subversive account of the destruction of Sevastopol that he witnessed firsthand while serving in the army. The author had not yet turned a moralizing eye to his own conduct, however, and in 1855 he went to St. Petersburg, where he led a dissipated life among the city's *literati.* There, he met the writer Turgenev, with whom he began what was to be a very long and turbulent friendship.

In 1862, Tolstoy married the eighteen-year-old Sofia. Their courtship and early marriage were blissfully happy; Tolstoy compared his love and his writing to "two drops of honey." Sofia was an educated woman who loved literature and, like her husband, kept a journal. For Tolstoy, writing was partly an act of expiation; but after Sofia pleaded with him to destroy his more unsavory descriptions of himself recorded in his journals, he no longer felt free to write whatever he wished. Their divergence of opinion on the nature of his writing underlies most of the Tolstoys' later marital conflicts.

Following his radical spiritual conversion, which earned him excommunication from the Russian Orthodox Church in 1901, Tolstoy's marriage deteriorated in earnest. Tolstoy wanted austerity; Sofia wanted security for their large family. Tolstoy published books to make them available to the masses; Sofia at the same time arranged for publication of her husband's complete works simply to make money to support the family. One work in particular, *The Death of Ivan Ilyich* (1886), reflects Tolstoy's distaste for marriage at this time. Shortly before his death, he and Sofia had bitter disputes over his copyrights and royalties; he wanted to bequeath these to the Russian people, she wanted them to be retained within the family. The acrimony between them led to his flight from home, but he died at a train station in Astapovo before reaching his destination.

A CRITICAL COMMENT

"Out of the spiritual crisis of the late 1870s, and testifying more decisively, if less directly, than his non-fiction to its importance for him, there comes a considerable sequence of stories and novels which may be said to deal in some way or other with the theme of conversion—with a crisis which leads towards the rejection of the inverted values and empty assumptions of the higher classes of society, and which involves the discovery of a new world of more stable spiritual values. In fact, it is possible to see all of Tolstoy's work after *A Confession,* with the notable exception of *Hadji Murat,* as related to some aspect of the conversion experience he describes there.

"This is most obviously true of such things as *Resurrection* or *The Death of Ivan Ilyich,* but it is true also of the masterly parabolic stories like *How Much Land Does a Man Need?,* which James Joyce felt to be 'the greatest story that the literature of the world knows'. This is only one of a large number of short stories aimed at a popular audience which Tolstoy wrote in the years following *A Confession*: in them he strips narrative detail to its barest minimum, avoiding what now seemed to him a trivial indulgence in detailed description, and concentrates his art with stringent economy on the communication of the moral lesson which is the *raison d'être* of each story. To speak of communicating a moral lesson, however, is to run the risk of misrepresenting the essential nature of these stories: in fact, the bareness of the narrative, Tolstoy's reliance on the method of parable rather than explication, saves them from becoming merely didactic *exempla.* Though their didacticism could scarcely be clearer, Tolstoy himself enters them much less than one would expect. They do not preach, but merely tell, and in the telling take on at their best a hard clarity of a kind that one associates with the finest folk art, and which goes some way to substantiate Joyce's admiration of one of the best of them.

"The relationship which these parabolic stories bear to Tolstoy's own crisis is clear, but tangential: they grow out of it in the sense that they set out to teach to a popular audience certain moral and religious truths which had become more clear to him since his conversion. Though they only occasionally deal with conversion itself, both their content and their form are dependent on the experience recounted in *A Confession:* they teach a rejection of material values, a subjugation of the physical and limited body to the spiritual and divine in man (what is called in *The Kingdom of God is Within You* his 'reasonable consciousness'), through a studiously 'universal' art that does not aim to please a small parasitic upper class, but which is intended to reach those great masses for whom, in Tolstoy's view, 'high art' could have no meaning or relevance."

—from Tolstoy, *T. G. S. Cain*

BIBLIOGRAPHY

Bloom, Harold, ed. *Leo Tolstoy.* New York: Chelsea House, 1986.

Cain, T. G. S. *Tolstoy.* New York: Barnes and Noble, 1977.

Courcel, Martine de. *Tolstoy: The Ultimate Reconciliation.* New York: Charles Scribner's Sons, 1988.

Smoluchowski, Louise. *Lev and Sonya: The Story of the Tolstoy Marriage.* New York: Putnam, 1987.

Tolstoy, Leo. *Twenty-Three Tales.* Trans. Louise and Aylmer Maude. Oxford: Oxford University Press.

A PROBLEM

Anton Chekhov ▼ Translated by Constance Garnett ▼ (Textbook page 1062)

SUMMARY

Sasha Uskov has brought potential dishonor to his family by cashing a fraudulent promissory note that has now come due for payment. Three of Sasha's uncles are holding a secret council to decide how to handle the matter. One uncle believes that Sasha should not be protected from the consequences of his action. The second uncle simply wants to keep the affair out of the newspapers. The third uncle argues that Sasha is not only young, but an orphan as well. He even questions whether a human being has the free will to commit a crime. Sasha is indifferent; he objects only to being called a criminal because he feels he did nothing unusual and meant no harm. When summoned by the uncles, he feels ashamed and is unable to defend himself. His uncles decide the family will pay the debt if Sasha repents and works in the country with the third uncle. As they prepare to depart, Sasha shocks his uncle by extorting one hundred rubles from him. Sasha then sets off for one of his friend's parties, only now feeling that he truly is a criminal.

MORE ABOUT THE AUTHOR

Chekhov first cultivated his gift for storytelling during his childhood, partly as a diversion from the rule of his tyrannical father. As a thirteen-year-old child he formed a small theater company composed of himself and his brothers and sister, who performed plays written by Chekhov for the entertainment of relatives and friends. But in spite of the literary pursuits of his youth and the hundreds of stories Chekhov later wrote while studying medicine, he had no ambition then to be a literary figure. All the same, he chafed against the restraints placed on his writing by his editors: he usually was allowed to write humorous material of one hundred lines only; and he could not make any ironic observations on religion or the government without being censored.

In 1884, in the midst of treating patients and writing, Chekhov noticed the first signs of tuberculosis, the disease that would later end his life. In the mid- and late 1880s, Chekhov began to acquire a literary reputation, without ever seeking it, from people who admired his published works. Chekhov entered literary circles in Moscow and St. Petersburg, and began to produce his mature work, although he continued to undertake medical projects. In 1889, Chekhov journeyed across Siberia to the prison island of Sakhalin, where he made a survey of the prisoners' living conditions that resulted in *The Island of Sakhalin* (1892), his only nonfiction work.

In 1895, Chekhov returned to drama, completing *The Seagull.* Though it is now recognized as one of his major works, Chekhov himself felt it was only a mediocre achievement, and indeed it debuted to a poor reception. However, writers such as Tolstoy and Gorky lent Chekhov their support. Gorky saw Chekhov as a pivotal writer, and saw in Chekhov's story "The Lady with the Dog" (1899) the end of the Realist era. The main ventures of Chekhov's final years were theatrical. *Uncle Vanya* (1900), *Three Sisters* (1901), and *The Cherry Orchard* (1904) were all performed at the Moscow Art Theater, founded in 1898, as was a later production of *The Seagull.* These productions brought greater recognition to the theater and to Chekhov himself.

A CRITICAL COMMENT

"Since Chekhov strove valiantly to avoid artificiality and insincerity, early critics deplored his lack of traditional plot structure. He often shuns orthodox beginnings and endings, choosing to focus on one quintessential action, when all that a character stands for is revealed. Life was his esthetic norm, and thus he uses real-life unity, probability, and structure or form. He avoids the "well-made" plot that moves towards a climax, since life too moves on invisible feet. His real plot is the "buried life" of one who is often too shy to star in a trumped-up melodrama.

"Plot is de-emphasized at the expense of character. Chekhov had a deep, intuitive understanding of human nature. His characters are almost always interesting and are sometimes unusual. Finding no heores or villains in life, he gives us none in his stories. But in a stroke we are instantly at home with his characters, for they live on our block. Chekhov shows deep compassion for his people, especially if they are underdogs or undervalued persons. The dramatic force of his stories generally grows out of his use of character contrasts.

"Chekhov's stories are provocative. They impel the reader to think, or more often to feel, in a new and sometimes oblique direction. His general theme is human inhumanity to fellow humans. In his stories the "enemies" are hypocrisy and the misuse of power, and the "heroes" are gentleness, forgiveness, simplicity, understanding, and work.

"Chekhov's language is simple and unadorned, but exceedingly accurate and precise. His language never violates the texture of his thought. Extreme accuracy and economy of diction give his stories a lyrical effect. His characters speak in natural dialogue. He rarely employs puns, symbols, or double entendres. . . .

"Along with Maupassant, Chekhov deserves credit for helping contribute to the evolution of the form of the modern short story. In Chekhov's hands the genre gained status as a high achievement of literary art."

—*from* Chekhov Criticism: 1880 through 1986,
Charles W. Meister

FOR FURTHER READING

Chekhov, Anton Pavlovich. *Letters on the Short Story, the Drama, and Other Literary Topics.* Ed. Louis S. Friedland. New York: B. Blom, 1964.
—.*The Tales of Chekhov.* Trans. Constance Garnett. Vol. 4. New York: Macmillan, 1917.
De Maegd-Soep, Carolina. *Chekhov and Women: Women in the Life and Work of Chekhov.* Columbus, OH: Slavica, 1987.
Troyat, Henri. *Chekhov.* Trans. Michael Henry Heim. New York: E. P. Dutton, 1986.
Williams, Lee J. *Anton Chekhov: The Iconoclast.* Scranton, PA: University of Scranton Press, 1989.

A DOLL'S HOUSE

Henrik Ibsen ▾ Translated by Michael Meyer ▾ (Textbook page 1071)

SUMMARY

ACT 1

Nora Helmer returns home from shopping on Christmas Eve. Her husband, Torvald, a banker, complains indulgently about her extravagant spending, calling her his "little squanderbird." He mistakenly believes that Nora spends his money on trivial things, a misconception Nora does not deny. Actually, as she reveals to Christine Linde, a childhood friend who comes calling, Nora is gradually repaying a debt she incurred to save Torvald's life when he was ill. Because women at this time could not legally borrow money, Nora has forged her father's signature. She believes that with Torvald's impending promotion to bank manager, their financial problems will be solved.

But her creditor, Nils Krogstad, calls on Nora later and blackmails her. He threatens to reveal her debt and her crime of forgery first to her moralistic husband and then to the authorities—unless she convinces Torvald to keep Krogstad on in his position at the bank. The act closes amid heightening suspense as Torvald forbids Nora to continue pleading Krogstad's case.

ACT 2

Torvald has decided to fire Krogstad and hire Mrs. Linde to fill his position, in spite of Nora's beseeching. Nora considers asking Dr. Rank, a terminally ill friend of the family, for money to repay her debt, but when he responds to her overtures with a protestation of love, she feels compelled to refuse his offer of assistance.

Since Nora is unable to ensure Krogstad's position at the bank, he carries out his threat, leaving a letter exposing her in Torvald's mailbox. Nora postpones Torvald's reading of the letter by persuading him to leave off business until after the holiday ball to take place the next night. In soliloquy, Nora reveals that once the ball is over, she will know by Torvald's reaction to the letter whether she will take her life or not, again heightening suspense.

Act 3

As Nora and Torvald attend the ball, Mrs. Linde and Krogstad, former lovers, become reconciled. His heart softened by love, Krogstad offers for Mrs. Linde's sake to retrieve his letter, but she insists that the truth must come out. After the ball, Torvald reads the letter. Far from being the protective and understanding husband Nora had hoped he would be, Torvald harshly condemns her. During his tirade, a messenger delivers an envelope from Krogstad, returning Nora's I.O.U. and absolving her of her debt. Ecstatically, Torvald forgives his wife. But the disillusioned Nora, who has already changed her clothes, is ready to change her life. Discussing her marriage with her husband, Nora says that Torvald does not love her as an independent adult but as a childlike, totally dependent doll. She also realizes that she can no longer play the role of the doll. She decides to leave him and their children to learn more about herself and the world, and immediately departs. The play ends with the slamming of the door as Nora leaves.

MORE ABOUT THE AUTHOR

As a young adult studying for the university, Ibsen became interested in the tumultuous political events taking place in France, such as Louis Philippe's abdication in 1848 and France's declaration of itself as a republic. At the university in Christiania (now Oslo), Ibsen became more deeply involved with social criticism and wrote literary and political commentaries in a weekly journal. He also became involved in the debate over whether Norwegian drama should be written in the vernacular or in the more formal, and elite, Danish-derived language; Ibsen favored the vernacular. Later that year, Ibsen wrote the drama *St. John's Night,* which shows the beginnings of the social criticism that is a key feature of his later works. In 1857, Ibsen accepted a position at the Norwegian Theater of Christiania. He eventually left the theater in disgrace, blamed in part for the theater's financial difficulties. This stress, plus his disillusionment with Norway when it failed to aid Denmark in its war with Germany, prompted him to leave his country in 1864.

During his self-imposed exile Ibsen wrote many of his greatest works. In Rome, he wrote a play based on Norwegian legend, *Peer Gynt,* which was published in 1867 and later set to music by Edvard Grieg. This verse drama pokes fun at Norwegian nationalism. While some critics admired its satire, others were offended by its lack of idealism. In 1868, the Ibsen family left Rome for Germany, where they would live for the next twenty-three years. Ibsen's reputation grew both in Norway and abroad. In 1879, *A Doll's House* was published in Copenhagen in an edition of 8,000 copies, the largest first printing of Ibsen's works. The play was inspired by true events befalling an acquaintance,

Laura Kieler, who had written a feminist novel entitled *Brand's Daughters* as a sequel to one of Ibsen's early plays, *Brand. A Doll's House* made Ibsen internationally famous; in spite of vociferous criticism in some sectors, the stage productions were a triumph.

In 1881, Ibsen met George Bernard Shaw, who would ten years later publish an article entitled "The Quintessence of Ibsenism," which helped to establish Ibsen as a major dramatist in England. In his mature years, Ibsen continued to write dramatic works that dealt with political and social themes, such as *Ghosts* (1881), *An Enemy of the People* (1882), and *Hedda Gabler* (1890). He also wrote plays exploring hypnosis and the forces of the unconscious, such as *The Master Builder* (1896); Sigmund Freud was a great admirer of these latter plays. In 1891, Ibsen returned to Norway for good after his self-imposed, twenty-seven-year exile. In his final years, the playwright was debilitated by apoplectic fits and strokes, and he died on May 23, 1906.

A CRITICAL COMMENT

"Immediately marriage becomes a microcosm of the prevailing male-dominated society at large, in which—as the preliminary notes to *A Doll's House* put it—'a woman cannot be herself. . . . It is an exclusively male society with laws drafted by men, and with counsel and judges who judge feminine conduct from the male point of view.' Nora's inbred faith in authority and in male domination clashes with her natural instincts, and it is very largely this that makes the drama. Relentlessly, Ibsen builds up by such means his case against the 'home': as the source of bigotry and hypocrisy and blinkered vision; as the abode of tyrannical affection and possessiveness; snug, smug places that confine, enfold, demand; ostensibly well-regulated institutions, . . . which deservedly burn down; facades, . . . which conceal obscenities; ways of life such as any right-thinking person slams the door on.

"Small wonder that strange things happen to truth in such surroundings; the suppressions, distortions, perversions that take place, the garbling and the dissembling that goes on, the sham and the pretence. Consider even *A Doll's House* alone, how much of the lives of the characters is spent in tampering in some way or other with the truth. Suppression first: Nora's big secret is of course the pivot about which the action turns, exploited by Krogstad, shared with Mrs. Linde, and withheld in terror from Torvald. And Rank's mortal secret is similarly a matter to share with some and withhold from others, entering into things by a kind of counterpoint. Then, secondly, both Torvald and Nora need the opiate of day-dreams to help them to bear the reality of their lives: Torvald indulges himself with the pretense that he and Nora are

A Doll's House **149**

secret lovers, newly and clandestinely wed; and Nora dreams of a rich admirer who will leave her all his money. And while they knowingly day-dream, they also unknowingly deceive themselves: Torvald with an image of himself as the broad-shouldered courageous male, longing only for the opportunity to save his wife from distress; and Nora with a belief that her marriage is a source of genuine happiness when in reality it is nothing but a hollow sham. The fancy dress ball at their neighbor's is not the only masquerade here, nor the tarantella the only performance Nora puts on. All the time she is acting a part, playing up to the role of irresponsible, scatter-brained wife that her marriage seems to have cast her for, masquerading as the helpless little thing so utterly dependent on her strong husband. The entire menage is based on misrepresentation, deception, falsity, in small things as well as big; it was a fraud that had to be exposed."

—*from* Ibsen and Meaning, *James McFarlane*

FOR FURTHER READING

Haugen, Einar. *Ibsen's Drama: Author to Audience*. Minneapolis: University of Minnesota Press, 1979.

Jaeger, Henrik. *Henrik Ibsen: A Critical Biography*. Trans. William Morton Payne. 2nd ed. New York: Haskell House, 1972.

Lyons, Charles R. *Critical Essays on Henrik Ibsen*. Boston: G. K. Hall & Co., 1987.

Marker, Frederick J. and Lise-Lone Marker. *Ibsen's Lively Art: A Performance Study of the Major Plays*. New York: Cambridge University Press, 1989.

McFarlane, James. *Ibsen and Meaning: Studies, Essays and Prefaces 1953–87*. Norwich, England: Norvik Press, 1989.

NOTES

UNIT 11: THE TWENTIETH CENTURY

(Textbook page 1138)

Unit Introduction: The Twentieth Century

The literature of the twentieth century is a literature of exploration, as it strives to describe and communicate the experiences of a fast-paced, ever-changing world of technological advances, continual warfare, and changing political and geographical borders. Yet, it is in part because of war, technology, and global realignment that twentieth-century literature now includes the voices of writers from emerging cultures and ethnic groups that had previously been silent or been ignored.

BACKGROUND

CHARACTERIZING RECENT WORLD LITERATURE

World literature in the twentieth century is difficult to characterize. More than the literatures of any other period or culture represented in this book, it is a diverse conglomeration of many, often overlapping, cultures, beliefs, and experiences. Reflecting a century of repeated armed conflicts, tremendous technological advances, and the increased empowerment and independence of groups that had previously had little power or influence, the literature of the twentieth century has pushed at the limits of traditional means of artistic expression, giving rise to new forms, new perspectives, and new schools of writing.

The strictures on literary expression have changed as the world has changed. At the beginning of the century, literature on the whole was Eurocentric; that is, it reflected the literary and philosophical movements such as modernism, existentialism, surrealism, dadaism, and psychological realism that were popular in western Europe. At the heart of these movements was the disillusionment brought on by the devastation of World War I. Writers of this period questioned the meaning of the world, experienced crises of faith, and explored the realm of the human psyche. After World War II, European power in the world declined greatly, and writers in the regions once held under tight imperial control now had the opportunity to speak out of their own experiences. As new nations emerged and former European colonies began to reestablish their own governments and traditions, so, too, did voices not previously heard become audible. Voices like those of African writers Chinua Achebe, Léopold Sédar Senghor, and Wole Soyinka

could speak of the problem of clashes with the West and within their own cultures; Korean writer Hwang Sun-won and Vietnamese author Nguyen Thi Vinh could write of the civil wars that have ravaged their countries; Aleksandr Solzhenitsyn and Anna Akhmatova could describe the trauma of Stalinist Russia; and women writers like Margaret Atwood, Jamaica Kincaid, and Zhang Jie could describe the world from a woman's perspective.

The literary movements that followed the First World War centered on the "inner experience" because, after all, the war had proven to many that there was no ultimate truth to count on and that one could only have faith in the individual human mind. The nihilistic, or fatalistic, philosophy of Friedrich Nietzsche and the scholarship of Sigmund Freud on the human psyche seemed to reduce life to a struggle of the individual to exist peacefully in the world and to know the workings of his or her own psyche. The effect of this emphasis on writers was to urge them to describe the world more accurately through the idiosyncratic perspective of individual minds.

EUROPEAN MOVEMENTS: IN SEARCH OF MEANING

Modernism was a movement that was at once a highly realistic expression of moment-to-moment perceptions of the world by a human mind, and a wistful desire for a return to prewar life where faith still had a role and the world seemed ordered and stable. The literature of the modernists is difficult: the poetry is urbane and structurally unconventional, the novels and stories are usually darkly psychological with narratives that are often disjointed and fragmented.

Other European movements, like **dadaism** and **surrealism,** were at once more playful than modernism and yet more daring in their detachment from ultimate meaning. Dadaism, the name of which is itself nonsensical and suggestive of meaningless babble, was a school of writing whose purpose was to render language meaningless and incomprehensible. In dadaism, poetry was no longer a means of expression of beauty or feeling but a linguistic experiment: words were broken up and scattered around the page, random sounds were used for an aural effect, and chaos and chance were the organizing principles of dadaist poems. On the other hand, surrealism, the offshoot of dadaism, was more deliberate in its search for a new expression of the modern experience. Influenced by Freud, surrealists plumbed the psychological depths for new symbols and visions to illustrate the chaos, uncertainty, and bizarre qualities of modern life.

The **existentialist** movement began before the Second World War and came to prominence afterwards, its basic precepts having been tested in Europe by the terrible trial of the war. The premise of existentialism is the assumption that the world is absurd and without meaning. Individuals create meaning by making responsible choices and taking deliberate actions. According to existential principles, every person is responsible for his or her every action: even the refusal to make a choice is a choice. The leading proponent of existentialism was Jean-Paul Sartre, a French philosopher and writer who believed that the individual's choice was intuitively based on what is best not only for the individual but for everyone. Fellow writer Albert Camus, however, felt that this philosophy did not consider the community enough, nor did it give any indication as to how a person could possibly know the effect of his or her choice and action on the community. Camus concluded that personal freedom was the value most important to every individual and that no choice should violate any other person's freedom.

THE LEGACY OF MODERNISM IN LATIN AMERICA

In Latin America, the existential and surrealist philosophies had a great impact on writers. The problems of identity and meaning were of utmost concern to the writers of a country of many different climactic regions, mixed heritages, and religions. At the beginning of the century, Nicaraguan poet Rubén Darío was strongly influenced by French Symbolist writers like Verlaine and Rimbaud, yet he expressed his own unique Latin voice. His work in turn influenced the work of many of the great Spanish poets of the twentieth century and brought Latin American literature to international attention for the first time.

Later, in the late 1940s and 1950s, other European movements were incorporated by Latin American writers. By mixing local customs, religious beliefs, and philosophy with European movements such as existentialism and surrealism, Latin American writers such as Gabriel García Márquez were able to create a distinctively Latin American literature. Their greatest innovation was **magical realism,** a literary movement that combined everyday events and believable characters with fantastic occurrences. The work of Gabriel García Márquez has a fairy-tale quality to it; his writing suspends the reader's disbelief and yet is compelling, so that readers of stories like *The Handsomest Drowned Man in the World* are willing to believe an entire village's love affair with a stranger's dead body. More recently, the writing of Chilean writer Isabel Allende has tapped into magical realism, creating stories that are highly political and yet feature such fantastic details as characters born with green hair. On the other hand, Jorge Luis Borges suffered from the same crisis of identity as many European writers. His conflict was compounded by his own self-perception, shared with other Argentinians, that he was a European transplanted to a foreign land. Borges's writings reflect a struggle to define an individual identity and are often set in cosmopolitan, vaguely European settings.

NEW VOICES WITH THE FREEDOM TO SPEAK

The question of freedom was a primary one in the postwar world. As the Western world recuperated from World War II and slid into the period of the Cold War, most other parts of the world continued in conflict, as new nations struggled to establish themselves in the international community and some established nations —China, for example— experimented with new forms of government. In China, the Cultural Revolution under Mao in the 1960s attempted to wipe out the cultural history of that country to make way for a new order that would be free of tradition. In Africa, former colonies fought hard to break free from the remnants of imperialism and to establish themselves as nations based on their ethnic groups. India and the Middle East worked to govern themselves independently of the British, but have been troubled by internal conflicts of race, class, and religion. Despite the statehood of Israel, for example, the region has been rife with conflict between Jews and Arabs, and India has been torn by struggles between different religious groups for decades. In South Africa, the struggle continues still against the minority rule of white South Africans over the black majority. Southeast Asia has found itself the battleground on two separate occasions—the Korean War in the 1950s and the Vietnam conflict of the 1960s and 1970s. Similarly, much of Central America has been embroiled in the conflict between Communist and democratic regimes for much of the 1970s and 1980s.

Other Movements of the New World Order

The **négritude** movement of the 1960s and 1970s was both a political and literary movement to explore and reclaim African traditions lost during the colonial period when blacks were expected to speak European languages and live in a European style. Négritude emphasizes a distinctly African world view, one that includes a sense of connection with tradition and with nature. Not all black African writers embrace négritude, however; Chinua Achebe, for example, recognizes that modern Africa is now something new, the result of the assimilation of Western culture, and it cannot afford to return to a strict adherence to tradition.

Feminism is another political and literary movement. Within feminism there are many arguments or traditions about the role of women in history and society. One school emphasizes the reclamation of "lost" or neglected women whose work was once considered minor and unimportant. The point of this effort is to increase awareness of women's contributions to literature, culture, and history. Other feminists concentrate on the argument that because women are biologically different from men, they automatically or innately perceive and experience the world differently from men, and that this difference is insurmountable. Yet another argument is that these differences of gender are the result of behavior and perceptions learned in a patriarchal culture, and that the only way to end discrimination and inequality is to adjust our Western cultural assumptions.

Beyond Modernism: Postmodernism

Overall, the literature of the postwar era points to a diversification and expansion of literary forms and voices. New voices from the margins, voices not previously heard before, are speaking loudly and are being responded to. Ironically enough, a new philosophical and literary movement, called **postmodernism**, has turned everything upside down by giving voice to issues and concerns that had once been left unsaid or only been hinted at in literature. The postmodern writer weaves together many different voices and perspectives (interior monologue, first-person narrative, second-person narrative, for example) to tell nonlinear and fragmented narratives in a way that attempts to reflect the modern conditions of chaos and confusion. Although this school of writing builds on the modernist tradition, the postmodernists do not yearn for another time or try to make sense of the world. They merely comment on what has been called the modern condition, using experimental literary techniques to portray a world in which every action has political ramifications, every voice is valid (though perhaps unheeded), and nothing is sacrosanct or secure.

Unit Projects

1. **Researching Twentieth-Century Art.** Like many writers, artists during the twentieth century gradually became less interested in depicting "reality" and more concerned with expressing ideas and concepts. Art was gradually pried away from its nineteenth-century rootedness in representation and realism and was allowed to find new and innovative shapes and forms. Some of the new schools of art in the twentieth century—such as dadaism and surrealism—closely paralleled their analogous literary movements. Research one of the following twentieth-century schools of art: postimpressionism, fauvism, cubism, expressionism, abstract expressionism, dadaism, surrealism, pop art, op art, nonobjective art, Tachism, futurism, minimal art. Prepare an oral report for the class. In your report, address such issues as the time period in which the movement took root, the characteristics of the art of that school, the major artists who practiced the form, and any parallels you can find between that type of art and a particular kind of twentieth-century literature. Reinforce your talk with plenty of examples of artworks in books and on slides.

2. **Adapting Stories for Film.** Imagine that you are an assistant at a major movie studio. Your job is to present three possible projects for films based on stories from the unit. Choose three of the selections you think are best suited for film and prepare a proposal for each explaining the appeal of your choices for modern audiences—the storyline, the setting, the believability of the characters, the potential for experimental camera angles. Work with a partner and act out the presentation.

3. **Presenting an Oral Report.** Elie Wiesel's memoir *Night* is based on personal experiences during the Holocaust. Prepare a report based on research of the events of the Holocaust. Rather than using strictly historical sources, explore also other autobiographical writings about that time, such as those of Primo Levi, for a different perspective. Other autobiographical sources include *The Diary of Anne Frank*. Present a report to the class.

4. **Researching World Film Directors.** Although we tend to associate film with America and Hollywood, other nations have produced film masterpieces, many of them the creations of highly regarded directors who are, both in their own and other cultures, considered to be artists as potent and influential as their nation's greatest writers. Choose one of the following film directors: Satajit Ray (India); Akira Kurosawa (Japan); Luis Buñuel (Spain); François Truffaut (France); Jean Renoir (France); Ingmar Bergman (Sweden); Werner Herzog (Germany); Fritz Lang (Germany); Michelangelo Antonini (Italy); Peter

Weir (Australia); Federico Fellini (Italy); Vittorio De Sica (Italy); Milos Forman (Czechoslovakia); or another director of your choice and research his or her life and works. Determine what subjects and themes this director is most known for and what his or her most famous films are. Try to view at least one of this filmmaker's works on video, if possible. Report your findings to the class. End your report with a brief review of the film you viewed.

5. **Creating a War Poetry Anthology.** Nguyen Thi Vinh's "Thoughts of Hanoi" and Yehuda Amichai's *Laments on the War Dead* are both poems that deal with the human response to war. Working with a partner, find other contemporary war poetry and consider what the poems have in common. Make an anthology of ten to fifteen poems that you find, complete with an introduction that explains the common themes and insights you have found in researching your anthology.

6. **Writing a Dialogue.** In many of the selections in this unit, characters interact without actually speaking to one another. Work with one or two other students to develop a five-minute dialogue between any set of characters who might have spoken had they the opportunity. For example, if Giovannino and Serenella had stayed in the villa with the young boy, what kind of dialogue might have occurred? Consider Gregor Samsa and his sister after his metamorphosis, the mother in "Love Must Not Be Forgotten" and the man she loved, Borges and his other self, Esteban and the villagers who find him.

7. **Illustrating a Selection.** Choose one or two of the African authors represented in this unit and illustrate a scene from his or her work. Draw or paint the scene or find appropriate illustrations in a journal or art book. You may have to do some research to accurately portray a place or person. Use a quotation from the selection itself as an accompanying caption. Display your work in class.

8. **Creating a World Music Anthology.** Create a music anthology of "world music" including traditional or modern popular music from some of the countries represented by selections in this unit. Include at least three different regions and their music. Play the tape you make for the class and present "liner notes" of the selections you have taped. These notes should include background on the nature of the musical selection and on the region where the music originated.

9. **Conducting a Radio Interview.** Imagine that you are a psychologist who also conducts a radio talk show. With a partner, choose a story from this unit whose protagonist's mind or actions interest both of you. Develop an interview between the psychologist and the character.

In the interview discuss the actions and motivations of the character. Present the finished interview to the class.

10. **Presenting an Oral Report.** Consider the typical images Americans often have of certain regions covered in this unit, such as the Caribbean or India. We often perceive the Caribbean, for example, as a vacation paradise. Choose a region of the world that interests you and prepare a report on what life is really like there. Present your report to the class and include illustrations that show both the typical view of that place and a more accurate depiction. Use the selection from the region you choose to show the flaws in stereotypes.

11. **A Conversation Between Authors.** With two classmates, write a script of a conversation between Gabriel García Márquez, Octavio Paz, and Jorge Luis Borges as they talk about their writing, Latin American literature, and/or the world in general. You may have to do some research into each of the author's philosophies. Perform your imagined conversation before the class.

12. **Conducting a Panel Discussion.** Imagine a panel discussion with at least four of the seven women writers represented in this unit. Have these women discuss the problems and issues of being women writers or being women writers from different cultures. After an initial discussion of five or ten minutes, have the women address questions from the class.

13. **Writing a Script.** Prepare an agenda for a political discussion between any two or three writers in the unit who address political problems, such as Wole Soyinka, Albert Camus, Aleksandr Solzhenitsyn, or Margaret Atwood. Before you begin, track down other writings by these authors—or, better yet, transcripts of interviews—so that you can get a better idea of the author's probable opinions and responses. Work with classmates to write a script of the resulting discussion and perform it for the class.

14. **Interviewing an Author.** Imagine interviewing your favorite author from this unit. Write a list of questions about his or her work, life, and the selection, and prepare the answers you imagine the author would give. You may have to do some research into the author's philosophies. Work with a classmate to act out the interview in class.

15. **Researching the Nobel Prize for Literature.** Many of the authors represented in the *World Literature* text were recipients of the Nobel Prize for Literature: Selma Lagerlöf, Gabriela Mistral, Albert Camus, Aleksandr Solzhenitsyn, Pablo Neruda, Gabriel García Márquez, Wole Soyinka, Naguib Mahfouz, and Octavio Paz. Find out more about the Nobel Prize. You may

wish to research the background of the prize, including the selection process involved, or choose one of the writers mentioned above (or another recipient of you choice) and find out the circumstances of his or her selection and acceptance of the prize. Try to find a copy of the author's acceptance speech.

16. **Researching Genre Fiction in Other Countries.** When you go to a bookstore, you see popular fiction books arranged according to various genres, or types: science fiction, horror, techno-thrillers, mystery, romance, Westerns, and so on. Choose your favorite genre of fiction and conduct research to find out about how that genre is expressed in other parts of the world. For example, what are some of the characteristics of science fiction from the former Soviet Union? What constitutes "popular fiction" in South Africa? Is there such a thing as a German Western? Do the Japanese read and write mysteries? Report your findings to the class.

BLACK CAT

Rainer Maria Rilke ▼ Translated by Stephen Mitchell ▼ (Textbook page 1150)

THE SWAN

Rainer Maria Rilke ▼ Translated by Robert Bly ▼ (Textbook page 1051)

SUMMARY

Rilke's *Black Cat* compares a black cat to unusual images, a ghost and the padded walls of a mad person's cell. Similarly, *The Swan* compares the awkwardness of daily human life, in which we grasp and cling to things, with the graceless gait of a swan on dry land, and the ease and naturalness of death—the "letting go"—with the grace of a swan in its natural element of water.

MORE ABOUT THE AUTHOR

In August of 1902, Rilke journeyed alone to Paris in order to write a monograph about the then famous French sculptor Auguste Rodin. Rodin indirectly became responsible for the observations of animals Rilke developed in poems like *Black Cat* and *The Swan*. Rodin's admonition to observe carefully and work in a disciplined manner enabled Rilke to describe with his pen what Rodin and other great visual artists could create with a chisel or paintbrush.

In addition to the influence of Rodin, Rilke became absorbed in the pioneering work of Paul Cézanne, the French painter considered by some to be the founder of modern art. Through viewing Cézanne's work, Rilke learned what he called the "thingness" of objects. The discoveries and enthusiasm he felt for the work of Cézanne, as well as the art of Rodin, Van Gogh, and others of that period, are fortunately preserved in letters Rilke wrote to his wife Clara.

Rilke could not stay long in the same locale or with the same people. His temperament required him to change his environment in order to fit the needs of whatever work he was then writing. At the same time, though, he did not want to abandon those who had been close to him. Eloquent, insightful correspondence exists between Rilke and his wife Clara, Paula Becker-Modersohn, the Russian writers Boris Pasternak and Marina Tsvetayeva, and many others.

The correspondence by which Rilke is best known, *Letters to a Young Poet,* was published after his death. It testifies to the seriousness with which Rilke related to others, even strangers like the young poet Franz Xaver Kappus, who sought Rilke's professional advice. In addition to the volume in which the animal poems of this selection appeared, Rilke published a volume of poems, *The Book of Hours.* After *New Poems,* other publications included *The Notebooks of Malte Laurid Brigge, Duino Elegies,* and *Sonnets to Orpheus.* His voluminous correspondence with various people has been published in many different volumes and translated into many languages.

A CRITICAL COMMENT

This excerpt comes from a letter written by Rilke dated Monday, June 24, 1907:

. . . Early this morning your long letter, with all your thoughts . . . Surely all art is the result of one's having been in danger, of having gone through an experience all the way to the end, to where no one can go any further. The further one goes, the more private, the more personal, the more singular an experience becomes, and the thing one is making is, finally, the necessary, irrepressible, and, as nearly as possible, definitive utterance of this singularity . . . Therein lies the enormous aid the work of art brings to the life of the one who must make it,—: that it is his epitome; the knot in the rosary at which his life recites a prayer, the ever-returning proof to himself of his unity and genuineness, which presents itself only to him while appearing anonymous to the outside, nameless, existing merely as necessity, as reality, as being—.

"So we are most definitely called upon to test

and try ourselves against the utmost, but probably
we are also bound to keep silence regarding this
utmost, to beware of sharing it, of parting with it in
communication so long as it has not entered the
work of art: for the utmost represents nothing other
than that singularity in us which no one would or
even should understand, and which must enter into
the work as such, as our personal madness, so to
speak, in order to find its justification in the work
and reveal the law in it, like an inborn drawing that
is invisible until it emerges in the transparency of
the artistic.—

—from Letters on Cézanne, *Rainer Maria Rilke,*
translated by Joel Agee

FOR FURTHER READING

Freedman, Ralph. *Rilke: A Biography.* New York:
Random House. 1988.

Hendry, J. F. *The Sacred Threshold: A Life of Rilke.*
Manchester, England: Carcanet New Press Ltd.
1983

Rainer Maria Rilke. Clara Rilke, ed. *Letters on
Cézanne.* Trans. Joel Agee. New York: Fromm
International Publishing Co., 1985.

——. *Letters to a Young Poet.* Trans. Stephen
Mitchell. New York: Random House, 1984.

——. *Selected Poems of Rainer Maria Rilke.* Trans.
Robert Bly. New York: Harper and Row, 1981.

THE METAMORPHOSIS

Franz Kafka ▾ Translated by Stanley Corngold ▾ (Textbook page 1156)

SUMMARY

Gregor Samsa wakes and discovers that he has
transformed into a roach-like insect. He cannot get
out of bed because he has not adjusted to his new
body and its movements. When he appears to his
family, they are terrified, and his horrified father
drives him back into his room. His sister, Grete,
takes upon herself the responsibility of caring for
Gregor in his altered state. He wishes that he could
communicate with her, but does not try. Although
he misses his family, he gradually finds himself less
and less interested in human affairs.

Later, Grete and her mother hope to give Gregor
more space by removing some furniture from his
room. When they try to remove other furniture,
however, Gregor becomes bold and moves out into
the open, where his mother sees him and becomes
hysterical. Gregor, suddenly worried and anxious,
follows them out of the room in order to help. At
this point, his father returns home, sees the
commotion, and begins pitching apples at Gregor as
he flees back to his room. One of the apples
severely wounds Gregor and remains wedged in his
side.

After this last episode, the family's attitude
towards Gregor changes dramatically. Less
attention is paid to him, and his door is kept closed.
A cleaning woman is hired to clean and take care of
Gregor, and boarders are taken in. One evening,
the boarders hear Grete playing her violin and invite
her to play. Drawn by his sister's playing and
careless of his appearance, Gregor creeps out of his
room into the dining room, where he is seen by the
boarders. They indignantly tell the family they will
not stay in their rooms any longer and will leave in
the morning. The family becomes very upset, Grete
most of all. As Gregor makes his way painfully back
to his room, Grete slams the door and locks it. Early
the next morning, Gregor quietly dies.

MORE ABOUT THE AUTHOR

Like the character of Gregor Samsa, who
experienced a transformation at night, Franz Kafka
also experienced a kind of nightly metamorphosis.
By day, he worked for the Workers' Accident
Insurance Institution. By night, he changed from a
Prague professional into a writer who plunged into
investigations of the human psyche, particularly the
problems of isolation and alienation.

In November of 1912, Kafka was working on
Amerika, a novel published posthumously, in 1927,
by his friend and executor of his will, Max Brod.
Displeased with the progress of his novel, the story
of the isolation of a newcomer in a foreign land, a
new idea came to Kafka. This idea became *The
Metamorphosis* (1915), which was written in an
extraordinarily short and feverish one-month
period. *The Trial* (published in 1925 by Max Brod),
tells of an individual's incarceration and persecution
for a crime he does not know he has committed.
The Castle (published in 1926) depicts the struggle
of a protagonist who attempts to attain recognition
by mysterious rulers. In each of these novellas, the
protagonists become alienated as they struggle to
find meaning to their existence, if meaning can be
determined at all.

Kafka prepared collections of short prose and
stories based on themes similar to his novels and
novellas. They include *Meditation* (1913), *The
Judgment* (1913), *In the Penal Colony* (1919), *The
Country Doctor* (1919), and his last work, *A Hunger
Artist* (1924).

A CRITICAL COMMENT

In his book *Conversations with Kafka,* the writer
Gustav Janouch remembers a conversation with
Franz Kafka in which Janouch suggests that the
family name Samsa is really a substitute for Kafka:

"'The hero of the story is called Samsa,' I said. 'It sounds like a cryptogram for Kafka. Five letters in each word. The S in the word Samsa has the same position as the K in the word Kafka. The A . . .'

"Kafka interrupted me.

"'It is not a cryptogram. Samsa is not merely Kafka, and nothing else. *The Metamorphosis* is not a confession, although it is—in a certain sense—an indiscretion.'

"'I know nothing about that.'

"'It is perhaps delicate and discreet to talk about the bugs in one's own family?'

"'It isn't usual in good society.'

"'You see what bad manners I have.'

"Kafka smiled. He wished to dismiss the subject. But I did not wish to.

"'It seems to me that the distinction between good and bad manners hardly applies here,' I said. '*The Metamorphosis* is a terrible dream, a terrible conception.'

"Kafka stood still.

"'The dream reveals the reality, which conception lags behind. That is the horror of life—the terror of art. But now I must go home.'

"He took a curt farewell.

"Had I driven him away?

"I felt ashamed."
—*from* Conversations With Kafka, *Gustav Janouch, translated by Gorownwy Rees*

FOR FURTHER READING

Brod, Max. *Franz Kafka,* 2nd ed. New York: Schocken Books, 1960.

Citati, Pietro. *Kafka.* Trans. Raymond Rosenthal. New York: Alfred A. Knopf, 1990.

Kafka, Franz. *The Metamorphosis*. Trans. Stanley Corngold. New York: Bantam Books, 1972.

Prawl, Ernst. *The Nightmare of Reason: A Life of Franz Kafka*. New York: Farrar, Straus, & Giroux, 1984.

Udoff, Alan, ed. *Kafka and the Contemporary Critical Performance*. Bloomington, Indiana: Indiana University Press, 1987.

THE RAT TRAP

Selma Lagerlöf ▾ Translated by Florence and Naboth Hedin ▾ (Textbook page 1198)

SUMMARY

A nameless wanderer who makes and sells rat traps develops a theory that the world is really a rat trap. He sees riches, joys, and comforts as baits which tempt people and ensnare them, just as bits of pork or cheese entice rats to his traps. One night, the rat-trap peddler stops for the night at the home of an old man. The old man shows him where he keeps his money, and the next morning the peddler steals it. He hides in the woods, but promptly gets lost. After finding his way to an ironworks for a warm place to spend the night, he is awakened by Willmansson, the owner, who mistakes him for an old friend and invites him to his house. The peddler refuses, but soon the owner's daughter Edla convinces him.

Once the rat-trap peddler has bathed, dressed, and shaved, Willmansson sees that he is an imposter and threatens to call the sheriff. Edla intervenes and insists that he stay for Christmas. On Christmas morning, Edla and her father go to church, where they hear the story of the poor old man who has been robbed by a peddler of rat traps. Willmansson worries that the peddler will also rob him. When he and Edla return, though, they find that the peddler has left a Christmas package for Edla, in which she finds a small rat-trap containing the money the peddler had stolen from the old man and a note.

MORE ABOUT THE AUTHOR

The story of "The Rat Trap," in which the peddler is caught in a trap of his own making but then released by kindness, illustrates the mix of realism and romanticism for which Lagerlöf is noted. The social relations between the owner of the ironworks and the farmer, the presence of poor beggars, and even the soot and grime of the ironworks are realistic details from the years of Lagerlöf's childhood in the Värmland district. At the same time, the young woman's defiant kindness and the way it transforms the peddler links Lagerlöf with the Romantics, who often discovered miraculous principles at work in humble, everyday scenes.

By using just enough detail to make her characters and their actions vivid and believable, but not enough to make them depressingly realistic, Lagerlöf successfully imitates the fairy tales she was familiar with as a child. Like a fairy tale, "The Rat Trap" spends little time developing a plot, includes little dialogue, and is told with an economy of detail. And, most important, as in fairy tales, a lesson is learned in conjunction with a happy ending.

Lagerlöf was fascinated by Christmas scenes, which appear repeatedly in her work. *Gösta Berling's Saga,* her first successful novel, begins in the smithy room of an ironworks on Christmas Eve. "The Legend of the Christmas Rose" and *The Christ Stories* focus on Christmas lore. "Liliecrona's Home" is another story which opens on Christmas. The contrast between the harsh Swedish winter and the warmth of Christmas celebrations perhaps symbolizes the contrast between hardheartedness and generosity.

A CRITICAL COMMENT

The following comment on *Gösta Berling's Saga,* another of Lagerlöf's works, clarifies the relationship between realism and traditional storytelling in her work.

"The realism in *Gösta Berling's Saga* manifests itself in many ways. Although the place names are fictive, the actual setting of the story can be found on a map of Värmland, and the industry and economic conditions of the area form the basis of the story. The action is set at the end of the 1820's—the end of the romantic period. Lagerlöf evokes with much precision the atmosphere of the time—the heyday of the great iron foundries in Värmland, the golden age of rich foundry owners and beautiful country estates. Like many of Lagerlöf's books, *Gösta Berling's Saga* gives evidence of her deep interest in history and her command of a whole spectrum of styles from different periods. What she sought in the past was primarily 'the inner history of the people.' Folkloristic material from Värmland and other regions determined the substance of *Gösta Berling's Saga,* one of the original aims of which was a cultural-historical one; Lagerlöf wanted to preserve the knowledge of customs and folklore, which she believed to be threatened.

"The narrative also makes use of the great treasures of fairy tale motifs and archetypes. The novel is grounded in the social history of Värmland, but it also has a symbolic dimension. As in the works of many other writers of world literature—Gogol and Gabriel García Márquez, for example—the dual levels of myth and reality form a very rich artistic pattern."

—*from* Selma Lagerlöf, *Vivi Edstrom*

FOR FURTHER READING

Berendsohn, Walter A. *Selma Lagerlöf, Her Life and Works.* Adapted from the German by George F. Timpson. Port Washington, New York: Kennikat Press, 1968.

Edstrom, Vivi. *Selma Lagerlöf.* Boston: Twayne Publishers, 1984.

Lagerlöf, Selma. *The Harvest.* Trans. Florence and Naboth Hedin. New York: Doubleday, Doran and Company, Inc., 1935.

——. *The Story of Gösta Berling.* Trans. and with an afterword by Robert Bly. New York: New American Library (Signet Classic), 1962.

EVELINE

James Joyce ▾ (Textbook page 1209)

SUMMARY

The story opens with Eveline contemplating her plans to run away with her fiancé to South America. She will be glad to leave a life of drudgery and abuse, and yet feels obligated to a promise she made to her dying mother to keep the family together. She wavers in her decision, but remembering her mother's difficult life, she is determined to leave. Yet at the docks, as the ship prepares to leave port, and her fiancé calls to her and pulls at her, she is transfixed and cannot move or sense a thing. She fails to escape from the life of her family.

MORE ABOUT THE AUTHOR

James Joyce was unusual among the early twentieth-century Irish writers in that he came from a Catholic, rather than a Protestant, background. Because Ireland had been under British rule for centuries, most of the key cultural figures of the day in Ireland came from the Anglo-Protestant upper classes. The setting of "Eveline" is Dublin, the capital and largest city of what is now the Republic of Ireland, which in 1921 won its independence from Britain. However, when Joyce wrote his story, Dublin was still under British domination. This made Joyce's subject matter, the lives of middle-class Dublin Catholics, distinctive when his work first appeared.

It was not so much his subject matter, though, as his candid treatment of family and religious entanglements that caused readers and would-be publishers to be outraged. *Dubliners* was prepared for publication in 1906, but the printer was so upset by what he read of the stories that he destroyed the pages of the book he was preparing. The book finally appeared in altered form in 1914.

It is hard for us, as modern readers, to imagine the effect that Joyce's writing had on his largely Victorian, Anglo-Irish and Irish-Catholic audience at the turn of the century. His exposure of the family as an essentially destructive institution was seen as a genuine threat to social order. Stories like "Eveline" gave a candid view into the lives of Dublin Catholics, condemning not only their hopeless cycle of poverty and violence but also, by implication, their religion. All this came at a time when Irish intellectuals, favoring the establishment of an independent Irish Republic, were promoting pride in the distinctive heritage of Ireland. Joyce's disinterested eye refused to pass over the ugliness of what he saw. In writing frankly, he threw over allegiance to a parochial Irish state for his interest in a modern approach to writing.

Joyce was more interested in the psychological existence of his characters than in their actions. "Eveline" exemplifies this approach, using the stream-of-consciousness technique to bring the inner reality of a character to life. For the majority of the story, Eveline sits in one place; it is her thoughts, rather than her actions, which interest the author. There are only two significant actions in the entire story. The first is when Eveline, panicked by the thought of her mother's life, stands up from her chair. The second is when Eveline grips the barricade at the dock and refuses to move forward. Even these actions appear as isolated moments amidst the continuous activity of Eveline's thinking. By choosing this approach, Joyce suggests that the imaginative inner life of a character explains much that a simple account of his or her actions fails to reveal.

A CRITICAL COMMENT

"So in *Dubliners* the self-contained world of Dublin is one unifying element. Another is the characteristic style. If I had to choose one word to apply to the style of *Dubliners,* that word would be 'economy.' Nothing is wasted. Every word and every phrase are made to carry their own burdens in the story and in the collection as a whole. Although some of the tales may appear to be slight at first reading, the more the reader examines them the more comprehensive they are seen to be. Joyce relies on implication, on suggestion and symbol, to extend the impact of his tightly constructed scenes. This technique he learned from many sources, but particularly from the French writers Maupassant and Flaubert; indeed, it may be said that *Dubliners* accomplished for English fiction what Flaubert had earlier accomplished for French fiction in his *Trois Contes.* . . .

"In Joyce's hands prose takes on the destiny and order of poetry and when we read the stories in *Dubliners,* we must exercise the same care in weighing and evaluating each line that we would exercise in the reading of poetry. . . .

"In Joyce's statement of intention he refers to the style of *Dubliners* as one of 'scrupulous meanness.' Most readers have taken 'meanness' as a description of Joyce's unsentimental attitude toward Irish life, and of course they are right. But 'meanness' can also signify strict economy, a passion to make the smallest detail carry its full burden. In this sense, 'scrupulous meanness' is a perfect description of Joyce's techniques in *Dubliners.* Nothing is ornamental; nothing can be classified as 'good description.' In his desire to create 'epiphanies' of Irish life Joyce has renounced direct commentary in favor of an allusive method in which dialogue and setting express the author's opinions of his characters."

—*from* James Joyce, *A. Walton Litz*

FOR FURTHER READING

Deane, Seamus. *A Short History of Irish Literature.* London: Hutchinson and Co., 1986.

Ellman, Richard. *James Joyce.* New York: Oxford University Press, 1959.

Joyce, James. *Dubliners.* New York: The Viking Press, 1967.

Litz, A. Walton. *James Joyce.* New York: Twayne Publishers, 1972.

THE RING
Isak Dinesen ▾ (Textbook page 1216)

SUMMARY

This selection is from the short-story collection *Anecdotes of Destiny,* published in 1958. Like many of Dinesen's stories, "The Ring" is written in a Gothic style that combines a sense of high romance with realism. "The Ring" is a tale of a young woman's coming-of-age as she is jarred from her newly-married, aristocratic complacency.

As the story begins, Lovisa, or Lise, and her husband Sigismund are enjoying a walk on Sigismund's estate when they hear news of a murdering sheep thief stalking nearby estates. As her husband tends to the sheep, Lise becomes bored, and Sigismund sends her along with the promise that he will catch up with her.

Walking away, Lise remembers a secret glade she had found days before. She imagines that by hiding there her husband would become worried and lonely. What she finds in the glade is not solitude, but the sheep thief. Lise and the thief silently study each other. Lise, unused to danger does not scream for help or run but offers her wedding ring to the thief, dropping her handkerchief in the process. The thief threatens her with his knife, but then puts it away. He does not take the ring, but touches Lise's outstretched hand, allowing the ring to fall to the ground. He then kicks the ring away, and after a moment, takes the handkerchief and suddenly vanishes. For Lise, the moment of their touching is somehow significant. Later, Lise tells her husband that she has lost her ring and does not remember where she saw it last.

MORE ABOUT THE AUTHOR

Isak Dinesen was a woman of many names. Her given name was Karen Christenze Dinesen, but she was called Tanne by family and friends. When she first began writing and publishing in Denmark, she used the names Osceola and Peter Lawless. Once married to Bror Blixen, she took the title Baroness von Blixen, and when she ran her African farm alone, her nickname was "The Lioness." Finally, when she returned to Denmark from Africa and began to write the stories and memoirs that are most familiar to modern readers, she used the pseudonym Isak Dinesen. *Isak,* meaning "the one who laughs," is an ironic name in light of the sorrows she had experienced during her last years in Africa: the loss of husband, lover, and farm, as well as a debilitating illness.

Upon returning to Denmark at age 46, Dinesen began in earnest her career as a writer. She wrote and published numerous collections of stories and memoirs, including *Seven Gothic Tales* (1934), *Out of Africa* (1937), *Winter's Tales* (1942), *Last Tales* (1957), and *Shadows on the Grass* (1961). Most of her work was written in English, the language of her married years in Kenya, then an English colony. Some of her stories, including "Tempests" in *Anecdotes of Destiny,* were originally written in Danish. The posthumously published book *On Modern Marriage and Other Observations* (1977) includes an essay about marriage.

A CRITICAL COMMENT

"As 'Isak Dinesen' Karen Blixen also recreated herself in a style of life harmonizing with the literary style, and a glance at her work will indicate its nature. For, although it remains true that there is no Dinesen figure in the tales as a main character, like Childe Harold, for example, or Lord Illingworth, there is still one person who is present in every single story—the storyteller herself. In reading Isak Dinesen one receives a quite indelible impression of the *persona* of the narrator, always present as a kind of reflective intelligence, speculating, describing, narrating, commenting, but doing all these things with a curious air of aloof detachment—curious, because there is abundant evidence from people who knew Isak Dinesen personally that she was utterly different from this in private life. Although a highly unusual, even strange person at times, she was also a gay, witty, charming woman with a compelling personality, possessed of great gifts of warm sympathy and understanding. But in her tales, the sense of distance is maintained throughout, and even deliberately cultivated by her steadfast refusal ever to identify herself overtly with any of her characters or to sympathize with their actions by explicit comment. This effect of studied detachment is a crucial element in her writing; it is one which is further strengthened by the technique. . . ."

"In addition to this, as readers, we are never made contemporaries of the characters in time, in the sense of living through the story's action, side by side with them. Knowing all the while that this is a story, we are not so much made aware what is happening, as told what has happened. Isak Dinesen's tales are not meant as a representation of events taking place in life; instead they are accounts of what has already taken place. Consequently, they are narrated, not in response to the demands of realistic presentation, but according to the dictates of artistic exposition and the requirements of their structural arrangement. In short, they are not organized as an imitation of life; instead, they preserve an unapproachable distance from—like their author.

—*from* Isak Dinesen and Karen Blixen: The Mask and the Reality, *Donald Hannah*

FOR FURTHER READING

Dinesen, Isak. *Anecdotes of Destiny*. New York: Random House, 1953.

——. *Out of Africa and Shadows on the Grass*. New York: Random House, 1985.

Hannah, Donald. *Isak Dinesen and Karen Blixen: The Mask and the Reality*. New York: Random House, 1971.

Thurman, Judith. *Isak Dinesen: The Life of a Storyteller*. New York: St. Martin's Press, 1982.

Westenholz, Anders. *The Powers of Aires: Myth and Reality in Karen Blixen's Life*. Baton Rouge, LA: Louisiana State University Press, 1987.

LOT'S WIFE

Anna Akhmatova ▼ Translated by Richard Wilbur ▼ (Textbook page 1225)

SUMMARY

The poem "Lot's Wife" describes the departure of Lot and his wife from their home in the city of Sodom. Lot obediently follows the angel who is guiding them along the road to safety. Lot's wife, however, turns for a last look at her native city and is transformed into a pillar of transparent salt. The speaker adds that she will never forget this woman who gave up her life to look back at what mattered most to her.

MORE ABOUT THE AUTHOR

After Akhmatova's marriage to Nikolai Gumilev, the couple moved to St. Petersburg, where their son Lev was born in 1912. The poem "Lot's Wife" comes from *Anno Domini MCMXXI* (1922), the book of poems she wrote after Gumilev's execution. Although Akhmatova and Gumilev had been divorced in 1918, she was clearly upset by his execution. Many of her friends decided to leave Russia at this time, but she decided that she had no choice other than to stay in her homeland. "Lot's Wife" is one of the poems in *Anno Domini MCMXXI* that contemplates the necessity of her decision. It also makes clear that it was a decision which brought her pain and loneliness.

One of the things that staying in Russia cost Akhmatova was publication. Shortly after *Anno Domini MCMXXI,* she was blacklisted by the Communist party. Although she "redeemed" herself in the party's eyes with poems that celebrated Russia during World War II, she was later officially expelled from the Writer's Union. In spite of sporadic publication, her work remained immensely popular with Russian readers.

In 1935, Akhmatova's son Lev was imprisoned, as was the man she was living with at the time. For seventeen months, Akhmatova went daily to stand in line with the other women outside the Leningrad prison, hoping for news of the prisoners. Discovering who she was, another woman in line asked her if she could describe their daily vigil. The result was the fifteen-part *Requiem,* a poem about the Stalinist years, which Akhmatova composed but did not dare to write down. Instead, she recited pieces of the poem to friends, who memorized and later recorded them.

During the last ten years of her life, Akhmatova was allowed to publish again and to make a little extra money by translating. She acted as a mentor to several younger poets and helped them find small jobs to support themselves. Before her death in 1966, she traveled to Rome and to Oxford to receive honors for her poetry.

A CRITICAL COMMENT

"Akhmatova's poems are modern in the sense that they do not idealize love: each love is unique in its character and brings pain when it ends, but it is never the only love or the last one. Her love lyrics are lessons in courage. Some of her other poems evoke her beloved city of St. Petersburg with its beautiful architecture and illustrious past, a city which defines her identity. A less frequent but still very important theme is that of the muse, a stern disciplinarian who deprives the poet of personal happiness for the sake of a greater reward. Each of Akhmatova's poems is a separate and complete entity. Although their subject matter is apparently quite intimate, her *oeuvre* as a whole is impersonal.

"Though she describes her country as bleak, unpropitious, and even sinful, she displays a fierce loyalty to it, and is ready to face the deaths of her men, a lover, a son. In the last of her major collections, *Anno Domini MCMXXI* (1922), her poems on personal subjects are even more complicated, more effective, and more arid than before. Now she expressed her love of country in the form of a refusal to emigrate to the peaceful west. And so she remained in the Soviet Union for the remainder of her life even though during much of that time she was unable to publish her poetry."
—*from* "Turn of a Century: Modernism, 1880–95,"
Evelyn Bristol

FOR FURTHER READING

Akhmatova, Anna. "Lot's Wife." *Walking to Sleep: New Poems and Translations*. Trans. Richard Wilbur. New York: Harcourt Brace Jovanovich, 1969.

Bristol, Evelyn. "Turn of a Century: Modernism, 1880–95." *The Cambridge History of Russian Literature*. Ed. Charles Moser. Cambridge: Cambridge University Press, 1989.

Haight, Amanda. *Anna Akhmatova: A Poetic Pilgrimage*. New York: Oxford University Press, 1976.

Hemschemeyer, Judith, trans. and Roberta Reeder, ed. *The Complete Poems of Anna Akhmatova*. 2 vols. Somerville, MA: Zephyr Press, 1990.

Mandelstam, Nadezhda. *Hope Against Hope*. Trans. Max Hayward. New York: Atheneum, 1970.

THE GUITAR

Federico García Lorca ▾ Translated by Rachel Benson and Robert O'Brien
(Textbook page 1230)

SUMMARY

In "The Guitar," García Lorca describes the sound of the guitar as a cry, an idea that serves as a sort of refrain throughout the poem.

This poem appears early in the volume *Poema del Cante Jondo,* originally published in Spain in 1931, ten years after it was written. *Cante jondo* is a traditional Spanish song most often associated with the Gypsy population that migrated to Spain from

India in the mid-to-late fifteenth century. These people, who settled in Andalusia, developed the *cante jondo*, which translates as "deep song," in which a singer communicates his or her most intense, often tragic feelings. By the late nineteenth century, *cante jondo* developed into the more popular, commercial art of flamenco dancing. Both the earlier *cante jondo* and flamenco are sung or danced to the accompaniment of a guitar, the subject of this poem.

MORE ABOUT THE AUTHOR

García Lorca's interest in *cante jondo* was strongly influenced by the Spanish composer Manuel de Falla, who settled in Granada in 1920. At that time, García Lorca and other artists found Granada an important cultural and artistic Spanish center. Before literature became the focus of García Lorca's artistic output, he had studied music seriously. On this subject, de Falla had much to teach García Lorca. Manuel de Falla had a strong influence not only on García Lorca but on the entire group of artists, called the *Rinconcillo,* that met and shared their work and ideas in Granada.

In 1922, Spanish and international writers, musicians, and flamenco dancers participated in a festival based on a series of songs written by García Lorca. "The Guitar" was one of the early songs written in this series, from the section of *Poema del Cante Jondo* called *The Gypsy Siguiriya. Siguiriyas* are intense songs in which emotions rise to a crescendo, indicated by alternating cries and silences, before the singer's voice and guitar fade altogether.

In addition to his connection with *cante jondo,* García Lorca is known for the term *duende,* which he applies to his verse. In a famous lecture he delivered in 1933, García Lorca explains what he means by this term. *Duende* is something with an intense and dark spirit, often related to death and suffering and things mysterious. He believed poets who read their work in public, along with musicians and dancers (such as flamenco dancers of Spain), communicated this sense of the world. This sensibility, for which García Lorca is famous, may easily be seen as a result of his involvement with *cante jondo.*

A CRITICAL COMMENT

"A study of *cante jondo* had led [García] Lorca to the conclusion, moreover, that Andalusians are 'a sad people, a static people,' and not at all the merry, extroverted songsters that they often lead foreigners to believe. Not only the music of *cante jondo* but its words had made him see this. In the second part of his lecture, much more original than the first, he subjected to scrutiny the little verses, known as *coplas,* used by the singers of *cante jondo* and which undergo constant variations. Speaking now as a young poet in contact with the avant-garde tendencies of Madrid, themselves inspired by the latest trends in Europe, Lorca told his audience that he and his friends found these verses astonishing—for their concision, their subtle gradations of anguish (*pena*), their striking imagery and their obsession with death.

"Lorca also mentioned another feature of the *coplas* that had caught his attention. It is what he called their 'pantheism,' their tendency to personify what the modern mind would consider inanimate objects or forces. . . .

"It seems certain that Lorca's careful study of *cante jondo* in 1921 and 1922 revived what he called the 'poetic memory' of his childhood in the Vega of Granada, when he used to speak to the insects and, as he said, assign, like all children, 'to each thing, piece of furniture, object, tree or stone, its personality.'"
—*from* Federico García Lorca: A Life, *Ian Gibson*

FOR FURTHER READING

Duran, Manuel, ed. *Lorca: A Collection of Critical Essays.* Englewood Cliffs, NJ: Prentice-Hall Inc., 1962.

Flores, Angel, ed. *An Anthology of Spanish Poetry from Garcilaso to García Lorca in English Translation with Spanish Originals.* New York: Anchor Books, 1961.

Gibson, Ian. *Federico García Lorca: A Life.* New York: Pantheon Books, 1989.

Londre, F. H. *Federico García Lorca.* New York: Ungar Publishing Co., 1985.

from NIGHT

Elie Wiesel ▼ Translated by Stella Rodway ▼ (Textbook page 1234)

SUMMARY

The excerpt begins as Wiesel and his family are herded with other Jews from their town into a cattle car and deported. The crowded, unsanitary, and terrifying conditions affect everyone in the car. But Wiesel focuses on the reactions of Madame Schächter, who sees from the window of the cattle car fires burning on the Czech frontier when, in reality, there are no fires. She cannot stop talking or crying about these fires of destruction. As her screams continue, the others begin to fear for their sanity and safety, but they cannot stop her cries.

When the train reaches its final destination, Auschwitz, cries of fire are heard again, but this time they come not from Madame Schächter, who is silent, but from others who actually see the flames from the Nazi crematoria. Immediately after debarking from the train, men and women are separated, and Wiesel and his father are assigned to a line destined, they are told, for the crematorium. While waiting on this line, Wiesel sees a truckload of children to be burned and the ditch dug for the bodies of cremated adults. Wiesel can only hope that it is all a nightmare and decides to throw himself against the electric fence rather than be burned to death.

At this point, someone begins to recite the Kaddish, the Jewish prayer for the dead. Wiesel is not comforted by this gesture, but enraged that God could allow such atrocities to take place. As the prayer is recited, his line moves closer and closer to the ditch of burning bodies. Two steps away from the pit, the line is ordered to the barracks, and Wiesel and his father are saved. Wiesel's father asks him if he remembers Madame Schächter's prophetic warnings of fire. Wiesel states that he has forgotten nothing of that entire night— the flames, the faces of the burning children. These sights have deprived him forever of his soul and his God, and he will never forget them.

MORE ABOUT THE AUTHOR

Elie Wiesel recounts in *One Generation After* (1965) the destruction by the Nazis of his home town in the Carpathian mountains of Rumania. Many years after the war, however, Wiesel returned to the town in a personal quest for the past. He sought in particular a spot where, on his Bar Mitzvah day (a Jewish celebration in which a boy of thirteen is welcomed as a man into the Jewish religion) he buried a gold watch. Both the spot and the watch were irreversibly changed from the innocent, pure memory of his Bar Mitzvah day; both had disintegrated and been ruined by the war and the passage of time.

For ten years after the war, Wiesel kept silent about his experiences. He questioned his adequacy to speak of such an event and for so many people, each with his or her story. In Paris, after working at a number of odd jobs to keep alive and continue his education, he became a journalist. Through his life as a journalist, he came to know the Nobel Prize winner and French Catholic writer, François Mauriac. Mauriac, in a moving personal interview, convinced Wiesel to write about his war experience; the result of this was *Night*.

In 1952, Elie Wiesel emigrated to the United States. He became a professor at the City University of New York. He was awarded the Nobel Peace Prize in 1986. Although he lives in New York City, his work is usually written in French. He has also written in Yiddish, the language of European

Jews across Europe before the war. He has written both fiction and nonfiction. Among his many books, in addition to *Night* (1960), are *Dawn* (1961), *The Town Behind the Wall* (1964), *A Beggar in Jerusalem* (1970), *The Testament* (1981), and *The Fifth Son* (1984).

A CRITICAL COMMENT

In his collection of essays and reminiscences, *A Jew Today* (published in 1978), Elie Wiesel recalls the interview he conducted with François Mauriac, a Roman Catholic writer and scholar, that provoked the writing of *Night* and, subsequently, Wiesel's lifelong quest as a speaker for the memory of the Holocaust.

"'. . . Well, I want you to know that ten years ago, not very far from here, I knew Jewish children everyone of whom suffered a thousand times more, six million times more, than Christ on the cross. And we don't speak about them. Can you understand that, sir? We don't speak about them.'

"(Mauriac) turned pale. Slumped on the sofa, muffled in a woolen blanket, he held my gaze without flinching, waiting for what else was to come. But I no longer felt like continuing. Abruptly, without shaking his hand, I turned toward the door. Finding myself in the hallway, facing the elevator, I mechanically pressed the button, and the elevator started to rise. At the same moment I heard the door opening behind me. With an infinitely humble gesture the old writer was touching my arm, asking me to come back. . . .

"Bathed in cold sweat, I wanted to vanish, to erase myself from his memory, or at least, to ask his forgiveness and alleviate the effect my words had produced. I was on the verge of saying something, but he prevented me: he did not want my apologies. Instead, he bade me continue speaking. But the words left my mouth with difficulty. He questioned me, and with considerable effort, I answered. In brief, staccato sentences: 'Yes, I come from that country. Yes, I lived through *those events*. Yes, I have known the sealed trains. Yes, I have seen darkness cover man's faith. Yes, I was present at the end of the world.'"

—from A Jew Today, *Elie Wiesel*

FOR FURTHER READING

Brown, Robert M. *Elie Wiesel: Messenger to All Humanity.* Notre Dame, Indiana: University of Notre Dame Press, 1990.

Ritter, Carol. *Elie Wiesel: Between Memory and Hope.* New York: New York University Press, 1989.

Wiesel, Elie. *A Jew Today.* Trans. Marian Wiesel. New York: Random House, 1978.

——. *Night.* Trans. Stella Rodway. New York: Bantam, 1982.

THE GUEST

Albert Camus ▾ Translated by Justin O'Brien ▾ (Textbook page 1246)

SUMMARY

Albert Camus's "The Guest" is the fourth in a series of six short stories titled *Exile and the Kingdom*. The collection explores the theme of exile—both geographical and moral: the loneliness of the individual, the sense of foreignness in one's own land, and the feeling of isolation in one's own society.

As the story begins, Daru, a French schoolmaster, is alone in the small schoolhouse that serves as both his home and the place where he teaches impoverished Arab children. On a high plateau, after a sudden snowstorm, he watches as the local gendarme, Balducci, ascends the steep slope through the snow to the school on horseback. With him, on foot, is an Arab prisoner who has brutally murdered one of his cousins in a family quarrel.

Balducci informs Daru that, in order to avoid the trouble that is brewing up in the Arab's village, Daru must escort this Arab to the police station fifteen miles away. Daru refuses to deliver the prisoner, but accepts custody of the Arab. Balducci is not pleased with Daru's attitude, and they part on bad terms. During the night Daru feeds and looks after the Arab, refusing to tie him up. He is disappointed that the Arab does not escape, thus saving Daru from having to decide what to do with him.

The next morning, Daru escorts the Arab to a point where he can walk either toward the town where prison awaits him, or toward the desert where nomad tribes will shelter him. Daru gives him food for two day's journey, and leaves him to make the choice. When Daru looks back, he sees the Arab marching towards the town. On his return to the school, Daru finds a threatening message from the Arab's family scrawled on the chalkboard.

MORE ABOUT THE AUTHOR

After his father was killed in battle when Camus was only a few months old, Camus's mother, an illiterate Spanish cleaning woman, raised him and his brother Lucien in the slums of Algiers. One of his teachers, Louis Germain, recognized Camus's exceptional intelligence, facilitated his education, and obtained a scholarship for him to attend secondary school. Here professor and philosopher Jean Grenier, also a writer, became his mentor.

At fourteen, Camus became an soccer enthusiast, a sport he was forced to abstain from in 1930 when he was diagnosed with tuberculosis, a disease that was to plague him throughout his life. He remained a lifelong fan of the sport that he later attributed to giving him his sure sense of morality and duty.

Chronic and progressive, tuberculosis affected not only Camus's physical well-being, but his attitudes and thoughts as well. Out of this experience he gleaned a philosophical conviction that human existence is both a constant movement toward death and a deep attachment to life. As a result, Camus was at once involved in and detached from his life's experiences.

From the age of seventeen Albert Camus was aware that he wished to become a writer. He was writing and publishing for local magazines by 1932, the same year he entered the University of Algiers. His illness and economic situation precluded further studies after he received his degree in 1935. After his university studies, he worked in various poorly paid positions—as a meteorologist, automobile parts salesman, government clerk, and maritime stockbroker's agent. He performed as an actor with the Radio-Algiers theatrical group, where he acquired a lasting passion for the theater that would express itself in his own acting and theater writing. For Camus, the theater was not only an art form but also a vehicle for political expression. From his background of poverty, Camus expressed in his writings a solidarity with the oppressed of this earth and a hatred of those who dominated and exploited them.

In 1934, Camus married Simon Hie, an attractive and well-to-do but unstable woman with a serious drug addiction problem. This marriage ended in divorce two years later. Camus was married for the second time in December of 1940 to Francine Faure, a mathematics specialist from Oran, Algeria. They had twins, a boy and a girl, in 1945.

Camus's first novel, *The Stranger,* appeared in June 1942, followed by *The Myth of Sisyphus,* a philosophical treatise. The 1947 publication of his novel *The Plague* became both an immediate and immense literary and financial success. In October 1957, at the age of forty-four, Camus was awarded the Nobel Prize for Literature.

While returning to Paris after the Christmas holidays, Camus was killed in an accident in a car driven by his friend Michel Gallimard.

A CRITICAL COMMENT

"Viewed as a whole, the narrative moves from one form of solitude to another. In the beginning, Daru was alone but thought of himself as a lord of his environment. Because of the intervention of men (their jealousies, their hate, their blood lust) he now finds himself alone, but in definitive exile. The rocky expanse he once viewed as his kingdom has now become his prison; he is now vulnerable, subject to the wrath of the Arab's 'brothers.' On one level, there is great injustice in the message on the chalkboard. Daru, the solicitous host, did not, in fact, deliver the Arab to the authorities. In some ways, he may have treated him in a more 'brotherly' fashion than the Arab's own violent family. On a deeper level, however, the reader cannot overlook the fact that Daru refused to make a moral choice. By leaving the choice to the prisoner, Daru did not act; he set himself apart from his fellow humans and presumed to pursue his existence in isolation from them and in isolation from the escalating political conflict in the country. Daru refused to heed the message of John Donne's much-quoted line: 'No man is an island.' By living as if he were alone and not engaged in the messy complexities of Algerian reality, he separated himself, despite his good intentions, from those human beings who most needed his support. The ultimate lesson of this story of high moral drama is that, in some circumstances, the refusal to choose is already a choice. Daru may not wish to be part of a judicial process or part of a social/political conflict, but his non-action, in the eyes of others, is action. To Balducci he is a traitor and to the 'brothers' of the Arab he is the enemy. The unwelcoming host turns out to be merely a guest, now an unwelcome one, in a land that has interpreted his love of solitude as a failure to grasp the constraints and asperities of human solidarity."

—*from* Understanding Albert Camus,
David R. Ellison

FOR FURTHER READING

Bree, Germaine. *Camus.* Rev. ed. New Brunswick, NJ: Rutgers University Press, 1964.

Camus, Albert. *Exile and the Kingdom.* Trans. Justin O'Brien. New York: Alfred A. Knopf, 1957, 1958.

Ellison, David R. *Understanding Albert Camus.* Columbia, SC: University of South Carolina Press, 1990.

Lottman, Herbert R. *Albert Camus, a Biography.* New York: Doubleday & Company, Inc., 1979.

THE ENCHANTED GARDEN

Italo Calvino ▼ Translated by Archibald Colquhoun and Peggy Wright ▼ (Textbook page 1259)

SUMMARY

A boy, Giovannino, and a girl, Serenella, are walking along the railroad tracks, playing as they are accustomed to play every day in this seaside town. A train approaches, so they duck through a hole in a hedge and find themselves in a beautiful but apparently deserted garden. They are afraid of being discovered and sent away, or, worse, having dogs set on them. In spite of this, they continue to explore and play. The anxiety that they may be discovered playing with things which are not their own, however, hinders their enjoyment.

Two servants appear from the villa at the end of the garden, each bearing a large tray of food. The children help themselves to the food, but they are still uncomfortable. Curious, Giovannino and Serenella tiptoe up to the villa, and through a window they spy a pale boy, dressed in pajamas, looking through a picture book. The boy seems as anxious and uncomfortable as they are. Giovannino and Serenella become afraid, and they make their way back along the paths and through the hole in the hedge.

MORE ABOUT THE AUTHOR

Allegory, a device which Italo Calvino used frequently, is a form of storytelling which relies on definite symbolism to make a point or teach a lesson. It is a purposely unrealistic mode of expression which was popular in medieval morality plays as well as in moral tales of the nineteenth century. "The Enchanted Garden" has the feel of allegory in that the setting and events seem to be highly symbolic. At the same time, the lesson is enigmatic, leaving the reader to puzzle out the story's intention for him- or herself. Something is wrong in the garden, but what is it? And what garden is this, anyway? One question opens into another until the whole story becomes an engaging puzzle.

One of the key achievements of Calvino's storytelling is that he avoids giving the reader the answers, even though he uses the framework of a highly symbolic story—the sort of story that is usually used to teach a lesson. As a result, the reader gets involved in puzzling out the "lesson" that the allegory may intend.

Calvino was less concerned with a correct answer than with the infinite suggestibility of narratives. He saw stories as multivalent—that is, capable of having more than one meaning at the same time. Thus, the setting of "The Enchanted Garden" may be the Garden of Eden, or it may be a symbol for the decadence of the rich. In Calvino's scheme, the two interpretations are not mutually exclusive.

Calvino is frequently lauded for his scientific powers of detached observation. One of the things he was most interested in observing was the way stories work. In later books, like *Cosmicomics* and *T-Zero*, Calvino actually told stories about the way stories are made. "The Enchanted Garden" does not go to this extreme, but it does demonstrate the detached relationship between author and subject which lays the ground for his later, more experimental work.

A CRITICAL COMMENT

In the preface to the collection *Italian Folktales*, Calvino discusses his own understanding of the folktale and the ways in which it relates to modern existence.

"Now my journey through folklore is over, the book is done. As I write this preface I feel aloof, detached. Will it be possible to come down to earth again? For two years I have lived in woodlands and enchanted castles, torn between contemplation and action: on the one hand hoping to catch a glimpse of the face of the beautiful creature of mystery who, each night, lies down beside her knight; on the other, having to choose between the cloak of invisibility or the magical foot, feather, or claw that could metamorphose me into an animal. And during these two years the world about me gradually took on the attributes of fairyland, where everything that happened was a spell or metamorphosis, where individuals, plucked from the chiaroscuro of a state of mind, were carried away by predestined loves, or were bewitched; where sudden disappearances, monstrous transformations occurred, where right had to be discerned from wrong, where paths bristling with obstacles led to a happiness held captive by dragons. Also in the lives of peoples and nations, which until now seemed to be at a standstill, anything seemed possible: snake pits opened up and were transformed into rivers of milk; kings who had been thought kindly turned out to be brutal parents; silent, bewitched kingdoms suddenly came back to life. I had the impression that the lost rules which govern the world of folklore were tumbling out of the magic box I had opened.

"Now that the book is finished, I know that this was not a hallucination, a sort of professional malady, but the confirmation of something I already suspected—folktales are real.

"Taken all together, they offer, in their oft-repeated and constantly varying examinations of human vicissitudes, a general explanation of life preserved in the slow ripening of rustic consciences; these folk stories are the catalog of the potential destinies of men and women, especially for that stage in life where destiny is formed, i.e., youth, beginning with birth, which itself often foreshadows the future; then the departure from home, and, finally, through the trials of growing up, the attainment of maturity and the proof of one's humanity. This sketch, though summary, encompasses everything: the arbitrary division of humans, albeit in essence equal, into kings and poor people; the persecution of the innocent and their subsequent vindication, which are the terms inherent in every life; love unrecognized when first encountered and then no sooner experienced than lost; the common fate of subjection to spells, or having one's existence predetermined by complex and unknown forces. This complexity pervades one's entire existence and forces one to struggle to free oneself, to determine one's own fate; at the same time we can liberate ourselves only if we liberate other people, for this is a sine qua non of one's own liberation. There must be fidelity to a goal and purity of heart, values fundamental to salvation and triumph. There must also be beauty, a sign of grace that can be masked only by the humble, ugly guise of a frog; and above all, there must be present the infinite possibilities of mutation, the unifying element in everything: men, beasts, plants, things."

—from Italian Folktales, *Italo Calvino*
translated by George Martin

FOR FURTHER READING

Calvino, Italo. *Italian Folktales*. Trans. George Martin. New York: Harcourt Brace Jovanovich, 1980.

——. *Difficult Loves*. Trans. William Weaver, Archibald Colquhoun, and Peggy Wright. New York: Harcourt Brace Jovanovich, 1984.

Carter, Albert H. *Italo Calvino: Metamorphoses of Fantasy*. Ed. Robert Scholes. Ann Arbor: University of Michigan Press, 1986.

Olken, I. T. *With Pleated Eye and Garnet Wing: Symmetries of Italo Calvino*. Ann Arbor, MI: University of Michigan Press, 1984.

FREEDOM TO BREATHE

Aleksandr Solzhenitsyn ▾ Translated by Michael Glenny ▾ (Textbook page 1266)

A JOURNEY ALONG THE OKA

Aleksandr Solzhenitsyn ▾ Translated by Michael Glenny ▾ (Textbook page 1267)

SUMMARY

In the first of these prose poems, "Freedom to Breathe," Solzhenitsyn celebrates his ability to breathe deeply and freely. He says that this freedom is the most important thing that imprisonment takes away, and that no other pleasure—kisses, wine, food—can surpass it.

In the prose poem, "A Journey Along the Oka," the narrator reflects that it is the great Russian churches that are responsible for the beauty and grace of the country's landscape. The speaker reflects that things were better when churches were used for eternal matters rather than for earthly concerns.

MORE ABOUT THE AUTHOR

Aleksandr Solzhenitsyn moved to Riakan, on the banks of the Oka River, shortly after the end of eight years of imprisonment in 1956. Prior to his release, he had been sentenced to "eternal" deportation to Kazakhstan. That sentence was lifted after Soviet premier Joseph Stalin died. Solzhenitsyn's relief at being allowed to return to the West, and to freedom, is evident in both of these prose poems.

We know Solzhenitsyn primarily as a writer, but he was trained as a mathematician. During his years in Riakan, he taught math and physics at a local university. He also continued writing, which he had begun to do in earnest in the last years of his exile; however, only his wife was aware of his writing activity. When *One Day in the Life of Ivan Denisovich* was approved by the censors and published in 1962, "Solzhenitsyn the writer" was an unknown entity even to his closest friends. From being a small-town, "rehabilitated" college professor, Solzhenitsyn became a literary and political sensation overnight.

The volume *Prose Poems* (1965), from which these selections are taken, was the first of Solzhenitsyn's works to be published outside of what used to be the U.S.S.R. Although Solzhenitsyn had not authorized foreign publication, he was severely criticized on the charge that he was supplying the enemies of the Soviet Union with anti-Soviet propaganda. One of the immediate results of this was the confiscation of *The First Circle* by Soviet officials. Solzhenitsyn responded by writing a letter to the Writer's Union, which called for the end of censorship. He was expelled from the Soviet Union two years later.

Interest in Solzhenitsyn's sensational political life sometimes eclipses the achievement of his work. But the style of Solzhenitsyn's writing is perhaps as revolutionary as the content. In choosing to speak in the voice of a humble average citizen, he rejects the elevated rhetorical stance that was favored in most social realist writing of the period. In these selections, he also uses the contrast between an ideal thought and the actual, physical reality that confronts him to make a point. This differs from the didactic approach of most of the literature and news writing of the time.

Solzhenitsyn was deported to West Germany and stripped of his citizenship in 1974. The immediate cause was probably the writing of *The Gulag Archipelago*, which had been confiscated in manuscript outside of the former U.S.S.R. Solzhenitsyn now lives in Cavendish, Vermont, where he maintains a library of Russian works in the hope that he will one day be able to return them to his native land.

A CRITICAL COMMENT

"Immediately upon publication of Solzhenitsyn's first book, his readers and critics recognized two vital characteristics of his art—his language, and his straightforward depiction of the inhumanity of Stalin's labor camps. Solzhenitsyn's Russian readers appreciated the innovative form and content of his fiction from his initial appearance on the literary scene. His style—which contrasts sharply with the bleak, stereotyped language of contemporary Soviet fiction—is based upon the Russian vernacular, flavored with the jargon of the labor camp and with archaic, long-forgotten word formations. The latter are often so surprising and refreshing that one might think Solzhenitsyn had invented his own neologisms. Actually, he has for the most part merely restored the beauty and richness of the Russian language, which entered a decline after the revolution of 1917.

"The idiosyncrasies of Solzhenitsyn's style blend organically with the content of his various works. His use of the vernacular and the jargon of the labor camp enables him to create in *One Day in the Life of Ivan Denisovich* a very effective *skaz,* or oral narration, that adds credibility to the story and contributes to its powerful effect upon the reader. The oral character of Solzhenitsyn's narration coupled with his use of archaic word formations, makes his prose unusually dynamic; and the exceptionally rich content of his lexicon lends additional nuances to the text. By concentrating a large amount of information within relatively brief passages, Solzhenitsyn engenders a rapid flow of ideas and images which create the impression of a totally spontaneous, improvised account. This apparent spontaneity of Solzhenitsyn's narrative makes his works unusually convincing and powerful.

"Solzhenitsyn's language also serves to distinguish his prose stylistically from standardized contemporary Soviet literature and the mass media, and thus to bridge the "credibility gap"; if one may apply this term to the distrust of the average Soviet citizen for the printed word in his country. The press and the literati have for so long abused the language with clichés of official rhetoric that its effect upon the reader has been reduced to a minimum. Solzhenitsyn's immediate success may to a large extent have been due to his new and fresh use of language."

—*from* Alexander Solzhenitsyn, *Andrej Kodjak*

FOR FURTHER READING

Bjorkegren, Hans. *Alexander Solzhenitsyn: A Biography.* Trans. Kaarina Eneburg. New York: The Third Press, 1972.

Kodjak, Andrej. *Alexander Solzhenitsyn.* Boston: Twayne Publishers, 1978.

Moser, Charles A. ed. *The Cambridge History of Russian Literature.* Cambridge, England: Cambridge University Press, 1989.

Solzhenitsyn, Alexander. *Stories and Prose Poems.* Trans. Michael Glenny. New York: Farrar, Straus and Giroux, 1971.

TRURL'S MACHINE

Stanislaw Lem ▾ Translated by Michael Kandel ▾ (Textbook page 1273)

SUMMARY

Trurl, who has just completed his eight-story, steel thinking machine, asks the machine a question to verify that it is working properly. He asks for the sum of two and two. The machine's answer is seven. Despite Trurl's attempts to correct the error, the machine seems determined to believe that two plus two is seven. Trurl's colleague Klapaucius suggests that Trurl could make the most of the situation by turning the stupid machine into a sideshow attraction. Trurl grows angry and kicks the machine until it wrests itself from its foundation and takes off after Trurl, intending to crush him.

The two constructors head for the mountains. They take refuge in a village, but the machine tears down houses in an effort to reach them. They hide in a deep cellar, but the mayor threatens to hand them over. Finally, Trurl and Klapaucius make a run for the mountains and hide in a cave. There, they think, they will be safe, but the machine blockades the mouth of the cave. Desperate, the two constructors try to appease the machine by agreeing with its math, but Trurl loses his temper and dares it to pound the mountains into dust. The enraged machine promptly smashes its bulk against the cliff until a great boulder flies off and smashes it. The machine declares with its last creak that the answer to the problem is, and always has been, seven.

MORE ABOUT THE AUTHOR

On one level, "Trurl's Machine" can be seen as an amusing and lighthearted story about the slapstick adventures of the two constructors and the thinking machine one of them has invented. On another level, this short story reflects much deeper considerations that arise from Stanislaw Lem's involvement with issues of a philosophical and scientific nature.

One issue that concerns Lem profoundly is the essentially flawed nature of human beings. In the selection "Trurl's Machine," the thinking machine's insistence on the answer "seven," despite Trurl's tinkering, illustrates the caprice of the kind of evolutionary mutation which brought human beings about. It is only through chance that the thinking machine's mutation fails to be successful.

To complicate matters, one learns as one reads on in *The Cyberiad*, the collection from which this story is taken, that Trurl and Klapaucius are themselves robots. Their personalities allow them to function like human characters in the story, but the fact remains that they are the products of essentially flawed human reasoning. This serves as a comment on Lem's own doubts about the perfection of human beings and their ability to control what they create.

One idea which recurs frequently in Lem's fiction, as well as in his nonfiction essays, is that there is a moral need for scientists to take responsibility for the impact of the things they create. The application of this idea to "Trurl's Machine" is clear in the scene involving the mayor of the destroyed town. Though Trurl begs for mercy, the mayor makes clear that logically the constructor has to take responsibility for the destruction of property and lives that Trurl's machine has wrought. Though Trurl asks the town officials to take pity on him, he does not show any remorse or feeling for the townspeople whom his rebellious machine has killed.

All of these ideas might be too ponderous for a story if Lem did not also give free rein to his quirky sense of humor. The exchanges between Trurl, Klapaucius, and the thinking machine as they kick, insult, abuse, and chase each other through the story are classic slapstick. But the story also reveals how close to slapstick certain aspects of existence really are. By insisting that the machine is "stupid," the constructors refuse to consider the possibility that it is also genuinely dangerous until it is nearly too late. Language, in this case, functions as another "machine" that works improperly.

A CRITICAL COMMENT

In his introduction to *Microworlds: Writings on Science Fiction and Fantasy,* Franz Rottensteiner notes that Lem expects more in the way of philosophical exploration than most science-fiction writers deliver. As a result, though he himself is classified as a writer of science-fiction, Lem is sharply critical of science fiction as a genre.

"Lem has an insatiable thirst for knowledge and more of a philosophical than a poetic bent; scientific and philosophical inquiry have always played an important part in his work. Even in his fiction there is a strong essayistic element. Learned disquisitions are frequently woven into the plot, and if anything this practice has grown stronger with the passage of time. The stories in the various cycles (such as the Ijon Trichy tales, the Pirx stories, and the philosophical tales of *The Cyberiad*) become more complex with time; sometimes they carry so heavy an intellectual load that the story is in danger of being smothered. . . .

"A Polish reviewer has remarked that Lem is not interested in literature *per se* at all; his main interest is in the structure of the world, not the structure of the literary work. Lem is more interested in intellectual problems than in their literary expression. He has no patience with the notion of science fiction as entertainment or art for art's sake, and fiction without intellectual problems bores him. He is filled with curiosity about what is not yet known. For him, science fiction is a laboratory for trying out experiments in new ways of thinking; it should be a spearhead of cognition. It should attempt what hasn't been thought or done before.

"These goals are of course impossible to achieve, let alone in a literature of mass entertainment. Lem sees science fiction with great potential—a potential that naive apologists often claim has already been achieved—and he is all the more disappointed that it falls so far short of his expectations. He complains that it is only a rehash of old myths and fairy tales, that it avoids all kinds of real problems, and that it resorts to narrative patterns of primitive adventure literature, which are wholly inadequate to express what is claimed for science fiction. For him, science fiction plays "empty games"—the tired old vaudeville of time travel, robots, supermen, mutants, extrasensory perception, and the rest."

—*from the Introduction to* Microworlds,
Franz Rottensteiner

FOR FURTHER READING

Davis, J. Madison. *Stanislaw Lem.* Mercer Island, WA: Starmont Reader's Guide, 1989.

Lem, Stanislaw. *The Cyberiad: Fables for the Cybernetic Age.* Trans. Michael Kandel. London: Martin Secker and Warburg Limited, 1975.

——. *Microworlds.* Ed. Franz Rottensteiner. New York: Harcourt Brace Jovanovich, 1984.

Milosz, Czeslaw, ed. *The History of Polish Literature.* Berkeley, CA: University of California Press, 1983.

Ziegfield, Richard E. *Stanislaw Lem.* New York: Ungar, 1986.

A CANARY'S IDEAS

Joaquim Maria Machado de Assis ▾ Translated by Lorie Ishimatsu and Jack Schmitt
(Textbook page 1283)

SUMMARY

The story begins as Macedo steps into a secondhand shop and finds a lively canary in an old cage. The canary is no ordinary canary; it can speak to Macedo, and it tells him that the shop owner is its servant and that it is lord of its world. Macedo purchases the bird and begins to study its language and psychology. Totally absorbed in his work, he neither leaves his house nor permits any interruptions. He is particularly interested in the canary's conception of the world, which it now defines as a spacious cage in a garden.

The intensity of Macedo's labors causes him to fall ill. When he recovers, he learns that the canary has escaped and cannot be found. Later, however, while visiting a friend, Macedo is greeted by the canary, perched on a tree, who asks him where he disappeared to. Macedo greets the bird joyously, not noticing that his friend presumes him mad. He invites the canary to return home with him, but the canary denies any knowledge of the cage and the garden. Having forgotten about the garden and the secondhand shop, the bird now says that the world is the infinite blue space of the sky.

MORE ABOUT THE AUTHOR

Joaquim Maria Machado de Assis is now regarded as a giant of South American—indeed of world—literature. A pessimistic author, he views human nature as irrational, life as absurd, and relationships as treacherous. Nevertheless, his attitude in most of his writings is not dismal and self-pitying but amused and serene. He is bitter but also playful, a disenchanted spectator of the human comedy, one who saw dreams—even madness—as an alternative to the misery of reality. Some critics believe his themes reveal a sense of inferiority about his mixed ancestry, his modest background, his childhood stuttering, and his epilepsy. A central theme—human egoism and selfishness—may have arisen from guilt about his stepmother, who probably first introduced him to literature but whom he abandoned early in his career.

Machado de Assis' early dramas, collections of poetry, and Romantic novels are generally regarded as lesser works than his realistic and psychological novels. These include *Epitaph of a Small Winner,* about an ordinary man who sees his life as devoid of meaning but for one small victory—he has remained childless and has thus not added to the number of those who must suffer the misery of existence; *Dom Casmurro,* considered his masterpiece, about a man consumed with jealousy over an affair between his wife and his friend that may or may not be imagined; *Esau and Jacob,* about twin brothers whose feuds are seen as allegorical representations of Brazilian conflicts; and *Counselor Ayres' Memorial,* again an allegory for the concerns of Brazilian society that raises the possibility of salvation through selfless love.

In his novels and stories, Machado de Assis explores how self-interest distorts perception and judgment of "truth," using techniques that would later characterize many modern authors: reflective commentary, unreliable narrators, and probing irony. His shorter works, many of which mingle elements of fantasy and realism, are considered as worthy as his novels.

A CRITICAL COMMENT

"The themes of Machado's short stories are subtopics of one broad basic concept of human life and the world in which men live. If there is a purpose in Machado's writing, other than simply to entertain his readers, it is to reveal to them this concept by combining fantasy, irony, and reality, blended in innumerable and original juxtapositions. . . .

"Imagined or existing philosophical notions are often presented in Machado's stories. In 'O segredo de bonzo' ['The Secret of the Lottery Ticket'] the theory that belief is the equivalent of truth is treated humorously. 'Idéias de canário' ['A Canary's Ideas'] deals with the concept that a man's philosophy is entirely dependent upon his own limited experience. Most of the philosophical elements in Machado's stories are related to his idea of an incongruous world. For example, in 'Lágrimas de Xerxes' ['Xerxes' Tears'] he points out that both life and love are fleeting in spite of the strong human yearning for permanency. . . .

"Machado's writings are a testimony of his own possession of the talent of spontaneous creativity which he admired so much. Many of his stories are pure fancies—highly original and entertaining. One marvels at his ability to conjure up an imaginary situation and to follow it along from association to association in a bold and bizarre progression.

"An ancient Greek returns to earth in modern times in 'Uma vista de Alcebíades' ['A Vision of Alcibíades'] and cannot tolerate the wearing of hats. In 'O dicionário' ['The Dictionary'] the king's ministers decide to invent a dictionary with entirely new words. The protagonist of 'Idéias de canário' ['A Canary's Ideas'] is a bird that informs its owner about its concept of the world. The statues of saints in a church described in 'Entre santos' ['Between Saints'] come to life and engage in a discussion. In 'O cônego' ['The Canon'] a writer supposes that nouns and adjectives occupy opposite sides of the brain, that they may come to love one another, and that their marriages produce style.

"These and many similar samples of Machado's remarkable flights of fancy show that he clearly champions the literary value of make-believe, as well as of realism, to develop his themes. . . .

"With regard to general attitudes reflected in Machado's stories, one notes a tendency toward equanimity. Although dealing with weird aberrations, strange incongruities, and discouraging twists of fate, the author never openly expresses despair or strong emotions. If there is a trace of attitude, it is usually that of humor born of irony. The follies of fate do not seem greatly to perturb Machado as he describes their ironic absurdities. . . .

"As to the language element in the author's style, highly literary or abstruse terms are infrequent. Machado writes concretely, tersely—one might say, almost in a journalistic fashion. He avoids an excessive use of adjectives and affective expressions. His language is clear, straightforward, and restrained. It provokes thought, enjoyment, and often amusement in the reader—as the concise writings of the Chinese have done for centuries.

"Although varied, the short stories of Machado de Assis, taken as a whole, have a basic unity—reflecting the same general concept of the 'Devil's world.' They are products of an ingenious craftsman gifted with a deep understanding of human motives, a flair for a spontaneously fanciful and original treatment, and a clear and restrained manner of expression. Reading them affords an enjoyable literary experience."

—from *"Machado de Assis:
Short Story Craftsman"*
Donald M. Decker

FOR FURTHER READING

Caldwell, Helen. *Machado de Assis: The Brazilian Master and His Novels.* Berkeley: University of California Press, 1970.

Decker, Donald M. "Machado de Assis: Short Story Craftsman." *Hispania* Mar. 1965: 76–81.

Fitz, Earl E. *Machado de Assis.* Twayne's World Author Ser. Boston: G.K. Hall and Company, 1989.

Machado de Assis, Joaquim Maria. *The Devil's Church and Other Stories.* Texas Pan American Ser. Trans. Jack Schmitt and Lorie Ishimatsu. Austin: University of Texas Press, 1977.

Sontag, Susan. "Afterlives: The Case of Machado de Assis." *The New Yorker* 7 May 1990: 102–108.

I Am Not Lonely

Gabriela Mistral ▾ Translated by Langston Hughes ▾ (Textbook page 1290)

The Little Girl That Lost a Finger

Gabriela Mistral ▾ Translated by Muna Lee de Muñoz Marín ▾ (Textbook page 1291)

Summary

Both selections have a sing-song, repetitive quality reminiscent of children's nursery rhymes. In the three stanzas of "I Am Not Lonely," the speaker notes that the night, the sky, and the world are lonely, but she is not because she has "you" (an infant) to cradle, to cling to, and to hug.

In "The Little Girl That Lost a Finger," the speaker, a little girl, describes the chain of events by which her lost finger ends up in Gibraltar, where the fishermen call for her to come retrieve it. She asks for a boat, a captain, and the wages to pay him.

More About the Author

Passion, loss, despair, maternal feelings, ties to the earth, concern for the oppressed, and death—these are the subjects of Gabriela Mistral, whose personal, traditional poetry contrasts with the Modernism of her contemporaries. She was a humanitarian poet, deeply concerned about all people but especially children, women, and country folk.

As a young country schoolteacher, Mistral began publishing poems and articles in local newspapers. She became an avid Bible reader at a time when Catholics were discouraged from personal readings. The Bible, particularly the Book of Psalms, was to have a lifelong influence on her work, as well as some tenets of Judaism, Buddhism, and Theosophy, which she explored later in life. Ultimately, she found in activist Christianity a hope for native consciousness and the betterment of society.

Mistral's first major success sprang from tragedy. The suicide of her fiancé led almost immediately to "Sonetos de la muerte" ("Sonnets of Death"), which won first prize in the literary contest Juegos Florales (Floral Games). Her first book of poetry, *Desolación* (*Desolation,* 1922), which includes "Sonetos de la muerte," deals with love, death and eternity, God, nature, and peasant life. Her second volume, *Ternura* (*Tenderness,* 1925), explores motherhood, both anticipated and fulfilled, and the world of childhood.

The next period of Mistral's work reflected her new sense of serenity and a growing interest in the indigenous traditions of Latin America. The death of her mother led to a number of works evoking her rural childhood, published in *Tala* (*Felling,* 1938), along with hymns to the Incas and Mayas and to the beauty of her native Chile. Mistral donated the proceeds from this book to aid the infant victims of the Spanish Civil War.

Mistral's final collection, *Lagar* (*Wine Press,* 1954), is a reflective celebration of the beauty of the Americas. In these poems she sees death as a threshold, a source of mystical beauty, part of the rhythm of the cosmos.

A Critical Comment

"The title, *Tenderness,* is well suited to the general character of the book and to the principal emotion that is the source of its poetry. All the poems sing to the pleasure of motherhood, the miracle of having a child, the charm of little animals, the loving understanding between the earth and its creatures. After the tremendous passionate, sensual energy of *Desolation,* this second work reveals to us the powerful vitality, the hunger for happiness, 'the spiritualization of voluptuousness which is tenderness,' the other poles of the poet's spirit.

"The themes of *Tenderness* duplicate almost all the major motifs of her poetry: maternal love, its pleasures, enchantments, fears, fantasies; the child, his games and legends; the earth (nature, landscape, heavens, constellations); matter (animals, vegetables, minerals, things made by man); toil; America, sleep, death, peace, cosmic harmony, Jesus Christ, God the Father. The poetic development of such rich, varied material keeps these poems free from monotony, trivia, foolishness, and the shoddy prosiness too often found in this genre."

—*from* Gabriela Mistral: The Poet and Her Work,
Margot Arce de Vasquez

For Further Reading

Arce de Vasquez, Margot. "Poetry." *Gabriela Mistral: The Poet and Her Work.* Trans. Helene Masslo Anderson. New York: New York University Press, 1964.

Fitts, Dudley, ed. *Anthology of Contemporary Latin-American Poetry.* Norfolk, CT: New Directions, 1947.

Gazarian-Gautier, Marie-Lise. *Gabriela Mistral.* Chicago: Franciscan Herald Press, 1974.

Mistral, Gabriela. *Selected Poems of Gabriela Mistral.* Trans. Langston Hughes. Bloomington: Indiana University Press, 1957.

Ortiz-Vargas, A. "Gabriela Mistral." *Poet Lore* Winter 1940: 339–52.

DISCOVERERS OF CHILE

Pablo Neruda ▾ Translated by Robert Bly ▾ (Textbook page 1296)

SUMMARY

The speaker metaphorically describes how the conquistador Diego de Almagro used Spanish guns to move south through Chile, reading the country as he might read a letter. Almagro's body is dry, like the shadows of thorn or thistle or wax, and totally unlike the body of Chile, with its varied terrain, its long coastline full of silence and foam, its wealth of coal, gold, silver, and caliche. No matter what Almagro sees, says the speaker, he does not understand the mystical wonder of Chile.

MORE ABOUT THE AUTHOR

Pablo Neruda is considered one of the most important and influential of twentieth-century Latin American poets, both because of his prolific range of subjects and styles and because of his innovative techniques. Because Neruda's work reflected the changes in his personal and social consciousness, he does not fit easily within any one group or movement. Certain dominant themes and stylistic features can be identified, however, including the pleasures of both human life and relationships and of the natural world; the myths and archetypes of Chile; the role of the poet in giving voice to the chaotic beauty of dreams. Neruda expressed personal concerns, visions of nature, evocations of history, and the yearnings of people everywhere for justice and dignity.

Stylistically, Neruda's work is characterized by complex metaphors and images in some works, dizzying lists of objects or natural features in others. He frequently uses repetition, alliteration, and internal rhyme, and writes in both free verse and conventional forms. Many voices speak in his poems, and he shifts easily between different points of view and time periods.

Neruda wrote love poetry all his life, but his earliest work, *Twenty Love Poems and a Song of Despair* (1924), remains the best known. Considered too erotic by one publisher, these poems interweave images of woman and nature. *Residence on Earth* (1933) is full of anguished poems and surrealistic images of nature; they reflect Neruda's personal loneliness at this point in his life.

Neruda's poems became more political after he became involved in diplomatic affairs and joined the Communist party. *Canto general* (1950), a collection regarded as his masterpiece, includes both historical and mythological explorations of Spanish America ("Discoverers of Chile" is one) and militant, political criticism of his native land. Among the three hundred poems is "The Heights of Machu Picchu," a masterful series describing the poet's isolation among the living dead of the cities, his ascent to the hills of the dead, and his discovery there of a different kind of living dead. In the process, he gains a new consciousness of life in the present and the past. *Elemental Odes* (1954) marked in Neruda's work a movement to a simpler style and to a celebration of everyday objects. His odes are hymns to life.

A CRITICAL COMMENT

"There is a cosmic intensity throughout ["The Heights of Macchu Picchu"], an intermittent awareness of totality that gives the miniscule a special importance, one I would call Blakean were it not for the inevitable associations with mysticism. Neruda is no mystic, certainly. But his vision of the earth, of its evolution and engendering of man with his own peculiar, tragic history, makes the terrestrial sacred. Neruda loves the earth as Lorca did: not its rose gardens and seascapes alone, but first its minute creatures and basic elements—ants, seeds, sand, quartz, water, air, and of course stone. . . .

"Into the realm of the untouchable and indeed, the intangible, Neruda persists in his quest: to touch, even in disappearing matter, man. His insistently physical probing reveals a poet convinced of the power of every atom of life on the earth and determined to stay close to the organic matter that nourishes him.

"He, the living, hopes to perpetuate those gone; and as poet, hopes to unite us with them. He offers his words and his body to join men. The closing line of ["The Heights of Machu Picchu"] is:

Speak through my words and blood.

"A testimony to Pablo Neruda's concept of art and life."

—*from* Pablo Neruda at Machu Picchu, *Agnes Gullon*

FOR FURTHER READING

Agosin, Marjorie. *Pablo Neruda* (Twayne's World Authors Series). Boston: G.K. Hall and Company, 1986.

Bloom, Harold, ed. *Pablo Neruda.* Modern Critical Views Ser. New York: Chelsea House Publishers, 1989.

Bly, Robert, ed. *Neruda and Vallejo: Selected Poems.* Trans. Robert Bly, John Knoepfle, and James Wright. Boston: Beacon Press, 1971.

Gullon, Agnes. "Pablo Neruda at Machu Picchu." *Chicago Review* 27 (1975): 138–45.

Neruda, Pablo. *Canto General.* Trans. Jack Schmitt. Berkeley: University of California Press, 1991.

BORGES AND MYSELF

Jorge Luis Borges ▾ Translated by N. T. di Giovanni and Jorge Luis Borges
(Textbook page 1300)

SUMMARY

In this short piece, the speaker—perhaps Borges the man or perhaps the voice of Borges's essential self—claims that things happen to the other Borges: Borges the writer. The speaker explains how he is at once within Borges and yet separate from him and his experiences. The speaker worries about being lost in the "showy," exaggerated Borges (the writer), but living completely without Borges has proved impossible. The speaker is confused, not certain whether he or the other Borges has written this piece.

MORE ABOUT THE AUTHOR

The wide-ranging interests of Jorge Luis Borges led him to write stories, novels, poems, essays, literary criticism, travelogues, and scripts. The wellsprings of his creativity, he once said, arose in his extensive reading of literature, as well as of philosophy, theology, history, and psychology, subjects which he found fascinating but incapable of truth. Thus, in his own writing, Borges shows the absurdity of any search for meaning or transcendence, often using such techniques as paradox and oxymoron to highlight the contradictions in life and the universe.

Given this background and outlook, it is not surprising that Borges's fiction, nonfiction, and poetry often overlap, the techniques of one genre used freely in the others. In the essay "The Approach to al-Mu'tasim," for example, Borges uses a review of a nonexistent detective novel to demonstrate that the reality of literature lies not in the concrete book but in the mind of the reader. (He "reviewed" the book so successfully that some of his readers were moved to order it!) Similarly, Borges demonstrates in "Borges and Myself" that his imagination has a real existence separate from Borges the writer.

Borges is best known, however, for his remarkable short stories. Characters and plots are frequently minimal in these stories, most of which are developed around philosophical themes like time, memory, and identity. Most, too, use elements of fantasy—the fusion of dream and reality. Borges did not see fiction as a representation of reality, but as a recreation of the labyrinthine ways human beings use to try to understand it. Indeed, mirror images and labyrinths are frequent motifs in his work.

Among his most famous stories are "Tlön, Uqbar, Orbis Tertius" (1941), which explores the shadowy line between the imagination and the real: as a group of men try to create an ideal world, some of its elements become real; "The Library of Babel" (1941), which reveals the books in the library, a supposed repository of human rationality, as illegible; "Death and the Compass" (1942), in which a rational detective and the irrational criminal he seeks are antithetical doubles, each bent on destroying the other; and "The Aleph" (1945), in which a stone in a Buenos Aires cellar contains all points in space, all the visual images of the world.

The story in the text, "Borges and Myself," appeared in the 1970 English language version of *The Aleph and Other Stories,* translated by Borges himself and Norman Thomas di Giovanni. The results of this collaboration have been acclaimed for their authenticity and grace, as if the stories had originally been written in English. According to one reviewer, the work actually involved three translators: di Giovanni, the Borges who first wrote the stories in Spanish, and the Borges who now rewrote each line in English, a language he loved for its "verbal music." "Borges and I" reflects the theme that identity is an illusion. (Borges uses his own double again in "The Other," a story in which the seventy-year-old narrator, Jorge Luis Borges, sitting on a riverside bench in Cambridge, Massachusetts, meets and converses with the twenty-year-old Borges sitting on a riverside bench in Geneva.)

A CRITICAL COMMENT

"[Borges's] stories and his poems are the inventions of a poet and a metaphysician. Thus they satisfy two of mankind's central faculties: reason and fantasy. It is true that Borges does not provoke the complicity of our feelings and passions, dark or light: piety, sensuality, anger, compassion. It is also true that his works tell us little or nothing about the mysteries of race, sex, and the appetite for power. Perhaps literature has only two themes—one, man among men, his fellows and his adversaries; the other, man alone against the universe and against himself. The first is the theme of the epic poet, the dramaturge, and the novelist; the second, the theme of the lyric and metaphysical poet. In Borges's works, human society and its many and complex manifestations, which run from the love of two people to great collective deeds, do not appear. His works belong to the other half of literature, and all have a single theme: time, and our repeated and futile attempts to abolish it. Eternities are paradises that become prison sentences, chimeras that are more real than reality—or perhaps I should say, chimeras that are no less unreal than reality.

"Through prodigious variations and obsessive repetitions, Borges ceaselessly explored that single theme: man lost in the labyrinth of a time made of changes that are repetitions, man preening before the mirror of unbroken eternity, man who has found immortality and has conquered death but neither time nor old age. . . . These are works of rare perfection, verbal and mental objects made according to a geometry at once rigorous and fantastic, rational and capricious, solid and crystalline. All these variations on a singe theme tell us one thing: the works of man, and man himself, are nothing but configurations of evanescent time. He said it with impressive lucidity: 'Time is the substance of which I am made. Time is a river which carries me off, but I am that river; it is a fire which consumes me, but I am that fire.' The mission of poetry is to throw light upon what is hidden in the folds of time. It took a great poet to remind us that we are, at the same time, the archer, the arrow, and the target."

—from "In Time's Labyrinth,"
Octavio Paz

FOR FURTHER READING

Bloom, Harold, ed. *Jorge Luis Borges*. Modern Critical Views Ser. New York: Chelsea House Publishers, 1986.

Borges, Jorge Luis. *The Aleph and Other Stories 1933–1969*. Trans. Jorge Luis Borges and Norman Thomas di Giovanni. New York: E.P. Dutton, 1979.

——. *Labyrinths: Selected Short Stories and Other Writings*. Donald A. Yates and James E. Irby, eds. New York: Random House, Inc., 1984.

Paz, Octavio. "In Time's Labyrinth." Trans. Charles Lane. *The New Republic* 3 November 1986: 30–34.

WIND AND WATER AND STONE

Octavio Paz ▾ Translated by Mark Strand ▾ (Textbook page 1305)

SUMMARY

In four stanzas the poet describes the interaction of wind, water, and stone, both as natural processes (water and wind erosion, dispersion, and evaporation) and as symbols of the rise and fall of human empires. More specifically, the stone may be Mexico (from the Aztec city of Tenochtitlan, "stone rising in water"), a quieter force than wind or water. In these eternal cycles, one element becomes the other, losing itself and disappearing. But, the poet implies, the elements also endure beyond human history and language—and the cycle begins anew.

MORE ABOUT THE AUTHOR

An epic poet, regionalist, and social thinker, Octavio Paz bridges the gap between the personal and the universal, between the individual and society, between symbol and reality, between poet and reader. His great themes are alienation and isolation, but he shows how communion—physical love, social interaction, and poetry—allows people to overcome these barriers and achieve wholeness.

Paz is often viewed as a surrealist writer more interested in the workings of the unconscious than in linear time or reality, trusting in poetry and love to counter life's contradictions, absorbed in a search for the timeless, ecstatic moment, for utopia, for the true life.

Though many of Paz's poems employ conventional meter and structure, others are experimental. In his famous long poem "Sun Stone" (1957), Paz links personal memories and social observation. Written in 584 unpunctuated lines addressed to the planet Venus, the poem reflects the design of the Aztec Sun Stone, a basalt disk twelve feet in diameter that represents the cosmos, including references to past creations, contemporary theology, and calendar symbols. Like the stone, the poem is circular, beginning in the middle of one reminiscence, concluding with the opening lines of that story. In "Blanco" (1967), Paz actively involves readers, inviting them to read the poem, written in three columns, in any of several ways: each section of each column separately, each column as a unit, or individual sections of the left column with individual sections of the right column.

Paz has also published many volumes of "literary essays," primarily dealing with social issues, with arts and letters, and with the connections between these spheres. He frequently explores the historical and mythological roots of present situations and the contribution of art as a form of social communion. In one controversial work, "The Labyrinth of Solitude" (1950), Paz explored the Mexican character, finding the source of current insecurities and suspicions in the conquests of the past. According to Paz, Mexico (and by extension, all of South America) is still searching for a national identity and a future it can call its own.

A CRITICAL COMMENT

"Paz's poetry *is* its imagery far more than it is any ideas that can be extracted from it, and anyway the ideas are inseparable from the images in which they are embodied. If we as readers ever come near to experiencing the ecstatic *instante* that Paz is aiming for, it is thanks to the exuberant evocativeness of his images. Yet alas whatever can be written about them will not do them justice. The language of Paz's poetry is energetically plurivalent. No word is allowed to settle down, or to attach itself to one single referent. . . .

"Paz's most famous poem is called 'Piedra de sol'—'Sun Stone' (1957). Much of his poetry constitutes an enterprise that is summarized in that title: the attempt to turn *stones* into *sun*. The title refers to the famous Aztec Calendar Stone, a vast stone block engraved with signs that embrace astronomy, history, and legend, and which bears the head of the Sun-God at its center. Yet it is not essential to be expert in Aztec mythology to gauge the significance of sun and stone in Paz's work. The Calendar Stone embodies the infinity of the Aztec universe. But it is nothing without the sun. Stone without sun—or without free-flowing water—is petrification. The task of poetry is to unpetrify stone, to bring sun to it and to make it live and breathe like an organism. If not, it will be a dead symbol of a dead people—as dead as the Aztecs, who, too, must be resuscitated. So when poetry is flourishing, 'the stone awakens: / it bears a sun in its belly.'"

—*from* Modern Latin American Literature, *D. P. Gallagher*

FOR FURTHER READING

Gallagher, D. P. *Modern Latin American Literature.* New York: Oxford University Press, 1973.

Paz, Octavio. *The Collected Poems, 1957–1987: Bilingual Edition.* Ed. Eliot Weinberger. Trans. Eliot Weinberger, Elizabeth Bishop, Paul Blackburn, and Lysander Kemp. New York: New Directions Publishing Corp., 1987.

Wilson, Jason. *Octavio Paz.* Twayne's World Authors Ser. Boston: G.K. Hall and Company, 1986.

THE HANDSOMEST DROWNED MAN IN THE WORLD

Gabriel García Márquez ▼ Translated by Gregory Rabassa ▼ (Textbook page 1309)

SUMMARY

In a small fishing village, children discover the enormous body of a stranger washed up on the shore. As the women prepare the body for burial, they discover that the dead man was beautiful beyond imagination. Because none of the villagers' clothes will fit him, the women make him some. As they sew, they imagine what his life must have been like, and they name him Esteban.

According to custom, the dead must be thrown into the sea from the cliffs, and the men want to dispose of the corpse quickly, before the heat of the day. They become impatient with the women's fussing over the corpse—until one of the women removes the cover on the dead man's face, revealing Esteban's beauty. The village gives Esteban a splendid funeral, and the villagers become aware for the first time of the barrenness of their lives and their dreams. They throw Esteban into the sea without an anchor so that he can return to the village if he wishes, and they promise to improve their lives and their village in honor of his memory.

MORE ABOUT THE AUTHOR

Gabriel García Márquez once said that all his writings are about things he knew or had heard before he was eight years old. Most critics, too, see those years as crucially important to his development. He spent his childhood with his grandparents in Aracataca, Colombia, and his grandmother's tales, the long decline of the town, and the myths and superstitions of its residents powerfully influenced García Márquez, particularly in the contrast they provided to his years of city life. Both García Márquez's use of the theme of solitude and the form of magical realism—surreal marvels set matter-of-factly alongside everyday events—can be traced to his youth in the Colombian village where folklore was still a part of daily life.

In García Márquez's first important work, the novella *No One Writes to the Colonel* (1961), a retired colonel futilely waiting for his pension sinks through dreams into illusion. His first novel, *In Evil Hour* (1962), is the story of an isolated town where the corrupt authorities and residents allow one young man to be killed for the posting of some mysterious lampoons. The book that catapulted García Márquez into the international spotlight, however, was *One Hundred Years of Solitude* (1967), the story of the founding, growth, and decay of the town of Macondo—in microcosm, the history of Colombia, of South America, indeed of the world "from Eden to Apocalypse." (Macondo, a backwater off in the marshes and the setting of other García Márquez stories as well, has been likened to William Faulkner's Yoknapatawpha County.) In *The Autumn of the Patriarch* (1975), the lichen-covered body of a dictator who ruled over an unnamed Caribbean country for over two hundred years is discovered, unleashing a stream of collective and individual memories.

The more recent *Love in the Time of Cholera* (1988) marks García Márquez's departure from magical realism and presents a lush celebration of life through the story of an elderly widow and a man from her past. *The General in His Labyrinth* (1990) is a more somber story, a novel framed within the last days of Simon Bolivar as the great Liberator wanders frustrated and bitter, unwilling to accept exile and death.

Three of García Márquez's works reveal his journalistic skills as well as sheer storytelling ability. *The Story of a Shipwrecked Sailor* (1970), among the best of modern sea tales, was originally published in installments in a newspaper, with García Márquez as the ghost writer. Called a novella, *Chronicles of a Death Foretold* (1981) is based on an actual murder, a tragedy that residents of another backwater town conspired in rather than prevented, unable to escape their own myths and customs. *Clandestine in Chile: The Adventures of Miguel Littin* (1987) is an unusual first-person account of the film director's underground return to his native Chile to document life under the Pinochet regime.

A CRITICAL COMMENT

"['The Handsomest Drowned Man in the World'] illustrates the manner in which García Márquez utilizes a heroic figure to revolutionize mundane reality. To achieve the appropriate reaction from the reader to the disparate elements in the story, García Márquez creates a constant tension between a small fishing village and the sea which borders it. The tension heightens as the story progresses, and it remains unresolved at the open-ended conclusion. The meaning of the story must be developed in the mind of the reader, for it is not readily apparent from the various elements of the plot. . . .

"[The] expansion of consciousness provoked by a visitor from afar reveals itself in four stages. The first is manifest in the children, who naturally participate in supernatural reality. The women gradually traverse the second stage, in which their atrophied interior lives begin to bloom for the first time. The men grudgingly participate in the third stage, which combines a vision of sublime beauty with the ritual enactment of the burial of the hero. The last, and most significant stage is that of the whole community. During the last seconds of Stephen's presence, they see their village as it really is and determine to change it to fit their new self. The validity of their communal vision is manifest in the fame the village gains, a fame always connected with the legend of Stephen.

"How does García Márquez justify the reversal of a way of life within the span of twenty-four hours?

He convinces the reader that Stephen transforms the village through the introduction and constant reinforcement of heroic constructs. Four modes of heroic allusion interact throughout the text. The most complex group of allusions refers to what may be termed the classical construct of the hero, as he appears in Homer and other ancient writers. The most puzzling attributes of Stephen result from a configuration of traits traditionally connected with Quetzalcoatl. Then there follows a group of figures representing the Renaissance man: Sir Walter Raleigh, Gulliver, and a nameless sea captain. Finally, operating throughout the story are both subtle and obvious allusions to Odysseus. . . .

"In his combination of Homeric and modern aspects of Odysseus' personality with pre-Columbian heroic constructs, García Márquez creates still another embodiment of the archetype of man's refusal to accept reality as it is. His villagers, incited by a lively dead man, completely change from within, and their new self is reflected in their village, famous for the legend of Stephen, the martyr whose death stimulates new life."

—from "The Voyage beyond the Map:
'El ahogado más hermoso del mundo,'
Mary E. Davis

FOR FURTHER READING

Bell-Villada, Gene H. *García Márquez: The Man and His Work*. Chapel Hill: University of North Carolina Press, 1990.

Bloom, Harold, ed. *Gabriel García Márquez*. Modern Critical Views Ser. New York: Chelsea House Publishers, 1989.

Davis, Mary E. "The Voyage beyond the Map: 'El ahogado más hermoso del mundo.'" *Kentucky Romance Quarterly* 26, no. 2 (1979): 25–33. Rpt. in *Critical Essays on Gabriel García Márquez*. Ed. George R. McMurray. Boston: G.K. Hall, 1987.

García Márquez, Gabriel. *Collected Stories*. Trans. Gregory Rabassa and S. J. Bernstein. New York: Harper Collins Publishers, Inc., 1991.

McMurray, George R. *Gabriel García Márquez*. New York: Frederick Ungar Publishing Co., Inc., 1977.

Williams, Raymond L. *Gabriel García Márquez*. Twayne's World Authors Ser. Boston: G.K. Hall and Company, 1984.

ELEGY FOR THE GIANT TORTOISES

Margaret Atwood ▾ (Textbook page 1318)

SUMMARY

The poem is about the speaker's appreciation for the awkward but persevering giant tortoises.

MORE ABOUT THE AUTHOR

As a poet and as a novelist, Margaret Atwood has achieved both critical and popular acclaim. Hers is a distinctive Canadian voice articulating nationalistic, feminist, and environmental concerns.

In both her poetry and fiction, Atwood deals with such themes as deceptiveness in human relations, the search for identity, and the desirability of a more natural way of life. In much of her work, Atwood borrows from myths, legends, and fairy tales to create a kind of modern Gothic. Her tone ranges widely, from highly melodramatic and symbolic in some works, to bleak and harsh, or comic and pointed in others.

Atwood came to prominence in the 1960s with a number of collections of poetry, beginning with *Double Persephone* in 1961. By the end of the decade she had written her first novel, *Edible Woman* (1969). Her second novel, *Surfacing* (1972), is widely regarded as a contemporary classic. One of her newer books, *Cat's Eye* (1989) is the story of a middle-aged woman artist reflecting on her own development and on her relationship with a childhood friend. Her short stories, collected in *Dancing Girls* (1977) and *Wilderness Tips* (1991), have been described as almost novels-in-miniature, intelligent, perceptive examinations of the human heart.

Herself a critic of note, Atwood has written a thematic study of Canadian literature (*Survival,* 1972) and has edited *The New Oxford Book of Canadian Verse in English* (1982) and, with Robert Weaver, *The Oxford Book of Canadian Short Stories in English* (1988). An avid birdwatcher, Atwood recently wrote *For the Birds* (1991), a young adult novel about a girl turned into a bird who then learns how human activity affects the ecosystem. Royalties from this book will be donated to a number of environmental causes.

A CRITICAL COMMENT

Margaret Atwood is an extraordinarily good writer who has produced widely different books: so far, two novels, five books of poetry, and a critical guide to Canadian literature. She possesses an unusual combination of wit and satiric edge, a fine critical intelligence, and an ability to go deep into the irrational earth of the psyche. Her books are varied in genre yet through everyone of them run victor/victim and quest for self themes, a set of symbols, and a developing underlay of theory. Some themes she shares with other Canadians, and others are characteristic of our developing women's culture. All are vital and juicy. Technique she has in plenty; what I want to look at is her matter.

"In *Survival: a Thematic Guide to Canadian Literature*, Atwood finds throughout a preoccupation with survival; survival in a bare and hostile place; survival in crisis—shipwreck, snowstorm; cultural survival for the French; survival as obsolescence (those who consider Canada a relic); survival in the face of economic take-over by the United States. Considering Canada as a colony, she finds this obsession with the obstacles to physical and/or spiritual survival unsurprising. She outlines what she calls the Basic Victim Positions.

"1. Deny that you're a victim. Direct anger against your fellow victims.

"2. Acknowledge victimhood but explain it as God's will, history, fate: you may play it out as resigned or rebellious, but of course you will lose. The explanation displaces the cause of oppression to something too vast to change.

"3. Acknowledge victimization but don't accept it as inevitable. This dynamic position can slide back to no. 2 or attempt to move on to no. 4. Here you can make real decisions about what can be changed and what can't; anger can be directed against what is oppressing you.

"4. Be a creative nonvictim. She describes this as almost impossible in an oppressive society. I would conclude from her work that basically position 4 is achievable in moments from which insight can be brought back to the normal life of struggle and confusion in no. 3.

"*Survival* is an extremely canny and witty book, but I am using it, or misusing it, not for its insight into Canadian literature, but for what it tells us about Atwood's ideas. I find in *Survival* a license to apply it to her own work, as she argues that discovery of a writer's tradition may be of use, in that it makes available a conscious choice of how to deal with that body of themes. She suggests that exploring a given tradition consciously can lead to writing in new and more interesting ways. I think her work demonstrates that a consciousness of Canadian themes has enriched her ability to manipulate them

—from "Margaret Atwood: Beyond Victimhood," Marge Piercy

FOR FURTHER READING

Atwood, Margaret. *Selected Poems*. New York: Simon and Schuster, 1976.

———. *Selected Poems II: Poems Selected and New, 1976–1986*. Boston: Houghton Mifflin Company, 1987.

Ingersoll, Earl G., ed. *Margaret Atwood: Conversations*. Princeton, NJ: Ontario Review Press, 1991.

McCombs, Judith, ed. *Critical Essays on Margaret Atwood* Critical Essays on World Literature Ser. Boston: G.K. Hall and Company, 1988.

Oates, Joyce Carol. "Margaret Atwood: Poems and Poet." *New York Times Book Review* 21 May 1978: 15, 43–45.

Piercy, Marge. "Margaret Atwood: Beyond Victimhood." *Parti-Colored Blocks for a Quilt: Poets on Poetry*. Ann Arbor: University of Michigan Press, 1982.

Trueblood, Valerie. "Conscience and Spirit." *The American Poetry Review* March/April 1977: 19–20.

VanSpanckeren, Kathryn and Jan Garden Castro, eds. *Margaret Atwood: Vision and Forms*. Carbondale, IL: Southern Illinois University Press, 1988.

A WALK TO THE JETTY
from ANNIE JOHN
Jamaica Kincaid ▼ (Textbook page 1322)

SUMMARY

Walking to the jetty with her parents on the morning when she will leave Antigua for England, young Annie John is assaulted by memories. Among the memories are her first trip to the store by herself, walks at night with her father and fears of falling through the slats of the jetty, her desire to wear glasses, and a recollection of a seamstress who treated her badly. Arriving at the jetty, Annie has nothing to distract her from the reality of her departure. She simultaneously feels hollow, held down, burning up, torn up. With great joy and great pain she realizes that she will never see this place and these people again.

In the launch on the way to the wharf, Annie is struck by all the familiar images she will never see again: the sea, the gulls, the fishermen, the shore, the houses. She realizes she is gripping her parents' hands and fears their scorn, but instead they kiss her. For just a moment she fears her decision was a mistake. Goodbyes are hurried. Annie has the feeling her father wants to say something to her, but he does not. Her mother cries, and so does Annie until she inwardly withdraws, wondering if her mother is up to something. Yet her mother's last words hit her painfully. As the launch pulls away with her parents in it, Annie and her mother wave frantically. Annie goes to her cabin and lies down and hears the sound of the waves on the ship.

MORE ABOUT THE AUTHOR

Jamaica Kincaid's fiction centers on the struggles of girls and young women as they try to define their identity, deal with relationships with others, especially their mothers, and understand the ambivalent feelings inherent in those relationships.

Kincaid's first work, *At the Bottom of the River* (1983), is a collection of short stories praised for their poetic images and lyrical language evocative of Caribbean folktales. That praise is tempered, however, by critics who find some of the stories lacking in narrative rigor and obscure in meaning. Two themes dominate the collection: the wonderful, terrible ties between mother and daughter, and the strangeness and magic of ordinary life.

Annie John (1985), published as a novel, was originally written as a series of short stories for *The New Yorker* magazine. It chronicles the childhood and adolescence of the narrator as she comes to grips with the reality of death, a growing love-hate relationship with her once adored mother, both conventional and unconventional friendships, the rigidity of school life, and the nature of her own heart.

A Small Place (1988) is Kincaid's bitter nonfiction account of the history and current condition of her native Antigua. Kincaid shows tourists what they would otherwise miss: the contrast between the haves and the have-nots, the discrepancies between the idyllic world of tourists and former colonialists and the distress of natives and descendants of slaves.

Annie, Gwen, Lilly, Pam and Tulip (1989) is an unusual collaboration between Kincaid and artist Eric Fisch, originally published in a limited edition for collectors. Kincaid's text is a lyrical dialogue between five girls who muse about life, love, and the future, and Fisch's lithographs illustrate their mysteries and revelations.

Kincaid's newest book, *Lucy* (1990), was also first serialized in *The New Yorker*. It is the story of a West Indian teenager who comes as an *au pair* to a seemingly happy New York family whose disintegration Lucy observes. At the same time, Lucy makes discoveries about America and about herself. Lucy believes she has renounced her past, yet her views are colored by the culture she rejected.

A CRITICAL COMMENT

"This singular gift [a tactile sensibility] has been applied in [Kincaid's] first novel, *Annie John*. Set on Antigua, it covers almost the same ground as *At the Bottom of the River*. It too is an account of a young girl's transition to womanhood and her discovery that she must leave her familial paradise for the uncertainties of the adult world. To this universal and well-explored theme Kincaid brings to bear a discipline that renders fleeting moments in the passage of a life with evocative clarity.

"Annie John is a carpenter's daughter, a sensitive and precocious child whose morbid curiosity for the unlovelier side of life brings her, like the twice-born, to an early maturity. Her naive but none the less wise judgments concerning the nature of the universal and permanent amid transience are artfully expressed in the idiom of childhood. But the ambivalence of her love for her mother, her realization of the inevitability of suffering and death, are trials which she must successively overcome. In an ambience of confused affections Annie John learns that wisdom often lies in pursuing the broad path of honesty while fawning with a false heart.

"The book is episodic in structure, and autobiographical—its development is that of Annie John herself. Her personal crises overflow into her perceptions and her triumphs lend the book new resonance.

"Jamaica Kincaid uses language that is poetic without affectation. She has a deft eye for salient detail while avoiding heavy symbolism and diverting exotica. The result captures powerfully the essence of vulnerability."

—*from* Wising Up, *Ike Onwordi*

FOR FURTHER READING

Edwards, Audrey. "Jamaica Kincaid: Writes of Passage." *Essence Magazine* May 1991: 86–89.

Garis, Leslie. "Through West Indian Eyes." *The New York Times Magazine* 7 October 1990: 42.

Kincaid, Jamaica. *Annie John.* New York: Farrar, Straus, & Giroux, 1988.

Onwordi, Ike. "Wising Up." *The Times Literary Supplement,* 29 November 1985: 1374.

AND WE SHALL BE STEEPED

Léopold Sédar Senghor ▾ Translated by John Reed and Clive Wake ▾ (Textbook page 1332)

SUMMARY

"And We Shall Be Steeped" is a short, unrhymed poem intended to be accompanied by a khalam, an African four-string guitar. The poem is evocative of Africa through its vivid, colorful, and culturally specific images of the different ethnic groups and nations of Africa.

MORE ABOUT THE AUTHOR

Léopold Sédar Senghor was born in the small village of Joal in Senegal in 1906, just four years after Africa was officially divided up among various European powers. Senegal had been under French administration since 1904.

Senghor belonged to the Serere tribe, and his father was a farmer, a cattle-breeder, and an exporter of ground nuts. In keeping with the Serere's matriarchal system, young Senghor spent a great deal of time with his mother's family and did not, therefore, take up an apprenticeship on his father's farm—a situation that did not please his father. In part as punishment, the father sent the boy in 1913 to the Catholic mission school at Joal, where he was taught French grammar and Latin by Holy Ghost Fathers. Senghor's ambition was to become either a priest or a teacher. In 1914, he went to live at a boarding house at Ngasobil, where he stayed for eight years, then entered the Libermann Junior Seminary at Dakar, the capital and major port of French West Africa. After four years in the seminary, he was informed that he had no vocation to be a priest, so he turned his attention to his second career choice, teaching. Senghor finished secondary school in Dakar, then left for Paris in 1928 with a partial government scholarship to study at the Lycée Louis Grand.

Senghor was the first West African to graduate from the Sorbonne. He then became a teacher in France. At the same time he was becoming known as a political leader of West Africa. Among other political appointments, he was a member of the Council of Europe and first Deputy for Senegal in the French National Assembly. In 1960, he became the first President of the independent Republic of Senegal, and held the presidency until 1980. His best-known volumes of poetry are *Chants d'Ombre* (*Songs of Shadow*, poems written mostly between 1930 and 1939, published in 1945), *Hostiles Noires* (mostly written during the Second World War, published in 1948), *Ethiopiques* (published in 1956), and *Nocturnes* (published in 1961).

A CRITICAL COMMENT

"Négritude's atavistic posturings deny a legitimate place for the continent in today's community of nations and peoples. . . . As a historical phenomenon, Négritude was a legitimate revolt, a meaningful assertion of the black self. Its ontological system was an expected response to centuries of European racism and downright arrogance. Yet there was something elegantly dilettantish about it, its contradictions exposed in the political sterility of Senghor as the President of Senegal, where French commercial and cultural power is still paramount.

"Senghor has been accused of being a poseur and, at best, a mediocre poet. His reading of some of his poetry to African musical instruments . . . has been dismissed as a bogus and forced attempt to yoke two disparate cultures together. But his mastery of French has been acclaimed and it is not for nothing that he is a respected member of the French Academy. He has illustrated very well in his poetry the thematic concerns and mannerisms of Négritude . . . Senghor illustrates the essential music of French in an unconventional poetic mold. It is he who created the magic of that African world, with its kingdom of childhood, an innocent yet preternaturally aware state of mind, the pastoralism of a lost Eden, which he fondly belives is out there in Africa. . . . He is the poet of two vicarious experiences, a veritable sample of Africa's own history. Senegal was colonized over three hundred years and the Serer, Senghor's people, became one of the most Europeanized groups in West Africa, accepting Roman Catholicism. At an early age he moved from the *lycée* at Dakar to the Sorbonne in

Paris, to the *agrégation* based on a study of Baudelaire, and to a German prisoner-of-war camp. Europe was a happy and at times, sad experience. His poety is the attempt to fashion out of the European experience a language and testament that will constitute homage to his African past. . . . For him Négritude becomes a cultural instrument of fusion, fashioned for the survival of man in a world gone mad with machines and industry. Basing a great deal of his thinking on the work of the French Jesuit philosopher Teilhard de Chardin, Senghor affirms the need for the achievement of the final human evolution through the pulling together of disparate and, at times, opposing elements of this revolution.

—*from* The Breast of the Earth,
Kofi Awoonor

FOR FURTHER READING

Awoonor, Kofi. *The Breast of the Earth: A Survey of the History, Culture and Literature of Africa South of the Sahara.* New York: NOK Publishers International, 1975.

Jones, Eldred Durosimi, ed. *African Literature Today*: Poetry in Africa, No. 6. London: Heinemann Educational Books Ltd., 1973.

Mezu, S. Okechukwu. *The Poetry of Léopold Sédar Senghor.* London: Heinemann Educational Books Ltd., 1973.

Senghor, Léopold Sédar. *Nocturnes.* Trans. John Reed and Clive Wake. New York: The Third Press, 1971.

LIFE IS SWEET AT KUMANSENU

Abioseh Nicol ▾ (Textbook page 1336)

SUMMARY

"Life Is Sweet at Kumansenu" is the story of a son's mysterious visit to his mother and daughter in the village of Kumansenu. Meji, the seventh and only surviving child of Bola, shows up unexpectedly one evening at his mother's house. Bola rejoices, but Meji does not want anyone to know he is there.

The following day, Meji takes his daughter, Asi, for a walk, during which she notices that he doesn't cast a shadow, that his watch has stopped at twelve o'clock, that he does not eat, and that he wears a red handkerchief around his neck so that his head will not fall off, he tells her. In the evening Meji, Bola, and Asi visit Meji's father's gravesite, but only Meji is able to "communicate" with his father through a ritual of kola nuts. Upon their return home, Bola notices that Meji has been discarding his uneaten meals and that his room smells of decay. Late at night, Meji wakes his mother to tell her he is leaving and to thank her, and he disappears into the rainy night.

The next day brings news that Meji had in fact died several days before from a broken neck. Bola and Asi are bewildered, but Bola understands that Meji came back from death in order to thank her for his life and to remind her that life is sweet.

MORE ABOUT THE AUTHOR

As Abioseh Nicol, the author has published short stories and poetry in numerous English and American publications, and many have been broadcast by the BBC in London. He was the 1952 winner of the Margaret Wrong Prize and Medal for African Literature.

As Dr. Davidson Nicol, the author is a scientist, educator, and diplomat. He earned his M.D. and Ph.D. from Cambridge University. He has written on scientific and medical subjects and has edited political and historical essays.

Various West African tribal cultures feature a belief in "born-to-die" children. The Yoruba people call this child "abiku"; Ibo society calls this child "ogbanje." *Abiku* means "child born to die" and refers to the belief that some children are reborn over and over to the same mother, dying soon after each birth. Both Wole Soyinka and J. P. Clark wrote poems which they entitled "Abiku," and Soyinka again uses the abiku child at the end of his play "A Dance of the Forests."

A CRITICAL COMMENT

"The wonder and thunder of the African scene must be understood because of the increasingly important role that Africa is now playing in world affairs. A most useful introduction to the mind of the modern African can be found in this literature, which has been greatly stimulated by the surge of national independence sweeping over the continent. The great opportunities for self-government and self-expression have gone hand-in-hand and are amply reflected in the wide variety of imaginative and realistic writing. . . .

"Africa itself has many languages. In any one African country alone there may be many vernacular languages. Sierra Leone, for example, officially an English-speaking territory, has a population of three million, among whom there are fourteen languages, with Temne, Mende, and Limba being dominant. People from the different language communities speak or write to each other in the language of the European power of which they were once colonies. Thus the European language is not only a medium of expression to the outside world, . . . but it is also an internal unifying force for each nation. It may be argued that a second language learned at school cannot be used with sufficient conviction and skill. It should be remembered, however, that great writers of English prose like Arthur Koestler, and before him, Joseph Conrad, were not originally English-speaking. The mastery of European languages by Africans is another evidence of the adaptability to world currents of scholarship and literature.

"There is a great deal of imagination and style in African writing and this is displayed against the background of the experience of an individual, his community, his nation, and his race. These exotic qualities give African literature a flavor which is both attractive and educative. . . .

"In African literature, the crackle of lightning of past memories gives a vivid flash of the African landscape before we hear the long roar of thunder; and then all is silence. But the wonder will always remain."

—from the Introduction to
Africa Is Thunder and Wonder, *Abioseh Nicol*

FOR FURTHER READING

Laurence, Margaret. *Long Drums and Cannons: Nigerian Dramatists and Novelists 1952–1966.* London: MacMillan and Company, Ltd., 1968.

Nicol, Abioseh. *The Truly Married Woman and Other Stories.* London: Oxford University Press, 1965.

——. Introduction. Africa Is Thuder and Wonder: Contemporary Voices from African Literature. Ed. Barbara Nolen. New York: Charles Scribner's Sons, 1972.

Parrinder, Geoffrey. *African Traditional Religion.* New York: Harper & Row, 1976.

——. *Religion in Africa.* Middlesex, England: Penguin Books, Ltd., 1969.

MARRIAGE IS A PRIVATE AFFAIR

Chinua Achebe ▾ (Textbook page 1345)

SUMMARY

When Nene, a young woman reared in Lagos, the former capital of Nigeria, and Nnaemeka, a young man from a remote African village, decide to marry, she assumes that his father, who still lives in the Ibo village, will be happy to learn of his son's engagement. But Nnaemeka is apprehensive, aware that they are violating the Ibo tradition of arranged marriages. His father, Okeke, not only knows nothing of Nnaemeka's plans with Nene, but has selected an Ibo girl, daughter of a neighbor, to be Nnaemeka's wife.

When Nnaemeka explains that he cannot marry his father's choice and is engaged to marry another woman, Okeke rejects him. Okeke refuses to meet Nene and for the next eight years refuses to allow Nnaemeka into his house. The Ibo villagers avoid even the mention of Nnaemeka's name in Okeke's presence. Even Nnaemeka's Ibo friends are slow to accept Nene as Nnaemeka's wife though their frequent contact with her eventually breaks through their prejudice, and they come to admit that she keeps her home better than they keep theirs. Despite this unfriendly environment, Nnaemeka and Nene are a happy couple to whom two sons are born.

Finally Nene writes to Okeke, explaining that the two boys have learned that they have a grandfather and insist upon seeing him. She requests that they be allowed to visit him. The sudden knowledge that he has two grandsons pierces Okeke's resolution. Despite his desperate struggle to maintain an unyielding heart, Okeke finds himself fearing that he might die before he can make up to them for shutting them out of his life.

MORE ABOUT THE AUTHOR

Chinua Achebe's father, Isaiah Okafor Achebe, was one of the earliest Ibo converts to Christianity and became a mission teacher for the Church Missionary Society. As a young man, he had left his ancestral home of Ogidi and only returned when his son, Albert Chinualumogu Achebe, was born. Achebe's primary schooling was at the Society's school and his first lessons were in Ibo. He was about eight years old when he first began to learn English. At age 14, he was selected for the distinction of attending the Government College at Umuahia, one of the best schools in West Africa. Shortly before turning 18, he entered University College, at Ibadan.

While a student at Ibadan, from 1948 to 1953, Achebe began to combine his understanding of Nigerian history and tradition with his growing interest in literature. He published four short stories in *The University Herald*. One of these was "Marriage Is a Private Affair," which was reprinted in 1972 in his short-story anthology *Girls at War and Other Stories*.

Achebe is best known as a novelist and is generally considered one of Africa's most prominent novelists. His four novels (*Things Fall Apart,* 1958; *No Longer At Ease,* 1960; *Arrow of God,* 1964; and *A Man of the People,* 1966) together form a history lesson on the making of modern Africa. The first describes Ibo society before the coming of whites and the early impact of the white missionaries; the last predicted the military coup that overthrew the civilian government of Nigeria in 1966—the year the novel was published. In addition to writing novels and short stories, Achebe has published two volumes of poetry: *Beware, Soul Brother, and Other Poems* (1971) and *Christmas in Biafra and Other Poems* (1973).

A CRITICAL COMMENT

"'Marriage Is a Private Affair' (May 1952) . . . develops a theme many Ibadan undergraduates had to give serious thought to—marriage for love in violation of rural custom. The story anticipates *No Longer at Ease,* but in contrast to the novel the story has a happy ending. . . .

"The story is an immature exploration of a problem largely created by the University itself. By bringing young people of both sexes together from variant language groups and then requiring them to work and speak in a common language, the University threatened all family and communal ties. The significance of the story does not lie in its unrealistic happy ending, but in its pitting of the new intellectual against his home and tradition. The greatest weakness of the story is not the ending, but the inadequacy of the portrait of the father. Achebe had not yet seen the traditional values that underlay the old man's intransigence. The story

shows no sense of community with the past. Its theme is the freedom of the modern world created by urban (i.e. European) values. Tradition has so little strength that the single idea, 'grandsons,' crushes it. Achebe accompanies the reading of Nene's letter with the first violent storm that signals the change of the year. 'Nature' will cure the foolishness of tradition. Marriage is not an affair of the family, of the community—it is 'private.' The whole thrust of Achebe's first two novels will say the opposite: that the clan is king, that nothing is private."

—*from* Achebe's World: The Historical and Cultural Context of the Novels, *Robert M. Wren*

FOR FURTHER READING

Achebe, Chinua. *Girls at War and Other Stories.* New York: Fawcett Premier, 1973.

Carroll, David. *Chinua Achebe.* New York: Twayne Publishers, Inc., 1970.

Killam, G. D. *The Novels of Chinua Achebe.* New York: Africana Publishing Corporation, 1969.

Palmer, Eustace. *An Introduction to the African Novel.* New York: Africana Publishing Corporation, 1972.

Wren, Robert M. *Achebe's World: The Historical and Cultural Context of the Novels.* Washington, D.C.: Three Continents Press, Inc., 1980.

TELEPHONE CONVERSATION

Wole Soyinka ▼ (Textbook page 1353)

SUMMARY

The poem "Telephone Conversation" is set in a red telephone booth in London in the late 1950s. The caller is a black African who is attempting to rent lodging, apparently responding to an ad. Having settled upon a reasonable rent and deciding that the location is acceptable, he has only to disclose his race, not wanting to waste a journey to see the rooms should Africans not be accepted. The poem describes the speaker's response to the racist landlady's questions about the darkness of his skin.

MORE ABOUT THE AUTHOR

Born in Abeokuta in Nigeria, Soyinka is a member of the Yoruba people, for whom farming is the most important occupation, followed by hunting, fishing, weaving, dyeing, and trading. The culture is dominated by religion; in fact, the Yoruba have a popular expression that ascribes to themselves four hundred and one gods.

Soyinka attended schools in Abeokuta and Ibadan, including what is now the University of Ibadan, until age 20, when he became a student at

the University of Leeds in England. He graduated from Leeds in 1957 with an honors degree in English. His education, in Nigeria as well as in England, was basically Christian-European. In much of his work, the influences of Christianity and of the many gods of the Yoruba are readily apparent.

Soyinka was very prolific at a young age in several literary formats. He was already publishing short stories by the time he was 23, and within two years he was attached to the Royal Court Theatre in London, with plays produced in London and in Nigeria. *The Swamp-Dwellers* was produced in London in 1959, while *The Lion and the Jewel* played in Ibadan the same year. By 1960, when he was 26, he had added poetry to his published literary work. He also directed and acted in his own plays and formed two theater groups, The 1960 Masks and Orisun Theatre. From 1962 to 1964 he was a lecturer at the University of Ife, while continuing to write poetry and plays. His novel, *The Interpreters,* followed in 1965. From 1965 to 1967 he was senior lecturer at the University of Lagos and Acting Head of the Department of English.

In August 1967, Soyinka was arrested by the Federal Military Government of Nigeria and remained in jail during most of the Nigerian Civil War until October 1969. While he was incarcerated, his translation of a Yoruba novel was published (*The Forest of a Thousand Daemons,* 1968), as were two more volumes of plays and poems. Though he had been appointed Head of the Department of Theatre Arts at the University of Ibadan in early summer of 1967, he was not able to assume the responsibilities of the position until after his release.

Among Soyinka's plays are *A Dance of the Forests* (1963), *The Strong Breed* (1964), *The Road* (1965), *Kongi's Harvest* (1967), and *Madmen and Specialists* (1970). His volumes of poetry include *Indanre and Other Poems* (1967) and *Poems from Prison* (1969).

A CRITICAL COMMENT

"Wole Soyinka was detained in prison from August 1967 until 1970 [sic]. In 1969 Rex Collings published two poems written in prison. There was no doubt in the minds of those who were familiar with Soyinka's work that the poems were his. The characteristic of making the immediate environment yield larger meanings, the ability to light upon the apt fixing image, the economical style were all there. But more importantly, and to the great relief of his admirers, the ideas were also there—the assertion of the individual will; the lonely figure separate, yet a part of the society—even a victim of the society; the concern for that society even as one groans under it.

"Soyinka's . . . poetry has the reputation of being difficult. What this really means is that it demands close and sensitive reading. . . . Very few writers, however, repay this attention more copiously than Soyinka does. However complex he may be, though, it seems ludicrous that in Africa, reading lists which include T.S. Eliot's poetry with its background of classical European mythology and mysticism, should exclude Soyinka on grounds of difficulty.

"The essential ideas which emerge from a reading of Soyinka's work are not specifically African ideas although his characters and their mannerisms are African. His concern is with man on earth. Man is dressed for the nonce in African dress and lives in the sun and the tropical forest, but he represents the whole race. The duality of man's personality, his simultaneous capacity for creation and destruction which makes him almost at every moment a potential victim of his own ingenuity, is a universal trait of *homo sapiens* who has been given by his creator the gift of free will. . . .

"Soyinka sees society as being in continual need of salvation from itself. This act of salvation is not a mass act; it comes about through the vision and dedication of individuals who doggedly pursue their vision in spite of the opposition of the very society which benefits from their vision. The salvation of the society then depends on the exercise of individual will."

—from The Writing of Wole Soyinka, *Eldred Durosimi Jones*

FOR FURTHER READING

Ademola, Frances, ed. *Reflections: Nigerian Prose and Verse*. Lagos: African Universities Press, 1962.

Dathorne, D. R. *African Literature in the Twentieth Century*. Minneapolis: University of Minnesota Press, 1975.

Duerden, Dennis and Cosmo Pieterse, eds. *African Writers Talking: A Collection of Interviews*. London: Heinemann Educational Books Ltd., 1972.

Jones, Eldred Durosimi. *The Writing of Wole Soyinka*. London: Heinemann Educational Books Ltd., 1973.

Moore, Gerald. *Modern African Writers: Wole Soyinka*. New York: Africana Publishing Corporation, 1971.

THE PIG

Barbara Kimenye ▼ (Textbook page 1356)

SUMMARY

Old Kibuka lives alone in a little cottage beside a stream in the Ugandan village of Kalasanda. Recently retired, he feels depressed. He is thinking he might as well be dead when his oldest grandson drives up and gives him a hug and a piglet that will make a nice meal. Kibuka is delighted, but the pig soon wins his heart. By evening the old man is no longer thinking of eating the animal and, in fact, is feeding it scraps from his own plate.

Within a few days, the pig's appetite grows so

that Kibuka is gathering food scraps from all the neighbors. At night, the pig sleeps at the foot of Kibuka's bed—a practice that continues even as it gains more and more weight and begins to disrupt Kibuka's sleep by snoring. Finally Kibuka tethers the pig outside at night, allowing it to roam free during the day until it begins to make a habit of falling into the stream. From this point on, the pig is kept tethered all the time, and every evening Kibuka walks the pig on a rope. The walks are agony for Kibuka, whose corns are very painful.

During one of these outings, while Kibuka rests

his feet, a motorcycle strikes the pig and kills it. A crowd gathers. Kibuka agrees to have the pig butchered so the villagers can enjoy the meat, asking only that a back leg be sent to the home of his friend Yosefu Mukasa. He declines any of the meat himself, saying he is not a great lover of pork. That night Kibuka has the best night's sleep he's had in months, and the next day he visits the Mukasas, where he is treated to a wonderful lunch. Suddenly, Kibuka realizes that his lunch is his late pig, but his dismay passes, and he fills his plate with meat, glad that he won't have to be taking an afternoon walk.

MORE ABOUT THE AUTHOR

Barbara Kimenye's work as a writer has taken her in several different directions: journalism, which made her well known in Africa; juvenile fiction, with seventeen titles published between 1966 and 1978; and adult fiction in the form of short stories, published by the Oxford University Press in two volumes in 1965 and 1966.

Interestingly, Kimenye's adult fiction is very different from her fiction for children. Her short stories for adults are set in rural Uganda and feature the interwoven lives of ordinary villagers, but while the characters in her juvenile fiction seem ordinary they have extraordinary adventures and experiences that are very much detached from real life worries of unpaid bills and conflicts with parents.

A CRITICAL COMMENT

"We can see that Miss Kimenye is certainly aware of what is going on in the outside world! But . . . she is interested in dealing with the ordinary people who live outside the pale of modern society and who seldom hit the headlines.

"And she does with such skill that I am at a loss to understand why her two books have not received greater critical acclaim. Her two books are very skillfully structured, each volume consisting of seven inter-linked short stories and an introduction. *Kalasanda* begins with 'The Village,' a description of the village, its physical and human assets and failings. . . .

"When she depicts 'simple' people, she reveals them as complex in their own way; and in order to reveal them, she uses language very appropriately. . . . When her 'simple' characters speak, Miss Kimenye uses the same kind of 'neutral' 'primary school' English as Narayan does; but when a character who has been trained in England speaks, she uses English expressions. . . .

"The good uncommitted writer makes us see and feel how such apparently dull lives existing in little backwaters of society and ignored by the world are actually full of interest."

—from An African View of Literature,
Peter Nazareth

FOR FURTHER READING

Herrick, Allison Butler, et al. *Area Handbook for Uganda*. Washington, D.C.: The American University, Foreign Area Studies, 1969.

Kimenye, Barbara. *Kalasanda Revisited*. London/Nairobi: Oxford University Press, 1966.

Nazareth, Peter. "An Uncommitted Writer." *An African View of Literature*. Evanston: Northwestern University Press, 1974.

Schmidt, Nancy J. "The Writer As Teacher: A Comparison of the African Adventure Stories of G. A. Henty, Rene Guillot, and Barbara Kimenye." *The African Studies Review,* September 1976: 69–80.

---

from KAFFIR BOY

Mark Mathabane ▾ (Textbook page 1365)

SUMMARY

The selection is an excerpt from Mathabane's memoir of growing up black in South Africa. The excerpt describes Mathabane's first trip as a child to the white world. He travels by bus with his grandmother Ellen and sees for the first time skyscrapers, traffic lights, and white school children.

Ellen works as a gardener for a white woman, Mrs. Smith, whose son Clyde has learned racist notions at school. When Clyde tells his mother that he does not play with Kaffirs—a disparaging term for blacks—his mother reprimands him. Clyde then shows Mathabane his room, which is roughly the same size as the house in which the black family lives. What most captures Mathabane's attention are the stacks of comic books and shelves of books. The Bantu school he attends does not have half as many books. Choosing a book by Shakespeare, Clyde tests Mathabane's ability to read English, then taunts him, saying that Kaffirs can't read, speak, or write English because they have smaller brains than white people do.

Clyde's remarks wound Mathabane, and he vows to master English and read, write, and speak it as well as any white man. As he leaves, Mrs. Smith gives the boy a box containing some clothing and a copy of *Treasure Island*.

MORE ABOUT THE AUTHOR

To discuss Mark Mathabane's early years in South Africa is to discuss the effect of apartheid on a black family in a South African ghetto. Mathabane was born in Alexandra, a black ghetto of Johannesburg, in 1960—a few months before the Sharpesville massacre, considered to be the first wave of black nationalism in its fight against apartheid. Sixty-nine unarmed black protesters were killed and 186 were wounded by South African police bullets.

Mathabane's parents came from tribal reserves: his father was one of the Venda people, from northwestern Transvaal; his mother, one of the Tsongas from northeastern Transvaal. Both parents were illiterate, but his mother so thoroughly believed that education was the means by which her children could rise above the squalor that she constantly encouraged them to get an education.

In 1976, Mathabane was deeply involved in the Soweto protests, in which some 10,000 black students of all ages marched and almost 5,000 were killed by the police. (Mathabane changed his first name from Johannes to Mark during this period in an effort to elude the police.) The spark that ignited the Soweto riot was a declaration by the Department of Bantu Education that all black schools were to teach courses not in English but in Afrikaans—considered by black Africans to be the language of their oppressors.

By age 13, Mathabane had received a tennis racket from the Smith family and had begun to learn the game. Arthur Ashe's trip to South Africa in 1973 convinced Mathabane that tennis was a viable route out of the black ghetto. By the time he was 17, he was playing regularly in a white tennis club, and as a participant in the South African Breweries Open, he met American tennis star Stan Smith, who was later instrumental not only in Mathabane's receipt of a tennis scholarship to attend college in the United States but also in providing significant financial support.

Mathabane arrived in the United States in 1978, transferring to various schools until he found an educational home at Dowling College in New York, where he graduated with honors in 1983.

Mathabane has written three books since coming to the United States: *Kaffir Boy: The True Story of a Black Youth's Coming of Age in Apartheid South Africa* (1986), *Kaffir Boy in America: An Encounter with Apartheid* (1989), and *Love in Black and White* (1992), the latest an account of his marriage to a white American woman. Along with autobiographical books, he has written articles on Apartheid in such publications as *U.S. News & World Report,* and lectures on college campuses. He has brought three of his five siblings out of Africa to be educated in the United States.

A CRITICAL COMMENT

"The free flow of books, information and ideas to South Africa has historically served to undermine the apartheid system. As a black South African, the most formidable form of oppression I had to overcome while imprisoned in a Johannesburg ghetto was mental slavery. Throughout my childhood and youth, I was confined to inferior and segregated schools and was persistently told by a racist society that I was subhuman and incapable of doing anything meaningful.

"I was able to emancipate my mind and gain control over my destiny only when I began reading books. Some of these books were given to me by a benevolent white family for whom my grandmother worked as a gardener; others I checked out of the ghetto's only library. They included *Treasure Island, David Copperfield,* and *Alice in Wonderland.*

"They became potent weapons in my battle against apartheid. First, reading them gave me respite in a world replete with suffering, pain, hunger, violence, hopelessness, oppression, and death. Their riveting stories lifted the shroud of anguish, despair and fatalism from my soul by offering visions of a more humane and delightful world, even if such a world existed only in the imagination. Ultimately, they became a source of hope in a seemingly hopeless environment. . . .

"In these times of momentous change in their country, black and white South Africans need more, not less, information about events around the world. They need to know about the way other societies are organized, about how others have dealt with racism and inequality and about the nature and responsibilities of democracy and freedom."

—*from "An Embargo That Backfires,"*
Mark Mathabane

FOR FURTHER READING

Mathabane, Mark. "An Embargo That Backfires." *U.S. News & World Report* 2 July 1990: 36.

——. *Kaffir Boy: The True Story of a Black Youth's Coming of Age in Apartheid South Africa.* New York: MacMillan Publishing Company, 1986.

——. *Kaffir Boy in America: An Encounter with Apartheid.* New York: Charles Scribner's Sons, 1989.

Nelan, Bruce W. "Taking the Measure of American Racism." *Time* 12 November 1990: 16–19.

"South African Struggles." The Oprah Winfrey Show. Harpo Productions. King World Syndication, Inc. KXAN, Austin. 8 July 1987. Transcript from Journal Graphics, Inc., New York.

HALF A DAY

Naguib Mahfouz ▾ Translated by Denys Johnson-Davies ▾ (Textbook page 1377)

SUMMARY

"Half a Day" is at once the story of a child's first day of school and the passing of most of a man's lifetime. As a boy, outfitted in new clothes and clutching his father's hand, the speaker walks to school for the first time. The street is lined with gardens and fields of crops. At the school gate, the father tells the boy to be a man and to go in by himself. The father promises to be at the gate waiting for him at the end of the day. As the school day progresses, the boy sets patterns for his whole life: making friends with boys, falling in love with girls, playing games, chanting songs, learning language and geography, studying religion, eating, napping. He also learns about rivalries, patience, pain, and hatred.

When the school day ends, the speaker can find no trace of his father at the gate. After waiting for some time, he sets off to find home on his own. En route, a middle-aged man passes. There is mutual recognition and hand-shaking. Continuing on his way he notices that the gardens and fields of crops are replaced by vehicles, crowds of people, piles of garbage, and skyscrapers. He wonders how all this could have happened in half a day, between early morning and sunset. He wants only to get home, so that he can ask his father for the answer to this question, but he finds he cannot get across the intersection because of the unbroken stream of cars. After a long time, a young man employed at a shop on the corner comes up to him, offers his arm, and asks if he may help the speaker as an old man across the street.

MORE ABOUT THE AUTHOR

Naguib Mahfouz (sometimes spelled *Nagib Mahfuz*) was born in an old quarter of Cairo, Egypt, where his father held a minor post in the government. He began writing as a young boy and continued into his late seventies, producing thirty-five novels, twelve collections of short stories, several scripts for stage and screen, and, in later years, a weekly newspaper column. He is considered the leading Arabic novelist and is generally credited with introducing the stream of consciousness technique into Arabic literature. His works have been widely translated, resulting in honorary awards and degrees from Denmark, France, and the Soviet Union, including the Nobel Prize for Literature in 1988.

Winning the Nobel Prize brought Mahfouz a great deal of media and public attention, the worst of which were death threats from Islamic fundamentalists—similar to those received by Salman Rushdie for *The Satanic Verses*. The stated cause of the threats against Mahfouz's life was the novel *Children of Gebelawi* (1959), an allegory in which the three main characters were said to represent Moses, Jesus, and Mohammed. The recognized Muslim leaders in the late 1950s declared the book to be offensive to Islam and it was never published in book form in Egypt; however, no death threats were provoked at that time. Then, in the late 1970s, Mahfouz was banned throughout much of the Arab world because of his strong support of the Camp David peace agreement worked out between Egyptian President Sadat and Israeli Prime Minister Begin, with the assistance of U.S. President Carter. Current students of Mahfouz believe that the true reason behind the death threats received by him in the late 1980s was not, in fact, the earlier book but rather his public support of the Camp David accords.

Born shortly before World War I, Mahfouz has witnessed a significant amount of war and political turmoil in his lifetime. The 1919 riots against the British presence in Egypt occurred when he was a young child. He was a student of philosophy at Cairo University (then called Fouad University) during the years of economic depression and graduated with a B.A. in 1934. While an undergraduate, he wrote a number of essays on philosophical subjects and translated a book entitled *Ancient Egypt from English to Arabic*. His first book, *A Game of Fates,* set in the age of the Pharaohs, was published in 1939 when he was 28 years old. Throughout World War II and the subsequent strife in Egypt, Mahfouz wrote prolifically, ceasing for several years when the Revolution of 1952 brought great changes to Egyptian society. His next published effort was his Cairo Trilogy (1956–57).

Along with pursuing his writing career, Mahfouz worked as a civil servant in Egypt for more than thirty years, assigned to various governmental departments, including the Ministry of Religious Endowments and the Ministry of Culture. He retired from civil service in the early 1970s.

The novel as a literary form has a very short history in Arabic, so novelistic influences on Mahfouz's work were largely European. He read in French the writings of Flaubert, Balzac, Zola, Camus, Tolstoy, and Dostoevsky. Proust is above all considered to be the most important Western influence on his work.

A CRITICAL COMMENT

"Between 1945 and 1957 Mahfouz published what one can describe as 'realist' novels, including *Khan el-Khalili, Midaq Alley, The Mirage, The Beginning* and the End, and the Cairo Trilogy, for which he was awarded the State Prize for Literature in 1957. Since 1959 Mahfouz's novels have taken a different turn, making use of symbolism and allegory to achieve fresh philosophical and psychological dimensions. Critics regard much of his more recent work as experimental.

"Time is a constant theme in all his novels and a constant preoccupation of his characters. Mahfouz's works are typically laced with sentences—such as 'Time is a terrible companion,' 'What has time done to my friend? It has imposed a hideous mask on his face'—that suggest almost a *horror temporis*.

"Avoiding such commonplace information as the age of the protagonists, Mahfouz gives us instead an evocation of what has happened to their features, their bodies, the looks in their eyes, the despair in their hearts. The techniques he favors for such evocation—stream of consciousness and interior monologue—lead to narratives in the first person. Each of his main characters thus tells his or her own story, supplies us with only a personal interpretation, creates in effect his or her own

theatrical drama out of the raw materials of life. The future of each may be unknown, lost in the intricacies of the present and past which are woven by each character into a single dark strand that he or she follows alone. . . . "
—*from the introduction to* Wedding Song,
Mursi Saad El Din

FOR FURTHER READING

Ghosh, Amitav. "The Human Comedy in Cairo," *The New Republic* 7 May 1990: 33–36.

Mahfouz, Naguib. *The Beggar.* Cairo, Egypt: The American University in Cairo Press, 1986.

——. *The Time and the Place and Other Stories.* New York: Doubleday, 1991.

——. *Wedding Song.* Introduction by Mursi Saad El Din. New York: Doubleday, 1989.

"A Novelist's Inspiration," *World Press Review.* January 1989: 61.

Steif, William. "Naguib Mahfouz: Fifteen Minutes with Egypt's Nobel Laureate," *The Progressive* February 1989: 38–39.

from LAMENTS ON THE WAR DEAD

Yehuda Amichai ▾ Translated by Warren Bargad and Stanley F. Chyet ▾ (Textbook page 1383)

SUMMARY

This excerpt from *Laments on the War Dead*, a poem translated in free verse, is a progression of thoughts that pass through the mind of a speaker who stands in a cemetery and contemplates the graves of those killed in war.

MORE ABOUT THE AUTHOR

Born in 1924 in Wurzburg, Germany, Yehuda Amichai has lived in Israel since 1936 and is a naturalized Israeli citizen. Generally considered Israel's best-known living poet, Amichai has published numerous volumes of poetry, many of which have not been translated from Hebrew to English. Those that have been translated to English include *Poems* (1969), *Selected Poems of Yehuda Amichai* (1971), *Songs of Jerusalem and Myself* (1973), *Amen* (1977), *Time* (1979), *Love Poems* (1981), *Great Tranquillity: Questions and Answers* (1983), and *Even a Fist Was Once an Open Palm with Fingers* (1991). He represented Israel at the International Poetry Festival in London in 1967 and was Visiting Poet at the University of Berkeley, California, in 1971. His poems have been published in several American magazines, including *Atlantic Monthly.* His novel, *Not of This Time, Not of This Place,* has been published in Israel (1963) and in the United States (1968).

Though Amichai's first language was German, he studied Hebrew as a young student while still living

in Germany as well as after relocating to Israel. Composed in Hebrew, his work has been translated into twenty languages. He has also translated German works into Hebrew. Amichai has won awards not only for poetry and prose, but also for original radio plays. His play *Bells and Trains* won the Israeli Radio Play Prize in 1962 and translations of it have been broadcast in ten European countries.

A CRITICAL COMMENT

"Israel is probably one of the few remaining countries where verse, far from being a dying technique, has managed to stay at the vital center of literary culture. To an American, who is accustomed to having his poetry in coffeehouses, summer workshops, graduate seminars, and other suitable places of solitary confinement, it is pleasant if puzzling to discover abundant signs in Israel of the presence of a body of contemporary verse that is read as well as written. Israel may conceivably have the highest per capita production of poetry in the world. . . .

"Amichai is the most influential of the younger poets who, partly in emulation of modern British and American models, have attempted to introduce the rhythms of ordinary speech and the flatness or harshness of everyday language into their verse. Such a program was clearly necessary for the younger generation in order to close the gap they felt between poetic convention and lived experience, though the success of the program has been at best a mixed one. . . . What is interesting about Amichai is that this avowed poet of fragmented, tarnished realities . . . should stud the jagged textures of his poems with shining bits from classical Hebrew texts.

"One of the important expressive effects of Amichai's verse derives from the pointed contrast between traditional idioms and the colloquial poetic environment in which they occur.

"The business of poetry, it has often been observed, is to relate the unrelated, to pull disparate fragments into significant wholes. To the Israeli, in his peculiar predicament of apparent but not absolute cultural uprootedness, this act of relating is especially vital, and the language of Hebrew poetry . . . renders it especially fit as an instrument for making meaningful connections. . . . The past is imaginatively linked with the present; the reverberations of historical catastrophe are caught in the exploration of private crisis; the unassimilable elements of both individual and collective experience are thus for a moment controlled, ordered, related."

—from After the Tradition: Essays on Modern Jewish Writing, *Robert Alter*

FOR FURTHER READING

Alter, Robert. *After the Tradition: Essays on Modern Jewish Writing.* New York: E.P. Dutton & Co., Inc., 1969.

Amichai, Yehuda. *Selected Poems of Yehuda Amichai.* Introduction by Michael Hamburger. Middlesex, Eng.: Penguin Books, 1971.

Anderson, Elliott, ed. *Contemporary Israeli Literature.* Philadelphia: The Jewish Publication Society of America, 1977.

Bargad, Warren, and Stanley F. Chyet, ed. and trans. *Israeli Poetry: A Contemporary Anthology.* Bloomington, IN: Indiana University Press, 1986.

Locher, Frances Carol, ed. *Contemporary Authors.* Vol. 85–88. Detroit: Gale Research Company, 1980.

BY ANY OTHER NAME

Santha Rama Rau ▾ (Textbook page 1387)

SUMMARY

At the age of five and a half, Rau is sent to the Anglo-Indian school in Zorinabad with her sister Premila, age eight. Prior to this time, the girls' mother has tutored her daughters herself, but when her health breaks down she is unable to continue the lessons.

School is very different from home life—the lessons are boring, the games are competitive, and Santha is separated from her sister. Also, the British headmistress gives the girls English names—Santha becomes Cynthia, and Premila, Pamela. This sudden change of names causes Santha to develop a second personality and a detachment and disbelief in the actions of "Cynthia." Nevertheless, her sister decides after the first day that they both should act more like the British students.

A week later, the day of Premila's first test, she marches into Santha's classroom and orders her to go home with her—with her pencils and notebook. On the long, hot walk home, Premila says that they will not ever return to school. When their mother asks Premila what happened, she reveals that during the test, she and the other Indian children were made to sit at the back of the room, with a desk between each one, because the teacher believed that Indians cheat. Both Premila and her mother agree that the girls should not go back to the British school. Premila and her mother think that Santha is too young to understand. Santha, of course, understands only too well, but knows that the events of the previous week had all happened to a girl called Cynthia.

MORE ABOUT THE AUTHOR

Santha Rama Rau has written a number of travel books—*East of Home, My Russian Journey, This Is India,* and *View to the Southeast.* Her two autobiographies, *Home to India* and *Gifts of Passage,* her two novels—*Remember the House* and *The Adventure*—plus *The Cooking of India* take the form of travel journals as well. She has also written a play based on E.M. Forster's *A Passage to India* (1960).

She writes from her experiences, but without sentimentality. From her autobiograpical writings, we can learn of her girlhood at Jalnabad. And her travel books are fascinating journeys through the Orient and India, offering information about people, their manners and customs, Oriental theater and dance, and a variety of Asian peoples and their ways of thinking and living.

A CRITICAL COMMENT

"Two of [Santha Rama Rau's] early stories dealing with her childhood experiences—her experience at an Anglo-Indian day school in Zorinabad and her experience as a child in her mother's home, just outside Allahabad—are included in *Gifts of Passage,* and they show a remarkable power of observation and an equally remarkable attitude of detachment, which, of course, go together. . . . "

"Santha Rama Rau must have realized with her characteristic objectivity both the strong and the weak points of her talent. She must have realised, for instance, that she was not essentially an inventive or imaginative writer, that her real forte was in the depiction of her own unique experience of people and situations and that her imagination, if at all she forced it to function, would operate within the limits of her actual experience. She must have also realised that she had a remarkable eye for the color and variety of life and, what is more, a fine command of the language which she could handle with classical dignity, subtlety and tact. . . . Her tremendous control and discipline bred its own enemy—a fear of the unknown, the hidden and the mysterious, the innate desire for which had to express itself in overt, physical terms of life—actual journeys into unknown lands instead of the unknown within. She developed a sophisticated, urbane attitude of an intelligent and cultivated 'outsider' which helped her to be a citizen of the world and wander about gypsy-like with enviable ease and enjoyment. She fashioned herself into an ideal observer looking at the world as a spectacle, content to record the details of her observation with accuracy and sympathy without experiencing any disturbing involvement.

"The personal is used to lend interest and authenticity to the travelogue and never to attract attention to itself. . . .

"It is actually a collection of stories, articles, and pieces of travelogue, strung together with autobiographical comments. . . . She has always remained the same—an exceptionally observant, civilized, cultivated person, capable of making balanced, perceptive comments on life and of presenting her observations with remarkable tact and sympathy. What comes out most convincingly in this book is her essential attitude to life which runs through all her books—an attitude which is deeply curious, profoundly understanding but essentially detached. She is critical, but never impatient or bitter; she has the modern questioning attitude, but she is never restless; she has a firm sense of values ingrained in her, but she is never dogmatic; she has the supreme sense of acceptance, but that hasn't blunted her sensibility. . . .

—*from* Santha Rama Rau,
Shantinath Kuber Desai

FOR FURTHER READING

Rama Rau, Santha. *East of Home.* New York: Harper and Brothers Publishers, 1950.

——. *Gifts of Passage.* New York: Harper and Brothers, 1951.

Desai, Shantinath Kuber. *Santha Rama Rau.* New Delhi: Arnold-Heinemann Publishers (India) Private Ltd., 1976.

Iyengar, K. R. Srinivasa. *Indian Writing in English.* New York: Asia Publishing House, 1973.

THE NOSE

Akutagawa Ryunosuke ▾ Translated by Takashi Kojima ▾ (Textbook page 1395)

SUMMARY

"The Nose," one of Akutagawa Ryunosuke's bizarre moralistic tales, is set in ancient Japan. The story portrays a renowned Buddhist priest, Zenchi Naigu, who suffers with his inordinately long and bulbous nose. Zenchi hides his distress, but in his heart, he is deeply mortified. He dedicates himself to his prayers yet lives in dread of the word *nose*.

Aside from pride, his nose is so large that it's always in his way—to the point where he must have someone hold it up for him at meals. Practical attempts to shorten his nose himself fail. Finally, he is introduced to a physician from China who succeeds in shrinking his nose. After a long and gruesome treatment he discovers to his horror that he now attracts even more attention. People stare and laugh at his nose and regard with envy his new fortune. Zenchi comes to regret his new short nose, but to his relief one morning it is restored to its original size, and he believes that now, finally, people will stop laughing at him.

MORE ABOUT THE AUTHOR

It is said that his father named him Ryunosuke, which means Dragon-helper, because he was born at the dragon hour on a dragon day in the dragon month of a dragon year. Perhaps this unique circumstance was responsible for his superb intellect and sensitivity. Akutagawa attended the first high school in Tokyo on recommendation without examination, graduated with honors, and went on to study English literature at the Imperial University of Tokyo, graduating in 1916. He lived most of his thirty-five years in Tokyo—eighteen years in school and eleven at his desk writing and rewriting over 150 short stories.

Published in a revival issue of the magazine *Shinshicho (New Thought)* in 1916, Akutagawa Ryunosuke's "Hana" ("The Nose") served as the catalyst that propelled him to prominence as a writer. Often described as more individualistic than any other writer of his time, he was an expert craftsperson, adapting his style and point of view to fit the piece. He differs from the majority of Japanese writers because he primarily wrote short stories, unique to Japanese literature at that time, and his writing is, for the most part, not based on personal experience, a dominant characteristic in modern Japanese literature.

Akutagawa's stories were translated into English, French, German, Spanish, Russian, and Esperanto. Yet he despaired of his lack of originality and never felt confident of his own writing—the reason, perhaps, that he often chose to write about remote topics. In fact, detachment appears to be a key strategy in his questioning of the values of society and his dramatization of the complexities of human psychology and the balance between illusion and reality.

He also seemed to have an inability to deal with the practical aspects of everyday life. Forever shadowed with the fear of inheriting his mother's insanity, he remained distanced from himself and from his work. Sensitive, precocious, and in delicate health, his only happiness came through his work.

Toward the end of his life, he wrote autobiographical sketches in imitation of Shiga Naoya, his contemporary whom he thought to be a superior writer. One phrase he used in a final composition became famous: *bon'yari shita fuan* (a vague uneasiness).

He had become a physical and nervous wreck— an accumulation of a lifetime of nervousness and frailty. For years he had contemplated taking his own life, and just before he drank a fatal cup of poison, he wrote a lengthy suicide note giving justification for his final action. It is thought that not even Akutagawa himself really understood why he finally did it.

A CRITICAL COMMENT

"'The Nose' is based mainly on an episode about the famous long-nosed priest, found in the *Konjaku* and *Ujishui,* two ancient collections of stories and tales; in psychological treatment it was inspired by Gogol's story of the same title. Yet Akutagawa's story retains nothing of the crudely simple narration and earthy humor of the original anecdote; nor does it echo the bizarre twist and sardonic laughter of the Russian writer. Sober and serious, as Soseki said, the tone is ironic, and this sense of irony derives from the author's angle of vision, the uncertainty of being human in a fickle world. The story revolves around the very attitude of the author who neither condemns nor condones. Using the human nose as a focal point Akutagawa pits his protagonist against the world and shows that neither side wins or loses completely. While his clear-eyed intelligence does not miss the slightest shade of psychological tension, his subtle comic sense contemplates human frailty with serene pity.

"Already apparent in 'The Nose' are three motifs: the manipulation of the absurd; the uncertainty of being human; and the morbidity of obsession. . . .

"It was written in an effort to get over a recent disappointment in love, and Akutagawa meant to be pleasant and remote from reality. Fresh in conception, dexterous in execution, and cumulative in effect, the story both puzzled and delighted the reading public."

—from Akutagawa: an Introduction,
Beongcheon Yu

FOR FURTHER READING

Akutagawa Ryunosuke. *Japanese Short Stories.* Trans. Takashi Kojima. New York: Liveright Publishing Corporation, 1962.

Keene, Donald. *Dawn to the West: Japanese Literature of the Modern Era.* New York: Holt, Rinehart and Winston, 1984.

Kato, Shuichi. *A History of Japanese Literature.* Trans. Don Sanderson. Vol. 3 of *The Modern Years.* Tokyo: Kodansha International Ltd., 1983.

Yu, Beongcheon. *Akutagawa: an Introduction.* Detroit: Wayne State University Press, 1972.

CRANES

Hwang Sun-won ▾ Translated by Peter H. Lee ▾ (Textbook page 1404)

SUMMARY

"Cranes" begins outside an empty northern village farmhouse. Through the boyhood recollections of Song-sam, a security officer, we see the changes in attitude and fears that the war has brought to him. He reminisces about smoking gourd leaves, nearly getting caught while stealing chestnuts, and having chestnut needles removed from his seat by his best friend, Tok-chae.

At first, Song-sam is surprised and then suspicious of his old friend, Tok-chae, who is now a prisoner of war from the north, but he learns of Tok-chae's poverty and his loyalty to his father. Song-sam feels guilty for having left his own family behind during the war. The two men reach a field where in their childhood they had trapped a wild crane and treated it as a pet. Song-sam remembers how they had let it free in order to save it from being shot. Inspired by this memory, Song-sam unties his friend's hands and suggests they hunt for cranes as they had done in their youth. Tok-chae is at first suspicious until it becomes clear that he, like the crane, is being given a chance to escape.

MORE ABOUT THE AUTHOR

His first poem published in 1931, Hwang Sun-won went on to write seven novels, more than one hundred short stories, and five collections of poems. Stylish yet simple, his work encompasses many themes and utilizes various narrative techniques.

In 1946, shortly after Japanese colonial rule ended, he fled south with his family, where he lived and wrote, publishing only fiction, until the mid-1970s. Most of his stories center around the everyday happenings in people's lives, capturing aspects of human emotion. His novels depict human existence in conflict with history, cultural confrontations, and other contemporary problems.

A meticulous, careful writer, all of his work is thoroughly researched. Employing either traditional or self-created imagery, he is renowned as an astute storyteller. Many of the short fiction works that he wrote during his days of hiding have become Korean literary classics. Sun-won is also admired for refusing to discuss the meaning of his work—and for not giving in to commercialism. A member of the Korean Academy of Arts since 1957, Sun-won is a professor at Kyonghui University in Seoul.

A CRITICAL COMMENT

"When one compares the various social values and morals of the west and Korea, probably one of the most striking contrasts one encounters is in the area of friendship and gratitude. It is of utmost importance to an understanding of Korean societies. In the west, the traditional virtue in this respect is centered around the individual. Each man is expected to stand on his own two feet. One can observe this fundamental reality of westerner's life when one has dealings with other people. If one individual helps a second individual, the second individual must repay the favor. If he does not repay, the first individual will be insulted; or if the first individual desires no repayment for his help, then the second individual, not wanting to owe the first individual anything, will be insulted. Possibly it is inevitable that this outlook would exist in such a heterogeneous society as there is in the west. Nevertheless, westerners are only slowly moving toward a different position, a position which is closer to the Korean outlook. A perfect manifestation of this entire process is the trend in the west today towards a more socialized society in which backward and underprivileged elements may be raised to a more favorable level of existence. In this connection, the Korean position with respect to friendship and gratitude is highly interesting.

"Many authors tried to show the ridiculousness and stupidity of trying to divide north and south simply by a political agreement. The point is brought out in many different ways. How can a country which is not divided naturally by a river or a mountain range be divided by the mark of a pen? The deep feelings of the people toward the armistice and the demarcation line are brought out in many forms.

"The views such as a love for country and land, hatred of communist aggression, the want for revenge of fallen comrades, a hope for a reunified Korea and continued peace and cooperation seem to be the view of South Koreans and her allies in the free world. This love of freedom and dignity of man is one of many admirable Korean traits.

". . . Korean literature is rich with the sentiments of self-determination and justice."

—*from* A Guide to Korean Literature,
In-sob Zong

FOR FURTHER READING

Han-sook, Chung, Kim Yoon-shik, and Kim Young-moo, eds. *Nineteen Contemporary Korean Novelists*. Seoul: The Korean Culture & Arts Foundation, 1985.

Hwang Sun-won. *Shadows of a Sound*. Ed. J. Martin Holman. San Francisco: Mercury House, Incorporated, 1990.

——. *The Book of Masks*. Ed. J. Martin Holman. London: Readers International Inc., 1989.

Lee, Peter H., ed. *Flowers of Fire*. Honolulu: University of Hawaii, 1974.

Zong, In-sob. *A Guide to Korean Literature*. New Jersey: Hollym International Corp., 1982.

THOUGHTS OF HANOI

Nguyen Thi Vinh ▼ Translated by Nguyen Ngoc Bich ▼ (Textbook page 1411)

SUMMARY

This simple poem is a "then and now" treatment of the recent war that tore apart North and South Vietnam. It compares childhood memories with the present, which serves to emphasize contrasting times and emotions.

MORE ABOUT THE CULTURE

The Vietnamese have always considered themselves poets. Vietnamese poetic heritage dates from the Bronze Age (the fifth century B.C.) and the Dong Son civilization. As part of their celebrations, they played music. Poetry was probably a part of these celebrations, because in the Vietnamese tradition, poetry and music go hand in hand.

The Vietnamese began to record their poetry during the period of Chinese rule (111 B.C. to A.D. 939). The influence of Chinese language and culture was felt into the nineteenth century; in fact, the first written version of Vietnamese was a version of Chinese.

Although greatly influenced by the Chinese, the Vietnamese retained their own culture, adapting Chinese classical style to their own purposes and in their own language. After their independence, they developed a national written language called *chu nom,* "Southern Writing." Although poetry in the Sino-Vietnamese tradition continued to be written for some time, many authors wrote in both languages. The tradition of two languages probably had its roots in the hierarchical structure of Vietnamese society, but it was facilitated by the country's political disunity.

By the 1600s, a Jesuit priest developed a system of transcribing Vietnamese, and eventually replaced *chu nom.* Called *quoc ngu* ("The National language"), this Roman script rapidly came to dominate Vietnamese literature. World War II (Japanese takeover, followed by the Viet Minh Revolution, occupation by Chinese and English troops, then the return of the French) brought a considerable influx of modern vocabulary, although poetry suffered. Experiencing a resurgence during the resistance war with the French and the war between the North and the South, *quoc ngu* is now the language of Vietnamese literature.

A CRITICAL COMMENT

"With the coming of the French, Vietnam was flung into contact with the West and the worldwide upheavals of the twentieth century. It experienced in turn colonization, world war, a resistance war, and revolution (with the added difficulties of overwhelming great-power involvement). Traditional Vietnam did not come through this onslaught intact. Its values and beliefs were overturned, its society and political structure thrown into turmoil. The language and literature underwent similar changes, although like the country both have survived and have become, perhaps, even stronger.

"A method of transcribing vernacular Vietnamese with the Roman alphabet, which was originated by the Jesuit missionaries and kept alive by the Catholic Church, came into general use in the early part of the century. It was called *quoc ngu,* or 'National Language'. The first *quoc ngu* literary efforts were transcriptions of *chu nom* or Sino-Vietnamese works, or, if original, derivative of the old poetry. By the thirties, however, a generation had grown up using the new language, and, influenced by the literary forms and philosophies coming from France and the West, it began to create another distinct tradition of Vietnamese poetry. The poems reflect the existential agonies of colonization and political domination, and, released from the limitations of old poetic forms, they also show a tendency to explore personal thoughts and philosophies in the modern manner. Another modern departure occurred in love poems. Traditional Vietnamese love poetry—except for folk poems—was symbolic and formal. The modern poems are sensuous and immediate."
—*from* A Thousand Years of Vietnamese Poetry, *Nguyen Ngoc Bich*

FOR FURTHER READING

Durand, Maurice M., and Nguyen Tran Huan. *An Introduction to Vietnamese Literature.* Trans. D. M. Hawke. New York: Columbia University Press, 1985.

Freeman, James M. *Hearts of Sorrow: Vietnamese-American Lives.* Stanford: Stanford University Press, 1989.

Huynh Sanh Thong, ed. & trans. *The Heritage of Vietnamese Poetry.* New Haven: Yale University Press, 1979.

Nguyen Ngoc Bich, ed. *A Thousand Years of Vietnamese Poetry.* New York: Alfred A. Knopf, 1975.

Shimer, Dorothy Blair, ed. *Voices of Modern Asia: An Anthology of Twentieth-Century Asian Literature.* New York: New American Library, 1973.

The Way of the Willow. Niagara Falls: Beacon Films. [A dramatization of the problems faced by a family of Vietnamese boat people as they first settle into a Canadian community.]

LOVE MUST NOT BE FORGOTTEN

Zhang Jie ▾ Translated by Gladys Yang ▾ (Textbook page 1416)

SUMMARY

Because it sanctions love outside marriage, "Love Must Not Be Forgotten" was quite controversial when it was first published in 1979. The narrator begins the story by explaining that she is thirty years old—nearly past marriageable age in her culture. She then paints an attractive picture of her suitor, but she is unable to make up her mind to marry him because he has nothing to say—and she does not love him. She feels very lonely, and thinks perhaps she takes things too seriously. She then reflects on her mother's failed marriage and her warning to live on your own if you're not sure what you want—and to marry only if you meet the right person.

The narrator then tells of her mother's own notions of love, how she had married a man she did not love, divorced him, and loved from a distance a man who was married. Through her mother's diaries, the narrator is able to piece together the story of her mother's unrequited love. She learns that her mother's set of Chekhov stories was so precious to her because it had been given to her by the man she loved. The narrator believes that, in spirit, her mother and the man were together day and night, although they had not spent more than twenty-four hours together in person. Considering her mother's unhappy love life, the narrator wonders if there will always be marriage without love, love where marriage is impossible. Her own choice not to marry is a challenge to tradition and cultural values, and she wishes the outside world would mind its own business.

MORE ABOUT THE AUTHOR

Active in politics from an early age, Zhang Jie is a committed Communist. Early in her writing career, she wrote mainly about the problems of youth and love. She is a strong advocate of Chinese modernization, and has branched out to write about key contemporary social issues: discrimination against women, hypocrisy, corruption, bureaucracy, and others.

Taking her responsibility as a writer seriously, she uses it to educate her readers to societal problems in order to effect change. She is considered a pioneer who highlighted women's problems long before authorities ever recognized them or took official action. The stance she took in "Love Must Not Be Forgotten" caused her to be accused of undermining social morality, because it is expected in China that everyone marry.

Whatever the theme, her style is sensitive, romantic, and insightful, and all of her stories offer to the Western reader a glimpse into the daily lives, feelings, and thoughts of Chinese peoples today.

A member of the Chinese Writers' Association, Zhang Jie now works for the China Federation of Literary and Art Circles in Beijing.

A CRITICAL COMMENT

"The publication of a short story can be a major event in China. In 1980, this particular story of Zhang Jie's became a *cause célèbre*.

"'Love Must Not Be Forgotten' describes an idealized, chaste love which an old woman, the narrator's mother, has borne throughout her life for a man she seldom sees, a man who, from 'class' obligation, married another woman. Older critics criticized the story for its Western-style idealization of romantic love, saying, as [G]od knows older people have always said, that if these two had actually married, their grand imaginary passion would have soon gone by the boards, and anyway, what would have become of the wronged wife? And young people in China said, as [God] knows young people have always said, that such love is true and grand, a possibility very much on their minds, and anyway, China's many loveless marriages are a feudal hangover, and it was high time somebody brought up the subject. The spicy thing about this apparently innocuous story, however, is that it dared to treat—and sympathetically!—love between unmarried partners.

"This story, which no critic here or there considers her best work, made Zhang Jie famous. Another of her stories, 'Heavy Wings,' drew political criticism for its 'gloominess.' According to Western China-watchers, Zhang Jie, who has been divorced twice, 'is the object of much gossip in China's literary scene'—but this isn't surprising, for so is every other writer."

—*from* Encounters with Chinese Writers,
Annie Dillard

FOR FURTHER READING

Dillard, Annie. *Encounters with Chinese Writers*. Middletown, CT: Wesleyan University Press, 1984.

Jung Palandri, Angela. *Women Writers of Twentieth-Century China*. Eugene, Oregon: University Printing Press, 1982.

Zhang Jie. *Love Must Not Be Forgotten*. San Francisco: China Books & Periodicals, Inc., 1986.

TEACHING STRATEGIES

WRITING ABOUT LITERATURE

Integrating composition with the study of literature produces numerous benefits for both students and teachers. To write about a literary work, students must read it closely and formulate their thoughts about it clearly. By doing so, they gain a deeper understanding of what they have read and of how it applies to their own lives and values. At the same time, they practice essential critical thinking and composition skills as they use the basic aims and modes of writing: narration, description, persuasion, and, primarily, exposition, the form they will use most frequently throughout their lives.

Having students write about their reading provides advantages for you as well. When all students write on the same topic, you can evaluate their essays more easily, and when they write on different topics, their common knowledge of the literary work makes collaborative writing, evaluating, and revising especially fruitful. Students' written work can also alert you to individual problems in reading comprehension and, sometimes with more challenging works, to a general need for reteaching. If many essays show signs of the same deficiencies, you will know what needs to be clarified.

Draw students' attention to the "Writing About Literature" section in the backmatter of their text (text page 1434) early in the term, explaining that it provides strategies for answering the text's essay questions and for choosing and writing about their own topics for essays on literary works. Throughout the year, remind students to refer to this section when they are writing or preparing for an essay test.

You may want to devote one or two lessons to teaching this section. This is a good time to explain whether you will regularly set aside class time for writing, how often you will give timed essay tests, and how you will grade students' papers.

WRITING ANSWERS TO ESSAY QUESTIONS

You probably cannot overemphasize to students the importance of understanding exactly what an essay question is asking. What thinking tasks are required? What specifics of the literary work are to be dealt with? What kind of support, and how much, is stipulated? Suggest that students read a question more than once as they work, to make sure they are following all of the directions.

In discussing the key verbs that are listed in the text, whenever possible use examples from selections the class has already read. As a further illustration of *analyze*, for example, you could ask students how they would proceed to analyze Chekhov's use of irony in "A Problem." As they answer, emphasize that they are *isolating* elements (dialogue, the revelation of characters' thoughts, the author's tone). In other words, they are "taking apart" the ironic elements in order to understand them and see how they work in the story.

When you discuss *compare* and *contrast*, remind students of the two methods for organizing this type of paragraph or essay. In *block organization*, students write about one work (or element) and then the other. When they use point-by-point organization, they alternate between the two works or elements as they cover each feature of comparison or contrast. Be sure to emphasize that a direction to compare may mean to look for both similarities and differences. Suggest that students check with you when they are not sure whether *compare* means *compare and contrast.*

Few students are likely to misinterpret a direction to *describe*; however, you might spend a few minutes reviewing spatial order as a method for organizing details of physical description. Also emphasize the importance of using precise words and including a variety of sensory details.

Students may have more difficulty with a question that requires them to *discuss*. Explain that even though *discuss* allows a broader response than some other key verbs, it does not permit superficiality or vagueness. Suggest that *examine* is a good synonym for *discuss* in an essay question, but also point out that, in order to discuss, one must almost always first analyze.

Another way for students to think of *evaluate* is as a judgment of how well a literary element or technique "works"—how effectively it creates a desired effect. Emphasize that evaluation is not merely an expression of personal preference: It is a test against certain criteria, or standards. For evaluation questions, suggest that students first clarify the criteria they will use to judge a work. (For more information on developing criteria, see "Writing a Literary Review" on text pages 1132–1133.) They can then judge how the work fulfills or falls short of those standards, citing evidence from the work to "prove" their evaluations.

For the next verb, *illustrate* (similar verbs are *demonstrate* and *show*), stress that students must always provide examples from the work (details, dialogue, figurative language, and so on) to support their ideas. Without supporting details, even good ideas appear as mere opinions, lacking force.

Students should see that such support is especially important when a question asks them to *interpret* meaning or significance. Explain that the verb *interpret* implies that no single, or absolute, statement of meaning exists. Students must therefore carefully explain what has led them to their interpretation.

Finally, point out that a direction to *explain your response* allows students a purely personal reaction to a work. But once again, support is required in the form of reasons. Offer an example: The statement "Rumi's 'Unmarked Boxes' is the best poem in the book" is acceptable—but not by itself; the student must tell why he or she thinks so.

Be sure students see that a question may contain or imply more than one key verb. For example, in *discussing* the use of irony in "A Problem," a student might use both *illustration* and *description* to develop the essay's thesis. In every question, however, one key verb is usually emphasized.

The next step, item 3, is crucial for students and should be stressed: Write a brief, direct, and specific thesis statement. For practice, you could ask students to rephrase actual essay questions from the text as thesis statements. Then note that in gathering supporting ideas and evidence, students usually can draw from class discussion of a selection. In fact, class work on the study questions that follow each selection can be thought of as prewriting. Explain that active participation in discussing these questions and note-taking will help students think of ideas and data for later writing.

In discussing items 4 and 5, be sure students see that an essay's main ideas will come from the information gathered to support the thesis statement. Emphasize that each paragraph should contain a single idea, supported by evidence, and suggest that students draft a thesis statement and a topic sentence for each paragraph before writing the complete answer.

Make clear to students that all of this thinking, note-taking, and organizing is essential no matter what form the rough outline takes. It is not time wasted, *especially* when time is limited. If students begin writing without planning, their essays will be incomplete or disorganized no matter how correct the grammar and mechanics. Emphasize that, in timed writing, students must set a schedule for themselves, allowing time for all major stages of the writing process: prewriting, writing, evaluating and revising, and proofreading. (On occasions that seem to warrant it, you may want to consider allowing students who run out of time to turn in their prewriting notes along with their papers. The notes may demonstrate that a student understood the question and had planned a sound answer but simply did not have time to execute it.)

WRITING AND REVISING AN ESSAY

Students should learn to choose a limited topic narrow enough to cover in detail in a fairly brief essay. If they are afraid they won't find enough to say about a narrow topic, assure them that developing a limited idea is actually easier than thoroughly supporting a broad generalization. Suggest that they find limited topics by asking themselves further questions about information discussed in class. They might look at *why* a character changed in attitude, *which* conflict or conflicts revealed a major theme, or *how* word choice set a particular tone. Students should skim a selection they want to write about and review their reading and class notes. Encourage them to take more notes as they reread, even if they haven't yet settled on a topic. These notes can help them define their thesis and gather supporting evidence.

Go over each of the remaining prewriting steps with the students, illustrating how the wording of their thesis statement will control, or direct, the subsequent steps. Remind students to write an informal plan or outline.

The text's outline of essay form is a good general reference. Emphasize that students should write their first drafts by working steadily through to the end, referring as needed to their outlines and notes. Warn them against overusing direct quotations to pad the body of an essay. Students should get in the habit of asking themselves whether the precise wording of the quotation is important to their point or whether a shorter reference or paraphrase will suffice.

When you discuss revision, note that this final step is tied to evaluation. Students must first read a draft to evaluate its strengths and weaknesses; then they can make the changes—adding, deleting, replacing, or reordering words and phrases—that will improve the draft. Suggest that students go through their drafts once for content and organization, a second time for style (wordiness, monotonous sentence structure, and so on), and a third time for mechanical errors (spelling, punctuation, and the like). Unless students do not correct hard copy and instead do corrections directly onto a word processor screen, they can use proofreader's symbols to streamline this part of the process. Encourage the use of peer evaluation, illustrating appropriate constructive criticism if your students do not regularly exchange work. As students revise their writing, refer them to Grammar, Usage, and Mechanics: A Reference Guide on pages 1455–1473 of their texts.

You might guide the class through the model essay (text pages 1437–1439) twice, to focus attention on different aspects. First have students concentrate on content and organization, using the sidenotes that highlight development of the thesis. The second time, they can focus on the writer's revisions. Ask students why they think the changes were made and how each change improves the essay.

DOCUMENTING SOURCES

Specify the style you prefer for documenting sources, and be sure to make available a reference containing several examples of citations, whether a published style book, your own information sheet, or the students' composition and grammar text. Students could also use good essays from your previous classes as models of correct documentation.

MODEL STUDENT ESSAYS

The following papers were written by high-school students. They are included here as samples of the writing you can expect from students using the *World Literature* text.

The following paper was written by a student in John Williamson's English class at Johnson Central High School in Paintsville, Kentucky, in response to the creative writing assignment following Guy de Maupassant's story "The Jewels" (text page 1041).

A Character Sketch in the Form of a Diary Entry

After he had been married several months, Lantin's new wife thought it silly of him to leave his late wife's room untouched. Lantin, with no spirit for argument, agreed to clear it of her things.

As he was emptying her drawer of personal belongings, he came upon a small, leather cased book. He opened it and discovered that it was his late wife's diary. Lantin took a great interest in this, for he had known little of her past.

He did not tell his wife of his discovery, nor did he give her an opportunity to find out. Being an early riser, she retired before nine o'clock every evening, and Lantin would take this opportunity to delve into his late wife's past.

Her style was flowing, but simple, and it brought back the memory of her charm that he so dearly missed. He nearly wept every time he read a word, because he longed to hear her speak them.

Lantin learned much of her past. He read of her experiences as a child; her first love, her first kiss. He read of her life in their small village, and of the sorrow at the loss of her father. Every detail of her life seemed to be in this book.

Lantin looked forward to reading her thoughts during their marriage, but when he reached the date where her entries should begin, he saw nothing but blank pages, save one. On this one page, she had written things that he had not read in the previous pages. As he read, everything suddenly became very clear.

Dear Diary,

I am writing to you for the last time. You have been a trusting friend throughout my life, and I will surely miss you. I am writing today the one thing I haven't written before, for fear of its discovery. When I was fourteen, I found out a horrible secret that my father had been keeping from my mother and myself. My father, whom I had always known as a kind and generous man, was nothing but a scandalous embezzler. Being the tax collector for many years, he robbed the country of hundreds of thousands of francs and kept them hidden away in a secret account. I didn't learn of this until after his death, when at that time, my mother took the money and myself and fled to Paris. When my mother died, the money became mine. I never told my husband of the money, because I wanted him to love me for myself. He is the kindest, gentlest, and most honest man I have ever known, and I wanted to make sure he was the kind of man I wanted to marry. He is a very hard worker, but his meager income could not support us in the fashion to which I have become accustomed, so I volunteered to take care of money matters. I use the money that he earns along with the money of my own, so we can live a luxurious life. My husband, the silly tot! He thinks that I just manage our money wisely. I shall never tell him of this though, because the marriage we have couldn't be better. I love him today more than I did in our first meeting. I must now say good-bye to you, my old friend, for it is time to start a new chapter in my life. Fear not, for thou shalt always be special in my heart.

After reading this, Monsieur Lantin sat with tear-filled eyes. He realized that he still had a very strong love for his late wife, and for the rest of the night, he was happy.

Jimmy Wheeler
Johnson Central High School
Paintsville, KY

The next paper was written by a student in a world literature English class at Austin High School in Austin, Texas. This paper was written in response to the instructor's own critical writing assignment to explore ways that the Book of Ruth reveals aspects of the Hebrew culture of its time.

Hebrew Culture in the Book of Ruth

When the Book of Ruth was written, the Hebrews had just returned from exile in Babylon. Throughout this exile, they had attempted to maintain their culture despite the persecution that they were enduring. Naturally, on returning to their homeland, they continued to be very concerned with their culture and its preservation. In dealing with this issue, the Book of Ruth reveals many aspects of the Hebrew culture.

One of these aspects which is dealt with extensively in the Book of Ruth is the Hebrew religion. It is obvious from the story that the Jews placed great emphasis on religious beliefs. In fact, one reason why the Moabites were not accepted by the Hebrews was the fact that they did not worship God, as is stated in the introduction to the story. Also, references to God are utilized throughout the story; for example, Naomi returns from Moab because "she had heard . . . that the Lord had visited his people in giving them bread." Historically, the story took place immediately after the Hebrews' successful return from exile. This indicates that the Hebrews attributed their good fortune (symbolized by the gift of the bread) to God. Naomi also believes that her misfortune in the beginning of the story was due to the Lord's works, as is illustrated when she says to the Jews, "Call me not Naomi, call me Mara: for the Almighty hath dealt very bitterly with me. I went out full, and the Lord hath brought me home again empty: why then call ye me Naomi, seeing the Lord hath testified against me, and the Almighty hath afflicted me?" Since Naomi, who was a Hebrew, attributed her misfortune to God, it is apparent that God and religion were very important to the Hebrews.

Another element of the Hebrew culture that is present in the Book of Ruth is the Hebrew system of social roles. For example, Ruth is poor and a Moabitess and therefore has a low status in the Hebrew community. In fact, she has to gather individual bits of food from the ground behind the reapers in order to have enough food to live. However, Boaz is higher in the social system, owning a field and being respected by all of the servants. This system was probably rarely violated, as is apparent in Ruth's surprise at Boaz's favorable reaction to her: ". . . she fell on her face and bowed herself to the ground and said unto him, 'Why have I found grace in thine eyes, that thou shouldest take knowledge of me, seeing I am a stranger?'" This indication of the societal hierarchy is yet another way in which the Book of Ruth reflects the Hebrew culture.

The Hebrews' desire to preserve their culture is perhaps most evident in their system of values, particularly their attitude toward marriage outside the Hebrew people. The Jews of that time period valued their family lineage, and many refused to accept foreigners into their culture. For example, the unnamed "kinsman" in chapter four refused to marry Ruth in order to carry on her deceased husband's name, saying "'I cannot redeem it for myself, lest I mar mine own inheritance: redeem thou my right to thyself; for I cannot redeem it.'" The kinsman didn't want any non-Hebrew blood in his family, so he refused to allow Ruth to affect his lineage. Understandably, the Hebrews had a great desire to maintain a pure culture, even to the point of each man refusing to allow foreigners in his family. It is interesting, though, that even though Boaz married Ruth, an outsider, his great-grandson David was Israel's greatest king. Some people think that this irony shows that the Book of Ruth was ultimately written as a plea for more compassion and tolerance toward those of different cultural or religious backgrounds.

All three of these elements of Hebrew culture are reflected in the Book of Ruth. In fact, one of the story's fundamental themes deals with the people's struggle to maintain their culture despite tremendous oppression. However, the Book of Ruth also makes the point that it is possible to go overboard in the desire to preserve a culture, especially when the result is prejudice toward foreigners. Just because the Moabites differed from the Hebrews in their religion, Ruth was considered a slave, and one man refused to marry her because she would mar his lineage. What makes this particularly unfair is the fact that Ruth had accepted the Jewish religion as her own: ". . . thy people shall be my people, and they God my God. . . ." The Book of Ruth makes the statement that such prejudice is unjust, and that all people should be treated equally regardless of their origins.

Kristi McGarity
Austin High School
Austin, TX

ASSESSING STUDENTS' MASTERY OF SUBJECT MATTER AND CONCEPTS

Students' writing is an excellent measure of their understanding of literary works and concepts. Whether writing compositions or answers to essay questions, students must organize and apply the knowledge they have acquired through reading, note-taking, and class discussion. They must demonstrate their understanding of particular selections as well as their understanding of literary genres and techniques.

With the aids in these Teaching Notes, you can plan your evaluation strategies carefully and reduce the time needed for grading or reviewing papers. For example, the sample essay that appears in "Writing About Literature" can serve as an assessment aid. In addition, the Annotated Teacher's Edition includes suggested criteria for evaluating the success of the student's responses to creative and critical writing assignments. You can also make use of the following evaluation methods, which include checklists, written comments, self-evaluation, and peer evaluation.

HOLISTIC SCORING

For some writing assignments, you may want to use holistic scoring, a method in which you read each paper quickly and respond to it as a whole, making no comments or corrections. With a carefully prepared scoring guide, holistic evaluation is an efficient and consistent means of judging students' work. Even though it does not provide students with your personal comments, it is not superficial or vague: Students receive an evaluation of key features of their papers. Two types of holistic evaluation are the analytic scale and the general impression scale, discussed in the following section.

ANALYTIC SCALES

Using an analytic scale, you rank each of several features of a piece of writing from high to low. The following scale lists features common to all writing and uses a numerical ranking.

ANALYTIC SCALE

	Low	Middle			High	
Ideas	2	4	6	8	10	
Organization	2	4	6	8	10	
Word choice	1	2	3	4	5	
Tone	1	2	3	4	5	_____
Usage, grammar	1	2	3	4	5	
Punctuation, capitalization	1	2	3	4	5	
Spelling	1	2	3	4	5	
Legibility	1	2	3	4	5	_____
					Total	_____

Adapted from Paul B. Diederich, Measuring Growth in Writing (Urbana, IL: NCTE, 1974).

In other analytic scales, the features are specific to a particular form of writing (description, narration, and so on) Such scales can be adapted for many different assignments.

The scales that follow cover four common writing tasks, each applied to a different genre. These examples use the dichotomous, or yes-no, scale.

FICTION: SUMMARIZING A PLOT ANALYTIC SCALE

	Yes	No
The story's title and author are cited.		
The summary includes the story's most important events.		
The events are summarized in the order in which they occur.		
The summary explains how one event causes or leads to another.		
The setting is briefly described.		
Extraneous details are omitted.		
The student primarily uses his or her own words.		
Word choice is precise and appropriate.		
Sentence structure is varied.		
Grammar, usage, and mechanics errors do not interfere with reading.		

POETRY: RESPONDING TO A POEM ANALYTIC SCALE

	Yes	No
The poem's title, author, and subject are stated.		
The student describes his or her general response to the poem.		
At least two details about the poem's content are used to explain the response.		
At least two details about the poem's construction are used to explain the response.		
Quotations from the poem are exact and are cited correctly.		
A concluding or summary statement ends the composition.		
Word choice is precise and appropriate.		
Sentence structure is varied.		
Grammar, usage, and mechanics errors do not interfere with reading.		

NONFICTION: ANALYZING A REPORT ANALYTIC SCALE

	Yes	No
The report's title and author are cited.		
The main idea of the report is stated.		
A sufficient number of the strongest facts supporting the main idea are cited.		
The facts in the report are distinguished from the author's opinions.		
Any appeals to emotion are identified and discussed.		
Significant narrative techniques are identified and discussed.		
Organization is clear and coherent.		
The conclusion summarizes main points of the analysis.		
Word choice is precise and appropriate.		
Sentence structure is varied.		
Grammar, usage, and mechanics errors do not interfere with reading.		

DRAMA: ANALYZING AND EVALUATING A THEME ANALYTIC SCALE

	Yes	No
The play's title and author are cited.		
A clear theme statement is presented.		
The theme statement is supported with at least three examples of action and dialogue.		
The student expresses an evaluation of the theme.		
The student presents at least two reasons for the evaluation, supported by evidence from the play.		
Quotations are exact and are cited correctly.		
The conclusion summarizes or restates the statement of theme and the student's evaluation.		
Word choice is precise and appropriate.		
Sentence structure is varied.		
Grammar, usage, and mechanics errors do not interfere with reading.		

GENERAL IMPRESSION SCALES

A general impression scale is also keyed to the form of writing, but the individual features of the paper are not ranked separately. Instead, the paper as a whole is judged high, average, or low. In this case, developing a scoring guide entails outlining the general characteristics of high, average, and low papers for the assignment. For example, you could use the following general impression scale to evaluate a descriptive paragraph:

There is no one prescribed format for writing the general characteristics for this type of scale. What is important—whether you use complete sentences, a series of phrases, or even a list of items—is that you cover the key features of the writing assignment and that you address the same features in each ranking. Here is a second example of a general impression scale, one for use in evaluating an essay comparing and contrasting elements in two stories.

DESCRIPTIVE PARAGRAPH GENERAL IMPRESSION SCALE

Assignment: To write a subjective description of a person, place, or object

4 The topic sentence expresses a main impression of the topic. Many concrete and sensory details create a vivid picture. Each sentence supports the main idea in the topic sentence. The organization is clear. Ideas flow smoothly with effective transitions. Sentences are varied and diction fresh. Errors in grammar and mechanics are minimal.

3 The topic sentence expresses a main impression of the topic. Concrete and sensory details are used, but the description could be fuller and more vivid. The organization is clear. Some transitions could be added or improved. Sentences are varied and the diction is accurate but unoriginal. Occasional grammatical and mechanical errors appear.

2 The topic sentence is vague or inexact. Details are not specific or are insufficient. The organization is flawed but can be followed. Few transitions are provided between ideas. Sentences are correct but often awkward or monotonous, with some inexact wording. Occasional grammatical and mechanical errors interfere with reading.

1 The topic sentence is missing or does not clearly identify the topic. Details are not specific and are insufficient to develop the description. Organization is unclear. Ideas are missing or irrelevant. Word choice is often inaccurate. Frequent syntax and mechanical errors interfere with reading.

0 The paragraph does not develop a description.

COMPARISON AND CONTRAST ESSAY GENERAL IMPRESSION SCALE

Assignment: To compare and contrast the themes and tones of two stories

4 The essay addresses both similarities and differences. The essay insightfully interprets the stories' themes and tones. Main ideas are supported with appropriate detail. The essay is well organized (a clear thesis statement in the first paragraph, a main supporting idea in each body paragraph, and a concluding paragraph). Ideas flow smoothly, with effective transitions. The essay contains few errors in grammar and mechanics.

3 The essay addresses both similarities and differences. The essay interprets the stories' themes and tones thoughtfully. The essay is well organized. Main ideas are not adequately supported. Some sentences are awkward or monotonous. The essay contains occasional errors in grammar and mechanics.

2 The essay does not address (or does not address equally) both similarities and differences. The essay interprets the stories' themes and tones sketchily. Much necessary supporting detail is omitted. In some places, ideas are difficult to follow. Errors in grammar and mechanics occasionally interfere with reading.

1 The essay does not address both similarities and differences. The essay lacks insight into or misinterprets the stories' themes and tones. The essay does not support main ideas with sufficient evidence. The essay is disorganized and lacks clarity of expression. The essay contains errors in grammar and mechanics that frequently interfere with reading.

0 The essay does not follow the assignment or does not develop its thesis.

When you use a general impression scale, be sure to provide students with your scoring guide before they write so that they know the specific criteria that determines their score. If possible, provide each student with a copy. Students with lower scores should use the guide to identify the errors and weaknesses in their papers, and all students should use the guide when developing similar papers in the future.

Remember that holistic scoring, while allowing you to evaluate many papers rapidly, does not preclude your giving more personal attention to students who need help. For example, you can invite students to consult with you individually when they cannot pinpoint the errors in their papers. You can also ask students to submit their revised papers. The revisions will show you exactly where they need further instruction.

COMMENTS AND CORRECTIONS

Some papers you will want to mark thoroughly, commenting on students' ideas and writing style and indicating errors. Many teachers prefer to do this in an oral conference; others prefer to write their comments on students' papers. You won't have the time and energy to do this for all assignments, but you should do it for some. Students respond remarkably well to such personal attention and specific guidance.

Whether you are agreeing or disagreeing, praising or finding fault, your comments show that you are paying attention to students' ideas and that you care about students' skills. Always include some praise or encouragement. Even when a student has written poorly, you can often offer encouragement by referring to real strengths: "You used some fresh, original words in last week's character sketch. I *know* you have the vocabulary to go beyond the trite expressions I've marked in this essay. I'll be looking for your vivid wording in the next assignment."

Keep in mind that a heavy marking of a paper is not a rewriting. Even if you suggest some specific content revisions, students must decide how to make the changes. Even though you isolate errors in grammar, usage, and mechanics, students must correct them. (Don't hesitate occasionally, however, to show students how to rework or correct a passage; students need models when they are acquiring skills.)

Using correction symbols will speed your marking of papers. You may want to distribute a list such as the following one with students' first marked papers. After students have worked with the list, you can ask for questions about particular symbols and writing problems.

CORRECTION SYMBOLS

CONTENT

Symbol	Meaning	What to Do
concl	conclusion missing, weak, or unrelated to main idea	Add or rephrase summarizing statement or paragraph.
irr	irrelevant detail	Delete or replace phrase or sentence.
spec	needs to be more specific	Clarify a detail, or add supporting details.
ts	thesis statement or topic sentence missing or not clear	Add or revise thesis statement or topic sentence to express main idea.

ORGANIZATION		
Symbol	**Meaning**	**What to Do**
org	organization not clear	Rearrange ideas in a more logical order.
tr	transition between ideas missing or confusing	Add or replace connecting words or phrases.
¶, no ¶	paragraphing problem	Begin new paragraph (¶), or join paragraphs (no ¶).
STYLE		
agr	agreement error	Make a subject and verb or an antecedent and pronoun agree in number.
awk	awkward sentence or passage	Rephrase sentence or section.
cap	capitalization error	Add capital, or lower-case capital.
frag	sentence fragment	Add subject or verb, or attach fragment to nearby sentence.
gr	grammatical error	Determine type of error, and correct it.
p	punctuation error	Add, replace, or delete punctuation.
pv	unnecessary shift in point of view	Eliminate shift in person.
ref	pronoun reference error	Clarify reference of a pronoun to its antecedent.
ro	run-on sentence	Correct with needed punctuation and capitals.
sp	misspelled word	Correct spelling.
t	tense error	Correct verb tense.
var	sentences lack variety	Vary structure and length of sentences.
wc	word choice problem	Replace with correct, more exact, or livelier word.

GRADING

In grading students' writing about literature, you will want to focus on the quality of their ideas. Without diminishing the importance of mechanics and style, let students know that *what* they have to say is of first importance in their grades: An error-free paper that is either shallow or incomplete should not receive an *A*.

Some teachers use a double grade on papers, for example *B+/C,* to distinguish between content and mechanics. Whatever system you use, explain clearly to students how your marking relates to their grades. Sample papers are especially helpful for this purpose. From previous classes, accumulate a file of marked and graded papers that students may examine, and review in class *A, B, C, D,* and *F* papers for a typical assignment. These papers will illustrate for students exactly what you expect.

SELF-EVALUATION

Students help both themselves and you by evaluating their own papers. Good writers evaluate automatically, although usually not in writing. Most students, however, skip this essential step altogether. By assigning even brief and informal evaluations, you can show students the importance of evaluation and instill a habit of lasting benefit. You will gain not only improved papers, but also insight into the students' ideas about writing. You may uncover misconceptions (a student is more concerned with correct spelling than with organization) and problems in composing (a student is a perfectionist and writes and rewrites an opening sentence). You can then help individual students or plan class sessions on particular aspects of the writing process.

One self-evaluation assignment is to have students rank the papers they are submitting as either high, average, or low and to explain their criteria for the ranking. Stress that you are not grading the evaluations and simply want honest, thoughtful responses to this question: What do you think of your paper and *why*? If you combine this self-evaluation with your own evaluation, students will see how their judgments compare to yours and can use the discrepancies to improve their evaluation skills. You can also use a simple form, such as the following one, for self-evaluation.

SELF-EVALUATION COMMENTS

Name _____ Date _____

Assignment or Title of Paper _____

1. I think one strength of this paper, or one thing that works well, is _____

_____

2. The weakest aspect of this paper is _____

_____

3. One problem I faced and was not sure how best to solve was _____

_____

Students should evaluate and revise the first draft of every paper. Emphasize that no first draft is ever perfect. If students evaluate and revise for themselves—rather than submitting first drafts—they will take a great step toward improved writing and better grades. Students can use the following general checklist to evaluate and then revise their writing about literature. (If you use holistic scoring guides, also alert students that the guides may be reused as evaluation checklists for particular assignments.)

Self-Evaluation Checklist for Writing about Literature

	Yes	No
1. Have I followed all of the directions for the assignment?		
2. Have I understood the literary terms and used them correctly?		
3. Have I clearly expressed a main idea in a strong topic sentence or thesis statement?		
4. Have I included enough details from the literary work to support my ideas?		
5. Are all the details accurate and directly related to the main idea?		
6. Does my paper have a clear beginning, middle, and end?		
7. Have I used precise words and avoided clichés and repetitious phrases?		
8. Have I correctly punctuated quotations and dialogue?		
9. Have I checked other punctuation, spelling, and use of capitals?		
10. Have I read the paper aloud to listen for missing words and awkward phrasing?		

PEER EVALUATION

When properly prepared for, peer evaluation can be highly rewarding and enjoyable for both writers and evaluators. It can produce new insights about the literary work and about the writing process. Unguided, though, peer evaluation can be ineffective or unpleasant. Irrelevant comments merely confuse, and heavy-handed criticisms wound. What is required is sensitivity, objectivity, and a common understanding of the evaluation criteria.

For successful peer evaluation, provide students with evaluation forms and demonstrate constructive criticism. First conduct a class evaluation of a paper from a previous class. Explain the writer's assignment, read the paper aloud, and offer samples of the comments you would make. As students enter the discussion, point out off-target comments or negative comments that serve no purpose; help students redirect or rephrase these criticisms. Remind them always to point out a

paper's good features: Evaluation identifies both strengths and weaknesses. You may want to go through two or three papers in this way before students work on their own.

At least for initial peer evaluations in small groups, use some type of prepared form. After students hear or read a paper, they can complete the form and then base group discussion on their written responses. Using a form need not limit discussion; always encourage students to react to each other's comments and brainstorm solutions for writing problems. After the discussion, the writer can use the completed forms for revising.

Depending on your students' abilities and maturity, you can use either a highly structured checklist or a form that elicits a more general impression. For example, you could adapt the preceding self-evaluation checklist for peer evaluation, providing room for the evaluator to explain every *No* response. A sample of a peer evaluation form follows.

PEER EVALUATION COMMENTS

Reader _____ Writer _____

Assignment or Title of Paper _____ Date _____

1. What I liked best in this paper was _____

   _____.

2. The most effective sentence was _____

   _____.

3. Good word choices were _____

   _____.

4. Ideas that I felt needed clarification or further support were _____

   _____.

5. Other positive comments are _____

   _____.

6. Other suggestions for revision are _____

   _____.

USING PORTFOLIOS TO EMPOWER STUDENT WRITERS

Winfield Cooper and B. J. Brown

For the past three years, we have been experimenting with student-writing portfolios, B. J. with her junior-high and Win with his high-school students. What is becoming especially interesting to us is the power of portfolios as teaching tools. Our research has shown us that, for students in an English language-arts classroom, the very act of compiling a portfolio can be a powerful process for many reasons, not least of which is that it helps students see themselves as writers, particularly when the process involves many opportunities for self-evaluation and reflection.

The criteria involved in selecting work to include in a portfolio are both internal and external (Linda Rief, 1990, "Finding the Value in Evaluation: Self-Assessment in a Middle School Classroom," *Educational Leadership* 47.6 [Mar.]:24–29). We set the external criteria by describing the kinds of writings which students must include; students choose the specific pieces they will include. The items our students include are quite similar because the external criteria were developed collaboratively by teachers at each grade level (7–12) to reflect the goals of the curriculum—which had also been created collaboratively. Teachers in our district designed a portfolio format that emphasizes a process approach to writing in an integrated language-arts program. At the same time we take into account, on one hand, the implications of a state-wide writing assessment which encourages students to become proficient in a variety of types of writing, and, on the other hand, the need for individual teachers to make decisions about how best to implement those goals in their own classrooms.

Our research is based on our work with the table of contents which has evolved in our district. (See the box page 212.) Each item in the portfolio has important implications for our teaching. We have found that selecting and preparing the various items provides students with many opportunities to reflect on their abilities as writers.

INTRODUCTION

In the introduction students speak to the audience, the readers of their portfolios, by introducing themselves, describing their characteristic writing process, and summarizing the contents of their portfolios. The introduction comes first in the portfolio but is written after students have assembled the body of their portfolios.

Diana, a twelfth grader, concludes her introduction by writing:

I am proud of the contents of this portfolio. It represents my hardest and best work, and I believe the three papers which get progressively more polished clearly track my progress as a writer.

Students' introductions are fascinating to read since they give insight into how students see themselves as writers. As Roberta J. Herter states (1991, "Writing Portfolios: Alternatives to Testing," *English Journal* 80.1 [Jan.]:90), "Portfolios involve students in assessing the development of their writing skills by inviting self-reflection and encouraging students to assume control over their writing." In their introductions, students invite us to look at what they can do, not what they can't; at what they have instead of what they haven't.

SAMPLE OF TIMED WRITING

The way the portfolio is set up, students are asked to include at least one example of a timed first-draft writing. While a process approach is at the core of the district writing program, teachers also acknowledge that academic situations frequently require students to formulate, organize, and write their thoughts in limited time periods. Asking students to include some sample of such writing is a way of ensuring that the portfolio reflects that aspect of school writing.

When teachers first decided to include timed writings in the portfolio, we asked students to include two examples of the same type of writing, both completed in a forty-five-minute time period (thus simulating the California direct writing assessment), one sample from the beginning of the year and the other from the end of the year. The assumption was that since the type of writing called for would be one of those that teachers had agreed

to concentrate on at that grade level, the students would have had multiple experiences with that kind of writing during the year. We hoped that the later sample would demonstrate higher achievement than the earlier one.

The timed writings for the portfolio need not be thought of as artifacts that are produced simply for inclusion in the portfolio outside the context of the curriculum. It may be possible, even desirable, to design a timed-writing experience as an integral part of an instructional unit, thus achieving one of the goals of authentic assessment, that assessment be virtually indistinguishable from instruction.

For example, Win incorporated a piece of interpretive writing on John Cheever's short story "Reunion" into a unit on rites of passage. After they had read the story, students wrote their responses within a time limit. Their essays went into their portfolios for future reference. Near the end of the year, Win asked his students to respond to a similar prompt requiring them to read and analyze a short prose passage in the context of a different instructional plan. As part of compiling their final portfolios, students re-read both papers and the scoring guide; they wrote comments about the differences they noted in their writing, speculating on what accounted for them and reflecting on the classroom experiences which had influenced the growth. The papers, as well as the self-evaluation and reflection, were included in the end-of-the-year portfolio. Advanced-placement students, who had been working on the kind of writing required for the AP literature exam, generally noted that the two samples showed they had become practiced at writing a focused essay using technical analysis; second-language students were able to point out dramatic evidence of their increased fluency in English; and other students often found that the comparison of the two papers offered concrete proof of their growth as writers.

DIFFERENT TYPES OF WRITING, ONE WITH EVIDENCE OF PROCESS

The statewide direct-writing test administered to eighth and eleventh graders by the California Assessment Program (CAP) identifies ten different types of writing. In our district, teachers have integrated these CAP writing types into our core literature units. It is from these writing types that we ask students to select three essays, one of which should be a packet including evidence of a complete process: prewriting, planning, writing, revising, editing, and rewriting. In most cases, students have several essays from which to choose their best three. They include their entire writing packet, for one essay of their choice, to show evidence of the writing process.

For example, before reading *Anne Frank: Diary of a Young Girl*, B.J.'s eighth-grade students interviewed someone who had firsthand experience in a war. James, an eighth grader, interviewed his father, who had been a child in London during World War II. His packet included notes from library research on WWII, his interview questions, the tape of his interview, his word-processed rough draft with revisions and corrections inked in, a response sheet completed by a classmate, and the computer printout of his final draft. As his other two choices, James selected an autobiographical incident he had written as a timed-writing sample for the NCTE Promising Young Writers' contest and a speculative essay written in response to "Flowers for Algernon." He chose not to include his short story, a tall tale, or his character analysis of Jeremy Finch in *To Kill a Mockingbird*. In order to make his selections, James had to reflect and evaluate the body of his work.

By showing examples of the whole process, the notion that it is the entire process which contributes to a satisfying finished product is reinforced. Since students include three essays in this section, they are able to show examples of writing for different purposes. These writing samples reflect the curriculum, the teacher's application of it, and the students' choices, making the portfolio inextricably tied to what goes on in the classroom.

WRITING TO LEARN

One of the most valuable lessons that students can learn is that writing is a powerful tool for learning—that writing, far from simply being the product of thinking, can actually shape thinking, a phenomenon that James Britton calls "shaping at the point of utterance" (1982, "Shaping at the Point of Utterance," *Prospect and Retrospect: Selected Essays of James Britton*, Ed. Gordon M. Pradl, Upper Montclair, NJ: Boynton, 143). Through exercises such as double-entry literary journals, classroom quickwrites, conscious imitation of an author's style, and other activities common to a student-centered, integrated language-arts classroom, students come to find out what they know through the act of writing.

Recognizing the importance of this aspect of writing has certain implications for teaching: teachers can reinforce the value of such writing in several ways: by designing such opportunities so that they build on one another, by providing students with the opportunity to clarify their thinking before discussing a text, by asking students to synthesize in writing their thoughts after discussion, and especially by encouraging students to go back to their "writing to learn" as they draft more formal papers based on ideas developed during their own discovery processes.

We have found the process of sharing their choices with other students provides a valuable lesson. The reasons students give are varied:

> because I wrote about a really personal connection I noticed between Stephen's experience and my own

because by the time I finished writing the different questions that the poem made me ask, I had already started to answer my own questions

I wrote some questions which I took to my collaborative group and they were the beginning of a really good discussion

this quickwrite was actually the inspiration for the final paper I wrote about the book

Seeing the uses others have made of such writing opportunities often is instructive to students, and it reinforces the importance of such writing more powerfully than our repeated assurances that such activities are good for them.

CREATIVE WRITING

We recognize that all writing that is not simple copying is creative, and we want our students to recognize that, too. The term springs from an unfortunate assumption that most academic writing is done according to some rigid formula or must somehow conform to strict guidelines which somehow constrain the writer. According to this thinking, all other writing in which the writer is not constrained is more spontaneous, more creative, more fun.

When we and our colleagues designed the first table of contents and looked at the kind of writing assignments we offered students, we recognized that some of our students' best work did not necessarily fit the other categories in the portfolio. We agreed that by requiring students to choose at least one creative-writing piece for the portfolio, we were implicitly providing more opportunities for students to do such writing.

Often the pieces chosen to fulfill the creative-writing requirement are written in response to a piece of literature or are written as a means of deepening understanding or appreciation of an author's technique or style. Win's students, for example, have chosen to include autobiographical pieces about early childhood written in the style of James Joyce's *Portrait of the Artist as a Young Man*, new chapters for *The Grapes of Wrath*, parodies of the style of Joseph Conrad, satires inspired by Jonathan Swift's "Modest Proposal," and "found poetry" based on *The Good Conscience*.

The creative-writing section might also contain a writing sample that was not written in response to a particular piece of literature or as a specific writing type. Students who write as a pastime can include their personal writing in this section. Poetry is a popular choice.

The creative-writing category reminds us that it is important to allow students the opportunity to write freely, to explore their ideas in their own way, thereby expanding the repertoire that they can present in their portfolios.

STUDENT-SELECTED BEST WRITING WITH A RATIONALE

By requiring students to select one piece of writing as their favorite, this category allows them additional personal choice, thus adding to their authority as writers. The best writing selection might be something that is included in another category also, or it might be something the student has saved for the special designation of "my best writing."

PORTFOLIO TABLE OF CONTENTS

1. Introduction
2. Sample of timed writing
3. Different types of writing, one with evidence of process
4. Sample(s) of writing to learn
   Possibilities include but are not limited to copy change, dialogue, word-weaving, creating a persona, imitation of author's style, transition from author to student voice, dialectical journal, reading log, quickwrite, drawing inferences, note-taking, learning log.
5. Creative writing sample
6. Student-selected best writing with rationale
7. Two pieces selected by student and/or teacher
   Possibilities include but are not limited to creative writing, special projects, evidence of collaboration, evaluation of oral presentations, evidence of listening, selections from other curricular areas, annotated reading list.

Although students have used their own criteria to evaluate each time they select a piece of writing for their portfolios, in the rationale they state their standards and show how the best writing sample reflects those standards.

Andrea, an eleventh grader, near the end of her first year in this country, wrote,

I chose the paper I wrote about *Glass Menagerie* because it was the first paper I am able to say in English exactly what I want to say. Even though it took me a lot of hard work to do it these are the ideas that I had in my head and I can say them. Before was frustrating because even with dictionary I knew I could not explain myself. When I finish this paper I know I have made a big step to learn English.

Carmen, an eighth grader, took a firm stance when she wrote her rationale.

I think that my best writing is my autobiographical incident because it's whole and pure. It was not anything I had to make up or lie about. All it says is the truth,

Tanya, an eighth grader, shows her enthusiasm for her best writing by commenting on her process.

I feel it is my best piece of writing because it was exactly what I wanted to write. I just knew the poem was perfect when I finished. The first sentence of my poem says, "Starvation and misery pluck at my heart." That is the exact way I wanted those words to come out. I could scream, I think my paper is so great.

Brian Johnston says, "Students do not learn writing simply through having many experiences of doing it. To learn to control the medium they must also reflect, conceptualize and experiment" (1987, *Assessing English: Helping Students to Reflect on Their Work*, Milton Kenyes, Eng.: Open UP, 105). Selecting their best writing allows students to evaluate their own work while the rationale asks them to internalize their own standards to support that choice in writing.

TWO PIECES SELECTED BY STUDENT AND/OR TEACHER

This vague requirement that the last two items in the portfolio be "two pieces selected by student and teacher" is perhaps the most obvious example of how an agreed-upon set of portfolio contents can be flexible enough to allow for diversity. Among the possibilities for these pieces are creative writing, special projects, a collaborative piece, evidence of reflection on collaboration, evaluations of oral presentations, evidence of listening activities, an annotated reading list, or writing for other content areas. A teacher may define the criteria for choosing one or both of these items in order to ensure that the portfolios reflect an important aspect of the curriculum, or the choice of one or more items may be left up to the student so that the portfolio includes what the student believes to be most important.

Since collaboration in both the writing process and in the process of making meaning from a piece of literature is central to the way he teaches English, Win wanted his students' portfolios to reflect the importance of collaboration, so he required them to include in their portfolios an item labeled "evidence of collaboration." During the course of the year, students were frequently asked to reflect on the collaborative process in various ways. For each major paper they wrote a metacognitive piece about their process, including an analysis of how collaborating had influenced the changes in their writing at various stages. Sometimes, to encourage collaboration, they were asked to list all the sources from which they had gotten help. Occasionally, after engaging in small-group discussion of literature, students would write notes to each other, commenting on what the others in the group had contributed to the discussion. They wrote self-analyses as well. At the end of the first semester and again at the end of the year, students looked over all this evidence, reflected on it, and attempted to synthesize what they had learned about themselves as collaborators and about the collaborative process.

A few examples of insights from their portfolio entries about collaboration serve to illustrate what happens when students are invited to engage in such reflection. Some students observed that collaboration had particularly influenced their understanding of literature.

> I am really grateful for those discussions in which the layers of my confusion are slowly peeled away by my peers.
>
> *Ronnie, twelfth grade*

> I like how my classmates can throw out their ideas, and how I can tell them mine, but then I can choose what I think is the "right answer." I also like collaborating because it is like figuring out a puzzle where you have to find the pieces first, and later put it together. The most important thing I have learned is that there is no definite right answer, and that my answer does have the potential, if supported, to be correct. I also have learned that I am capable of analyzing literature, that I can figure it out, that I can be right. It is not some process that only English wizards can do.
>
> *Donna, twelfth grade*

Others came to understand the role of collaboration in the writing process:

> [A]lso an important skill is knowing when to listen to your own writing intuitions and when to yield to the suggestions of the group. Although there may be a degree of safety in numbers, you have to be wary of losing your voice or original intent under the well-intended, but not always healthy . . . suggestions of the group.
>
> *Gary, twelfth grade*

After he explained how specific papers in his portfolio illustrate various stages in his struggles as a writer, Bruce concluded,

> even though there are occasional pieces with discouraging results, the fact that I can finally write outside the boundaries of the five-paragraph essay is refreshing enough to keep my full interest and attention for what I'm sure will be all year.

We have come to believe that, when students become more conscious of the many decisions they make in order to improve their writing, when they begin to be aware of the processes they must engage in to produce effective writing, and when they finally look over a body of their work, judging it against a set of criteria they have developed and internalized, they are engaged in the kind of thinking characteristic of writers.

*Torrey Pines High School
Encinitas, California 92024
Earl Warren Junior High School
Solana Beach, California 92075*

---

from WHAT I WISH I HAD KNOWN ABOUT PEER-RESPONSE GROUPS BUT DIDN'T

Ronald Barron

FORMING PEER-RESPONSE GROUPS

How many people should peer-response groups have, and how should their composition be determined?

Trial and error has taught me that <u>four people</u> is probably the best size for a group. Assuming a fifty-five to sixty-minute class period, an efficient peer group can provide useful feedback on four papers. Also, a four-member group seems to facilitate discussion of the paper. If a group gets too large, some students may be left out of the discussion, or a teacher may have to institute some "rule" to ensure equal participation opportunities. Neither alternative is desirable. On the other hand, if a group is too small, students do not get sufficiently diversified responses to their papers, thus limiting the value of peer response.

THE FINISHED PRODUCT

Assembling their portfolios at the end of the semester or year is a way for students to celebrate their accomplishment. Students agonize over which pieces to select and ask their classmates for advice. As Herter points out, "<u>authority as writers, editors, and audience is validated by their experience</u> with <u>one another's texts</u>" (91). The time students spend organizing portfolios is valuable time to reflect and evaluate. When we allow time for students to assemble their portfolios, they often revise their work and share it informally before it "goes public" in the finished portfolio.

Students can present their portfolios to the class, or a small group. B.J. asks students to show their parents the portfolio before presenting it to her. She includes a letter to parents which summarizes what the portfolio represents, and she encourages

AUTHOR'S NOTE: I would like to thank Cindy Houlton, the writer of the paper, and her three peer editors (Amy Swanson, Mary Schultz, and Peter Gilbertson) for allowing me to use a sample of their work in this article.

A brightly colored ribbon tied back my shoulder length black hair. All around I could feel the excitement. The stands were filled with expectant coaches, family and teammates. The morning sun was still cool and slowly making its way to its peak. I looked over at my coach Kim Case. ~~and my best friend. Kim~~ *She* raised a ~~fist~~ *fist* and smiled, nodding her head. She stood by the finish line (near the outside lane.)

delete

Unclear — Is this the start of the race?

All of these sentences are the same length.

With a burst of nervous energy I strided down the track towards the other girls in my race. My light weight ~~shoes~~ Nikes dug into the soft new red track. My energy pushed me forward with out my brain consciously ~~trying~~ working at each stride. ~~The~~ A mechanical voice called for us to line up in our lanes. One by one we were given our assignments. As the start neared the turning tenseness in my stomach tightened. By nature jumping around from foot to foot and up and down on both feet. I felt springs in my feet ~~legs~~ as I moved about to release my anxiety. The girl next to me tentatively wished me luck and I smiled only half hearing her voice.

Too many adjectives

Good image but revise wording

The starter raised his gun and all of us froze.

BANG!

The race had begun. ~~With a quick~~ In a matter of seconds we (filled) into a line. Many fought to keep up with the leader. I felt strong but I stayed back toward the back. I had run this race so many times yet regions was always different. This was my third year at regions even though I was only a sophomore in high school.

filed?

Would it be better to mention when this happened earlier?

~~The first lap~~ I had just finished my first lap with a good time even though I was in last place. As I ~~rounded the~~ began the second lap I ~~sti~~ quickened my stride. I began to near the next runner in front and passed her with ease. I could hear the heavy breathing and pounding of the feet of the girls that had gone out too quickly. One by one I passed girls on the outside of the pack.

Tell us more about you

By the end of the third lap I managed to pass every girl but one. My legs began to feel tired. I had to push myself for each stride. My arms felt like dead weights. My head was pounding as the last lap loomed in front of me like another mile. I had never felt this before. I ran out of sheer will to finish. As I rounded the last turn with 200 meters left, the pounding of feet came up behind out of nowhere I fought but one by one they began to race ahead of me.

Good sentence

cliche

good word choice

The short sentences give readers a sense of your lack of breath

I want to know more about the third lap. Try to build more tension.

I crossed the finish line in seventh as I heard the timer yell 5:40.

The disappointment of being passed drained from my body.   In a rush Kim and my other team-

mates circled around me with hugs and congradulations. *Sp*

The tired feeling had disappeared.   I had worked all season to get a 5:40 in the 1600 m, and I

had done it.

← Write out

The emotions you tell us about are interesting, but could you tell us more? It would help readers experience the event with you.

The conclusion is too quick. Work more on Bringing out the significance of the experience you have chosen a unique experience -- most people would only write about a race they won.

I like the subject you have chosen. Reveal more about what you were thinking. The little you tell us makes me want to know more.

The introduction isn't very catchy. Tell us more about Kim. I expected to find out more about her.

them to give positive, specific responses to their children. Sending portfolios home strengthens an important link among teacher and student and parents.

Once students submit their portfolios, we read the introductions and rationales carefully and page through the rest, which we've seen before as assignments, stopping to read whatever strikes us. We add a final positive comment, then return the portfolios to the students. We continue to experiment with how to incorporate the portfolio into end-of-term grades. Once we have returned portfolios to students, they are theirs to keep. And why not? They are the creators, the writers.

Portfolios can be a valuable source for summative evaluation by teacher and student; at the end of the year they can provide an accurate measure of what students have accomplished. By the same token, portfolios have potential for formative assessment. When students make tentative selections for portfolios and especially when they compile interim portfolios, evaluate them, and reflect on what they notice, they can reinforce their own learning processes and set goals for future learning. Often, writing about their reflections in such interim portfolios can help them see where they have come from and clarify where they want to go. For

example, at the end of the first semester Bruce, a twelfth grader, wrote,

This year a combination of techniques has finally allowed me to expand my abilities, which is wonderful. But it also means that I feel like I've started over, and I found that it is like learning how to write again. These techniques have revolved around two areas—expanding my reading capabilities with more original, personal responses in the form of homework, and then, in class sessions involving the gathering of so many different ideas and opinions. With these new concepts of responding to literature, it is impossible that my writing abilities and attitudes wouldn't change.

The membership of peer-response groups can be determined in a wide variety of ways, ranging from random assignment to balancing groups so all of the best or all of the poorest writers do not end up together. Since rapport contributes to the effectiveness of a group, I allow students the option of setting up their own peer groups; however, I tell them I will rearrange the groups if they do not function effectively. After the peer-group practice sessions, my students select their own groups if they have a preference. Students who do not express a preference are randomly assigned to groups. One suggestion I offer students prior to selecting their groups is that they probably should not be in a group with their best friends since they would likely seek their responses anyway. They will derive the most benefit by getting additional responses from students they would not normally ask to read their papers.

Periodic teacher monitoring of groups is extremely important and enables teachers to recognize problems and to try to solve them before they become critical. If problems arise that cannot be resolved, I change the composition of the groups. But using response groups is not a "miracle method" which works equally well with all students. Teachers need to understand that there may be some students who do not function well with any group. In such cases teachers have to work with those students to try to improve their group participation, but in the end they may have to be content with placing these students in groups where they do the least harm.

How often should peer groups meet, and what should they actually do?

I schedule peer groups to meet twice for each composition assignment. The first time the groups meet they focus on the global components of the composition such as the organizational pattern, additional material that may be needed, places where the paper could use emphasis or clarification, and unrelated or unnecessary material that may sidetrack the reader. These global components should be the subject of the first session because problems at the sentence and word level may change or disappear as the writers make large structural or conceptual changes during the revising process. To keep the focus on these larger components of a composition rather than on more limited items, I suggest that students read their papers to each other rather than exchange written drafts. However, I strongly recommend that students take notes during the discussion of their papers so they will not forget the advice they receive from their peer group. When students revise their drafts, they decide which advice has merit and which advice doesn't match their goals for the composition.

For the second peer session I require students to exchange drafts because the focus of this session should be on the word, sentence, or paragraph level, for example, sentence variety, word choice, punctuation, and the like. I also encourage students to provide copies of their papers to other group members prior to the day of the response group meeting. This practice allows other members of the group to provide a studied response rather than being restricted to a first impression.

Although I would like to devote more time to response groups, the time available in my composition course prevents it. However, my

students are encouraged to convene their groups outside of class when and if they feel the need. As the course progresses and students learn the benefits of peer response, groups meet more frequently on their own, or at least individuals exchange drafts of their compositions outside of class. I even see students going outside of their own group for additional feedback—probably the major testimonial to the value they place on peer feedback. Success with their first papers makes students believers in the technique.

Where does the teacher fit into the writing process once students learn the importance of peer response?

First, teachers sit in on group sessions to determine how efficiently the groups are operating. During those observations teachers can expect to be asked for advice about the drafts under consideration by the group. In these situations I attempt to act as any other member of the group, giving my frank response to the draft but consciously resisting the temptation to take over the group. A second way teachers can participate is by making individual conference time available for students who request it. In other words, the use of response groups does not preclude teacher input, but it does change the nature of the input. Rather than the teacher determining when and what input is necessary, students determine when they need such input and what specific help they require. Sometimes students request a great deal of help with a particular assignment; at other times they feel quite content to proceed on their own with little or no teacher assistance. I consciously strive to become only one source of advice about how to write a composition, rather than trying to be a "writing seer" who knows all and tells all about how to complete the assignment. This approach to composition closely resembles the way students will have to handle writing outside of school.

Prior to having students write a first draft, I have them study effective models, usually strong papers written by students during the previous year, but sometimes I also use professionally written examples. We then spend class time discussing the unique qualities of the types of writing students will be expected to do, as well as trying to reach a consensus about what makes the models effective. When students discuss what makes a piece of writing effective, they have a better understanding of how to write a composition of their own which incorporates those priorities. The discussion of quality papers can also lead to teacher and/or student-generated guide sheets which can be used both by the response groups in suggesting revisions of works-in-progress and by the teacher in evaluating final compositions. . . .

I encourage groups to set as a goal producing the four best papers in the class, not just one good paper. As one student said in her evaluation of my

All around me I could feel the excitement of Regions. The stands were filled with expectant coaches, family, and teammates while runners moved about trying desperately to relieve their ← *these two lines are too similar.* anxiety. Tears and pain along with joy and pride were evident in the expressions of those *Word choice* already done while anxiety and fear raced through the minds of those ^(of us) who were waiting for their → *Would "our" be better?* chance.

A brightly colored ribbon tied back my shoulder length black hair and my light-weight Nikes dug into the new red track. I slowly strided ~~down~~ towards the far end of the track to loosen my *Could these words be left out?* tightly coiled leg muscles. My mind replayed (fast forward) every race I had run since 8th grade as I tried to focus on today.

A (mechanical) voice called ~~for~~ us to line up in our lane assignments. One by one we stood in our positions as the starter announced we had five minutes until the start. I hopped from foot to foot ~~releasing sore~~ as I did before every race. I felt springs in my toes as I moved about to release the pent up butterflies in the pit of my stomach.

^(Kim) "You can do it!" exclaimed ~~Mim~~, my coach. *You capitalize "Regions" in the first line, but here you don't.*

I looked over, and nodded ~~only~~ half smiling. I had never worked so hard for anything as I had for regions that year. The long hot afternoons with Kim and that ever present stopwatch reminded me of how prepared I was. Together, Kim and I had planned nutrition, ^(and) ~~,~~ worked to improved my overall fitness. ~~not just my~~ She had been there for me ~~when~~ through the good ← *cliche* days and bad days. I had learned to depend on her support.

I looked over at ~~her~~ Kim again to see her confident smile and her raised stopwatch. I smiled back, this time with strength and no doubt in my eyes.

The starter raised his gun and ~~all~~ everyone froze.

"BANG!"

The race had begun. In a matter of seconds we filed into a line. Many girls fought to keep up *Was there any battle for position in the pack?* with the leader, but I stayed back. I had run this race so many times. I unconsciously picked up a *combined* rythym and strided along without thinking about each step. *How did you feel about your pace?*

Before I knew it, I finished my first lap with a good time, even though I was in last place. As I

I felt the excitement of Regions surround me.
Your second paragraph helps me understand what you were experiencing

rounded the ~~curve~~ first curve of the second lap I began to quicken my stride. I neared the runner

in front of me and passed her with ease. I could hear the pounding of my feet of the girls who *and the*

had gone out too fast. My mind never focused except on the girl in front of me. I felt nothing *heavy*

except the natural pace of my stride as I passed girls one by one on the outside of the pack. *breathing*

By the end of the third lap I managed to pass every girl but one. My mind cleared as I could

win *my effort*

sense victory. I wanted to ^more than anything else. I pushed my body forward with all as I ^

good→ began to feel the first signs of fatigue. Every stride became a tedious effort as the last lap

lines loomed in front of me like another mile. My arms and legs felt like lead weights as my mind

began to spin. The sweat was dripping off my face in a constant flow as I gasped for every

breath. I kept running ~~on the will to finish~~ only out on the sheer will to finish. I rounded the last

curve with only 200 meters left. My ears heard muffled tones of the crowd screaming as we

neared the finish.

I like → I pushed but my body resisted. Pounding from behind pushed me forward ~~to yet once more.~~

this line The other runners passed me. My last ounce of energy helped me reach the finish line in

seventh place as I heard the timer yell "5:40." The disappointment of placing seventh drained *Didn't you start*

from my body as I processed what I had just heard. *to react in the previous line?*

"You did it! You did it!" screamed Kim as she raced over to hug me before I could react.

In a rush my other teammates rushed over to congratulate me. They all seemed very distant

for

though. Everything was fuzzy ~~except~~ ^Kim and her stopwatch. She raised it slowly so I could see

the time. Dark digital numbers read 5:40. ← *One place you put it in quotes and in the other place you don't*

"I did it!" I said quietly with a grin.

I can imagine your emotional state much better after reading this draft. I also understand why you wrote about this event even though you didn't win the race.

Your new opening paragraph is more effective because it catches the excitement of the experience. Waiting until the second paragraph to focus on yourself is a good idea. The conclusion is stronger now than it was in your earlier version. The importance of achieving personal goals rather than winning the race is clearer in this version.

I understand Kim's role in the experience better.

composition course last year, "When someone in my group got an *A* on a paper, I also felt like I had received an *A*." Although that ideal goal of producing the four best papers is not always attainable, how will students and, for that matter, their teachers know if it can be reached unless students try to accomplish it? Trying sometimes leads to pleasant surprises. A more realistic group goal should be to produce four papers which are all better than what individual writers could have produced on their own. That goal is within the capabilities of all students.

One of the purposes of a composition course should be to make students more confident and more independent writers. Peer-response groups help accomplish this purpose. In addition, good responders tend to become better writers. For most students, as their ability as responders improves, their ability to revise their own compositions also improves because they have a better sense of how to approach the task.

However, teachers should not expect all members of response groups to gain the same benefits from the experience. Teachers need to tolerate some partial failures even though they may have worked extensively with individuals trying to improve their performance. The important point to keep in mind is not to junk the technique because it does not work well with all students. Also, teachers may not experience as much success with peer-response groups as they wish the first time they try them. My own experience is a good case in point. Experience and modification of the technique to fit the individual personalities of teacher and students are necessary for success with peer-response groups, just as with almost every other effective teaching technique. However, teachers who devote time and effort to instruction in the use of response groups will be rewarded when students write better papers, feel more confident about their writing skills, and view writing as a positive experience rather than one to be avoided.

Richfield Senior High School
Richfield, Minnesota 55423

TWENTY (BETTER) QUESTIONS

Kris L. Myers

Maybe you don't struggle getting your students to read literature assignments, but I do. Getting an edge on MTV, mall-walking, and girl- or boy-watching is difficult, but I am competing better since I've changed my tack in evaluating students' knowledge of literature and my view of what that knowledge should be.

Most of us have used the "pop quiz" as a quick check to see who has read last night's assignment. We rationalize that it is positive motivation—a reward for those who have read, rather than punishment for those who have not. We make quizzes "simple" so any fool who has skimmed the assignment can pass.

But do you remember *taking* one of those quizzes? I do. I remember heart palpitations, silent prayers that the teacher would ask what I'd remembered of the details (and they were always about details), and brain freeze. I couldn't remember the name of the main character, the author of the story, or even the setting. And I'd read it; I had!

Well, I'm guilty of having given those infernal quizzes, too. Why don't I give them any more? The influence of two people changed my approach to quizzing and my whole outlook on what is important to know about literature.

The first influence was a wide-eyed high achiever in my first period class three years ago. Heidi was an eager student, willing to participate in all class activities. She went beyond what most students did. Needless to say, she always read her assignments, often more than once. Yet she would come in panic-stricken the day after a reading assignment, begging to know if we were having a pop quiz.

On the day we quizzed on Thurber's "The Dog That Bit People," Heidi froze. It was a true/false quiz with "simple" questions, but Heidi missed them all. She left her paper totally blank; she didn't even record her name. But the agony for me was watching her face as I read each question. I saw various stages of panic, fear, agitation, and resignation, ending finally in silent tears.

She was silent the entire class period. As the classroom cleared at the bell, she came to my desk and stood for several moments. Then she apologized. She had read the story twice, she said, but didn't know the "important" parts; she would work harder, read again, do whatever I could suggest. But she didn't know how to figure out what I thought was important. That gave me pause. What *I* thought? Is this what I wanted her to do: psych out what *I* felt was important about Thurber's story? Is that what teaching literature should be?

The second influence was Maia Pank Mertz at The Ohio State University. She introduced me to reader-response criticism by opening to me the worlds of Louise Rosenblatt, David Bleich, Norman Holland, and Alan Purves. But, more importantly, her classroom procedures were response-centered theories in action.

So, do I still struggle to get my students to read their assignments? Well, yes, but less so. Do I still give pop quizzes? Not exactly. Instead, I have students keep response journals. I use David Bleich's response heuristic to help students define and refine their responses. In *Reading and Feelings* (Urbana: NCTE, 1975), Bleich suggests that readers respond first to their perception of the work (what it means), then to the connections and associations within them that caused the affective response.

Students are used to looking to teachers for answers. They are seldom asked to reflect on what they think about what they read, or even less so, why they think what they think. Bloom's Taxonomy levels of application, analysis, synthesis, and evaluation are still largely ignored in most classrooms. But my students are responding to literature on all of these levels. I give students the following list of questions at the beginning of the school year and ask them to keep the list in their response journals to use all year.

1. What character(s) was your favorite? Why?
2. What character(s) did you dislike? Why?
3. Does anyone in this work remind you of anyone you know? Explain.
4. Are you like any character in this work? Explain.
5. If you could be any character in this work, who would you be? Explain.
6. What quality(-ies) of which character strikes you as a good characteristic to develop within yourself over the years? Why? How does the character demonstrate this quality?
7. Overall, what kind of a feeling did you have after reading a few paragraphs of this work? Midway? After finishing the work?
8. Do any incidents, ideas, or actions in this work remind you of your own life or something that happened to you? Explain.
9. Do you like this piece of work? Why or why not?
10. Are there any parts of this work that were confusing to you? Which parts? Why do you think you got confused?
11. Do you feel there is an opinion expressed by the author through this work? What is it? How do you know this? Do you agree? Why or why not?
12. Do you think the title of this work is appropriate? Is it significant? Explain. What do

you think the title means?

13. Would you change the ending of this story in any way? Tell your ending. Why would you change it?
14. What kind of person do you feel the author is? What makes you feel this way?
15. How did this work make you feel? Explain.
16. Do you share any of the feelings of the characters in this work? Explain.
17. Sometimes works leave you with the feeling that there is more to tell. Did this work do this? What do you think might happen next?
18. Would you like to read something else by this author? Why or why not?
19. What do you feel is the most important word, phrase, passage, or paragraph in this work? Explain why it is important.
20. If you were an English teacher, would you want to share this work with your students? Why or why not?

 I am constantly revising this list, and students may use any of the questions when writing their responses, providing they answer all of the questions fully. What is important about this list is not the specific questions on it, but the nature of the questions, the attitude about literature that is fostered by the questions. The focus is constantly *on the students* and their perceptions, feelings, and associations which result from the work.

I still "check up" on my students' reading by randomly grading written responses, but students know what will be asked of them. Usually I require a minimum of a half a page of writing but nearly always get more. Sometimes I ask students to include in their response a reaction to a specific question on the list, but most students tend to drop the crutch the list provides.

How do I grade responses? I use Bleich's suggestions again and grade on seriousness of intent and obvious knowledge of the story. Unlike answers on the objective pop quiz, responses are impossible to fake; the reader knows immediately whether the student has read and thought about the work. Also, I do not grade every response. I try to include my own written response to their writing occasionally as well.

I encourage students to take their journals with them and respond to the work while it is fresh in their minds. I am available to read and respond to their writing upon request. Sometimes they write, discuss the work, then write again. Or we discuss and then write. And the work doesn't end when the students leave the classroom. It becomes something they "own" and is forever a part of them.

Yes, more of my students are reading their assignments more of the time. They do see response writings as a positive reward. But more than that, they see themselves as critics and meaning-carriers. They are less intimidated by and more intimate with the printed word. The mystery in the text has become the mystery in them. And that is a mystery they want to solve.

Granville Middle School
Granville, Ohio 43023

READING DEVELOPMENT IN *WORLD LITERATURE*:
The Student as Reader/The Teacher as Facilitator
Nancy E. Wiseman Seminoff

The *World Literature* anthology includes a wide range of significant literary works, as well as supporting instruction that helps students become more proficient readers and writers as they learn to analyze, interpret, and evaluate literature. The anthology presents a survey course of world literature organized into units by culture and chronology. A list of the selections organized by themes (see Annotated Teacher's Edition page T17) allows teachers the flexibility of using a thematic approach.

The instructional materials include background information for understanding the genres, the selections, and the writers' lives; factual and interpretive discussion questions; and creative and critical writing assignments. The questions and assignments, designed to stimulate critical thinking, emphasize reading and writing strategies in which students use their own experience and knowledge to comprehend and appreciate literature.

Additionally, exercises throughout the text use specific linguistic features of the selections as springboards to language and vocabulary instruction. The exercises cover literary terms and techniques, such as allusions and figures of speech, as well as word-study skills important in all reading, such as context clues and word roots. For a listing of all skills taught in the program, see the index on pupil's text pages 1488–1494 and the Integrating the Language Arts chart on pages T27–T52 of the Annotated Teacher's Edition.

World Literature provides you with excellent materials and tools to help your students become better readers. Your role in the classroom is pivotal to students' success. By understanding the reading process and basing your teaching strategies on it, you can make use of the anthology's full potential for reading development.

UNDERSTANDING THE READING PROCESS

In the past, educators viewed reading as a series of discrete skills, sequential and hierarchical in nature. They increasingly found, however, that students who learned these skills in the elementary grades did not necessarily develop into proficient readers in the higher grades. Something was missing in the traditional view of the reading process: the interaction between the reader and the text itself.

According to recent research, reading is a dynamic process that involves the reader, the text, and the situation in which the reading takes place. The assumption behind previous reading theory was that the writer bore sole responsibility for conveying meaning. Educators now recognize that readers must actively seek meaning as they read and must be able to modify their approach to a text if the approach doesn't yield meaning. The reader's characteristics and background (linguistic, social, cultural, and psychological) and the writer's characteristics (as evidenced in the text) necessarily influence the reader's understanding.

Students actually *construct* meaning as they read; they do not simply absorb it. They bring prior experience and knowledge (which includes expectations about the type of literature) to the work. They draw tentative conclusions as they begin to read and modify those conclusions as they continue. The reading process is thus one of accumulating meaning.

The development of schema theory by cognitive psychologists has helped illuminate this process, showing how people approach new information by setting it against a known framework. In reading, schemata (frameworks) enable a student to recall relevant facts and experiences, to anticipate what will happen next, to fill in missing information, and to know when a writer's meaning is not clear. Important to a student's framework for understanding, therefore, is experience not only with the topic of a reading selection, but also with the genre. In reading about a certain type of flower, for example, a student's comprehension is aided by prior knowledge of the flower's physical properties, no matter what the genre of the writing. But a student cannot approach the reading of Li Ch'ing-chao's poem "Peonies" (see text page 534) and the reading of a botanical text about peonies in the same way. To construct full meaning from "Peonies," the student must be familiar with such poetic conventions and techniques as personification and metaphor, as well as with stylistic variations within, in this case, the poetry genre. The student must have appropriate expectations against which to gauge understanding.

Teachers, in turn, must be alert to gaps in students' experience and knowledge that will prevent them from being "active" readers, supplying (or guiding students in finding) necessary background in the many ways suggested in the student text, the Annotated Teacher's Edition, and these Teaching Notes. If students face a literary work that seems thoroughly unfamiliar, the reading will seem a difficult chore. Students will not read with interest—and interest is another fundamental element in the dynamics of reading.

The purpose for reading a selection, either self- or teacher-imposed, is an additional variable in the reading situation. A student uses quite different reading strategies to gain an initial impression of an essayist's position and to read a dramatic soliloquy. For the first task, the student reads in "chunks," with wide eye sweeps. For the second task, the student reads closely, ideally aloud, with attention to specific phrasing and detail. ("Teaching Students to Vary Reading Rates," on pages 228–231 of these Teaching Notes, provides a discussion of different reading strategies as well as genre-specific guidelines for close reading.)

The conscious awareness and control of cognitive processes is termed *metacognition.* In reading, metacognition is the adjustment of reading strategies to control comprehension. Encourage students to monitor their own comprehension as they read: to pause and raise questions when they do not understand, to reread a section to seek clarity, to use context clues to determine meaning, and so on. You should help students see, in short, that the response to difficult reading is not to stop reading. Students can learn reading techniques that will help them to become flexible, responsive readers—a necessity if they are to participate in the experiences offered them in literature.

BEFORE READING—MOVING INTO THE SELECTION

The instructional materials that accompany the selections in the anthology provide a framework for your classroom activities. These can be grouped in three phases: preparation for reading the selection, an encounter with the selection, and extension beyond the selection.

Students' preparation for reading a selection often determines the success of their reading and therefore cannot be left to chance. The unit and selection introductions, the author biographies, the Reader's Guide pages, and the selection headnotes, as well as various special features such as "Behind the Scenes," "Primary Sources," and "The Art of Translation," supply background information, relate the selection to contemporary life, and help students anticipate topics and themes. The Annotated Teacher's Edition offers additional information and ideas for introducing the selections.

Also important are activities to bridge the gap between students' prior knowledge and an unfamiliar literary work, activities that will motivate them to want to begin reading. In the student edition, Writer's or Oral Responses on the Reader's Guide pages do much to fulfill this instructional need. In addition, the Annotated Teacher's Edition presents many hints for stimulating interest. Remember, however, that students do not need exhaustive introductions to begin reading, understanding, and appreciating a selection. Reading preparation should be stimulating and revealing, not oppressive. When students must learn many new facts, concepts, and terms, the introductory material should comprise a separate lesson.

DURING READING—MOVING THROUGH THE SELECTION

The questions that follow each selection are intended to assist students in understanding the literary work. The questions are offered for instruction, not testing, and students should refer freely to the selection when answering them. (You may on occasion select some questions for closed-book reading checks or essay tests.)

Good questions help students to tap into their own experiences and to engage more deeply with the text. The questions labeled "First Thoughts" and "Applying Meanings" are especially helpful in eliciting reader response. The goal of all the study questions is to help readers to *accumulate* understandings of the text while encouraging them to think on their own. As students answer the questions, they are continually gathering information, interpreting, and raising their own questions in a process that causes them to refine their understandings and to confirm or reject their initial predictions. Cognitively, they move between and among the questions as they build comprehension and understanding.

Consequently, you should encourage students to answer questions as fully as possible but to be open to revising their responses in light of new evidence. In this process of deepening comprehension, other students' responses also play an important role. Small groups are particularly effective for discussing questions and comparing written answers. In this way, students can refine, reconsider, reject, revise, or confirm their understandings in response to others' ideas.

Keep in mind that while questions should guide students to find meaning and contribute their own ideas, the amount and type of guidance they need can vary. Debate exists among reading experts about how structured the guidance should be, but your students' needs should be the determining factor. For some students and in some situations, highly structured questions may be best. In other cases, you may be able to use open-ended questions and provide minimal guidance. For

further discussion of questioning strategies, particularly to provoke critical thinking, see "Using Literature to Teach Higher-Level Thinking Skills" (page 224).

AFTER READING—MOVING BEYOND THE SELECTION

Activities after reading serve two purposes: assessing students' understanding of a selection and helping students apply what they have learned to a new situation or selection. Culminating small-group discussions—following your instruction and guided class discussion—are one simple but effective way for you to help students move beyond the selection. As students express and explain their final responses to the work, you should move among the groups, listening for problems. You should determine how many students still have not read successfully and how best to help them.

Creative and Critical Writing Responses, Language and Vocabulary activities, and Speaking and Listening activities require students to demonstrate comprehension and to go beyond the selections. Many of the writing assignments encourage students to use their imaginations in response or imitation of the literature selection. Other writing assignments require students to explore a literary element more deeply, to compare and contrast it with another selection, or to relate the work to other life situations. The Language and Vocabulary exercises, while assessing students' mastery of selection-related skills and terms, usually extend and apply the language study to other areas. Thus the students' understanding and abilities increase as they complete each exercise.

Discussing one or more selections in relation to each other is another successful technique. You may ask students to connect selections in terms of their theme, style, genre, historical period, or another element or combination of elements. You may ask them to create an original work. In these activities, students are synthesizing. They analyze the selections, but they arrive at understandings (comparisons, contrasts, original works) that are external to the selections. In applying elsewhere what they learn from a literary work, students learn how to use past reading to approach new reading. They expand those frameworks for understanding that makes them proficient, responsive readers.

FURTHER READING FOR THE TEACHER

Alvermann, D. E. "Metacognition." *Research Within Reach: Secondary School Reading*. Eds. D. E. Alvermann, D. W. Moore, and M. W. Conley. Newark, DE: International Reading Association, 1987. 153–168.

Armbruster, B. "The Problem of 'Inconsiderate Text.'" *Comprehension Instruction: Perspectives and Suggestions*. Eds. G. Duffy, L. Roehler, and J. Mason. New York: Longman, 1984. 202–217.

Atwell, Nancie. *In the Middle: Writing, Reading, and Learning with Adolescents*. Portsmouth: Heinemann, 1987. 149–221.

Baker, L., and A. L. Brown. "Cognitive Monitoring in Reading." *Understanding Reading Comprehension*. Ed. J. Flood. Newark, DE: International Reading Association, 1984. 21–44.

Langer, J. A. "Understanding Literature." *Language Arts* 8 (1990): 812–816.

——. "The Process of Understanding Reading for Literary and Informative Purposes." *Research in the Teaching of English* 24 (1990): 229–260.

Meyer, B. J. F. "Organizational Aspects of Text: Effects on Reading Comprehension and Applications for the Classroom." *Promoting Reading Comprehension*. Ed. J. Flood. Newark, DE: International Reading Association, 1984. 113–138.

Moffett, James, and Betty Jean Wagner. "Student-Centered Reading Activities." *English Journal*, Oct. 1991, 70–73.

Mosenthal, P. "Reading Comprehension Research from a Classroom Perspective." *Promoting Reading Comprehension*. Ed. J. Flood. Newark, DE: International Reading Association, 1984. 16–29.

Paris, S. G., M. Lipson, and K. K. Wilson. "Becoming a Strategic Reader." *Contemporary Educational Psychology* 8 (1982): 293–316.

Pearson, P. D., and R. J. Spiro. "Toward a Theory of Reading Comprehension Instruction." *Topics in Language Disorders* 1 (1980): 71–88.

Rosenblatt, L. M. *The Reader, the Text, the Poem*. Carbondale, IL: Southern Illinois University Press, 1978.

USING LITERATURE TO TEACH HIGHER-LEVEL THINKING SKILLS

Because human life is its subject, imagination its method, and words its medium, literature is rich and subtle in both meaning and form. Critical thinking is inherent in its study. In order to discuss and write about literature, students must use the very skills that define critical thinking, including analysis, inference, interpretation, comparison and contrast, hypothesis testing, argumentation, evaluation, and synthesis. Moreover, they must use these skills on a subject matter that requires them, as few other subjects do, to confront ambiguity and relativity; to comprehend irony; to arrive at moral and aesthetic judgments. They will also use critical thinking skills to make connections on many levels—concrete and abstract, personal and impersonal, literal and figurative. These sophisticated, but essential, mental processes are increasingly recognized as the realm of higher-order thinking.

CRITICAL THINKING IN THE *WORLD LITERATURE* TEXT

The *World Literature* text not only thoroughly exercises students' critical thinking skills in the interpretive questions and composition assignments following each selection, it also uses literature to teach thinking skills. At the end of each unit, a Critical Thinking and Writing exercise isolates an important cognitive skill to be applied to a writing assignment. (For a complete listing of these exercises, see the "Index of Skills" on text page 1494.) The "Background" material defines and explains the skill. Then the student is given detailed instruction—prewriting, writing, evaluating and revising, and proofreading and publishing—on using the skill in writing.

Students are not simply being put through the paces of an exercise; they are being shown how to think, how to approach problems, how to transfer cognitive skills from one setting to another, how to make critical thinking a habit of mind.

As you use *World Literature* to develop students' critical thinking, the following teaching strategies, derived from educational theory and cognitive psychology, will assist you.

THREE BASICS TEACHING STRATEGIES

First, continually lead students to relate literature to their own lives. This approach has several connected benefits: It makes unfamiliar material less threatening or alien, and it helps students find ways to discover writing and project topics of particular interest. It also enables students to make connections between an external reality and their personal experience—an important criterion of higher-level thinking. The student text, Annotated Teacher's Edition, and Teaching Notes demonstrate many ways to elicit these connections.

Second, take every opportunity to help students perceive the ambiguities, ironies, multiple meanings, and contrasting points of view that abound in literature. Emphasize exploration of a number of positions and supporting arguments, rather than the search for a single right answer. This attempt to see several sides of an issue is what philosopher Richard Paul calls dialogical, or dialectical, thinking. A related concept is Jean Piaget's ideal reciprocity, the ability to empathize with other people, ideas, and values.

Collaborative activities foster this kind of thinking, as do questions that require students to choose a position and assignments that concentrate on point of view. Especially important is the atmosphere you create in your classroom. When you communicate your willingness to accept students' responses and ideas, to consider differing interpretations, students will respond positively. They will learn to listen more open-mindedly to their classmates' conclusions, as well as to examine their own more carefully.

Students' assessment of their own reasoning is the third basic teaching strategy. Make students conscious of their critical thinking; make them think about their thinking. (The term for this awareness is metacognition.) The text establishes this method in the Critical Thinking and Writing exercises. You can extend it to daily classroom work in several ways. Call students' attention to their cognitive processes during discussion. Ask them how they arrived at an idea or opinion and insist that they justify interpretations with textual evidence. Whenever they disagree with a classmate's conclusion, ask them to explain how the argument is flawed. When you increase students' awareness of how they think, their thinking improves.

These three teaching strategies—guiding students to relate literature to their own lives, to think dialectically, and to consider their own thought processes—underlie the questions and exercises in the text, Annotated Teacher's Edition, and Teaching Notes. Some additional teaching ideas follow.

QUESTIONING STRATEGIES

By planning the questions you ask and when you ask them, you will be rewarded not only with students' increased enthusiasm for literature, but also with their keener thinking about it.

Initial Questions First, simply ask questions frequently. Use questions to stimulate discussion, not just to check comprehension. For example, begin the discussion of a selection with a question: Is "Borges and I" a short story? How does the speaker in Victor Hugo's "Russia 1812" feel about Napoleon? Don't force-feed your ideas about a work; let students offer theirs first. An initial question immediately creates an atmosphere of inquiry. It frees students to form their own hypotheses or to voice feelings without reference to your ideas, and it provides focal issues around which they can organize new information (Meyers 59–60).

Dialogue Questions Remember, too, that you can respond to students with questions, not statements. Meet a question with a question; turn a statement into a question; throw a problem back to the student who raised it or to the rest of the class. Whenever possible, do not "give" answers; help students find them.

A student may offer, for example, "The Metamorphosis isn't very realistic." Rather than disagreeing or agreeing and offering your own examples, draw out the student's thoughts: Why do you say that? Compelled to go beyond the vague statement, the student may reply, "Gregor's reactions to his transformation are unbelievable. He's too calm and accepting—like it's just an inconvenience and not a terrifying change." You can, of course, press the student further: Which specific reactions are you thinking of? But even at this point, the class has a specific judgment to explore (Gregor's reactions make the story unbelievable), and other students may want to jump in.

As the discussion unfolds, continue probing with questions: How do you think Gregor should have reacted? How do Gregor's reactions reveal his character? What might Kafka be trying to say by portraying Gregor this way? Use these questions to help students define their criteria for judgments, offer examples and evidence, generate hypotheses to explain inconsistencies, and so on. Such questions also create group dialogue and put students in dialogue with themselves. Pushed to elaborate, reflect, or defend, students will learn to clarify what they "really mean" and to be aware of how they arrived at a position or response.

Structured Questions When choosing or creating discussion questions, you can structure them to call forth particular types of critical thinking. Another approach is to focus on three areas: the literary work, the student's personal experience, and the external world (Christenbury and Kelly 12–15; Swope and Thompson).

About The Tempest, for example, you could ask: Why does Prospero encourage Ferdinand and Miranda's love? (The question elicits facts and inferences solely about the work.) Do you think Prospero abuses his power? Why or why not? (The question calls for the student's personal opinion.) How would Shakespeare's audience have responded to Prospero's freeing of Ariel? (The question seeks information external to the literary work.)

Each type of question can provoke critical thinking, but questions that combine two or three of the areas will lead students to more complex reasoning. A question that simultaneously elicits textual facts, opinion or personal experience, and outside information—what Christenbury and Kelly call a "dense question"—can be the focus of a class discussion, presented to the students in advance. (For example: If you were Prospero, would you have treated the conspirators the same way?) The single- and two-area questions that you ask during the discussion will help students approach the complex question by clarifying its issues and guiding students to a more fully thought-out response. (For example: What exactly does Prospero do to encourage Ferdinand and Miranda? What are his reasons, and how do you feel about them? How do you feel about his manipulations of the other characters in general?)

CLASSROOM ACTIVITIES

Experienced teachers report that students enjoy literature most when they actively participate in some way. The following sections suggest four kinds of activities that have worked successfully with high-school students.

Collaborative Interpretation Collaborative activities are especially conducive to critical thinking because they necessarily involve dialogue and exchange. Many teachers find, in fact, that lively whole-class discussions are greatly aided by initial small-group work. The following collaborative-learning activities can be used to discuss interpretive questions (Dragga).

Assign each group the same question, one that will generate different answers and require reference to the selection. Give each group about fifteen minutes to devise a collective answer, with supporting details from the text, to be reported by a group spokesperson. (Change speakers during the term so that each student serves in this role.) Because each group must arrive at a single answer, every group member is drawn into the discussion. Each student must offer, if not an original idea, at least a reasoned judgment of any suggested answer and evidence. As the groups work, you can move among them, monitoring the content and process of the discussions and helping students through impasses.

When the time limit is reached, have each spokesperson report the group's answer, explaining reasons for main ideas and citing support from the text. (For early collaborations, speakers may report from notes. Later, you may want groups to write collective essays, which the speakers will read.) In the ensuing class discussion, students will challenge each other's interpretations, defend their own arguments, build on another group's position by offering overlooked evidence, and attempt an evaluation of the differing interpretations.

The critical thinking benefits of this kind of collaboration and discussion are numerous. Students model their thinking processes for one another; examine literary works closely to find logical supporting evidence; synthesize their thoughts into a coherent spoken or written answer; and evaluate divergent interpretations of literature.

Courtroom Trials A more structured collaborative activity is a courtroom trial about a compelling conflict in a literary work (Segedy). The trial format captivates students' imaginations as it challenges their reasoning power. It keeps students' interest high not only because of its inherent drama but also because of the variety of activities required: close reading, research, debating, role-playing, and composition.

For this project, choose a narrative containing a conflict appropriate to courtroom investigation. Plan how you will delineate the actual "case" (who is bringing suit against whom for what), and decide the roles students will play. Stories, novels, and plays that focus on crimes are, of course, excellent choices. But any work that raises questions of social, ethical, or moral injustice may yield issues for prosecution and defense. (See student text page 557 for an example of a courtroom trial activity.)

Generally, you will appoint a team of three or four lawyers for each side of the case and will choose students to play characters who must appear at the trial. For some cases, you might need to involve some students as expert witnesses, such as psychologists or scientists. The attorneys must work together to develop the best possible cases to represent their clients, without contradicting the literary work in any way. They must prepare strong logical arguments, support their arguments with compelling evidence, plan their questioning of witnesses, create persuasive rhetoric, and practice their public speaking. The students playing characters must do in-depth character analyses, gleaning from the text all facts about the characters and making inferences about feelings, motives, and experiences not explicitly described. The expert witnesses must research their areas sufficiently to be able to offer sound and relevant testimony.

Any students not playing roles are paired with either a lawyer or a character as research aides. They actively participate in case preparation or in character analysis and can thus substitute for their partners during the trial if necessary.

After both sides have presented their cases, every student prepares a written summation to the jury. Students should be preparing for this persuasive composition during all pretrial work. They must also pay careful attention during the trial itself, for the proceedings may yield new ideas or arguments. For the essay, all students assume the persona of an attorney, address themselves to an imagined jury, and argue for conviction or acquittal as persuasively as possible.

Thus a courtroom trial project uses a variety of methods to improve students' critical thinking. As they work in small groups and pairs to prepare for their trial roles, students analyze, interpret, and synthesize many elements of a literary work. When they participate in the trial itself, students think on their feet as they present and defend logical arguments in dynamic, unrehearsed exchanges. Students listening to the trial observe and evaluate others' thought processes and refine their own positions accordingly. Finally, as they write the summations, students work individually to synthesize all of their experience into strong persuasive compositions.

Expert Groups In addition to having groups of students research and report on particular aspects of a literary work (see "Varying Teaching Techniques" on pages 234–237 of these Teaching Notes), you can have an expert group take complete responsibility for teaching one of the text selections (Bonfiglio). This more sophisticated collaborative activity should be reserved for later in the term, after students have worked through many selections with you, and should be assigned only to students capable of independent work. The expert groups must devise an entire project plan, not simply follow directions, and must accomplish their plans without supervision.

Assign an appropriate text selection, and explain that the group is to serve as teacher for that selection. They must decide how to present the work (classroom methods and teaching focus), conduct necessary research, and decide how to divide the labor. Members of the group can use or create visual aids, and you can also require a written outline of the presentation. Encourage students to use their imaginations, to think of innovative ways to engage their classmates' interest while presenting sound insights into the literary work.

This activity requires critical thinking on two levels. First, students must analyze, interpret, and evaluate the literary work, and they must also propose, prepare, and execute a teaching plan. Throughout the project, they must make judgments both about the selection and about their presentation; they must solve problems of interpretation and of group interaction, compare and contrast teaching methods, organize their presentation into a coherent sequence, and so on. The task is challenging but extremely beneficial, and satisfying, particularly for advanced students, who use higher-level reasoning not only to investigate literature but also to communicate their findings to others.

Oral Composition Oral composition is a collaborative activity that specifically develops metacognition (awareness of one's thinking processes). Again, students need some preparation for this technique. You should attempt it only after students have completed several of the text's Critical Thinking and Writing exercises or after you have accustomed students—through comments and questions during discussion—to the exercise of reflecting on their own and their classmates' reasoning processes. Vinz describes an effective paired-student approach to oral composition.

Give each student in the pair a different interpretive essay question about a selection. Select or create questions that do not have clear right and wrong answers, such as those requiring decision making or problem solving. (For example: Does Daru in Camus' "The Guest" make an ethical decision or avoid making a decision? Could you change the setting of "The Guest" and yet preserve the story's existential theme?) You may use the same two questions for all pairs in the class.

For this open-book activity, students take turns as speaker-writers and listeners. The speaking-writing student is to compose *aloud* an answer to the question. The listening student is to take notes on the speaker's composition process. Explain that the speaker-writers are simply to say aloud exactly what they are thinking as they plan and draft their essays. Remind them of what they do normally during prewriting: brainstorm, consider and reject ideas, articulate a possible thesis, look for supporting evidence, contemplate how best to arrange their main points. The point of oral composition is to get students to recognize and verbalize these processes. Speaker-writers should write down important prewriting notes and then begin to draft their essays.

The listeners are to observe, interpret, and record the composers' thought processes; they do not comment aloud. They might note how much time their partners spend on different processes (free-associating ideas, searching for supporting facts, evaluating their own thoughts, rereading and revising a draft paragraph). They should note how often good ideas come from chance associations and what seems most often to stop the flow of the composer's ideas. Listeners should also observe whether the composer is methodical, completing each line of thought before starting another, or more unstructured, willing to leave a difficulty unresolved and move on to something else.

You may want to set aside portions of two class periods for each speaker-writer to generate a first draft (students can work alone to write final versions of their essays). Then have the pairs exchange and discuss their listener-notes.

As a summarizing activity, both students should write, perhaps as a journal assignment, what they learned about their own thinking processes. The oral composition process itself, as well as the listener's written observations, should lead to some insight for all students. They may ask themselves: exactly how, and how well, do I think my way through problems? What could I change, improve? What did I learn from my partner's reasoning and composing process that I could adopt?

REFERENCES AND FURTHER READING FOR THE TEACHER

Bonfiglio, Joseph F. "Collection, Connection, Projection: Using Written and Oral Presentation to Encourage Thinking Skills." NCTE 93–96.
Christenbury, Leila, and Patricia P. Kelly. *Questioning: A Path to Critical Thinking*. Urbana,

IL: ERIC Clearinghouse on Reading and Communication Skills and National Council of Teachers of English, 1983.

Dragga, Sam. "Collaborative Interpretation." NCTE 84–87.

Educational Leadership 42 (1984).

Lazere, Donald. "Critical Thinking in College English Studies." Urbana, IL: ERIC Clearinghouse on Reading and Communication Skills and National Council of Teachers of English, 1987.

Meyers, Chet. *Teaching Students to Think Critically.* San Francisco: Jossey-Bass, 1986.

Muldoon, Phyllis A. "Challenging Students to Think: Shaping Questions, Building Community." *English Journal*, April 1990, 34–40.

NCTE (National Council of Teachers of English) Committee on Classroom Practices. Chair Jeff Golub. *Activities to Promote Critical Thinking.* Urbana, IL: NCTE, 1986.

Parker, Walter C. "Teaching Thinking: The Pervasive Approach." *Journal of Teacher Education* 38.3 (1987): 50–56.

Segedy, Michael. "Adapting the Courtroom Trial Format to Literature." NCTE 88–92.

Swope, John W., and Edgar H. Thompson. "Three R's for Critical Thinking About Literature: Reading, 'Riting, and Responding." NCTE 75–79.

Vinz, Ruth. "Thinking Through Dilemmas." NCTE 107–111.

TEACHING STUDENTS TO VARY READING RATES

The ability to read flexibly (that is, at different rates according to purpose and subject matter) is a valuable skill for students of literature. If students learn to adjust their reading rates and habits, they are likely both to improve their comprehension and to increase their enjoyment of literature.

To introduce the concept of reading flexibility, draw on students' experience with recreational reading. Suppose they have just acquired a new novel by a favorite author. Ask what they read first, how many times they read all or part of the novel, and what they look for as they read. Responses might run along these lines: They first read the title and any other information on the cover and may glance at any illustrations or chapter titles, all to get an idea of the subject and the plot. They may also read a few pages quickly to see whether the setting, characters, tone, and style are familiar. Then they probably settle on a comfortable pace to read the whole story, perhaps stopping occasionally to think about what a character says or does. Later they may come back to the story, rereading certain pages quickly to locate a character's exact words or more slowly to recapture the feeling of a favorite scene. They may even reread the whole story to see more clearly how early events led to the climax. Use this example to show students that they (1) usually read something more than once to get the most out of it, (2) do sometimes vary the speed at which they read, and (3) choose a pace based on their purpose for reading.

SETTING A PURPOSE

Students often mistakenly believe that studying and enjoying literature are two mutually exclusive purposes. Some may argue that their main purpose in reading a literature anthology's selections should be pleasure—having to "appreciate" each selection through study spoils the fun. These students don't realize that enjoyment is built on understanding,

and that the mental struggle itself can be a pleasure. Readers will take more pleasure in the irony of a story when they recognize the technique and understand how the writer uses it to manipulate our responses. Furthermore, students can better articulate a personal response to a work if they possess the terms to talk about it. Full enjoyment of literature, then, requires reading for several purposes: to get an overview, to respond to ideas and literary techniques, to locate important details, to refresh the memory, or to generate new ideas.

Naming one of these purposes for a particular reading is just the first step. An active reader takes another important step: formulating initial questions to be answered while reading. For example, to get an overview, a reader might ask: What type of work is it? What is the topic? When was it written, and by whom? To locate particular details, a reader might ask: What key words or phrases will help me find the details? Am I likely to find them near the beginning, the middle, or the end of the work? Such reading-purpose questions not only further define the purpose but also provide an active reading plan.

With a definite purpose in mind, students should more easily identify a suitable reading rate. In general, they should use an average, or "most comfortable," rate when reading for pleasure. They should read faster when reading to get an overview, locate details, refresh the memory, or generate ideas. And they should learn to slow down when reading to respond to the writer's ideas and language. Students can apply this approach to literature by using the following reading techniques.

SKIMMING

Skimming is reading quickly for main ideas—just how quickly, in terms of words per minute, will vary from person to person. A rule of thumb is that the skimming speed should be twice as fast as the individual's average reading rate (Fry). To achieve the higher speed, the reader skips some sentences or details, concentrating instead on reading just enough of each paragraph to get its main idea. Since the reader does not consider every detail, the level of comprehension necessarily decreases somewhat. Some teachers like to describe skimming as a "prereading" or "rereading" activity; this distinction often helps students decide when to use the technique.

Perhaps most important is the use of skimming as a prereading activity. Explain to students that the common habit of simply opening the book to the right page and reading straight through once at an average rate is not the most efficient—or rewarding—reading approach. When they open the book to read a selection, they should first skim the title, the headnote, background information about the writer and the work, chapter or section titles, the questions and assignments that follow the selection, and their own notes from preliminary class instruction. The purpose of skimming a work before they read is to obtain an overview of the work. This skimming will help students prepare specific questions to be explored in a close reading.

As a rereading activity, skimming is an efficient way to review main ideas of a work and mentally summarize a personal response to it. A student might quickly go over a selection with questions such as these in mind: What does the writer say about life or about people? What literary devices does the writer use? Does the work end as I expected it to? How did it make me feel, and why? If skimming reveals a point of confusion, the student can slow down for a more careful rereading. Note that students may also use skimming to review their class discussion notes.

Skimming is useful, too, for generating writing topics. To questions like those above, a student searching for a topic might add these: Why was I drawn to a particular character, passage, or scene? Which literary element of the work seems most effective? Does this work have something in common with another I have read? How does the theme of the work relate to my own life?

CLOSE READING

A close reading is a slow and careful reading for the purpose of analyzing and evaluating a literary work. For class discussion and many assignments, mature readers may need to read at this "thoughtful" pace only once. When reading a difficult or lengthy work and when writing essays, almost all students should do two or more close readings, at least of portions of the work.

What all of your students should begin to realize is that in reading literature closely, they are seeking three levels of understanding: literal, inferential, and critical. Put another way, they must read the lines, read between the lines, and read beyond the lines (Poindexter and Prescott). You no doubt have found students to be most comfortable, and most practiced, at the literal level—understanding directly stated details. They usually need more help at the inferential level—understanding implied ideas—and at the critical level—understanding a writer's purposes and making value judgments about a piece of literature.

Posing Questions Before students begin a close reading, have them list a few questions about the selection to guide their initial reading. Use the text's Reader's Guide pages and headnotes and the teaching suggestions in the Annotated Teacher's Edition and these Teaching Notes to help them ask appropriate and specific questions. The Background, Writer's Response, and Literary Focus sections of each Reader's Guide will contain several suggestions for a guided reading. The headnote introducing each selection directs attention to a particular aspect of the work, and often ends by posing a reading purpose question. Several sections in the Annotated Teacher's Edition, such as the Objectives, Prereading Focus, and reading skills annotations will give you additional ideas for elements that students can look for and consider as they read. Posing initial questions sets a precise purpose for close reading, activates students' prior knowledge of both literature and cultural values, and arouses personal interest in a literary work.

Predicting Outcomes For several selections, the student text and the Annotated Teacher's Edition suggest a stopping place in the reading, a point at which students are asked to predict what will happen and give reasons for their opinions. Take full advantage of this strategy, and use it for other selections whenever practicable. Many teachers have found that predicting outcomes encourages not only a rich exchange of ideas in the classroom but also multilevel comprehension, more so than would a traditional review of what has been read so far (Nessel). In order to predict the resolution of events, students must recall essential literal details, draw inferences about the situation and characters, and evaluate the writer's intent. Thus, the class gains a review as well as practice in critical thinking. Evaluate the predictions not on how close students come to the writer's conclusion but rather on how logically they form and support their hypotheses.

Responding Personally Suggest to students that their ultimate goal in reading closely is to understand their own intellectual and emotional responses to a literary work—what they liked or disliked and why, how the work affected them, and why. They should think about their reactions as they read and when they discuss the work in class.

Alert students to the questions and assignments that follow each selection. These features will help guide them, during a close reading, through the three levels of comprehension and will lead them,

---

after the reading, to an organized expression of their personal responses through creative and critical writing and/or speaking and listening activities.

FOLLOWING GUIDELINES FOR READING

Certain close-reading techniques apply generally to literature; others are important to particular types of literary works. You may want to duplicate and hand out the following guidelines, which are addressed to students.

GUIDELINES FOR READING LITERATURE CLOSELY

1. Write down a few questions you would like to answer as you read the selection. The skimming you did to get an overview of the work will help you pose questions, as will your teacher's introduction. Perhaps your question will relate to something you read on the Reader's Guide page, to a suggestion in the headnote, or even to the title of the selection.

2. Take notes as you read. Jot down answers you find to your initial questions as well as any further questions that come to mind. Note your impression of the characters. Note passages that seem to hint at the writer's purpose or theme, passages that are particularly vivid to you, and passages that seem confusing. Identify how different parts of the work make you feel.

3. Stop occasionally to think about what you have read. Ask yourself these questions: What main ideas or events have been presented so far? What do I think will happen next?

4. Look up unfamiliar words and allusions or use context clues to make educated guesses. Some definitions will be found in the textbook's Glossary (text pages 1474–1487). Keep your dictionary handy for words that seem important but that you can't figure out.

5. Keep in mind the type of literature you are reading. The questions you ask often relate to the literary form. Here are some specific hints:

Fiction. Look for the elements of story-telling: What is the point of view? The narrator's tone? What conflict or conflicts does the writer create? What complicates the problem? What are the main events of the plot? How does one event cause another to happen? How does the setting affect the story? What passage marks the climax? How is the main conflict resolved? What is the theme of the story?

Poetry. Read a poem several times, at least once out loud. (If the poetry is in an epic or a play, read each section or scene several times.) Pay particular attention to punctuation; it will help you follow the writer's ideas and help you "hear" the emphasized words. Paraphrase lines or passages that are not immediately clear. Which words or lines do you think are most important in the poem. Make a note of figures of speech, and look for the writer's main idea. Is a central thought or emotion expressed? Or is the poet telling a story? Try to state the main idea in one or two sentences.

Nonfiction. Be alert for the writer's attitudes toward the topic and toward the people described. Is the writer's tone humorous, serious, sympathetic, hostile, or some combination of these feelings? Is the work objective, or is it written from a subjective, or personal, point of view? Does the writer use narrative techniques, such as foreshadowing or suspense, to hold your interest? Decide what the writer's main purpose is: to tell a story, to explain or inform, to describe, or to persuade. Notice how the writer organizes information, and make an informal outline of the main points. Then determine the main idea of the work. Is it directly stated? Implied? How do you feel about the idea?

Drama. Who wants what, and what steps are taken to get it? What complications arise? Who drives the action? What feeling about life or people is the writer expressing?

SCANNING

Scanning is reading very rapidly to locate details. Students unfamiliar with the term are likely to recognize the technique when it is explained. They use scanning to find a name and number in the telephone book, a listing in the television program guide, or a definition in the dictionary. Scanning is faster than skimming, because the reader is searching for key words rather than reading sentences or phrases to isolate ideas. The reader may focus the mind and eye by moving a finger rapidly across and down the page, not stopping until the key word or phrase is found.

In the study of literature, scanning is most useful as a rereading activity. When students have already read a work and know its organization, they can use scanning to answer certain kinds of follow-up questions, usually ones of literal comprehension (Who? What? Where? When?). For example, you may ask a student to identify Homeric similes that help describe a certain episode in an epic. The student would first locate the episode and then find the similes by scanning for key words such as *like* and *as*.

Two things essential to scanning successfully are having a sense of a work's organization (Should I look first in the beginning, middle, or end? Didn't that scene close an early chapter?) and choosing key words or phrases appropriate to the search (Which words in the question are keys? What key words are implied by the question?). When students think they have located the detail, they should stop to read the sentences around it to make sure they are correct. If they discover that they are frequently inaccurate when scanning, they should slow their pace for a while and check their choice of key words.

You can give the class a timed practice in scanning during your vocabulary exercises. List on the board five to ten vocabulary words, out of alphabetical order, that are defined in the Glossary. Tell students to write down for each one the word that follows it in the Glossary. Explain that you will start the stopwatch when they begin scanning and after one minute will begin putting the time on the board in ten-second intervals. When each student has finished the last item, he or she can then write down the last time given on the board. Check the answers and response times in class, and suggest further practice at home to increase speed or improve accuracy.

PROMOTING THE GROWTH OF STUDENTS' VOCABULARY

Many teachers have found that a concentrated effort on vocabulary during literature study results in great gains in students' active vocabularies. Often in such efforts you first must convince students of the value of a larger vocabulary. Besides continually sharing your own enthusiasm for words, you can easily demonstrate the necessity and power of language. Tell students to close their eyes for a few moments and to think thoughts for which there are no words. After a minute or so, the class will probably protest that it can't be done. This response is the point of the exercise: Words are essential to thought. Point out that the more words students know, the better they will be able to understand and communicate their ideas.

In guiding students through vocabulary for the selections, you will probably find that a multifaceted approach is most effective—a combination of dictionary use, context study, and structural analysis.

DICTIONARY USE

Here are a few ideas for encouraging the dictionary habit.

1. Have students turn to the Glossary (text pages 1474–1487) during your general introduction to the anthology. Go over the pronunciation key to review common symbols for sounds, and point out the abbreviations for parts of speech. Remind students that many words have multiple meanings, and note that the Glossary defines words according to their use in the selections.

2. Use a short, timed exercise to check students' basic dictionary skills. Provide dictionaries, and give the class five minutes to look up and write down the pronunciation and first definition of three words from a selection. Check responses for the third word, asking about problems in following guide words, alphabetization, or pronunciation symbols.

3. Show students how to use dictionaries quickly and effectively when reading literature. Tell them to keep handy a supply of blank index cards. As they encounter unfamiliar words, they can jot down each one on a card, with the page number for reference, and later look up several words at once. Direct them to write the pronunciation under the word, say the word aloud, and, on the back of the card, write the part of speech and meaning that fit the context. Have students bring in their cards every week or two and compare their collections.

4. Pay special attention to words with interesting histories. Help students understand how to read an etymology and give them some in-class practice. Give examples that will help them discover that a word is borrowed from another language, for example, or that it derives from an old custom. Show students how to use special dictionaries of word and phrase origins.

5. Review usage labels in the dictionary when the class studies Americanisms, jargon, colloquialisms, and so on.

6. Be sure students understand that a dictionary's method of numbering definitions is significant. Some dictionaries begin with the oldest sense of a word, others with the most frequent usage. Have the class look up words such as dashboard, temperance, and wardrobe to see how the use of certain words has changed over time.

7. Emphasize pronunciation in your dictionary drills to help students "sound out" new words.

CONTEXT STUDY

The following activities will help students learn *and use* new words through recognizing context clues, making connections between words, and creating new contexts through original writing. The following suggestions are ways to reinforce students' use of context clues when they are reading or listening.

1. Before class begins, write on the board a sentence about the day's literary topic. The sentence should contain two or three new vocabulary words, with some clue to their meanings. Underline the vocabulary words.

When students arrive, ask them to write a paraphrase of the sentence, without using the underlined words, while you call the roll. Discuss their responses, asking what context clues they used. Use the exercise as a springboard to your reading or discussion of the selection.

2. If you are reading a selection aloud, stop occasionally when you come to an unfamiliar word, and ask students for context clues to its meaning.

3. Use the vocabulary words in your comments to let students hear them in context.

4. When the vocabulary list for a selection is long, assign different words to different students. Ask them to find for each word a context clue, a synonym, and an antonym and then share these in a class discussion.

5. Have students look for vocabulary words in contexts other than the text selection. For example, ask them to locate and paraphrase famous quotations in which the words appear.

(Suggest that they look for quotations by using the index to *Bartlett's Familiar Quotations* or another book of quotations. If a word does not appear in such an index, searching for a quotation with a vocabulary word will probably be futile.)

6. For quick reviews, write on the chalkboard the sentences from the selection that contain the vocabulary words, but replace the words with blanks. Ask students to fill in the blanks with the correct word from an alphabetized list, and discuss how they made their choices.

The next two activities emphasize word relationships.

7. Review synonyms or antonyms for vocabulary words by devising short matching quizzes. You might have students create them: Assign a small group to select ten words and put together a scrambled list of synonyms (or antonyms). Check the group's work, and have them write the two lists on the chalkboard, one list numbered, the other lettered. Ask the rest of the class to match the words.

8. Review any group of related words with a simple crossword puzzle using the words' definitions as clues. You may create the puzzle yourself or have students volunteer to do it. Give the puzzle a title that classifies the group of words, such as "Vivid Adverbs" or "Words That Describe [a character's name]." Some teachers also find such puzzles effective as a review of literary terms: "The Elements of Drama," "Sound Effects in Poetry," and so on.

The following activities require students to write new contexts for the words they are studying. Several suggestions also take advantage of the strategy of centering word study on a concept.

9. Have students create their own direct context clues for new words. Ask them to write sentences for vocabulary words, giving a clue to meaning by definition, example, restatement, comparison, or contrast.

10. Explain that some words have *connotations* (emotional associations) as well as *denotations* (dictionary meanings). To explore connotative meaning, have students use five vocabulary words in original sentences and then substitute a synonym for each vocabulary word. How well does the synonym work in the same context? Does the synonym have exactly the same connotations? Ask students what difference in meaning or feeling is created.

11. Choose two or three vocabulary words that have distinctive multiple meanings, and ask students to write a sentence using each meaning.

12. If the vocabulary words for a selection number fewer than ten, offer students the challenge of writing one sentence using as many of the words as possible. However fanciful, the sentence must be intelligible.

13. When the vocabulary list for a selection is long, group the words by part of speech. Have students write a sentence using one word from each group and compare their sentences.

14. For a group of adjectives, ask students to create comparisons. For example, Sarah is more *disconsolate* than a lost kitten.

15. Encourage students' use of active verbs by having them write sentences in which they apply new verbs to a school situation.

16. When several vocabulary words for a selection relate to a particular geographical or cultural setting, introduce the words as a group. For example, *adobe, arroyo, mesa, mission* (church), and *tumbleweed* are words of the West or Southwest. Have students identify the common element through definitions and etymologies and then write sentences or a paragraph using the words.

17. If students are learning descriptive words that apply to a character in a selection, ask them to write sentences applying the words to other characters they have studied.

18. Assign different students, one or two at a time, to use vocabulary words in writing three or four quiz questions about a selection's plot, characters, or setting. At the beginning of class, the students can call on classmates to answer the questions, orally correcting the answers and clarifying the meanings of the vocabulary words when necessary.

19. For a review of words from several selections, group them according to an emotion or idea. Have students write new sentences using each word.

20. Encourage regular attention to new words by offering bonus points for the appropriate use of vocabulary words in the text writing assignments and in class discussions.

21. On Fridays, have students vote on their favorite new word from the week's vocabulary. Ask them to explain their choices.

STRUCTURAL ANALYSIS

Students can often learn and remember new words by breaking them into recognizable parts. Try these activities for an approach that focuses on roots and affixes. A list of common Greek and Latin word parts follows the activities.

1. Have students make a personal set of flashcards of Greek and Latin roots and affixes. Introduce a few roots, prefixes, and suffixes at a time, having students write each one on an index card. On the other side of the card, students should write the meaning of the root or affix, along with an example that you provide —preferably a vocabulary word or literary term already assigned. Tell students to be alert throughout the term to vocabulary words (as well as words from other sources) that contain these roots and affixes and to add the words to their cards. Remind them that some words, such as *infallible*, will be recorded on more than one card.

   Every week or two, ask students to bring in their collections of vocabulary flashcards. Divide the class into small groups for peer quizzing with the cards. Spot-check the cards and quizzing to evaluate students' progress and to decide on review strategies. (After you have introduced several groups of word parts, you may want the students themselves to begin presenting new roots and affixes from their assigned vocabulary or from other reading.)

2. In one lesson present prefixes that show position. Guide students in identifying and defining words with these prefixes. The examples might be vocabulary words from the selections, literary terms, or more familiar words encountered in the text.

3. Encourage students to recognize prefixes that create a negative or opposite meaning. Ask students to complete a list of "not" definitions with words they have studied.

4. To help students recognize the grammatical function of an unfamiliar word in context show them how suffixes often—*not always*—signal a particular part of speech. Students can make a note on their suffix flashcards or list the groups in a vocabulary notebook, but remind them to watch for exceptions. In some words the ending looks like a suffix but actually is part of a root or base word.

5. After you define a common Greek or Latin root in a new word, divide students into small groups, and, setting a time limit, have them list familiar words built on the same root. The group with the longest list could receive bonus points.

6. Occasionally review small groups of prefix, suffix, and root definitions with oral and written quizzes. For variety in the quizzes, you could create crossword puzzles or conduct a group competition on the pattern of a spelldown. There are hundreds of roots and affixes, and the following lists contain only a selection of those that students may learn through their vocabulary study in literature. As you introduce the study of word parts, point out that the spellings of roots and affixes sometimes vary, that affixes almost always alter the root's meaning in some way, and that the meanings of some Latin and Greek roots have undergone slight changes over time.

ROOTS

Greek

bio-	life (*biography*)
-chron-	time (*chronological*)
-crac-, -crat-	power, rule (*democracy, autocrat*)
-cris-, -crit-	separate, judge (*crisis, critical*)
-cycl-	circle (*Cyclops*)
-glos-, -glot-	tongue (*glossary, polygot*)
-graph-	write, record (*biography, photograph*)
-log-, -logy-	speaking, study (*chronology, dialogue*)
-ops-, -opt-	eye (*Cyclops, optical*)
-phon-	sound (*phonetic*)
-stereo-	firm, solid (*stereotype*)

Latin

-aud-	hear (*audible*)
-cred-	believe (*incredulous*)
-dict-	tell, say (*prediciton*)
-duc-, -duct-	load, draw (*deduction, produce*)
-fac-, -fic-	make, do (*benefactor, fiction*)
-flect-	bend (*deflect, reflection*)
-ject-	throw (*projectile, reject*)
-leg-, lect-	read (*legend, lecture*)
-loqu-	speak (*eloquent*)
-mis-, -mit-	send (*commission, noncommital*)
-mort-	die (*immortality*)
-quer-, -quest-, -quir-	seek, ask (*query, quest, inquiry*)
-sci-	know (*omniscient*)
-scrib-, -script-	write (*describe, manuscript*)
-spec-, -spic-, -spect-	look at, examine (*circumspect, speculate, inspect*)
-tens-, -tent-	hold (*tenant, untenable*)
-vers-, -vert-	turn (*averse, invert, versatile*)
-vid-, -vis-	see (*videotape, visage, visual*)
-viv-	live (*vivacious, vivid*)

PREFIXES

Greek

a-	not, without (*atheist, atypical*)
ant-	against (*antagonist*)
auto-	self (*autobiography*)
dia-	through, across, between (*dialogue*)
exo-	out of, outside (*exodus*)
mono-	one (*monologue*)
poly-	many (*polytheism*)
pro-	before, first (*protagonist*)
syn-	with, together (*synthesis*)

Latin

a-, ab-, abs-	away, from (*abominable, abscond, abhor*)
ad-	to, toward (*adversary, advocate*)
ante-	before (*antecedent*)
bene-	well (*benediction, benefactor*)
circum-	around, on all sides (*circumstances*)
com-, con-	with, together (*complicity, connotation*)
contra-	against (*contrary*)
de-	from, down (*denotation, denouement, depress*)
dis-	apart, away (*dispel, disrepute*)
e-, ex-	out (*evade, exorbitant*)
extra-	outside of, beyond (*extravagant, extraordinary*)
il-, im-, in-, ir-	not (*incredulous, irresolute*) or in, into, on (*impetus, inversion*)

inter-	between (*intermediary*)
non-	not (*nonentity*)
omni-	all, everywhere (*omniscient*)
per-	through (*perpetual*)
post-	after, behind (*postpone, postscript*)
pre-	before (*prewriting*)
pro-	forward (*projectile*)
re-	again, back (*redress, reference, resolution*)
soli-	alone, only (*soliloquy, solitude*)
sub-, sup-	under, beneath, below (*subversive, support*)
super-	above, over, outside (*superficial*)
trans-	across (*transluscent*)

SUFFIXES

-able, -ible	able to (*formidable, infallible*)
-age, -ance, -ence, -ity, -ment, -ness, -ship, -tion	a state or condition (*atonement, calamity, carnage, gyration, indulgence, patronage, vigilance*)
-al, -ic, -ly	similar to (*acutely, cynical, heroic*)
-an, -ee, -eer, -er, -ian, -ist, -ite, -or	a person, one who (*barbarian, mountaineer, civilian, strategist, writer, actor*)
-ate	to act or do (*evaluate, perpetrate*)
-er, -est	degree (*shadier, shadiest*)
-ful, -ous	full of (*fearful, ominous*)
-less	without (*artless, ruthless*)

VARYING TEACHING TECHNIQUES

Using a variety of teaching techniques keeps students' interest high and encourages their personal involvement with literature. A variety of approaches also allows you to accommodate individual learning styles. The following teaching suggestions make the study of literature an active, multifaceted experience for your class.

COLLABORATIVE LEARNING

To foster regular collaborative learning, you may want to assign students to groups (no more than five or six members) and to pairs early in the year. Use a random selection method such as counting-off. Then you will waste no time forming groups for each new activity. You may change the groups and pairs at some point, but do not change them too frequently. Students benefit from working with the same classmates for an extended period. They begin to appreciate different learning styles and abilities, and they develop a team spirit. The two group methods that follow have many applications in a literature course.

Expert Groups. In this technique, members of a small group become highly knowledgeable about one aspect of a topic or literary work and serve as experts for the other students. When you are reading *Oedipus Rex*, for example, one group might become experts on the Greek theater and another on the Aristotelian concept of tragedy. The expert groups report to the class and answer whatever questions their classmates may have about their area of expertise. The benefit of this strategy is twofold: Group members gain experience in intensive research, and all students gain more information about a topic or a work.

Jigsawing. Jigsawing, which uses two levels of groups, is another method by which students become each other's teachers. The method is particularly effective for covering lengthy or complex material when class time is limited. For example, suppose you want your class to paraphrase five paragraphs of difficult prose. Divide the students into five groups, assign one paragraph to each group, and set a time limit for the paraphrase. (Whenever possible, use any standing groups for this first jigsaw level.)

When the students have finished, make a second-level group assignment. Within each group, have students count off (or designate themselves by letters, colors, and so on) and then move into their second groups—all 1's, (A's, reds) together, 2's (B's, blues) together, and so on. Each student now becomes the "expert" for the paragraph paraphrased in his or her first group and presents the information to members of the second group.

Jigsawing also works well with lengthy vocabulary lists or an exercise containing many items. In those cases, divide the words or items equally among the first-level groups and then proceed as before to the second-level groups.

INTO, THROUGH, AND BEYOND TECHNIQUES

Many teachers think of three distinct stages in teaching a selection: preparing students for it; guiding them through it; and offering them bridges from it to other works, ideas, and activities. Here is a summary of types of activities appropriate to each stage. Detailed descriptions of concept formation, imaging, debating moral dilemmas, journal writing, sensory recall, and Readers' Theater follow the summary.

To lead students *into* a work:
1. Use filmstrips, films, or recordings to arouse students' interest.
2. Invite lecturers to provide special background on a selection. The speakers may be knowledgeable about a particular work, author, or literary topic or may have experience that relates to a selection. (Someone who has visited or lived in Egypt, for example, could provide background for Mahfouz's "Half a Day.")
3. Introduce the work with a variety of background information (history, the author's biography, technical explanations), using the text's introductions and the supplementary information in the Annotated Teacher's Edition.
4. Distribute plot summaries, study guides, or character lists for difficult or lengthy works.
5. Have students master vocabulary words before they begin to read, using a variety of strategies. (See "Promoting the Growth of Students' Vocabulary" pages 231–234 of these Teaching Notes.)
6. Encourage skimming as a prereading step, and guide students in posing questions for a close reading (see "Teaching Students to Vary Reading Rates," pages 228–231).
7. Use the techniques of concept formation, imaging, and journal quick-writes (see pages 235–236).
8. Read portions of the selection orally.

To guide students *through* a work:
1. Assign the questions following the text selections for discussion or writing. Assign the creative and critical writing exercises for individual or collaborative work.
2. Pause during in-class readings to allow students to predict outcomes.
3. Assign groups of students to dramatize and perform brief scenes from a story or novel.
4. Organize debates on issues and moral dilemmas raised by a work (see page 236).
5. Have students keep dialectical journals.
6. Schedule Readers' Theater presentations.
7. Lead imaging and sensory recall exercises (see page 236).
8. Assign reports and projects for class presentation, encouraging forms of expression other than writing (creating maps, illustrations, charts, timelines; performing; composing original music; and so on).

To lead students *beyond* a work:
1. Encourage students to make connections between the work and other works they have read. The connections may be with works in the same genre or in a different genre. Possible connections include subject, theme, major symbols, imagery, allusions, historical setting, and so on. Students may present their comparisons and contrasts in compositions, reports, and projects.
2. Suggest further reading of works by the same author, of books and articles related to the selection's background, and of works in the same genre.
3. Have a group of students write and produce an original video play inspired by some aspect of the selection (a moral dilemma, a character, a striking element such as horror).
4. Have students create games based on literary selections.
5. Have a group of students assume the personae of characters from different works and engage in a panel discussion on a specific topic. Instruct students to prepare carefully for their roles so that they can respond in character and in a way appropriate to their time.

CONCEPT FORMATION

When students use concept formation to approach a new work, they practice both classifying and predicting. To use this technique, present students—without any preliminary explanation—with a list of words, objects, names, or ideas taken from or related to the selection. (You may restrict the list to one category of information or mix the several categories.) Ask the students to group items that seem related and then to formulate predictions about the selection based on the items and their common elements. For example, from the vocabulary list for "The Nose," students might isolate *acolyte*, *prayer*, *disciple*, and *temple*, predicting—even without knowing the story's title—

that religion will figure largely in the tale. From a list that contains the names of characters in *"The Pig,"* students might predict that the novel is set in Africa.

Concept formation, in addition to sharpening critical thinking, involves students actively in a work even before they begin reading. An unexplained list can be an intriguing puzzle, and once students have made predictions based on such a list, they may read a selection with more eagerness and more purpose.

IMAGING

Imaging taps students' imaginations, leading them into a literary work through sensory awareness. Acting as guide, you ask students to close their eyes and then "talk" them into a specific time, place, or mental state. You may play mood-setting or period music, and tell students to draw on their sensory memories as you give them a description rich in sensory detail.

Imaging is effective with image-rich poetry as well as with narratives; you may use it to introduce a selection as well as to focus on individual passages and sections. For example, you may want to set the stage for Gabriel García Márquez's "The Handsomest Drowned Man in the World" by guiding students in imagining the sights, sounds, and smells of a coastal village in Central America. Imaging not only helps remove barriers to understanding of culture, time, and place but also shows students their own considerable power to evoke sensory experiences from words.

MORAL DILEMMAS

Moral dilemmas arising from conflicts within literary works are an approach that engages students' feelings and stimulates their critical thinking. You may use an actual situation from a work (the moral dilemma Daru faces in deciding what to do about the Arab prisoner in "The Guest") or an extrapolation from it (a similar situation involving a terrorist). Whichever you choose, describe the situation in such a way that students are forced to take sides. (Some other provocative conflicts are those pitting individual conscience against law and those forcing a choice between loyalties to two friends or two family members.)

Have students articulate the opposing positions. Then write each as a statement on the board, and ask students to take sides by a show of hands. Divide students on each side into smaller groups for developing supporting arguments. Allow sufficient time, and then, taking one side at a time, have each group's spokesperson present one supporting argument. Go from group to group until supporting arguments are exhausted, and then allow a free exchange of rebuttals, guiding the discussion as necessary. Be sure each student comes to some formal closure about the moral dilemma, perhaps through a journal entry or a brief essay.

JOURNALS

Journals are excellent tools for literature study: They encourage personal responses to literary works; allow freer, less formal writing; build a repository of writing ideas; and offer students a full year's record of their changing perspectives and thoughts. A loose-leaf notebook will allow students to make both private entries and assigned entries for your review. When you make journal assignments, specify those that must be turned in. Students should feel secure that no one has access to their private entries.

Two specialized uses of journals follow.

Dialectical Journals. Sometimes called dialogue journals, dialectical journals are double-entry records in which students take notes about a literary work and then add their own reflections about the notes. Each page is divided into two columns labeled "Note-taking" and "Note-making." Notes about the work may include facts, passages, quoted dialogue, significant plot developments, and so on. The students' recorded musings about these notes will be personal, but occasionally you may want to direct a particular kind of response. (For example, you could direct students to "take" notes about a poem's imagery and then to "make" notes about their emotional responses to the images).

A dialectical journal is valuable because students are forced to go beyond facts and think about what they read. Encourage students also to review all their entries for a selection, and then write a summary of their personal response.

Quick-Writes. The aim of a quick-write journal entry is an immediate, spontaneous, unedited response to a stimulus. Possible stimuli are many: a passage from a selection, an idea you supply, music, guided imaging and sensory recall, and so on. Quick-writes can be used in all three stages of teaching a selection (into, through, and beyond).

SENSORY RECALL

Literature presents all readers with emotions and situations far removed from their own experience. Sensory recall, a technique by which professionals prepare for acting roles, is one means of making these unfamiliar experiences more understandable. An actress playing a character who, after extreme provocation, physically attacks someone may have no experience with such violence, for example. To help her "get in touch" with her character's feelings, the director may ask her to remember being driven crazy by mosquitoes and then to act out the resulting scene. Under the director's coaching, the actress begins to understand her character's response to the provocation and can then build a believable series of emotions for her role.

An adaptation of this theatrical approach can help students identify with unfamiliar characters and understand emotions otherwise out of their reach. As an introduction, students may enjoy watching a classmate with acting experience demonstrate the technique, but all students can participate in sensory recall. First, isolate an experience in a selection, build an appropriate parallel situation (or brainstorm situations with students), and then have students put themselves in that situation and write their thoughts and feelings. You might use sensory recall, for example, to make accessible the bizarre events in "The Metamorphosis," beginning with the main character's awakening to find himself transformed into a giant bug. Ask students to recall awakening in the middle of the night after a disturbing dream. Elicit from them memories of the feelings of disorientation, and they will begin to feel more acutely the narrator's frame of mind in Kafka's story.

Initially, you will have to lead students in using sensory recall, but after some practice, they will be able to create their own parallel situations and record their responses in their journals.

READERS' THEATER

Readers' Theater is simply a group oral reading of a selection, whether the work is a play, story, poem, or essay. Effective Readers' Theater is not impromptu, however. Students are assigned roles, or passages, and practice their reading outside of class. Readers' Theater hones students' skills in oral interpretation and makes a work come alive for the whole class. It is a dramatic presentation with a minimum of production worries (you need only stools or chairs) and stage-fright problems (most students are much less frightened of sitting and reading than of acting).

Students may read whole plays or single acts or scenes; they may create their own scripts from short stories, novels, and epics; they may present poems and essays by alternating the reading of stanzas and paragraphs. One way to accomplish the latter is to count off the stanzas or paragraphs according to the number of readers. The first reader reads all the stanzas or paragraphs numbered one, the second reads those numbered two, and so on. Remember also that for scripts one reader should read aloud the scene setting, necessary stage directions, and any prologue or explanatory narrative.

You may want to assign roles for certain dramatic readings, but at other times students may form their own groups and choose roles. If students in a particular small group want to read a script in which the number of roles exceeds the number of members, some students can read more than one role. Whenever a student reads more than one role, he or she can indicate character changes with simple props (hats, glasses, shawls, and the like) or with name signs.

RESEARCH AND REFERENCE MATERIALS

OBTAINING AUDIOVISUAL RESOURCES

GUIDES AND INDEXES

The following sourcebooks contain information about the wealth of educational audio-visual materials available.

AV Instruction: Technology, Media, and Methods. Ed. James W. Brown, Richard B. Lewis, and Fred F. Harcleroad. 6th ed. 1983. McGraw-Hill Book Co., 1221 Avenue of the Americas, New York, NY 10020.

Educational Film/Video Locator. 4th ed. 2 vols. 1990–1991. R. R. Bowker Co., 245 W. Seventeenth St., New York, NY 10011. (This reference contains 51,900 videos and films viewed by 46 media library staffs across the country. It also contains 194,000 titles held by members of the Consortium of College and University Media Centers.)

Educational Media and Technology Yearbook. Ed. Elwood E. Miller. 17th vol. 1991. Libraries Unlimited, Inc. P.O. Box 3988, Englewood, CO 80155. (The yearbook is published in cooperation with the Association for Educational Communications and Technology.)

Educators Guide to Free Audio and Video Materials. Ed. James L. Berger. *Educators Guide to Free Films* and *Educators Guide to Free Filmstrips and Slides.* Ed. John C. Diffor and Elaine N. Diffor. Annual eds. Educators Progress Service, Inc., 214 Center St., Randolph, WI 53956.

NICEM Index Series. 1984, 1985, 1990 eds. in hardcover, monthly bulletins (separate multivolume sets for tapes, films, videotapes, slides, and transparencies). National Information Center for Educational Media, Access Innovations, Inc., P.O. Box 40130, Albuquerque, NM 87196. (The center works closely with the Library of Congress to update indexed titles.)

SUPPLIERS

The following producers and distributors publish catalogs of their offerings.

Agency for Instructional Technology (formerly AITelevision), Box A, Bloomington, IN 47402.

AIMS Media, 9710 DeSoto Ave., Chatsworth, CA 91311.

Allyn and Bacon, Inc., 160 Gold St., Needham Heights, MA 02194.

Association Films, Inc., 866 Third Ave., New York, NY 10022.

Barr Films, Box 7878, 12801 Schabarum Ave., Irwindale, CA 91706.

Blackhawk Films, Inc., 12636 Beatrice St., Los Angeles, CA 90066

Center for Humanities, Inc., Communications Park, Box 1000, Mount Kisco, NY 10549.

Churchill Films, 12210 Nebraska Ave., Los Angeles, CA 90025.

CRM Films LP, 110 Fifteenth St., Del Mar, CA 92014.

Encyclopaedia Britannica Educational Corp., 310 S. Michigan Ave., Chicago, IL 60604.

Epcot Educational Media (Walt Disney Co.), 500 S. Buena Vista St., Burbank, CA 91521.

Films for the Humanities, Inc., P.O. Box 2053, Princeton, NJ 08540.

Films, Inc. (also distributes Audio Brandon, Macmillan, and Texture Films), 1144 Wilmette Ave., Wilmette, IL 60091.

Great Plains National Instructional Television Library (GPN), University of Nebraska at Lincoln, P.O. Box 80669, Lincoln, NE 68501.

Grover Film Productions, P.O. Box 12, Helotes, TX 78023.

Guidance Associates, Communications Park, Box 3000, Mount Kisco, NY 10549.

Holt, Rinehart and Winston, School Division, 1627 Woodland Ave., Austin, TX 78741.

Indiana University Audio-Visual Center, Indiana University, Bloomington, IN 47405.

International Film Bureau, 332 S. Michigan Ave., Chicago, IL 60604.

Listening Library, Inc., Box 611, 1 Park Ave., Old Greenwich, CT 06870.

Lucerne Median, 37 Ground Pine Rd., Morris Plains, NJ 07950.

National Audiovisual Center, National Archives and Records Administration, 8700 Edgeworth Dr., Capitol Heights, MD 20743.

National Council of Teachers of English, 1111 Kenyon Rd., Urbana, IL 61801.

National Education Association, Audio-Visual Instruction, 1201 Sixteenth St. N.W., Washington, DC 20036.

National Film Board of Canada, 1251 Avenue of the Americas, New York, NY 10020.

National Public Radio, Educational Cassettes, 2025 M St. N.W., Washington, DC 20036.

National Video Clearinghouse, Inc., 100 Lafayette Dr., Syosset, NY 11791.

Phoenix/BFA Films and Video, Inc., 468 Park Ave. S., New York, NY 10016.

Public Television Library (Public Broadcasting System), 475 L'Enfant Plaza S.W., Washington, DC 20024.

Pyramid Film and Video, P.O. Box 1048, Santa Monica, CA 90406.

Silver Burdett Co., 250 James St., Morristown, NJ 07960.

Smithsonian Collection of Recordings, Division of Smithsonian Institution Press, Washington, DC 20560.

Society for Visual Education, Inc., 1345 Diversey Pkwy., Chicago, IL 60614.

Time-Life Video and Television, 777 Duke St., Alexandria, VA 22314.

Vineyard Video Productions, Elias Lane, West Tisbury, MA 02575.

INDEX OF AUTHORS AND TITLES